Unless Recalled Ear
DATE DUE

REFORGING THE IRON CROSS

REFORGING
THE IRON CROSS

The Search for Tradition
in the West German
Armed Forces

DONALD ABENHEIM

WITH A FOREWORD BY
Gordon A. Craig

PRINCETON UNIVERSITY PRESS

PRINCETON, NEW JERSEY

Copyright © 1988 by Princeton University Press

Published by Princeton University Press, 41 William Street,
Princeton, New Jersey 08540
In the United Kingdom: Princeton University Press,
Guildford, Surrey

All Rights Reserved

This book has been composed in Linotron Galliard type

Clothbound editions of Princeton University Press books are
printed on acid-free paper, and binding materials are chosen for
strength and durability. Paperbacks, although satisfactory
for personal collections, are not usually suitable for
library rebinding

Printed in the United States of America by Princeton
University Press, Princeton, New Jersey

Library of Congress Cataloging-in-Publication Data

Abenheim, Donald, 1953–
Reforging the Iron Cross.
Bibliography: p.
Includes index.
1. Germany (West)—Armed Forces—History. 2. Civil-military
relations—Germany (West)—History. I. Title. II. Title:
Tradition in the West German armed forces.
UA710.A594 1988   322'.5'0943   88-9969
ISBN 0-691-05534-3

Contents

CONTENTS

Illustrations

Abbreviations

AA	Auswärtiges Amt
a.D.	ausser Dienst
ADK	Arbeitsgemeinschaft demokratischer Kreise e.V.
AusbKp	Ausbilungskompanie
Az	Aktenzeichen
BA	Bundesarchiv, Koblenz
BA/MA	Bundesarchiv-Militärachiv, Freiburg
Befh	Befehlshaber
BMVg	Bundesministerium der Verteidigung
BW	Bundeswehr
CDU	Christlich Demokratische Union
ChdSt	Chef des Stabes
CSU	Christlich Soziale Union
DAG	Deutsche Angestellten-Gewerkschaft
DBWV	Deutscher Bundeswehr-Verband e.V.
DDR	Deutsche Demokratische Republik
DGB	Deutscher Gewerkschaftsbund
DKP	Deutsche Kommunistische Partei
DOKZENTBw	Dokumentations Zentrum der Bundeswehr, Bonn
d. Res.	der Reserve
EKD	Evangelische Kirche Deutschlands
e.V.	eingetragener Verein
EVG	Europäische Verteidigungsgemeinschaft
FAZ	Frankfurter Allgemeine Zeitung
FDP	Freie Demokratische Partei
Frhr	Freiherr
Fü B	Führungsstab Bundeswehr
Fü H	Führungsstab Heer
Fü L	Führungsstab Luftwaffe
Fü M	Führungsstab Marine
Fü TV	Führungsstab Territoriale Verteidigung

Fü S	Führungsstab Streitkräfte
GI	Führungsgebiet I (Personal)
Gen	General
GenInsp	Generalinspekteur der Bundeswehr
GG	Grundgesetz
HDv	Heeresdienstvorschrift
HIAG	Hilfsgemeinschaft auf Gegenseitigkeit der Angehörigen der ehemaligen Waffen SS
HOS	Heeresoffizierschule
IfdT	Information für die Truppe
i.G.	im Generalstabsdienst
InFüSBw	Schule für Innere Führung der Bundeswehr
IP Stab	Informations-und Pressestab
IR	Infanterieregiment
Insp	Inspekteur
K.Adm	Konteradmiral
KavDiv	Kavalleriedivision
Kdr	Kommandeur
KTV	Kommando Territotiale Verteidigung
M	Marine
MdB	Mitglied des Bundestages
MGFA	Militärgeschichtliches Forschungsamt
MGM	Militärgeschichtliche Mitteilungen
Min	Minister
NATO	North Atlantic Treaty Organization
NfD	Nur für den Dienstgebrauch
NS	Nationalsozialismus
NVA	Nationale Volksarmee
O	Oberst
ObdH	Oberbefehlshaber des Heeres
ÖTV	Gewerkschaft "Öffentliche Dienste, Transport und Verkehr"
OKH	Oberkommando des Heeres
PGA	Personalgutacterausschuss
Pz	Panzer
PzBtl	Panzerbataillon
PzDiv	Panzerdivision

Pz. Tr.	Panzertruppe
SDS	Sozialistischer deutscher Studentenbund
SED	Sozialistische Einheitspartei Deutschlands
SPD	Sozialdemokratische Partei Deutschlands
SG	Soldatengesetz
SS	Schutzstaffel
STAL	Stabsabteilunsgleiter
StS	Staatssekretär
SZ	Süddeutsche Zeitung
TF	Truppenführung
Tgb	Tagebuchnummer
UAL	Unterabteilungsleiter
VdS	Verband deutscher Soldaten
VS	Verschlusssache
WBK	Wehrbereichskommando
WBO	Wehrbeschwerdeordnung
VBK	Verteidigungsbezirkskommando
VKK	Verteidigungskreiskommando
ZDv	Zentrale Dienstvorschrift
ZIF/ZUA	Zentrum Innere Führung-Zentrales Unterstützungsarchiv, Koblenz
z.S.	zur See

Foreword

IN THE LAST months of 1954, I visited Germany for the first time since before the war. It was a kind of vacation, for I had just finished writing a large book on the rise and fall of the Prussian-German army from the seventeenth century to 1945, and I had certainly not expected that my trip would coincide with the rebirth of an institution I thought had been disposed of. But that is what happened, for I arrived immediately after the conclusion of the Paris agreements, which authorized the raising of a West German force of five hundred thousand officers and men for NATO, and the extent of that authorization and the plans being made to implement it filled the air and the columns of the press during my visit.

If one could believe what one read, few West Europeans were happy about the prospects of German rearmament. Newspaper stories dated from Holland and Denmark made this clear enough, as did a cartoon from *Le Rire*, which was widely reprinted in the local press, showing a disconsolate Marianne, obviously pregnant with "l'armée allemande," a condition that she blamed on a departing hussar with a strong resemblance to John Foster Dulles. But unhappiest of all were the West Germans themselves, not only the young men who would be called on to serve in the new force (hundreds of whom showed their displeasure during the first week of November by demonstrating before the railway station in Cologne, where officials from the *Amt Blank*, the provisional defense ministry, had arranged a public discussion of their plans), but citizens of all ages and professions. "One may dare the generalization," Paul Sethe wrote in an article called "The Will of the Twenty-Year Olds" in the *Frankfurter Allgemeine Zeitung* on 10 November 1954, "that at this time emotional opposition to military service is in no European country as strong as it is in the Federal Republic."

Under the subtitle "Zerissene Tradition," Sethe went on to explain why this was so:

The military tradition of the Germans was broken off in 1945. In the nine years since, memories and sentiments have become overwhelming among young people that make it difficult to link up with this heritage. Two lost wars with their terrible casualties; great parts of our cities will remain in rubble for long to come; the appeal to idealism and a sense of sacrifice have been brutally abused and arouse today only bitterness among many; the long struggle of the occupiers against German soldierly pride has not been without effect; the division of Germany paralyzes many.

In the disorderly discussion in Cologne, many different explanations were given for the prevalent antimilitarism, but basic to them all was the fear that, since the army had been the source of so much ill in the past, this would inevitably be so in the future also and that one could expect this new army to free itself as quickly as possible from constitutional and parliamentary restraints, to undermine the republic's democratic institutions, and to use its influence to inaugurate an adventurist, and inevitably disastrous, foreign policy.

Almost thirty-five years have passed since that turbulent autumn and winter of 1954. In that time the army that was projected has become a reality and a reliable and respected component of the western military alliance. The baleful consequences predicted in 1954 have not been realized, largely because parliament and the defense ministry, working in close collaboration, established at the outset rules for the selection of officers and for the civic education of all ranks that were based on the experiences of the past and designed to avoid its mistakes. Although their work in the years that followed was accompanied by continued public suspicion and a not inconsiderable amount of professional resistance, they succeeded in making their ideal of an army of citizens in uniform a reality, without in any way impairing its military skills.

The trials and tribulations that they encountered along the way, Donald Abenheim has described with admirable detail and insight in the pages that follow. It is clear from his account that the problem that has caused them most trouble and been least amenable to solution has been that of tradition, the articulation in a form acceptable to the Bundeswehr and to the civilian society that supports it of a connection with past German armies and their experience, insights, values, and achievements. Without a sense of tradition, a military force lacks perspective and orientation; its professional stature is diminished; and it is in danger of being degraded into a mere technical facility whose purpose is killing. Yet after 1945, with the shadow of Adolf Hitler hanging over their past, it was difficult for German soldiers to talk comfortably about tradition, let alone to devise a code of tradition that would meet general approval. If such a document passed over the National Socialist period in silence, it would seem to do a disservice to those soldiers of the Wehrmacht who had fought bravely and well for their country. On the other hand, to do justice to them by including their accomplishments in the tradition of the new Bundeswehr ran the risk of seeming to condone actions that could not, by the most casuistical verbal facility, be squared with soldierly honor—collusion with the Nazis of the basest kind, complicity in unspeakable atrocities.

The most fascinating pages in Donald Abenheim's book deal with the new German army's attempt to deal with this dilemma, in the course of which it has been submitted to a process of historical self-examination more rigorous than anything of the sort undergone by other major social groups in Germany. The problem of tradition has not been solved. Indeed, Professor Abenheim points out that it is inevitable that, in an evolving society, it will be posed anew with every generation. But the self-examination in itself has been healthy and, together with the principles of civic education laid down at the time of the Bundeswehr's establishment, has helped to integrate what, historically, was always a state within a state into Germany's new democratic society.

Gordon A. Craig

Acknowledgments

I WAS HELPED by many people in Germany and the United States who graciously made their time and knowledge available to me. Above all, I want to thank those senior officers and officials who participated in the creation of the West German armed forces, and who generously consented to be interviewed, to respond to my letters of inquiry, and to read versions of the manuscript: the late General a.D. Heusinger, the late Admiral a.D. Ruge, the late Generalmajor a.D. Weber, General a.D. Graf von Kielmansegg, General a.D. de Maizière, General a.D. Schmückle, Generalleutnant a.D. Schnez, Professor and Generalleutnant a.D. Graf von Baudissin, Generalleutnant a.D. von Ilsemann, General a.D. Schulze, General a.D. von zur Gathen, General a.D. Kiessling, Generalmajor a.D. Dr. Wagemann, Brigadegeneral a.D. Karst, Brigadegeneral a.D. Freiherr von Uslar-Gleichen, and Dr. phil habil Walz.

Among the officers serving in the Bundeswehr in the period from 1982 to 1986, I am particularly indebted to the officers of the *Innere Führung* staff (*Führungsstab der Bundeswehr I*) in the West German Ministry of Defense, Bonn, Brigadegeneral von Scheven, Oberst i.G. Kuse, Brigadegeneral Dr. Genschel, Oberst i.G. Dr. von Steinaecker, Oberstleutnant Knopf, and Dr. Loch; the commander and staff of the *Dokumentationszentrum der Bundeswehr*, Bonn, Oberst Beyer and Oberstleutnant Baumann; the commander of the 5th *Panzerdivision*, Diez, Generalmajor Uhle-Wettler; the commander and staff of *Zentrum Innere Führung*, Koblenz-Pfaffendorf, Brigadegeneral Baron von der Recke, Oberst i.G. Francke, Oberst Dr. Balke, Oberstleutnant Dr. Schubert, Major Dr. Wullich, Hauptmann Sailer, Obergefreiter Ritzler, Herr Scherhag, Herr Sonntag, Frau von Kracker and Frau Pindter; the staff of the *Kampftruppenschule 2*, Münster, Major Dr. Freiherr von Rosen; the commander and staff of the *Militärgeschichtliches Forschungsamt*, Freiburg, Brigadegeneral Dr. Roth, Brigadegeneral Dr. Hackl, Professor Dr. Messerschmidt, Kapitän zur

ACKNOWLEDGMENTS

See Dr. Rahn, Oberst Dr. Wiggershaus, Oberstleutnant Dr. Caspar, Oberstleutnant Dr. Harder; the staff of the *Bundesarchiv-Militärarchiv*, Freiburg, Herr Archivoberrat Montfort; the commander and staff of *Territorialkommando Süd,* Heidelberg, Generalmajor Komossa, Oberst i.G. Schweitzer, Major Fischer, Major Pölchau and Hauptmann Berewinkel; the staff of *Wehrbereichskommando IV,* Mainz, Major Eichstädt and Major Hochstädter; the commander and staff of *Verteidigungsbezirkskommando 45,* Neustadt/Weinstrasse, Oberst Herold, Oberstleutnant Ranck, Oberstleutnant Martin and Oberleutnant Konnes; the staff of *Verteidigungsbezirkskommando 54,* Tübingen, Kapitänleutnant Blashöfer; the staff of the *Wehrbereichsverwaltung IV,* Wiesbaden, Herr Dr. Orinsky; the staffs of the *Kreiswehrersatzämter* in Neustadt/Weinstrasse and Kaiserslautern, Herr Rick, Herr Trautmann, Herr Wittmann; the staff of the *Verband deutscher Soldaten,* Bad Godesberg; the staff of the *Konrad Adenauer Stiftung*, St. Augustin, Herr Haak; the staff of the *Friedrich Naumann Stiftung*, Königswinter, Oberst a.D. von Stechow; the staff of the *Friedrich Ebert Stiftung*, Bonn and Saarbrücken, Herr Dr. Kremp; the *Bundesbahndirektion*, Saarbrücken, Herr Dipl. Ing. Kratz; Generalleutnant a.D. Ranck, Hamburg; Professor Dr. Stroynowski, Cologne.

I must also thank my colleagues and mentors in U.S. Army Europe of the period 1982 to 1985: General Frederick Kroesen, Lieutenant General Nathaniel Thompson, Major General Robert Drudik, Lieutenant Colonel Lewis Flanders, Lieutenant Colonel John Fairlamb, Major George Kent, Sergeant Major Thomas Gulick, Dr. John Langellier, Mr. Bruce Siemon, Mr. Benton Moeller, Mr. Robert Garnett, Mrs. Lynne Sparks, and Mrs. Cary Stone.

I am indebted to my teachers at Stanford University: Professors Gordon Craig, Peter Paret, Alexander George, Gordon Wright, and James Sheehan; my advisers and friends at the Hoover Institution: Ambassador Richard Staar, Dr. Milorad Drachkovitch, Dr. Lewis Gann, Dr. David Gress, Mrs. Agnes Peterson, the late Professor George Duca, Dr. Elena Danielson, Mrs. Grace M. Hawes, and Mrs. Ella Wolfe. In particular, I should like to thank Dr. Ron Davies of Stanford and Dr. Dan Moran of the Institute for Advanced Study at Princeton for their insight and good humor in editing the manuscript.

Thanks are also due to my colleagues at the U.S. Naval Postgraduate School, Monterey, California: Professors James J. Tritten, Sherman Blandin, Russell Stolfi, Michael Clough, Edward Laurance, Stephen Jurika, Boyd Huff, Frank Teti, and Edward Olsen, as well as my students Michael Burns, Peggy Burns, and Jane Holl.

The following people generously read portions of the manuscript and provided helpful comments and criticism: Professors Felix Gilbert, Hans-Adolf Jacobsen, Michael Geyer, Catherine McArdle Kelleher, Charles Burdick, Condolezza Rice, Mark Cioc, Klaus von Schubert, and Dr. Gerhard Wettig. I am particularly indebted to Joanna Hitchcock, Deborah Tegarden, and Cynthia Halpern of Princeton University Press, who kindly guided me through the steps of preparing the manuscript for publication. Thanks also to Susan McReynolds and Phillip Carroll for their special help.

I would also like to thank my parents for their patience and encouragement during my work on this study.

For the shortcomings of this work, none of the above-named persons or institutions bears any responsibility. The merits it may have are due to their assistance.

The views expressed in this study are the author's own, and do not represent the official position of the U.S. Department of the Navy or the Department of Defense and they should not be construed as such.

All photographs were generously provided by the Information and Press Staff of the West German Ministry of Defense.

REFORGING THE IRON CROSS

Introduction

IN NOVEMBER 1985 the West German armed forces celebrated their thirtieth anniversary. The occasion went largely unnoticed in a world that three decades earlier had watched with concern the rebirth of a German army and feared the danger it might pose to the young democracy of the Federal Republic. In a speech in the Ministry of Defense in Bonn honoring the anniversary, the President of the Federal Republic, Richard von Weizsäcker, praised the achievements of the West German military and its contribution to the Atlantic alliance. Weizsäcker did not hesitate to lend his considerable moral authority to an institution that for much of its thirty years has been the object of intense debate and mistrust—an army created from the wreckage of Nazi Germany, which since its inception had struggled with the political ambiguities of its background as much as with the strategic and operational difficulties of its mission.

Looking to the past, Weizsäcker spoke of the West German army as having been founded on the traditions of the Prussian reformers of the early nineteenth century and of the military resistance to Hitler. His reference to the era of Prussian reform was reminiscent of an action by West Germany's first Minister of Defense, Theodor Blank, thirty years earlier. Blank chose 12 November 1955, the 200th birthday of Scharnhorst, the military leader of the Prussian reform movement, as the date for the induction of the first 101 volunteers of the new army. In a brief speech, Blank told the little group that it would have to build the new army without either glorifying Germany's military past or damning it totally. The new army would adopt nothing from the past without making certain that it was still valid for the present. In 1955 this injunction proved difficult to carry out because of memories of Nazism and the war and the feeling among many Germans that their history had ended ten years before. The seeming ease with which Weizsäcker now honored the Prussian reformers and the resistance to Hitler later belied the difficulty the selection of historical examples

3

had once caused the Bundeswehr. In the early 1950s, the need to select what might be called a usable past gave rise to a long debate about the army's role in German history and also about the position of the soldier in state and society. This controversy, and its accompanying effort to create a new type of German soldier, was a continuation of a much broader debate, which had been going on for a century and a half, about the nature of Germany's military institutions and their relationship to state power and society.

The Iron Cross, the emblem of the West German military, reveals within its own history the problem faced by those who have reforged the links between the German soldier and the past. Although for some people, the Iron Cross is synonymous with the swastika, its historical reality includes far more than merely the Third Reich. King Frederick William III of Prussia awarded the first Iron Cross in 1813, during the "iron time" of the wars of liberation against Napoleon. He gave the decoration for bravery in battle, without regard for the recipient's rank in society. The medal signified the democratization of the army and its unity with the nation and state in the struggle against the French occupier. When Prussia again led Germany to war against France in 1870, the Iron Cross symbolized the victory of arms in German unification and the outstanding role of the military in society and politics. The medal given out by the millions after 1914, however, became the badge of the front-line fighter and of Germany's refusal to accept the humiliation of defeat in 1918. Adolf Hitler, one of the millions who had received the Iron Cross in the trenches, reestablished the award in September 1939. This Iron Cross bore the swastika on its obverse side, signifying the bond between National Socialism and the wars of liberation, the unification of the empire and the First World War. As a result, German soldiers guilty of war crimes defaced this symbol even as they wore it themselves. Despite the events of the period between 1933 and 1945, the founders of the new West German army adopted the Iron Cross as an insignia after 1955, seeking to return it to its original, more democratic meaning.

This study examines the way professional soldiers, academics, and politicians in the 1950s created the self-image of the new West German soldier, an image that had to be acceptable to the new democratic Germany. When asked in 1953 what relevance the history of former German armies had to the new Bundeswehr, one of the leaders in the rearmament process declared that important threads of tradition had passed through the vacuum of Nazi Germany, and these threads should be taken up and spun into a new fabric. But what exactly were these durable threads? Opinions varied then as they do today. "The problem of tradition," as one of the major framers of reform policy, Wolf Count Baudissin, has observed, "is the traditional problem of the West German armed forces." In confronting this issue over the past thirty years, the participants in the official and public debate have reflected on the relationship between civil and military power in German history, the nature of command and leadership, the political importance of military symbolism, and—perhaps above all—the complicity of the German military in the rise of National Socialism and in carrying out its policies.

The following pages describe the context and development, formulating and applying, new historically rooted political and ethical standards to the German soldier, the solutions adopted by the leadership of the armed forces, and the fate of their policies during the last three decades. Needless to say, Germany's military past and the traditions that were a part of it constituted only one problem for the founders of the Bundeswehr. They had to deal with a daunting combination of political, operational, historical, and legal obstacles to rearmament, all of which would have to be examined in any full account of the creation of the West German armed forces, a work that remains to be written. Inherent in these issues of politics and strategy, however, was the relationship of the West German soldier to his past. In the sphere of international politics, the founding of the new army was linked to the future of West Germany within a united Western Europe. The new army was also clearly on the front line of a world divided between ideological antagonists. These facts complicated the task of motivating West German soldiers to fight in what would surely be, from the perspective of the Federal Republic, a nuclear civil war. In the arena of domestic politics, the place of the new soldier in state and society was worrisome for the fledgling democracy of West Germany. Would the soldier of tomorrow attempt to regain his former political and social position at the expense of the new democratic system? How could the soldier's rights be assured while training him realistically for combat that would be infinitely more brutal than that of World War II?

The arming of the Federal Republic in the 1950s occurred as the spread of nuclear weapons and the establishment of the alliance system were transforming the face of war. The West Germans were latecomers to these developments, and they had to adjust their operational ideas as well as their concepts of military tradition to them. The attempt to create a tradition for the future German soldier also influenced historical scholarship. The role of the military in the collapse of the Weimar Republic was an important issue in the scholarly debate over the failure of the republic. This debate took place during the years when the controversy about the West German soldier and his valid heritage was beginning, and it is not surprising that historians came to participate directly in formulating policy in the Ministry of Defense.

The founders of the West German armed forces promised that the future army would represent something fundamentally new in contrast to the era before 1945, and that it would avoid the political and social abuses of the past. This promise was to be fulfilled through a process of military reform of the political, social, legal, and historical role of the professional soldier in German life. During the initial period of growth of the Bundeswehr, through the mid-1960s, the question of the validity of the German soldier's heritage grew more pressing as the innovations in and reforms of the professional soldier's purpose and self-image encountered a variety of political and operational difficulties in the years after 1955. The separate debates about reform and tradition merged as time passed. Those who spoke of reform were forced to define what were valid and what were invalid traditions; often an argument that began over the cut of the West German army uniform ended in an exchange about the role of the military in German history and the nature of war in the modern world. This study reconstructs certain of the key episodes in this debate and highlights the main phases in which this exchange has taken place. The record of the controversy over the self-image of the West German soldier reflects the consolidation of the Bundeswehr within the political culture of the Federal Republic of Germany.

The problem tradition poses for the modernization and reform of armies is of course not unique to Germany. In the recent past, the French, the Russians, and the Chinese, to mention three prominent cases, have reformed and reconstituted their armies and have carefully selected elements of their military history for contemporary inspiration. Although the present work addresses solely the West Germans after 1945, it illustrates the general importance of coming to grips with a state's military heritage, and it highlights the difficulties faced by those who rebuild an army. The German professional soldier's image of himself, expressed in symbols and customs drawn from the past, probably has less to say about his effectiveness in combat (although that is surely important) than about his relationship to other social and political groups. This relationship was especially difficult to define in the West Germany of the 1950s, while memories of the 1920s and 1930s loomed over the enterprise of building a democracy.

The anxieties of civilians as they regard the profession of arms in today's world are a part of the story, as is the use of history in a modern bureaucratic organization. The West German experience illustrates the difficulty of enlisting history in the service of political aims, while attempting to preserve a measure of historical honesty in a pluralistic society. Although Germany's defeat in 1945 and the U.S. debacle in Vietnam in the 1970s are hardly comparable, the gradual emergence of public myths, traditions, and symbols explaining the Vietnam War offers an interesting counterpoint to the German case in the 1950s. For anyone who lived through the political turbulence of the 1960s, the apparent shift among Americans from condemnation to respect for the veterans of the Indochina war among Americans, and the renaissance of popular esteem for traditions of self-sacrifice and bravery in battle are quite remarkable.

Such a shift in attitudes always raises problems when the attempt is made to reconcile a nascent tradition with the historical record, as revealed by sound scholarship—as the Germans discovered repeatedly in their own debates. The soldier and his traditions in the Federal Republic of the 1950s are unique, defying easy comparison with other events in recent history. The historical memory that dominated the founding of the Federal Republic and the evolution of its political culture was shaped by the outcome of the two world wars and Germany's decline from political and cultural ascendancy into genocide and barbarism. The image of tradition in the armed forces and the society that had evolved from the late nineteenth century to 1945 was strongly linked to the perception of the past.

PART ONE

The New Army and the Past

1. The Maintenance of Tradition and the Burden of the Past

FOR GENERATIONS of Germans, the Garrison Church in Potsdam has symbolized the Prussian tradition, which the bells of its carillon recalled every hour with a verse set to a Mozart theme: "Be loyal and honest unto the cold grave."[1] Until 1945, the bells rang out over the town, joining the drums and fifes and the cadence of marching boots of the Potsdam regiments. In the crypt beneath the tower were the tombs of King Frederick William I, the creator of the Brandenburg-Prussian Army and the builder of Potsdam, and Frederick the Great, whose diplomatic and military genius made Prussia a great power, men whose elevated sense of the importance of the state became an important tradition of German life. For many, Potsdam symbolized an "authentic and strict soldierly spirit," which represented "simplicity, modesty, conscientiousness, and order, as well as the willingness to assume responsibility and sacrifice oneself for a greater idea and cause."[2] The exhilaration of Prussia's Icarus flight to power led succeeding generations to exaggerate these virtues and the military traditions they came to symbolize. As Friedrich Meinecke reflected in his *German Catastrophe*, popular adoration of the "young god lieutenant" and naive self-admiration of Prussian virtues revealed the degree to which these traditions had shrunk by the early twentieth century to a rigid convention all too often expressed in the forced Potsdam dialect of the officer's mess.[3]

[1] Werner Schwips, *Die Garnisonkirchen von Berlin und Potsdam* (Berlin, 1964), pp. 54ff.

[2] Kurt Hesse, cited in Wolfgang Paul, *Das Potsdamer Infanterie-Regiment 9, 1918–1945: Preussische Tradition in Krieg und Frieden*, 2d ed., 2 vols. (Osnabrück, 1985), 1: v.

[3] Friedrich Meinecke, *Die Deutsche Katastrophe*, in *Friedrich Meinecke Werke: Autobiographische Schriften*, 9 vols. (Stuttgart, 1969), 8: 336. For a full discussion of the problem of military tradition before 1945, see the excellent book by Gustav-Adolf Caspar et al., *Tradition in deutschen Streitkräften bis 1945*, vol. 1 in *Entwicklung*

11

To many Germans in the decade after 1945, the symbols and traditions of the soldier—often one-sided before 1933, abused by the Nazis, shattered by the violence of the war, and banned by the victors—had lost all positive meaning. Using the heritage of Germany's military past for his own ends, Hitler had reduced this legacy, along with so much else, to ruin.

Immediately after the war, the concept of military tradition shared the fate of William II's famous *Siegesallee*, the processional avenue near the Brandenburg Gate, where freezing and starving Berliners had cut down the trees around the monuments of past heros, and turned the grounds into potato fields. Men in tattered clothes plowed the soil under the splinter-scarred gaze of the great stone figures of Brandenburg-Prussian history—a scene that symbolized how strikingly the virtues of the past had given way to the catastrophe of the present. Unlike 1918, when the physical reality of defeat had been remote for most civilians, the destroyed cities and the film images of the liberated death camps forced Germans to reflect on their own roles in the Third Reich. Many blamed the party hacks and the professional soldiers for the defeat. There was a widespread revulsion toward those soldiers guilty of continuing the war long after all hope of victory had vanished. This hostility was common to many groups in postwar German society, and it resulted in an almost complete rejection of everything military in the years after 1945. Although many rank-and-file Nazis escaped public wrath by justifying their actions as responses to the dilemma faced by nearly every German, the professional soldier could point to little more than his tradition of obedience as an excuse, an offer that seemed ridiculous and criminal amid the ruins. In the aftermath of defeat, no one wanted to recall the traditions of the army that had once made Germany a great power.

In the wake of cataclysmic defeat, many Germans believed they had come to the end of their national development—the zero hour. Few could have imagined how quickly Germany would recover from the physical wounds of war. Although many institutions and traditions of the German past did disappear after 1945, Germany's startling return to economic strength and political power in the early 1950s re-

---

deutscher militärischer Tradition, ed. Militärgeschichtliches Forschungsamt (MGFA) (Herford, 1986).

vived numerous features of national life that had seemed extinct, among them the armed forces. The brutal experience of the "zero hour" combined with the rapid development of the cold war only exacerbated the controversy about the validity of the soldier's heritage.

There have been repeated attempts to define the tradition of the German soldier; observers of the German army have underscored both its universal and its unique qualities and described what succeeding generations should choose from this military past to guide them in the present. Such attempts, however, have precipitated an enduring debate that has yet to reach a resolution. It does seem clear that in describing the heritage of the German soldier, one should make a distinction between different aspects of the problem—the military tradition itself and the self-conscious maintenance of the military tradition in the present. Military tradition can be described as the sum of attitudes, customs, and symbols of military life that succeeding generations have preserved and adapted in armies over time. The second aspect of the problem—the maintenance of tradition (*Traditions-pflege*)—arises when the consensus about the meaning of these shared values and symbols breaks down. What some have called the cult of tradition is the self-conscious, emotionally charged, and sometimes openly political use of past customs and symbols to lend legitimacy to things in the present. The periodic resurgence of these practices more or less coincided with intense political and social changes that have taken place in the German military in this century. The return to tradition and to the problem of the maintenance of tradition as issues of policy in West Germany after 1950 form the chief subject of this study. But we must also be aware in general terms of what Germans mean by the term "military tradition." A simple way to come to do so is to summarize the two schools of thought on the subject: military tradition as viewed by its critics, and its proponents. The conflicting lines of argument—with their flaws of oversimplification, caricatures, and omissions—are described in the following section.

CRITICS of the German military tradition contend that the heritage of the army stemmed chiefly from the officer corps, which, in their view, resisted the social and political changes of the nineteenth and twentieth centuries. These critics agree with a general of the German

13

empire who asserted that "noncommissioned officers and soldiers come and go within a people's army. The officer corps forms the enduring part of the army; it carries on tradition."[4] According to these critics, the officer corps bears considerable responsibility and therefore guilt for leading Germany on its special path of political and social development; the rise of the Prussian army, with its officer corps drawn from the landed nobility, hindered the formation of a liberal, democratic society in Germany. The critics, in short, interchangeably use the terms "military tradition" and "militarism" in their analysis.

The ethos of the Prussian nobleman in arms stood in fundamental conflict with the principles of liberty, equality, and fraternity that were gaining adherents elsewhere. Closed off from other social groups, Prussian-German officers nurtured a common worldview that was increasingly at odds with the world beyond the barracks and the officers mess. Eckart Kehr, an important German historian of the interwar years and a critic of this outlook, characterized it as "that of a 'warrior caste' with its own code of honor, its own form of law, and its own set of beliefs," which had little in common with those of men in industry, science, commerce, and parliamentary politics.[5] The centerpiece of this tradition was the officer's code of honor.[6] "True honor," as the Emperor William I told his officers in 1874, "cannot exist without faithfulness unto death, unshakable courage, firm determination, self-denying obedience, simple truthfulness, and strict discretion, nor without self-sacrifice in what seems the fulfillment of a minor task."[7] The officer corps believed—or wanted to believe—themselves to be the heirs to medieval chivalry, whose values their military code handed down from one generation to the next.

The code of the officer caste, as Kehr described it, "mistook bra-

---

[4] Ludwig Hahn, ed., *Das Heer und das Vaterland: Ein Gedenkbuch für das deutsche Volk* (Berlin, 1883), p. 99.

[5] Eckart Kehr, "The Genesis of the Royal Prussian Reserve Officer," in *Economics, Interest, Militarism and Foreign Policy*, ed. Gordon Craig (Berkeley, 1977), p. 99.

[6] See the description of the officer's honor in Karl Demeter, *The German Officer Corps in Society and State, 1650–1965* (New York, 1965), pp. 111–54; Hans H. Driftmann, *Grundzüge des militärischen Erziehungs- und Bildungswesens in der Zeit 1871–1939* (Regensburg, 1980), pp. 94–99; also see generally, Bernhard Poten, *Geschichte des Militär-Erziehungs- und Bildungswesens in den Landen deutscher Zunge* (Berlin, 1889–1897), 5 vols., reprinted, Biblio Verlag, Osnabrück, 1982.

[7] "Introductory Order by William I to the Ordinance Tribunals of Honor," dated 2 May 1874, cited in Demeter, *The German Officer Corps*, p. 313.

vado for an expression of strength, arrogance and conceit for a manifestation of dignity, and swagger for sensibility."[8] For the critics of the German military tradition, the customs and symbols of the officer corps—the autumn maneuvers and troop reviews, the pageantry of the oath, the grand tattoo, the regimental flag, the duels, and the club atmosphere of the officers' mess—were the hallmarks of this antiliberal, antisocialist, anticatholic worldview, one which strongly influenced bourgeois behavior. The eagerness with which many members of the middle social groups in Germany aped the traditions and customs of the officer corps when they became reserve officers attested to this domination. Nonetheless, not all Germans were so captivated by the shine of an officer's shoulderboards. Satirists at the turn of the century depicted line and reserve officers as buffoons, striding down the street in pairs, their oversized spiked and plumed helmets pulled down over their eyes, with their sabers dragging behind them, as they boasted of their adventures with women and complained about their debts.

The lot of the common soldier, experienced by many of the critics themselves, further invalidated Germany's military heritage in the modern age. The officer corps could freely impose its will upon the Reich because of universal military service, an institution that its proponents lauded as the "people in arms" and the "school of the nation." Millions of men passed through the gates of the barracks, where, by donning the blue wool tunic of the king and emperor, they cast off their few civil rights. The Prussian nobleman had taken his whip from the fields of his East Elbian estates and brought it to the ranks of the armies of Frederick; although the army eventually did away with corporal punishment, its spirit remained. The formalized barbarism of the running of the gauntlet in the eighteenth century evolved into the rigors of the barracks square, ruled by the capricious, often brutal noncommissioned officers. These men drilled their recruits for hours on the parade ground, setting upon the reluctant among them with insults and humiliations, against which civil law provided no effective defense. On the barracks square, the soldier learned the senseless intricacies of presenting arms and the parade march, known to the English-speaking world as the "goose step," which struck many critics as

[8] Kehr, "The Genesis of the Royal Prussian Reserve Officer," p. 108.

the essence of the brutality of German military tradition. To its defenders, however, the soldier's mastery of drill showed the state of his
discipline and his preparation for battle, as well as his sense of order-
liness, obedience, and punctuality. Such customs, so prominent in the
everyday experience of soldiers, fostered a blind obedience in the "pu-
pils in the school of the nation," which others found antithetical to
the principles of a modern society, which required not pliant subjects
but self-reliant citizens.

Furthermore, argued the critics, the bearers of tradition in the
highest ranks of the army were guilty of a politically blind professionalism that elevated the military above the state and helped to bring on
the German catastrophe in the twentieth century. Here was the most
dangerous tradition of them all: a worldview embodied in the Prussian-German general staff that set war above and beyond the reach of
politics. This outlook was found to prevail in such personalities as
Alfred von Schlieffen, Erich Ludendorff, Hans von Seeckt, Kurt von
Schleicher, Werner von Blomberg and Wilhelm Keitel, all of whom,
as Gordon Craig suggests, mistook "cunning for intelligence and
frantic violence for statecraft."[9] Since the late nineteenth century, they
had used their technical mastery of the deployment and operations of
mass armies to overturn Carl von Clausewitz's dictum that war is a
continuation of politics by other means. With the logic implicit in
their mobilizing schedules and railway timetables, they had made war
an end in itself; they sought to separate it from its political purposes,
subordinating German society to the exigencies of total war. Many
such apolitical technicians of war, having failed in 1914–1918, eventually allied themselves with Adolf Hitler and his movement, where they
met another remnant of Germany's military past: the paramilitary des-
peradoes of the storm troops and Free Corps. These latter groups
consisted of soldiers and junior officers who returned from the
trenches in 1918 to join the civil war being fought in the streets of
German towns. It was here, in concert with embittered and socially
disenfranchised civilians, that they formed the vanguard of Nazism—
an alliance whose appalling results have cast a shadow over Germany's
military tradition that reaches to the present.

[9] Gordon A. Craig, introduction to Herbert Rosinski, *The German Army*, ed.
Gordon A. Craig (New York, 1966), p. 9.

THIS overwhelmingly negative image of the German military tradition has long been pervasive; in fact, outside the ranks of the German military itself and a handful of scholars and students of military history, this negative view predominates in the popular imagination. Yet the question must be asked, if the tradition of the German military has really been so brutal and backward, how could one explain the remarkable accomplishments and innovations of German soldiers in military organization and battle in the last two hundred years? The defenders of the German military tradition point to several factors that conflict with the harsh judgments of the critics.[10]

As a general said in the 1950s, not everything in the German soldier's past has been bad.[11] Gordon Craig, although he is a strong critic of the political effects of military tradition, acknowledges an important connection between the tradition of an army and its efficiency in battle.[12] This connection is to be found in what the Germans have long called the "inner cohesion" or "inner structure" of the army, that is the union of moral, social, and political factors in the ranks and in the different institutions of an army that holds it together in war. Soldiers of all armies recognize the fundamental importance of such inner structures; all are eager to select elements from the past that contribute to its strength. In the German case, the defenders of tradition argue, the inheritance passed down from the eighteenth- and nineteenth-century armies had great value, and it stemmed from many of the same personalities, institutions, and events the critics of tradition have described so negatively.

Gordon Craig summed up the findings of generations of historians by observing that Frederick the Great offered the German soldier the "sense of individual and regimental honor that inspired fortitude under fire and made retreat unthinkable." From Scharnhorst, the reformer of the early nineteenth century, the Prussian-German army took "the concept of discipline, not as robot-like obedience, but as

[10] For two examples of this recent interest in the German military, see Martin van Creveld, *Fighting Power: German and U.S. Army Performance, 1939–1945* (Westport, 1982), and Franz Uhle-Wettler, *Höhe und Wendepunkte Deutscher Militärgeschichte* (Mainz, 1984).

[11] Bundesarchiv/Militärarchiv (BA/MA) Bw 9/ 716, "Stenographisches Protokoll der 34. Sitzung des Ausschusses für Fragen der europäischen Sicherheit am 10. Juni 1953."

[12] Gordon Craig, introduction to Rosinski's *German Army*, p. 7.

willing subordination to the common interests of the fighting unit to which one belonged." Clausewitz gave the German soldier "the idea of war as a coherent, continuous whole, directed to the complete overthrow of the enemy's power of resistance." No less outstanding among the makers of German military tradition was Helmuth von Moltke, the organizer of victory in the wars of German unification of the mid-nineteenth century. His concept of strategy and operations in war demonstrated that "adherence to a battle plan must not be allowed to crush the initiative of individual commanders and that the *Feldherr* must have the courage and the wit to change his dispositions as the situation required." The American approach to war is focused on combat, removed from its political dimension, and on machines in battle that are supposed somehow to supplant the human element of war or to make it unnecessary; the tradition of the German soldier emphasized the role of men in battle and "traditions of command and obedience and good judgment handed down from each generation of German officer to their successors and transmitted by them to the units they commanded."[13]

These facets of the past as described by Craig are similar to those put forward by the advocates of the German military tradition. They also link the heritage of the German soldier to the code of honor of medieval chivalry—a connection justified by the fundamentally unchanging nature of war and its demands upon men in battle: the need for courage, camaraderie, honor, self-sacrifice, and intelligence. They describe the responsible manner in which German soldiers were trained and led in battle, emphasizing the sense of responsibility that existed at all levels of command. Contrary to the widespread impression that a robot-like obedience dominated the German military, the defenders of tradition recall that officers cultivated independent judgment in their subordinates to make difficult decisions on their own, as the situation dictated. A leader's character and his ability to establish a basis of trust with his subordinates was decisive. Although formal discipline could often be quite strict, German soldiers nevertheless had the right to make complaints against their superiors. A subordinate also could respond to a superior's orders with a countersuggestion, if he believed that the order should be carried out differ-

[13] Ibid.

ently. While this tradition applied particularly to general staff officers, it nevertheless affected the workings of the army at all levels.

The makers of these traditions of character and initiative are to be found in the ranks of the armies of Frederick William I and Frederick II, as well as among the men who sought to strengthen Prussia after the disaster of 1806, such figures as Grolman, Boyen, Scharnhorst, Gneisenau, and Clausewitz. The tradition guided the education and training of officers and noncommissioned officers, emphasizing the responsibility of the leader for his subordinates and the need for a sense of camaraderie that provided strength in adversity. Differences of opinion between, say, a captain and a colonel, were tolerated on the grounds that camaraderie should count for more than an officer's rank insignia. A strong intellectual foundation existed for this tradition as well. Officers came to embrace the idea of personal education and self-enlightenment that strengthened their capacity for judgment in the fog of war. An officer's written and oral self-expression had to be clear and simple. Those who denied the importance of education maintained that the native dash and daring of the nobleman alone were all an officer required for battle. In contrast, the tradition of the educated officer, versed in the most intellectually demanding aspects of his profession, sought to foster a harmony in the individual between character and intellect. A balance between courage and intelligence allowed the officer to master the friction of combat, where the simplest thing was the most difficult.

German victories in battle over three centuries, say the proponents, attest to the value of these traditions. The general staff, created by the Prussian reformers and expanded throughout the nineteenth century, provided the example for the brains of armies throughout the world. The relative effectiveness with which the Prussian general staff manipulated mass armies, rail transport, and telegraphic communication astounded the nineteenth century. "Work hard, do not stand out, and be more than you appear" became the watchwords not only for the general staff officer but for many Germans outside of the military, who saw Moltke as the moral personification of the Prussian-German state. German military traditions in operations and tactics, building on the achievements of the previous century, underwent an important metamorphosis in the twentieth century, which soon helped transform the face of war. The German front soldier of 1914–1918 amply demonstrated his heroism and his ability to innovate. The achievements of the German soldier in the lightning campaigns of the years 1939 to 1941, even if on behalf of an evil regime, revealed further examples of military ability and daring—fruits of a long tradition, and themselves examples for the future.

The profound tension between the need for tradition on the one hand and rigorous historical scholarship on the other renders this analysis of opposing opinions a frustrating enterprise. Lists of the good and the bad appear incomplete and historically simplistic. The negative viewpoint pays too much attention to civil-military relations, while ignoring the way soldiers see themselves, a crucial issue in the inner structure of any army. The positive point of view is guilty of lavishing far too much attention on the details of battles at the expense of politics. It also tends to downplay the role of National Socialism in the German military, an error that makes nonsense of German history between 1933 and 1945.

A note of caution is necessary in juxtaposing these two points of view. The schematic description of the debate offered here could suggest that the conflict simply pits the recent past against the healthier traditions of the eighteenth and nineteenth centuries. The historical reality, however, is quite different. The German military tradition has always consisted of many diverse components that have never been easy to reconcile. The failure to recognize this long historical conflict, which is but one aspect of the fragmented development of German politics, society, and culture, complicates the use of historical examples to lend legitimacy to present institutions. The era of Prussian reform perhaps best illustrates this phenomenon of a fragmented military tradition.

Frederick the Great was both admired and resented by the Prussian reformers of the early nineteenth century.[14] Many of the military reformers, who in Clausewitz's words, sought to reorganize the army "according to a new spirit . . . so that the burden was carried on all shoulders,"[15] felt an emotional antagonism toward Frederick as the "symbol of the old Prussia that needed to be reshaped and modern-

---

[14] This analysis is indebted to Professor Peter Paret; see especially his *Yorck and the Era of Prussian Reform* (Princeton, 1966), pp. 117–40; and *Clausewitz and the State: The Man, His Theories and His Times*, 2d ed. (Princeton, 1985), pp. 138–46.

[15] Cited in Paret, *Clausewitz*, p. 138.

ized."[16] They admired his martial qualities and strategic genius, but rejected his political and social views: he represented a system of government that had outlived its usefulness. The reformers wanted "to break up the old absolutist system, which had inhibited the rational execution of public business, and to achieve a fuller exploitation by the state of social and psychological energies that the Frederician class structure had repressed."[17]

Even after the reformers managed to draw unsuspected military energies from Prussian society in the years between 1813 and 1815, there still existed very profound conflicts in what some have all too easily described as a unitary "Prussian tradition." Clausewitz's critique of the growing narrowness and one-sided professionalism in the education of Prussian officers at this time indicates the shape of the continuing conflict between conservative and liberal forces in 1819.[18] Prussian officers of the time were educated by means of a system of formal lectures that emphasized learning by rote. Clausewitz, Peter Paret writes, argued that student officers should be turned "from passive listeners into participants" as part of a greater effort to strengthen their capacity for independent judgment and action in war.[19] Clausewitz's ideal of military education aimed toward the "free play" of the student's "intelligence and imagination." These qualities were necessary to overcome the frictions of war. But before Clausewitz's superiors acted on his memorandum, the course of politics in Germany led to the triumph of ultraconservatism over moderates and liberals.[20] The Prussian reformers had to fight for their political lives and Clausewitz's memorandum was put aside. "The Restoration," Paret writes, "turned the unrepentant reformer into something of an outsider."[21] The shelving of Clausewitz's forward-looking ideas about officer education, and his relegation to the margins of military life in the wake of the Carlsbad Decrees, illustrate the ambiguities and cross purposes that have always existed within Prussia's military tradition.

Nor, obviously, can we speak of a single "German" tradition before 1918. Rather, ideological tensions of the kind revealed by the Prussian reforms were further compounded by the autonomous, and often quite different, traditions of the other German lands. Advocates of a

[16] Ibid., p. 333.   [17] Ibid., p. 138.   [18] Ibid., pp. 272–85.
[19] Ibid., p. 278.   [20] Ibid., pp. 278–79.   [21] Ibid., p. 282.

unified tradition have often described German efficiency and discipline in battle as the product of a "Prussian tradition," thus overlooking the long military histories of states like Hannover, Saxony, Württemberg, and Bavaria, all of which, at one time or another, fought against Prussia. Perhaps the best-known German soldier of World War II in the English-speaking world, Field Marshall Erwin Rommel, was trained and commissioned in the army of Württemberg. One need not have been the product of a Prussian barracks square to be a good soldier in Germany. The armies of the medium-sized German states were heirs to very different concepts of discipline, military justice, and barracks square spit and polish than the Prussians.[22] Their contingents contained significant numbers of middle-class officers, and displayed greater openness to liberal political ideas; they were known for their combination of less rigorous military discipline and their efficiency and determination in battle.

In the end, arguments about military tradition of the kind considered here do not significantly improve an understanding of how tradition itself operates as a historical force. Their unending, circular quality will try the patience of even the most determined scholar, and, precisely because they depend on a selective, politically conditioned reading of the historical record, they resist resolution based on the record itself. A better approach to the problem of military tradition lies in an analysis of the context in which diverging views of it are articulated. One can learn more by following the development of the cult of the soldierly past, and placing it in its own historical and political context. Traditions, military or otherwise, make themselves felt most strongly precisely at those moments when their meaning is called into question, and when their maintenance becomes an issue for the present generation.

Although revulsion with the professional military and distaste for military tradition in West Germany has stemmed chiefly from the lost war of 1945, the cult of tradition and its political abuse had begun long before Hitler, and it cannot be attributed to the Nazi period alone. Military tradition became an object of controversy in the postwar era not only because of the catastrophe of 1945, but also because earlier

---

[22] These issues are developed in Hans Martin Ottmer, "Ursachen und Hintergründe zur Entwicklung deutscher militärischer Tradition vom Ende des 18. Jahrhundert bis 1914," in Caspar, *Tradition in deutschen Streikräften bis 1945*, pp. 67–208.

political and military figures in the German past had used the cult of tradition to put their stamp on the image of the soldier in the German state. This effort took place within the larger attempt to make the Reich a world power. William II, Hans von Seeckt, and Adolf Hitler each offered a version of the heritage of the German soldier, demonstrating the political nature of the maintenance of military tradition in German life.

GERMAN military reference works written after the old armies had ceased to exist in 1918 generally describe the maintenance of military tradition as the cultivation of the memory and glories of former German armies, which the soldiers of the present were to hand on (Latin: *tradere*) to the future.[23] Reference books before 1918 contain no entry on the maintenance of tradition (*Traditionspflege*), because it did not exist as a self-conscious practice on the national level.[24] The cultivation of tradition on a broad scale in the German military emerged only at the end of the nineteenth century, amid the social and political change of the Wilhelmine Reich. This growing emphasis on the maintenance of tradition represented an enlargement and political transformation of customs and practices that had long existed within the inner structure of the German military. In effect, the creators of the cult of tradition attributed exalted political and symbolic meanings to certain routine aspects of the training and education of troops.

The regiment was the chief place for German soldiers to maintain tradition in what, after 1918, came to be called the "old armies." It was in the soldier's "regimental home" that the traditional pageantry took place and that his officers and NCOs imparted the time-honored du-

---

[23] See, for example, Hermann Franke, ed., *Handbuch der neuzeitlichen Wehrwissenschaften: Das Heer*, 5 vols. (Berlin/Leipzig, 1937), 2: 702–03.

[24] See, for example, H. Frobenius, *Militärlexikon: Handwörterbuch der Militär Wissenschaften* (Berlin, 1901). For a discussion of the advent of the term "military tradition" after 1918, see Helmut Schubert, "Historisches Bewusstsein und soldatisches Selbstverständnis," in *Information für die Truppe* (No.9 1981), pp. 30ff.; and DOKZENT Bw PA 2718, Major Dr. Klaus Buschmann, "Der Traditionsbruch zwischen Bundeswehr und Wehrmacht: Ursachen, Folgerungen und gegenwärtiger Stand der Diskussion" (Thesis Führungsakademie der Bundeswehr, 1982), pp. 1–3. (DOKZENT Bw is Dokumentationszentrum der Bundeswehr, an automated reference library/archive for the use of the Bundeswehr. This document is a thesis by an officer at the staff academy of the Bundeswehr. The number is the ID number for recalling the document.)

ties and obligations of military service; within the walls of the barracks he learned the political and legal relationship of the solider to the state and witnessed the power of the army through the self-image contained in its symbols. Yet contemporaries generally did not describe the sum of these symbols and practices as *Traditionspflege* at the time.

Custom had long prescribed that soldiers swear their oath to the king on the regimental flag and that officers instruct their men about their duties to the crown as set down in the traditional Articles of War.[25] These practices formed an integral part of the training and education of the soldier at the regimental level—they were the essence of a kind of unreflective and natural maintenance of tradition.

The unit flag, which the king awarded to the regiment, occupied a central role in this heritage. As part of the soldier's code (*Pflichtenlehre*), the recruit learned the ninth paragraph of the articles of war, that "the regimental flag shall be sacred to the soldier." Officers taught their troops that the colors were "a symbol given to them by their king, by the grace of God." The soldier was "to rally to the flag in the peril of battle," and protect it with his life at all costs. He gave witness of his loyalty to king and fatherland, swearing his oath before God while placing his hand on the flag lowered before him.

The regimental flag also symbolized continuity between past and present, a presence that surrounded the soldier in his regimental education and training. "The soldier," directed the author of a leading handbook from the Prussian army, "should learn of the great deeds of the unit to which he belongs." He was to take pride in being a member of a famous regiment and should uphold the example of patriotism, loyalty, and heroism set by his regimental comrades before him.[26] Pride in the soldier's uniform, whose cut and color often varied from one regiment to the next, was also supposed to strengthen *esprit de corps* by recalling the glories of the past. Beyond instruction in regimental history, in the later years of Wilhelmine Germany soldiers

[25] Konrad Lehmann et al., *Dienstunterricht des Offiziers: Anleitung zur Erteilung des Mannschaftsunterrichts in Beispielen*, 3d ed. (Berlin, 1913), pp. 68–69. The oath could also be sworn on a sword or the barrel of a fieldgun. A discussion of the *Pflichtenlehre* is to be found in Rudolf Absolon, *Die Wehrmacht im Dritten Reich*, 4 vols. (Boppard, 1971), 2: 211ff.

[26] Lehmann et al. *Dienstunterricht des Offiziers*, pp. 50–51.

learned the history of the Reich. This instruction took the form of "the history of the fatherland," a subject that highlighted the heroic role of the army in the unification of Germany. It depicted opponents of the Prussian-dominated order—left-liberals, Catholic-particularists, and social democrats—in an unflattering light.

The *Pflichtenlehre* emphasized loyalty, comradeship, readiness for battle, bravery, and courage, but it also described how the soldier could make a complaint. Although the Articles of War included twenty-eight different paragraphs, the soldier had only to know the second one by heart, since it summed up the traditional values contained in the *Pflichtenlehre*. "The soldier's first duty is to maintain the unbreakable loyalty sworn in his oath on the flag. The soldierly profession further demands: readiness for battle, conviction in all matters of service, courage in war, obedience towards one's superiors, honorable demeanor in service and without, and good and honest behavior towards one's comrades."[27]

After William II became emperor in 1888, he began to transform the symbolic and political meaning of the maintenance of regimental tradition, especially in the elite guard regiments. He was eager to create traditions that would invigorate the connection between his rule, his ancestors, and his soldiers. His attention to the past also sought a soldierly heritage common to all German states. The army corps headquartered in Hannover and Hesse, for instance, received the lineage and honors of the Hannoverian Body Guards and the Hessian Life Guard Regiments, respectively, units that had been disbanded when Prussia consolidated northern Germany after the 1866 war.

In his efforts to maintain the soldierly tradition he focused on the externals of military life: parade uniforms, military accoutrements, and regimental flags—elements that seemed increasingly artificial and theatrical to many observers in an age of industry and mass politics. He reached back to the eighteenth century and the memory of Frederick William I and Frederick II. The young emperor had the surviving regimental flags and standards of the Prussian army restored, and awarded new ones patterned on those of the eighteenth century. He presented inscriptions on helmet plates to certain regiments, recalling great battles of the eighteenth century. One of his more striking acts

27 Ibid., p. 76.

of *Traditionspflege* took place in February 1894. He gave new grenadier caps to his Potsdam guard infantry, the First Guard Regiment of Foot, paying for them out of his own pocket.[28] The new headdress for the guards was a replica of the kind worn by the Fifteenth Guards in the reign of Frederick II. William wanted the new cap to symbolize an unbroken lineage between the Frederician regiment and his own First Guard Regiment of Foot, which had been created in 1807 after the defeats of Jena and Auerstedt the year before.

If the sight of the guards with the new cap on parade in the Lustgarten of Potsdam recalled the battle of Leuthen for some, the men who wore it in the years before 1914 only knew that the heavy and unbalanced cap often fell off their heads while they passed in review. Theodore Fontane, the great social novelist and a keen observer of Prussian military life, looked skeptically on the growing trend toward antiquarian excess. Commenting on the new headdress, he wrote that the young emperor would do better to assure his subjects "money, brains, and enthusiasm" rather than "grenadier tin hats, medals, and battle streamers on flags."[29] But this new use of "traditional" items of militaria to maintain unit lineage and honors became widespread in the course of the twentieth century.

William's love of old flags and caps notwithstanding, the maintenance of lineage and honors in the old armies also incorporated local traditions, in order to preserve the heritage of the particular German states. Such customs also relied upon personal loyalties stretching over generations. Young men of the upper-middle class in such an important garrison as the fortress city of Mainz, for instance, might volunteer for a particular local field artillery regiment because good families traditionally sent their sons there. Often the young men would have attended the same gymnasium. This bourgeois custom of joining a specific regiment imitated the aristocratic military tradition, and is another example of what Kehr describes as the "feudalization of the middle class" in Wilhelmine Germany. It was to certain elite and splendidly uniformed guards regiments, with Death's Head and

[28] Manfred Bresemann, "Die Parademützen des Königlich-Preussischen Ersten Garde-Regiments zu Fuss 1824–1918," *Zeitschrift für Heereskunde*, 39, 259 (May/June 1975): 102–11. Also see Paul Pietsch, *Die Formations und Uniformierungsgeschichte des preussischen Heeres, 1808–1914*, 2d ed. (Hamburg, 1963), p. 68.
[29] Kenneth Atwood, *Fontane und das Preussentum* (Berlin, 1970), p. 180.

"Suum Cuique" insignia, that the best noble families sent their sons over generations; regiments that generally refused commissions to commoners. This kind of social exclusivity of course contributed not only to the maintenance of tradition, but also to the political frictions that plagued professional German soldiers well into the twentieth century.

William II also liked to refer to tradition in his addresses on ceremonial occasions. On the two-hundredth anniversary of the Prussian monarchy on 18 January 1901, William II issued a decree reaffirming the bond between king and soldier in historical terms: "The spirit maintained in the army, from Frederick I and all his successors, the spirit of honor, of loyalty, of obedience, of bravery and chivalry, has made the army into what it should be and is: the sharp and reliable weapon of its kings, the shield of and the blessing of the fatherland." Until the outbreak of the war, William continued his cult of tradition by means of awards of unit lineage and honors and special insignia. But his habitual recalling of a simple, stirring past would prove all too conspicuously irrelevant to the realities of the Great War. William's self-serving attempts to maintain the traditional bond between the sovereign and the officer corps recalled the decadence of the monarchy before 1806, compounded now by the forces of total war and mass politics. Riven by ideological tensions that mirrored those of German society as a whole, and confronted with a defeat for which tradition offered no adequate solace, the leaders of the officer corps finally broke their oath and lent their voices to the call for abdication that would drive William from his throne.

THE WAR ended in 1918 with military defeat, social conflict, and finally a civil war that shook the military caste and finished the imperial armies. While the professional military survived by striking a deal with the reluctant leaders of the new republic, its self-image had been badly damaged. The professional officer was robbed of his sovereign—the personification of his oath. The social transformation that had taken place in the professional military during the war had its effects as well. The officer corps that had gone into action in 1914 with common perceptions and traditions had by 1915–16 been supplanted by a new breed of officer from lower social strata with a much different outlook. These new officers entered the military without the same education in the customs and traditions of their calling, and they lacked the intense traditional bond to the crown. They were dedicated to the handicraft of war in its increasingly technical forms, and they were open to new political ideologies. The old officers and the new officers entered the postwar military with very different notions about the relation between the soldier and the state. In the 1920s, many senior officers in the new army remained loyal to the aloof, imperial style; among their juniors, there was a tendency toward a more outspoken ideology of nationalism, ambition, and military daring. Fault lines developed in the army's inner structure that became more pronounced as the younger generation advanced in the ranks.[30]

The defeat and the military restrictions imposed by the Versailles treaty complicated the prospects of forming a military suited to the new German republic. General Hans von Seeckt became the chief of the new army that eventually emerged from the chaos of war's end and revolution. He wanted to preserve the ethos of the old professional military, and at the same time to make up for the loss of a king to whom the soldier could swear his oath. The absence of the traditional bonds of military service added to the other political difficulties faced by Seeckt. The left regarded the army as a dangerous remnant of the old regime; the right pitied it as a militarily useless bastard of the dictated peace. Seeckt himself saw the future one-hundred-thousand-man army as but a temporary expedient, which was supposed to fulfill contradictory missions: on the one hand, it was to defend the Reich against a Polish invasion; on the other, it was to serve as a cadre for a future national army on the old scale.

He first had to restore discipline in the ranks and prevent his men from joining the private political armies roaming the streets. His solution was to focus the officer corps and the ranks on their twofold

[30] On the social and political problems of the German officer corps after 1918, see Kurt Hesse, *Von der nahen Ära der "Jungen Armee"* (Berlin, 1925); Friedrich von Rabenau, *Die Alte Armee und die Junge Generation* (Berlin, 1925); Adolf Heusinger, *Befehl im Widerstreit* (Tübingen, 1950), pp. 9–22; Karl Demeter, *Das Deutsche Offizierkorps in Gesellschaft und Staat* (Frankfurt, 1965); Michael Geyer, "Die Wehrmacht der Deutschen Republik ist die Reichswehr," *Militärgeschichtliche Mitteilungen*, 2 (1973): 152–99; Detlef Bald, *Der deutsche Offizier: Sozial- und Bildungsgeschichte des deutschen Offizierkorps im 20. Jahrhundert* (München, 1982); Heinz Hürten, *Das Offizierkorps des Reichsheeres*, in *Das Deutsche Offizierkorps 1860–1960*, ed. Hanns Hubert Hofmann (Boppard, 1980), pp. 231–46.

28

mission, as a cadre and as a bulwark in the east. In the process, he elevated the cult of the soldierly past to a new and greater importance within the political culture of the new republic. This increased emphasis on tradition came quite naturally to him. He was a veteran of the Kaiser Alexander Guard Grenadiers, which, like the First Guard Regiment of Foot, had a very pronounced cult of tradition. The Alexander Grenadiers were immensely proud of their reputation as a crack unit—it was before them that William II had made his famous statement that his soldiers should be ready to shoot down their kin in the streets. Seeckt's emphasis on the continuity between the new and the old armies apparently reflected a widespread longing for the past in the officer corps and in the ranks. "All sides regard the preservation of the tradition of the old army," wrote a high-ranking officer as early as 1919, "as a pressing necessity in the Reichswehr."[31] In his first directive on military training and education, issued in January 1921, Seeckt began to put this desire into effect, using the very words employed by William I in 1874.[32]

Seeckt's aim, as he later described it, was to overcome distrust of an "alien and rootless mercenary army . . . by strengthening the army's deepest roots" by an appeal to the past.[33] As had been the case in the old armies, he hoped that the emphasis on soldierly tradition would stimulate *esprit de corps* in the ranks. "The consciousness that one carries on great historical fame has an undeniable effect upon the value of a unit, which helps distinguish it from others."[34] These traditions were to be symbolized by the externals of militaria: "Whoever refuses to see the uniqueness of the military psyche will fail to understand the deeper meaning of these externals and dismiss them as theatricalities." He believed in the importance of pathos, a point he underscored with

[31] This proposal was put forward in a document signed by Generalmajor Fritz von Lossberg, Chief of Staff of Reichswehrgruppenkommando 2 in Kassel: BA/MA, N 247, "Nachlass Seeckt, Reichswehrgruppenkommando 2, Ia Nr. 1000/664 A 1," ca. September 1919, cited in Gustav-Adolf Caspar, "Die militärische Tradition in der Reichswehr und in der Wehrmacht, 1919–1945," in *Tradition in Deutschen Streitkräften bis 1945*, ed. Militärgeschichtliches Forschungsamt (MGFA) (Herford, 1986), p. 228.

[32] "Heeresverordnungsblatt," vol. 3, no. 79 (30 December 1920), pp. 1041ff., cited in Caspar, "Tradition, 1919–1945," p. 229.

[33] Hans von Seeckt, *Die Reichswehr* (Leipzig, 1933), pp. 46–64. See also Buschmann, "Traditionsbruch," pp. 6–8.

[34] Seeckt, *Die Reichswehr*, p. 47.

a quotation from Schiller: "The soldier must be able to feel himself as a soldier."

In August 1921 Seeckt decreed that certain companies of the new army would maintain the lineage and honors of the regiments of the old army.[35] For example, the 1st company of the Potsdam Infantry Regiment 9 assumed the lineage and honors of the First Guard Regiment of Foot, while the thirteenth company of the same unit assumed the traditions of the colonial troops in German East Africa.[36] Although brightly colored regimental uniforms had disappeared before the war, Seeckt nonetheless provided some units with insignia and accoutrements for their nondescript field-gray uniform that recalled distinguished regiments of the old armies. The 2nd and 4th Squadrons of Cavalry Regiment No. 6 in Pasewalk wore the eagle of the old Schwedter Dragoons on their peaked caps, while the 1st and 2nd Squadrons of Mounted Regiment No. 5 wore the Death's Head of the Guard Hussars. Infantry Regiment No. 1 was awarded the unit tradition that recalled the dash of the 43rd Prussian Infantry Regiment at the battle of Königgrätz in 1866, where Prussians had captured an Austrian drum wagon pulled by a dog. This "drum dog" became a special, jealously guarded mascot of the 43rd Regiment that was then handed down to the 1st Infantry of the Reichswehr. The navy generally made a point of naming new ships after vessels lost in the last war. These measures were meant to forge a link between the old and the new, the spirit of which was symbolized by the memorial to the First Guard Regiment of Foot erected in Potsdam in 1924. The monument, which stood beneath the tower of the Garrison Church, depicted a guardsman of the mid-eighteenth century and a front soldier of the recent war grasping hands beneath the gaze of Frederick the Great. Like the figures in the monument, the soldiers of the new

[35] See Caspar, "Die militärische Tradition in der Reichswehr und in der Wehrmacht, 1919–1945," in *Tradition in deutschen Streitkräften*, pp. 229–30. Hanns Demeter, "Die Pflege der Traditionen der alten Armee im Reichsheer und in der Wehrmacht," *Feldgrau*, Sonderheft 7 (1956), contains a fairly complete list of these lineages and honors.
[36] These practices are fully described in Wolfgang Paul, *Das Potsdamer Infanterie Regiment 9, 1918–1945: Preussische Tradition in Krieg und Frieden*, 2d ed., 2 vols. (Osnabrück, 1985), especially vol. 1, pp. ix–134, and Christoph von L'Estocq, *Unser Potsdam* (Limburg, 1985).

and old armies were to join hands across the abyss of defeat and abdication.

Seeckt encouraged soldiers to collect old pieces of militaria, which were enshrined in regimental traditions rooms. These little museums became an important focus of barracks life. The traditions companies invited veterans groups and traditions associations to regimental and company celebrations, sports events, and unit hunts, making such customs major occasions in the social life of the garrison. That some troops regarded this practice with more amusement than reverence is illustrated by an example from Infantry Regiment No. 9, whose 3rd Battalion in Spandau maintained the lineage and honors of the Alexander Guard Grenadiers. Seeckt himself often came to Spandau to be with his "Alexander comrades," where he greatly enjoyed the club life among officers and soldiers alike. For the young recruits, however, the maintenance of tradition meant that, before visits by Seeckt or members of the traditions associations, they would have to polish the fittings of the old helmets and swords that hung on the walls of their otherwise drab barracks. One night, after a lively celebration in the unit squad room, several soldiers of the 3rd Battalion, dressed in night shirts and buckled up in belts and cartridge pouches, paraded into the hallway where they donned the old Grenadier caps and drew the ancestral swords for an unofficial reenactment of the battle of Cassano.[37]

Such incidents of military humor aside, Seeckt believed the union of veterans and young soldiers would educate the troops. And, as he observed in 1933, "this carry-over of the tradition would deeply benefit the younger generation. They were to preserve something of great significance for the present, and for future generations."[38] *Traditionspflege* was meant to form a bridge not just to the past but to the future as well.

Implicit in all this was Seeckt's hope that such a future would witness the end of party politics. Although Seeckt proved relatively loyal to the republic, his critics condemned his view of the military as embodying the state and thus as standing beyond the reach of politics. To these critics, the cult of tradition reflected Seeckt's resentment of civilian attempts to control the armed forces. The union of the old

[37] Guenter Heysing, "Alexander Tradition," in *Deutsches Soldatenjahrbuch 1985* (München, 1985), pp. 169ff.
[38] Seeckt, *Die Reichswehr*, p. 62.

and the new inevitably brought the soldiers of the republic together with veterans groups closely allied to the antirepublican right. All too often, when the veterans and young soldiers came together in the smoke- and alcohol-laden atmosphere of the traditions associations, the talk would turn from tales of heroism under the storm of steel to resentful reflections on the weakness of the republic and the decadence of the political parties and special interests.

As Wolfgang Sauer observed during the debate about the spirit of the new West German army in 1954, Seeckt had built a structure for the Reichswehr that was held together with the clamp of tradition.[39] This involved more than mere decoration. The officer corps itself constituted a human link with the past: almost 23 percent of its members were drawn from the nobility, which made up but two-tenths of one percent of the population as a whole. These noble officers were disproportionately concentrated in northern garrisons and saw themselves as charged with preserving the traditions of elite Prussian units from the past. They worked hard to preserve their old code of honor, and they fought for a separate system of military justice like that which had existed under the empire. They also worked hard to perpetuate themselves and to discourage the entry of bourgeois officers into the new army, a task made easier by a decentralized system of recruitment, which gave individual regiments control over the selection of officer candidates.

Decorated on the outside with garlands from a glorious past and held up by the timber work salvaged from the inner structure of the old armies, Seeckt's edifice was decried by contemporary observers as a state within a state. Liberal critics asserted that the emphasis on a continuous military tradition at the expense of a republican military ethos posed a threat to the already troubled democracy of Weimar Germany.

In fact most officers served with reasonable, if perhaps unenthusiastic, loyalty to the republic. Indeed, under the aegis of a group of military innovators, civil-military relations grew increasingly inter-

---

[39] On Seeckt, see Wolfgang Sauer, "Die Reichswehr," in *Die Auflösung der Weimarer Republik*, ed. Karl Dietrich Bracher (Villingen, 1960), pp. 229ff.; Hans Meier-Welcker, *Seeckt* (Frankfurt, 1967); Claus Guske, *Das politische Denken des Generals von Seeckt. Ein Beitrag zur Diskussion des Verhältnisses Seeckt-Reichswehr-Republik* (Lübeck/Hamburg, 1971); and Geyer, "Wehrmacht."

connected in the Hindenburg republic of the late 1920s. Too many observers of the Reichswehr have dismissed it as a miniature copy of the old army in all respects. The military innovators in the Reichswehr developed remarkably effective doctrines of operations and tactics that were anything but tradition-bound. Before the early 1930s, the military leadership selected the very best personnel and took advantage of long-term training in a professional army. With the passage of time, the tensions between innovation and the cult of the past tended to divide the generations of officers. These social and political cleavages in the officer corps intensified as the prewar generation departed or rose to senior positions, and less tradition-bound officers grew in number. While many officers of the earlier generation found the traditions associations, festooned with old headgear, a welcome atmosphere for recalling a golden past, those from the younger generations—among them those who were tried in 1930 for attempting contacts with the National Socialists—protested that the spirit of the army was dead. In place of its isolation and its enchantment with tradition, they believed that the army should join in a national uprising to rejuvenate the Reich and create a nation in arms prepared for total war.[40]

IN WHAT seemed to be a miracle to most Germans, the return to the army's golden past and a national uprising appeared to occur simultaneously on 21 March 1933. Beneath the tower of the Garrison Church in Potsdam, within earshot of the carillon's somber message, the President of the Reich, Field Marshal Paul von Hindenburg, and Chancellor Adolf Hitler joined hands atop the resting place of the Prussian kings to open the newly elected Reichstag. The Day of Potsdam demonstrated, as clearly as any episode in Germany's recent past, how the cult of tradition had become a means to advance political ends. It was the work of Joseph Goebbels, a man who understood the power of pathos far better than had Seeckt. After the new Reichstag election of 5 March 1933, Goebbels hit upon the idea of convening

---

[40] On the political radicalization of young officers, see Heinz Hürten, *Das Offizierkorps des Reichsheeres*, in *Das Deutsche Offizierkorps 1860–1960*, ed. Hanns Hubert Hofmann (Boppard, 1980), pp. 244–45. For a definitive survey of the *Reichswehr* in the late 1920s and early 1930s, see Michael Geyer, *Aufrüstung oder Sicherheit: Die Reichswehr in der Krise der Machtpolitik 1924–1936* (Wiesbaden, 1980).

parliament on the twenty-first of March, both the beginning of spring, symbolizing light and renewal, and the date on which Bismarck had opened the first Reichstag in 1871. Potsdam was to contrast with Weimar, which for Nazi publicists signified a conquered and deceived Germany. With remarkable energy and attention to detail, Goebbels planned and oversaw every aspect of the ceremony.[41] It was to be the first true spectacle in Nazi style, a combination of tradition, Wagnerian *mise-en-scène*, and technology in service of a secular deity. For the first time, moreover, all German radio stations would broadcast the event simultaneously throughout the Reich.

The interior of the church had been decorated with garlands of laurel and evergreen. The standards of the old regiments hung from the walls. As the deputies filled the church, the seats of the former kaiser, Queen Luise, Frederick, and Frederick William I remained empty. Hindenburg and Hitler both spoke of the need for recalling Prussian-German traditions in the face of the present crisis. At the conclusion of the ceremonies, while an artillery salute was being fired, Hindenburg placed a wreath on the graves of the Prussian kings and then reviewed the parade of tradition-laden Potsdam regiments, followed by the formations of the Nazi party.

"National Socialism," as Friedrich Meinecke wrote afterward, "was now to appear as the grand inheritor and propagator of all great and splendid Prussian traditions."[42] Although dismissed by some soldiers as kitsch, Goebbels's theatricality had a profound effect on many soldiers. "We German officers," Field Marshal August von Mackensen observed, "used to be called the representatives of reaction, whereas we were really the bearers of tradition. It is in the sense of that tradition that Hitler spoke to us, so wonderfully and so directly from the heart, at Potsdam."[43] Many of the younger generation of officers, as Goebbels himself soon found on a visit to Potsdam's Infantry Regiment No. 9, accepted the promises of the new regime with enthusiasm. Yet among this group of junior officers in Potsdam and else-

[41] Joseph Goebbels, *Vom Kaiserhof zur Reichskanzlei* (München, 1934), pp. 283–86; Manfred Schlenke, "Das 'preussische Beispiel' in Propaganda und Politik des Nationalsozialismus," *Aus Politik und Zeitgeschichte*, 3 July 1968.

[42] Meinecke, *Die Deutsche Katastrophe*, p. 336.

[43] Rüdt von Collenberg, *Mackensen* (Leipzig, 1944), p. 149, cited in Gordon A. Craig, *The Politics of the Prussian Army* (London, 1964), p. 470.

where were such future leaders of the military resistance as Henning von Tresckow and Klaus Graf von Stauffenberg.[44]

The artifice of the cult of tradition helped Hitler to establish his regime by reassuring many of those who were skeptical about the new government. More than ceremonies, however, were required for Hitler to consolidate his hold on the state and carry out his program. In particular, he needed the support of the military leadership, and he received it on 30 June 1934, when the SS gunned down not only the SA chiefs but also two politically active Reichswehr generals, Kurt von Schleicher and Ferdinand von Bredow, as well as a number of wholly innocent people. Shortly thereafter, Hindenburg died, and the military took the traditional oath to Hitler personally, as a man who appeared to personify the oath as it had existed before 1918. In so doing, German soldiers ceremonially bound themselves to the fate of a man intent on sweeping away the essence of the traditions of tolerance and the moral limits to power. Together with the Nazi party, the armed forces were to become, in Hitler's view, one of the two pillars upholding the National Socialist state.

Like William II and Seeckt, Hitler used the symbols and ceremonies embodied in the cult of tradition to increase the soldier's self-esteem and to win him over for his own purposes: a new parade uniform (nicknamed the Kaiser William memorial tunic) based on those in use before 1914, a new war flag with the iron cross, and new unit standards were designed and awarded with the Führer's personal involvement. Continuing the practice started by Seeckt, but on a much broader scale, the lineage and honors of the old armies were passed on to the newly formed units of the rapidly growing Wehrmacht.[45] In

---

[44] Goebbels, *Vom Kaiserhof zur Reichskanzlei*, p. 292.

[45] In his first major address to the Wehrmacht at the 1935 Party Congress, Hitler exhorted the new conscription army to maintain the tradition of the armies of the World War. See *Hitlers Reden und Proklamationen 1932–1945, kommentiert von einem deutschen Zeitgenossen*, ed. Max Domarus, 4 vols. (Wiesbaden, 1962ff.), vol. I/2 1935–38, p. 540. For a description of the maintenance of tradition in the military from 1933 to 1945, see Gustav-Adolf Caspar, "Die militärische Tradition in der Reichswehr und in der Wehrmacht, 1919–1945," in *Tradition in Deutschen Streitkräften bis 1945*, ed. MGFA (Herford, 1986), pp. 259ff.; Hanns Demeter, "Die Pflege der Traditionen der alten Armee im Reichsheer und in der Wehrmacht," *Feldgrau*, Sonderheft 7 (1956): 5ff. Details of the maintenance of tradition in the air force and navy, respectively, are found in: Oberst E. Tschoeltsch, "Die Tradition in der Luftwaffe," in *Jahrbuch der Deutschen Luftwaffe* (Leipzig, 1940), pp. 104–11 and Fritz Otto Busch, *Traditionshandbuch der Kriegsmarine* (München, 1937).

fact, the Nazis covered the Reich with their own militarized cult of tradition that went far beyond the barracks: the German salute with the raised right arm; the parade review of political soldiers at the party congresses; the identification of the Munich district as the birthplace of Nazi tradition (*Traditionsgau*); the "traditions" uniform of the party formations and the black uniform of the SS, an imitation, in part, of the Death's Head Hussar uniform of the old army; the ceremonial daggers for party political soldiers, and the route marches for the political leadership corps with drums and fife, backpack, and mess kit. Many features of barracks life in the old army became things of everyday experience for civilians who were confronted with a constant rolling of drums and a blaring of bugles amid a welter of uniforms and flags. The Nazis took an existing heritage and grafted it onto their ideology in an effort to justify it as a new tradition overnight.

The result of this hybrid was most visible in the SS. Fulfillment of one's duty became the motto, "My honor is loyalty," stamped on the SS man's silver belt buckle and engraved on the blade of his black-gripped dagger. The Prussian virtues recalled by the carillon of the *Garnisonkirche* were painted in foot-high letters on the walls of the concentration camps run by the SS. In the hands of the SS, virtues and traditions that had once meant the best in Germany became symbols for the rule of terror.

The social metamorphosis of the armed forces worked by the Nazis proved equally significant for the fate of military tradition as a political force, rendering its meaning increasingly problematic. The homogeneous cadre of Seeckt's Reichswehr was dwarfed by the sixteen million strong Wehrmacht at the height of the war, the true nation in arms desired by the Prussian reformers of the early nineteenth century. It was a people's army filled with men from social groups that the bearers of military tradition had long excluded. This social transformation had both its positive and negative sides. With the passage of time, military functionalism further asserted itself in the Wehrmacht, fostered by the nature of mechanized warfare and the impact of ideology. Such military functionalism promoted far better relations between officers and men than had obtained in the First World War, a strong emphasis being placed on the cohesion of small military units, symbolized by the crews of armored vehicles, aircraft, and submarines. For many, these changes became important features of German military tradition. On the shadow side of military life, especially in training and rear-area units, more Germans than ever before encountered the drillmaster mentality that, in the view of many critics, had always been the essence of German military tradition.

Nazi racist and imperialist ideology had a strong impact on the military traditions taken over by and formed in the Wehrmacht. Although some Germans after 1933 had joined the army as a form of "inner immigration" from National Socialism, the Wehrmacht was increasingly penetrated by Nazi ideology or by something that resembled it: a disturbing combination of traditional principles, personal ambition, and intense nationalism merged into a frenzy of action. The traditions of moderation and of the moral limits of obedience faded in the haste to rearm, and in the breathtaking series of victories and defeats in the years between 1939 and 1944. Although the German armed forces proved highly effective militarily, in part because of noteworthy traditions of operational leadership and tactical innovation, within the Nazi state too many soldiers became accomplices in a war of annihilation.[46] The dividing line between soldier and executioner, even murderer, vanished, especially in the struggle against Russia. The record of guilt is plain among numerous members of the high and highest military leadership as well as among many, but certainly not all, officers and men. The documented actions of many units in the killing of prisoners of war and their collaboration with the *Einsatzgruppen*—SS murder squads—placed an indelible stain on the army's record.

Although some soldiers became deeply implicated in the crimes of the Nazis, others conspired against the National Socialists. A few officers had tried to defeat Hitler in 1938, but they did not attempt any

---

[46] On the ideological aspects of the Wehrmacht and its inner structure, see Manfred Messerschmidt, *Die Wehrmacht im NS Staat: Zeit der Indoktrination* (Hamburg, 1969); Klaus-Jürgen Müller, *Das Heer und Hitler: Armee und nationalsozialistisches Regime 1933–1945* (Stuttgart, 1969); Michael Salewski, "Die bewaffnete Macht im dritten Reich, 1933–1939," in *Handbuch zur deutschen Militärgeschichte*, ed. MGFA, 6 vols. (München, 1979), 4: 13–287; Helmut Krausnick et al., *Die Truppe des Weltanschauungskrieges* (Stuttgart, 1981); Christian Streit, *Keine Kameraden: Die Wehrmacht und die sowjetischen Kriegsgefangenen 1941–1945* (Stuttgart, 1979); *Das Deutsche Reich und der Zweite Weltkrieg*, ed. MGFA (Stuttgart, 1979ff.); Jürgen Foerster, "Zur Rolle der Wehrmacht im Krieg gegen die Sowjetunion," in *Aus Politik und Zeitgeschichte*, No. B45/80 (8 November 1980), pp. 3–15; and Omer Bartov, *The Eastern Front* (Basingstoke, Hampshire, 1985).

significant action against the regime until late in the conflict, when defeat seemed at hand and Nazi popularity was clearly waning. When the soldiers did finally act, however, the step of trying to kill the head of state was unprecedented. Although Prussian-German military tradition knew men of conscience who had resisted their sovereign, none had attempted to overturn the entire political system like those officers who joined the Russian-sponsored *Komitee Freies Deutschland* after Stalingrad, or those who tried to kill Hitler on the Twentieth of July 1944 at Rastenburg.

The unsuccessful coup of the Twentieth of July marked the end of the cult of tradition in the German military, which had begun in the late nineteenth century. It forced moral questions on men who proudly regarded themselves as the bearers of past values, questions concerning resistance, guilt, complicity, and criminal participation. The explosion in the briefing hut at Rastenburg tore open the longstanding rift between those soldiers who adhered to pre-Nazi traditions and those who owed their careers to Hitler and his victories. With the blast still ringing in his ears, the Führer could freely liquidate his conservative allies of 1933. He declared open season on the old guard of the Prussian-German military way of life—men who had been enchanted with the dramaturgy of the Day of Potsdam, but who later saw behind Goebbels's stage setting and recognized the true aims of the regime. They were either gunned down in the aftermath of the putsch or brought into the courtroom of Roland Freisler for the greatest show trial in the history of Nazi Germany. Adept at using anything to serve their ends, the Nazi propagandists after the Twentieth of July could simply dismiss as reactionaries the group of military men from families and regiments with a long heritage who had joined with others from all walks of German life to topple Hitler. For the overwhelming majority of officers who had not resisted, the tradition became an alibi for those in positions of authority who had refused to break their oath to join the plot against Hitler. An officers' traditional court of honor ejected from the army high-ranking staff officers, generals, and even a fieldmarshal, handing these men over to the SS to be strung up on meat hooks in a slaughter recorded on film. The disastrous outcome of the Twentieth of July revealed the decadence of German military tradition under Nazism. The lack of sanctity of the soldier's oath in a moral vacuum and the unstable position of the soldier in the state, which made him grasp at military traditions empty of content, helped lead the German soldier to the crimes of the war.

THE EVENTS of the years from 1933 to 1944, which culminated in the plot against Hitler, laid bare the inner corruption of much in German military tradition. Germany's opponents, however, could hardly have been expected to care about such decay. On the contrary, they were eager to wipe out the soldierly tradition of the Reich, convinced that it expressed the inherent militarism of the German character. The allies rained unprecedented destruction on the Reich in part to eradicate this spirit root and branch. The Garrison Church in Potsdam caught fire on the night the British attacked in April 1945. The bells crashed to earth with a hellish sound, amid the fire and crumbling masonry. Long before then, however, the allies had begun to formulate a plan to wipe out whatever remnants of Germany's military heritage the bombs failed to destroy.

Already in 1943, Russia, the United Kingdom, and the United States had joined in the demand for the unconditional surrender of the German Reich. The leaders of the anti-Nazi alliance also agreed that they would work closely together in the postwar world, a vow which, in the event, none was able to keep. Two years later, with the prospect of victory plainly in sight, the allies met at Yalta to divide the Reich into zones of occupation, create a control commission for all of Germany, and plan the disarmament of Germany. The vow to root out Nazism and militarism became the watchwords of the occupiers in the years immediately after the war.

The fate of the professional soldier in the aftermath of 1945 made a mockery of the popular prewar song entitled "It's great to be a soldier!" Long used to being considered the first man in the state, he was now damned together with the SS leaders and the party bosses of the NSDAP. The victors imprisoned senior Wehrmacht officers, tried them for war crimes, and executed many of them. General staff officers were also rounded up and kept behind barbed wire. The political wounds of the professional officer corps festered in captivity. Officers were divided over their support for Hitler and their judgment of the Twentieth of July. Most viewed the participants in the plot as traitors, while others regarded those who had continued to serve Hitler as nothing more than obedient swine. Amid the choking dust and hunger of the zero hour, the Germans—particularly men in POW camps—were exposed to a new image of their history by teachers selected by the victors. Reeducation revealed to the average German that soldierly virtues and military tradition had been in reality camouflaged immorality. German history had been a tale of betrayal and human culpability from Hermann to Luther to Hitler. In the end, reeducation may have been more effective than denazification. With the liberated concentration camps, the ruined cities, and the heaps of dead as proof, many Germans could easily conclude that the work of statecraft begun by the Prussian kings had been a disaster. The history of the German Reich was at an end, and the professional soldier, so clearly linked with the creation of the state, was also finished in Germany. But soon enough, as in George Orwell's novel of the time, *1984*, the fronts changed. As Hitler and Goebbels had predicted in the bunker while waiting for a Frederickian miracle beneath the gaze of Anton Graff's portrait of Frederick II, the alliance between the western powers and the Soviet Union broke down. The intensification of the cold war led the western allies and the USSR to consolidate the temporary zones of occupation into two separate German states, each based on a different political order. The cold war and the division of the Reich forced the armament of the Federal Republic of Germany, raising anew the question of military tradition sooner than anyone had dreamed.[47]

[47] On the armament of the Federal Republic within the context of international relations after 1945, there is a growing literature. See Gerhard Wettig, *Entmilitarisierung und Wiederbewaffnung Deutschlands 1943–1955* (Stuttgart, 1967); Richard Löwenthal "Vom Kalten Krieg zur Ostpolitik," in *Die Zweite Republik, 25 Jahre Bundesrepublik Deutschland—eine Bilanz*, ed. Richard Löwenthal and Hans-Peter Schwarz (Stuttgart, 1974); Klaus von Schubert, *Wiederbewaffnung und Westintegration* (Stuttgart, 1970); *Aspekte der deutschen Wiederbewaffnung*, ed. MGFA (1974); Josef Fischepoth, ed., *Kalter Krieg und Deutsche Frage: Deutschland im Widerstreit der Mächte, 1945–1952* (Göttingen, 1985); Edward Fursdon, *The European Defense Community: A History* (London, 1980); John L. Gaddis, *Strategies of Containment: A Critical Appraisal of Postwar National Security* (New York, 1982); Andreas Hillgruber, *Europa in der Weltpolitik der Nachkriegszeit 1945–1963* (München, 1983); Wilfried Loth, *Die Teilung der Welt, Geschichte des Kalten Krieges, 1941–1955* (München, 1980); Olav Riste, ed., *Western Security: The Formative Years. European and Atlantic Defense 1947–1953* (Oslo, 1985); and Hans-Erich Volkmann and Walter Schwengler, eds., *Die Europäische Verteidigungsgemeinschaft: Stand und Probleme der Forschung* (Boppard, 1985). On the political, strategic, and domestic aspects of

THE ESTABLISHMENT of a new democratic political and legal foundation for Germans in the West provided the spiritual inspiration for a new army in West Germany. During 1948–49, the founders of the Federal Republic wrote a provisional constitution—the Basic Law—which has proved as successful as any in German history. This document has assured the rights of the citizen as never before in the German past. The framers of the Basic Law consciously sought to prevent the recurrence of the political abuses of the Weimar constitution and the illegalities of the Nazi regime. In so doing, they established the standard by which the future German soldier would judge his heritage, and offered the citizens of the nascent Federal Republic an image of military service that would correspond with the pluralistic spirit of the age.

The creators of the Basic Law addressed nearly all the questions of state power and the freedom of the individual save one: how would West Germany and its citizens be defended? The men at work on the Basic Law in Bonn plainly believed that, for the foreseeable future, the security of western Germany would rest with the occupying powers.[48] Aside from draft articles that forbade the preparation and the execution of an aggressive war, compelled the Federal Republic to

---

the Federal Republic in European defense from a West German perspective, see Roland G. Foerster, Christain Greiner et al., *Anfänge westdeutscher Sicherheitspolitik 1945–1956* (München, 1982); Anselm Doering–Manteuffel, *Katholizismus und Wiederbewaffnung. Die Haltung der deutschen Katholiken gegenüber der Wehrfrage 1948–1955* (Frankfurt, 1981); Alexander Fischer et al., eds., *Entmilitarisierung und Aufrüstung in Mitteleuropa, 1945–1956* (Boppard, 1983); Guther Mai, *Westliche Sicherheitspolitik im Kalten Krieg: Der Korea Konflikt und die deutsche Wiederbewaffnung* (Boppard, 1977); S. Thomas, *Der Weg in die NATO. Zur Integrations und Remilitarisierungspolitik der BRD 1949–1955* (Berlin, 1978); Ludger Borgert et al., *Dienstgruppen und westdeutscher Verteidigungsbeitrag. Vorüberlegungen zur Wiederbewaffnung der Bundesrepublik Deutschland* (Boppard, 1982); Christian Greiner, " 'Operational History (German) Section' und 'Naval History Team.' Deutsches militärstrategisches Denken im Dienst der amerikanischen Streitkräfte von 1946–1950," in *Militärgeschichte. Probleme—Thesen—Wege*, ed. Manfred Messerschmidt (Stuttgart, 1982); Manfred Messerschmidt et al., "West Germany's Strategic Position and her Role in Defence Policy as seen by the German Military, 1945–1949," in *Power in Europe? Great Britain, France, Italy and Germany in a Postwar World, 1945–1950*, ed. Josef Becker et al. (Berlin, 1986); Alexander Fischer, ed., *Wiederbewaffnung in Deutschland nach 1945* (Berlin, 1986).
[48] Georg Meyer, "Innenpolitische Voraussetzungen der westdeutschen Wiederbewaffnung," in *Wiederbewaffnung in Deutschland nach 1945*, ed. Alexander Fischer (Berlin, 1986), pp. 40–44.

41

join a system of collective security, and ensured that no individual could be forced into military service against his wishes, the Basic Law contained no further articles that dealt even indirectly with security policy. The spirit and letter of the West German Basic Law was, at the very least, neutral in its provisions for military power in the state, if indeed it was not antimilitary or pacifist in spirit. The law contained no specific guidelines on how a future army might be established or integrated into the new Federal Republic. This attitude also reflected the response of the first Chancellor of the republic, Konrad Adenauer, to the rumors during 1948 that an army would soon be formed. In November 1949, Adenauer publicly declared that he opposed the creation of German national armed forces, although in the most extreme case he was prepared to consider a German contingent within the army of a European confederation.

But as the 1940s ended, international developments began to suggest that what Adenauer described as the most extreme case might well come about. The detonation of a Soviet atomic bomb followed the Berlin crisis, ending the United States's nuclear monopoly and creating a state of affairs that grew even more disquieting for the West when the North Koreans attacked South Korea on 25 June 1950. The United States and its weakened French and British allies worried that what appeared to be a Soviet-led feint in Asia was the prelude to a worldwide Blitzkrieg. It was unlikely that the recently formed NATO could prevent a Russian advance to the English Channel and the Pyrenees. The dismembered Reich left an enormous gap in the central front of the Atlantic alliance. The United States had no ground troops to speak of in Europe; American units in West Germany were occupation forces in no condition to fight World War III. But the use of U.S. ground forces in Central Europe was not the chief intent of the Atlantic alliance, whose *ultima ratio* rested in the B–29 and B–36 bombers of the Strategic Air Command. If war came, the planners in the United States foresaw a withdrawal from the continent, as in 1940. The U.S. Air Force would have to drop atomic bombs on what it could and the alliance would gather its forces offshore over two years for a reenactment of 6 June 1944, a prospect that brought no joy to most Europeans privy to these plans. A growing number of policymakers argued that Europe would have to be defended as far to the east as possible, and to do that, the West would need the Germans.

Two months after the outbreak of war in Korea, Winston Churchill demanded a West German contribution to the European defense, thereby lending his authority to secret efforts by the United States in this direction that had been initiated after the Berlin crisis of 1948. As the pace of events quickened in the spring and summer of 1950, Adenauer decided to begin cautious planning for a West German contribution to western defense, a step that would address several of the Federal Republic's essential political goals. The new chancellor, worried about a war, eager to regain full rights for his still-occupied country, and convinced that the new state could only survive if it were integrated within Western Europe, suddenly gave a memorandum to the allied high commissioners in August 1950 that offered West German soldiers for a European Army. He did so much to the surprise not only of his own cabinet members, but of the West German people as well. Adenauer's Minister of Interior, Gustav Heinemann, promptly resigned in protest, convinced that Adenauer's step would seal the division of the Reich. Carlo Schmid's words of 1946 anticipated the popular shock at what Adenauer had done: "Never again do we want to send our sons to the barracks. And if again somewhere this insanity of war should break out, and if fate should want it that our land becomes a battlefield, then we shall simply perish and at least take with us the knowledge that we neither encouraged nor committed the crime."[49] The average German shortened Schmid's sentiment into the simple phrase *ohne mich* ("count me out"). As the summer of 1950 ended, former German officers and their previous opponents met secretly in Bonn to discuss the defense of the Federal Republic, scarcely five years after the unconditional surrender, the implementation of the demilitarization statutes, and even as military war criminals were still going to the gallows. For the third time in a single generation, after the creation of the Reichswehr in 1921 and of the Wehrmacht in 1935, a new army was to be raised on German soil, an event that shocked West Germany and the world.

Confronted with the unwanted prospect of new German soldiers, Adenauer and his advisers recognized the need to break with Germany's military tradition, much as the advocates of reform in Prussia had attempted to do after 1806, and as the Weimar Republic more

---

[49] Carlo Schmid, *Errinnerungen* (Bern/München, 1979), p. 490.

fatefully had failed to do with the Reichswehr. In the last week of September 1950, the French High Commissioner for Germany, André François Poncet, who as his country's ambassador to Berlin in the 1930s had been witness to the disastrous events of recent history, suggested in conversation with Federal President Theodor Heuss that the new West German government should prevent German generals from influencing domestic politics as they had done in the 1920s. In a similar exchange in late September 1950 with the American High Commissioner, John J. McCloy, Adenauer announced his intention to reform the German military and to choose future officers on the basis of their democratic attitudes as well as their technical skill.

THIS PROMISE of reform became one of the answers of the Federal Republic to the military abuses of the past, a pledge that evolved over the course of the 1950s into the concept of *Innere Führung*, a term that cannot really be translated into English.[50] Long the subject of an in-

---

[50] The English translations of this term are as varied as its definitions in German. It has been called "inner command," "inner leadership," "moral leadership," and "moral education." It has been left untranslated to avoid any of these inadequate terms. Among the many works on *Innere Führung* are *Handbuch Innere Führung: Hilfen zur Klärung der Begriffe*, Bundesministerium für Verteidigung (BMVg), Führungsstab der Bundeswehr (Fü B) I 6, ed. Führungsstab der Bundeswehr (Bonn, 1957); *Zentrale Dienstvorschrift (ZDv) 10/1, Hilfen für die Innere Führung*, BMVg, Fü S I, ed. Führungsstab der Bundeswehr (Bonn, 1972); Wolf Graf von Baudissin, *Soldat für den Frieden: Entwürfe für eine zeitgemässe Bundeswehr* (München, 1969); Dieter Walz, *Drei Jahrzehnte Innere Führung: Grundlagen, Entwicklungen, Perspektiven* (Baden-Baden, 1987); Heinz Karst, *Das Bild des Soldaten: Versuch eines Umrisses* (Boppard, 1964); Carl-Gero von Ilsemann, *Die Bundeswehr in der Demokratie: Die Zeit der Inneren Führung* (Hamburg, 1971); Ulrich de Maizière, *Führen im Frieden: 20 Jahre Dienst für Bundeswehr und Staat* (München, 1974); Gerd Schmückle, *Kommiss a.D.* (Stuttgart, 1970); Ulrich Simon, *Die Integration des Bundeswehr in die Gesellschaft: Das Ringen um die Innere Führung* (Heidelberg, 1980); Peter Wullich, *Die Konzeption der Inneren Führung der Bundeswehr als Grundlage der Allgemeinen Wehrpädagogik* (Regensburg, 1981); Jack Harris, "*Innere Führung*": *U.S. Army Training and Doctrine Command Monograph M-26-78* (US TRADOC Liaison Office, Cologne, 1978); "Bibliographie der Inneren Führung," ed. Streitkräfte Amt (Bonn, 1980); George Macioszek, *Das Problem der Tradition in der Bundeswehr: eine empirische Untersuchung unter jungen Offizieren des Heeres* (Hamburg, 1969); and Martin Esser, *Das Traditionsverständnis des Offizierkorps: eine empirische Untersuchung zur gesellschaftlichen Integration der Streitkräfte* (Heidelberg, 1982). The present study does not include any substantive discussion of military tradition in the German Democratic Republic. On this topic, see Alexander Fischer, "Tradition und Traditionspflege in der NVA," and Wilfried von Bredow, "Die Last der Traditionen," in *Deutsche Studien*, Sonderheft, January 1981, pp. 25–37, 55–66.

tense debate, it can be described as military leadership appropriate to the modern world, which enables the soldier to carry out his mission while assuring his rights as a citizen. Or, as one of the chief advocates of *Innere Führung*, Ulrich de Maizière, characterized it in 1984, *"Innere Führung* assures the Bundeswehr's readiness for action [while remaining] within the framework of our system of rights."[51] *Innere Führung* has been the Federal Republic's ongoing attempt to reconcile the citizen with the soldier, and to overcome the traditional antagonism between democracy and the military in German history. The adaptation of the new army to the West German Basic Law, which was militarily neutral in spirit, seemed a daunting task to most political and military thinkers of the 1950s. The creators of the new army foresaw that the program of reform would need to be carried out by adjusting, as nearly as possible, the relationships in everyday military life between officers, NCOs, and men to the new political realities of West Germany. Methods of leadership, and relationships between superiors and subordinates—which were specifically understood to incorporate an element of mutual responsibility and participation—were to be made to conform to the image of the citizen codified in the Basic Law. As it evolved, *Innere Führung* was also to be advanced through courses in political education and psychological warfare, and through a reform of military justice under the principle of the "citizen in uniform." This extraordinarily difficult task could not be accomplished overnight; time and again it raised questions about Germany's military traditions.

Adenauer's promise of military reform to the western allies was a bold one, given the burdens of Germany's past. In the event, as West Germans tried to make good on this pledge during the 1950s and 1960s, it proved even more problematic than anticipated, because of the tension between liberal, democratic values and the military requirements of an ideological war fought with atomic weapons. The obligation to carry out these reforms compelled the West German government and its military leadership to clear away the spiritual wreckage of the past, much as the *Trümmerfrauen* (women of the ruins) removed rubble by hand in the years after the war in the streets of Germany's towns, laboriously cleaning each brick and examining it

---

[51] Ulrich de Maizière, "Der Wehrbeauftragte, die Innere Führung und die Soldaten," *Europäische Wehrkunde*, May 1984, p. 291.

to see if it was still durable. In the judgment of the political leadership in the early 1950s, the inner structure of the new army could not be as Seeckt had built it. The clamp of tradition that had bound the inner structure of the old armies had given way under the weight of Germany's catastrophe. The Day of Potsdam, the Röhm Putsch, and the attempt on Hitler's life on the Twentieth of July 1944 had broken this bond, rendering unusable many customs, symbols, and ceremonies enshrined in the cult of tradition. The new structure would have to be located within, and remain open to, the democratic state that created it, a part of a united Europe made up of pluralistic societies. Nevertheless, the architects of the new army would still have to salvage material from the old, prompting them to find a new meaning for military tradition in German life.

2. The "Magna Carta" of the Bundeswehr: Tradition and Reform

THE CREATION of the West German military began shortly after the outbreak of the Korean War and culminated in the winter of 1955–56 with the commissioning of an initial group of volunteers and the induction of the first training cadres. Based on the proposal for a European army by René Pleven, the French foreign minister, the planning until 1954 foresaw a West German contribution to a united European force—later named the European Defense Community (EDC)—which expired stillborn in the summer of 1954. With the failure of the EDC, the West German planners were forced to direct their efforts toward an organization that Adenauer had vowed not to create: a West German national army. Political obstacles both at home and abroad and pressure to produce results quickly made their task even more difficult and the compromise solutions they reached were to have a longlasting effect on the nature of these West German forces. The planners at work in Bonn and Paris (at the EDC negotiations until 1954) had to deal with the criticism of foreign and domestic opponents against German rearmament as well as the diplomatic and operational difficulties of integrating West Germany into the Atlantic alliance. At the same time, the United States was pushing its European allies to establish the new army more quickly. The raising of the West German forces and their subordination to the peacetime NATO command structure went pretty much as planned, once these tasks were completed in the mid-1960s. But the historically unique character of the West German armed forces—a military organization established to help defend the West, yet also commanded and deployed to assure the West's security from a new Greater German threat—repeatedly forced West Germans to face the problem of how they could integrate this new army-within-an-alliance into the existing political, social, and legal institutions of the Federal Republic. The role of military tradition—especially the custom of *Traditionspflege* developed in the late 1890s—within the reform movement worried observers of the political evolution of the new army. Nonetheless, the Bundeswehr, hampered by the political and social conditions of its birth, was slow to formulate a policy on military tradition. The account that follows describes the genesis of the policy concerning this tradition in the Bundeswehr as it evolved before 1956 within the larger planning efforts for the future army.[1]

MAINTENANCE of military tradition as practiced in the Reichswehr and Wehrmacht, that is to say, as a means of preserving the exclusive position of the military in the state through the use of symbols and ceremonies drawn from the past, and as a method of operational and political education for soldiers,[2] played a minor role in the planning that took place during the period from 1950 to 1955. Neither the parliament nor the military staff and their outside advisers devoted as much attention to this subject during the years 1950 to 1956 as they were to do from 1958 to the mid–1980s.[3] Nevertheless, the very nature of the reform program that accompanied rearmament was, in the words of a prominent advocate of *Innere Führung*, an "anti-traditional concept" which continually forced to the fore the issue of what would be retained from the past.[4] In the beginning, it seemed as if the new army would keep very little; according to one leading military adviser to Adenauer's government, the word tradition "would have no place in the vocabulary of the future German soldier."[5] This pro-

[1] This chapter is indebted to the work of Norbert Wiggershaus and Hans-Jürgen Rautenberg of the Militärgeschichtliches Forschungsamt (MGFA and BMVg, Bonn), who provided the scope, direction, and key insights for research on the first years of the Bundeswehr.

[2] See the very useful definition offered by Hans-Jürgen Rautenberg in "Aspekte zur Entwicklung der Traditionsfrage in der Aufbauphase der Bundeswehr," in *Tradition als Last*, ed. Klaus M. Kodalle (Köln, 1981), pp. 133–34.

[3] This is the observation of three scholars of the early history of the Bundeswehr. See Claus Freiherr von Rosen, "Tradition als Last: Probleme mit dem Traditionsangebot der 'Gruppe Inneres Gefüge' (1951–1958) im Leitbild 'Staatsbürger in Uniform' für die Tradition der Bundeswehr," in *Tradition als Last*, ed. Klaus M. Kodalle (Köln, 1981); Dietrich Genschel, *Wehrreform und Reaktion: Die Vorbereitung der Inneren Führung 1951–1956* (Hamburg, 1972); and Rautenberg, "Aspekte zur Entwicklung der Traditionsfrage."

[4] Interview with Major General Dr. Eberhard Wagemann, June 1984.

[5] Rautenberg cites an unnamed air force officer who had been at the Abbey Him-

hibition would prove difficult to enforce, however, for questions of military tradition in all its forms, extending well beyond the pre-1945 cult of tradition, were implicit not only in the inner structure of the new force, but in its operational requirements as well. The creators of the new force, as well as political commentators in West Germany and abroad, understood that reform and tradition were intimately linked. The planners saw that the desire for the maintenance of tradition would be greatest "where revolutionary conditions had swept away the old order."[6] The confusion and apparent discontinuities that plagued Germany's present might well increase the longing for a return to the past, and to the honoring of traditional military symbols and customs. This widespread attitude complicated prospects for a quick and easy course of reform in West Germany. In addition, the speed in arming of the Federal Republic and the lingering side effects of this rapid build-up led to uncertainty about how to define and treat the cult of tradition in the new force, which in turn produced a cautious response. The leadership of the armed forces only began to advance an explicit policy on military tradition at a late stage in the establishment of the Bundeswehr during the years 1959 to 1965, and then very much as a reaction to the failure of the earlier policy of caution.[7]

In the first years of planning for the West German army, the Bonn government tended to define military tradition in a negative way: after the "zero hour" a "new army was created from nothing." If tradition was defined at all, it was done proverbially: "It must be the army's tradition to remain in conformity [with the times] and to march at the head of progress"—words mistakenly attributed to Scharnhorst, which were in fact those of the National Socialist historian Reinhard Höhn.[8] As long as the future West German soldier was

---

merod when the first major planning document for the new army was drafted. See Rautenberg, "Aspekte zur Entwicklung der Traditionsfrage," p. 137.

[6] Bundesarchiv-Militärarchiv (BA/MA) Bw 2/4025, "Aktennotiz der Sektion II/ IG, 27 January 1953," cited in Hans-Jürgen Rautenberg, "Zur Standortbestimmung für künftige deutsche Streitkräfte," in *Anfänge westdeutscher Sicherheitspolitik 1945–1956: Von der Kapitulation bis zum Pleven Plan,* ed. MGFA (München, 1982), vol. 1, p. 836.

[7] Interviews with General Johann Adolf Graf Kielmansegg, June 1984, with General Ulrich de Maizière, April and June 1984, and with Professor Wolf Graf von Baudissin, May 1984.

[8] "Tradition aber in der Armee muss es sein, in Form zu bleiben und an der

to serve in the armed forces of a united Europe, the question of military tradition, although it was present, stood in a kind of political and bureaucratic limbo. The silent hope of many West Germans was that whatever problem existed in this regard might solve itself within an integrated European army.[9] After the European Defense Community failed in August 1954 and it became evident that West Germany would have to create its own national army, a clearly formulated policy on military tradition became essential. This new policy, which amounted to a bureaucratic definition of military tradition, took years to formulate and generated considerable confusion and conflict. The requirement to adapt German military doctrine to a peacetime coalition armed with nuclear weapons, the fear of an antidemocratic revival in West Germany, the division of Germany into East and West, and domestic political anxieties about the place of the soldier in the young West German democracy all complicated this attempt by the military leadership to establish a usable past for its soldiers. Political differences among the planners and the civilian advisers to the new army made this task of defining tradition no easier, nor did certain material obstacles to the armament of the Federal Republic: inadequate personnel and a shortage of facilities. The attempt within the leadership of the Bundeswehr to define a valid heritage emerged from the difficulties of the new army in its first decade.[10]

Spitze des Fortschritts zu marschieren." See Reinhard Höhn, *Scharnhorsts Vermächtnis*, rev. ed. (Bonn, 1952), p. 89.

[9] Interviews with Lieutenant Colonel Dr. Helmuth Schubert, March and July 1984. See Rautenberg, "Aspekte zur Entwicklung der Traditionsfrage," p. 138.

[10] In 1969, during the political crisis that brought many of these latent difficulties of the Bundeswehr to the surface, the Deputy Chief of Staff of the West German Army, General Hellmut Grashey, asserted that *Innere Führung* had only been a mask to sell rearmament to its Social Democratic and Protestant critics in the Federal Republic. This remark moved Dietrich Genschel, then a young staff officer in the Ministry of Defense and a Ph.D. student, to write the first major scholarly examination of the sources, *Wehrreform und Reaktion: Die Vorbereitung der Inneren Führung 1951–1956* (Hamburg, 1972). Genschel's scholarly analysis tended to support Grashey's claim that the Ministry of Defense assigned the reforms a low priority once the armed forces were created. Genschel's book sparked much controversy, but it should be regarded as a *Streitschrift* within the turbulence of the late 1960s and early 1970s. Subsequent scholarly work has criticized Genschel in detail, especially Rautenberg's "Zur Standortbestimmung" and Wiggershaus's "Zum Problem der Tradition im Vorfeld eines westdeutschen Verteidgungbeitrages," unpublished manuscript, 1983, which subsequently appeared as Norbert Wiggershaus, "Zur Debatte um die Tradition künftiger Streitkräfte 1950–1955/6," in *Tradition und*

AFTER negotiations with the western allies in the late summer and early fall of 1950, Adenauer's government secretly began to prepare for the new armed forces, a step that violated the occupation control statutes. Adenauer's efforts in the fall were in part an extension of existing plans, and at the same time, they represented something fundamentally different.[11] In May of that year, the chancellor had en-

---

Reform in den Aufbaujahren der Bundeswehr, ed. MGFA (Herford, 1985). Citations in the present study refer to the unpublished versions of the manuscripts by Harder and Wiggershaus, which differ in some details from the published versions of their work. I could not reproduce the enormous scholarly work done by Genschel, but did spend nearly two hundred hours in conversation with many of the principal figures and examined most of the available files in the Bundesarchiv-Militärarchiv. The more recent historical work done by Rautenberg and Wiggershaus challenges Genschel's polemical position. In fact, evidence suggests that the reforms were ultimately the victim of the political and material circumstances engendered by the pace and scope of rearmament as well as the personal differences between certain of the key reformers. This combination of circumstances helped, in part, to produce the need for a policy on military tradition. Nonetheless, Genschel's work remains absolutely indispensable.

[11] On the armament of the Federal Republic within the context of international relations after 1945, there is a growing literature, see: Gerhard Wettig, *Entmilitarisierung und Wiederbewaffnung Deutschlands 1943–1955* (Stuttgart, 1967); Richard Löwenthal, "Vom Kalten Krieg zur Ostpolitik," in *Die Zweite Republik, 25 Jahre Bundesrepublik Deutschland—eine Bilanz*, ed. Richard Löwenthal and Hans-Peter Schwarz (Stuttgart, 1974); Klaus von Schubert, *Wiederbewaffnung und Westintegration* (Stuttgart, 1970); Militärgeschichtliches Forschungsamt (MGFA), ed., *Aspekte der deutschen Wiederbewaffnung* (1974); Josef Fischepoth, ed., *Kalter Krieg und Deutsche Frage: Deutschland im Widerstreit der Mächte, 1945–1952* (Göttingen, 1985); Edward Fursdon, *The European Defense Community: A History* (London, 1980); John L. Gaddis, *Strategies of Containment: A Critical Appraisal of Postwar National Security* (New York, 1982); Andreas Hillgruber, *Europa in der Weltpolitik der Nachkriegszeit 1945–1963* (München, 1983); Wilfried Loth, *Die Teilung der Welt, Geschichte des Kalten Krieges, 1941–1955* (München, 1980); Olav Riste, ed., *Western Security: The Formative Years. European and Atlantic Defense 1947–1953* (Oslo 1985). On the political, strategic, and domestic aspects of the Federal Republic in European defense from a West German perspective, see: Roland G. Foerster, Christian Greiner et al., *Anfänge westdeutscher Sicherheitspolitik 1945–1956* (München, 1982); Anselm Doering-Manteuffel, *Katholizismus und Wiederbewaffnung. Die Haltung der deutschen Katholiken gegenüber der Wehrfrage 1948–1955* (Frankfurt, 1981); Alexander Fischer et al., eds., *Entmilitarisierung und Aufrüstung in Mitteleuropa, 1945–1956* (Boppard, 1983); Guther Mai, *Westliche Sicherheitspolitik im Kalten Krieg: Der Korea Konflikt und die deutsche Wiederbewaffnung* (Boppard, 1977); S. Thomas, *Der Weg in die NATO. Zur Integrations und Remilitarisierungspolitik der BRD 1949–1955* (Berlin, 1978); Ludger Borgert et al., *Dienstgruppen und westdeutscher Verteidigungsbeitrag. Vorüberlegungen zur Wiederbewaffnung der Bundesrepublik Deutschland* (Boppard, 1982); Christian Greiner, " 'Operational History (German) Section' und 'Naval History Team.' Deutsches militärstrategisches Denken im

trusted a former armor general, identified with the resistance to Hitler, Gerhard Graf von Schwerin, with the task of planning for domestic security and of creating a federal police force.[12] Among Schwerin's small staff in the innocuously titled "Central Headquarters for Home Service" (*Zentrale für Heimatdienst*) were three well-known general staff officers also connected with the resistance to Hitler: Johann Adolf Graf von Kielmansegg, head of the committee of military experts, Axel von dem Bussche, press officer, and Achim Oster, the officer in charge of intelligence. All three later emerged as important advocates of reform in the West German armed forces, Kielmansegg becoming perhaps the most influential staff officer working behind the scenes in the first years of planning.[13] In early October 1950, Ade-

---

Dienst der amerikanischen Streitkräfte von 1946–1950," in *Militärgeschichte. Probleme—Thesen—Wege*, ed. Manfred Messerschmidt (Stuttgart, 1982); Manfred Messerschmidt et al., "West Germany's Strategic Position and her Role in Defence Policy as seen by the German Military, 1945–1949," in *Power in Europe? Great Britain, France, Italy and Germany in a Postwar World, 1945–1950*, ed. Josef Becker et al. (Berlin, 1986). See especially Gerhard Wettig, *Entmilitarisierung und Wiederbewaffnung in Deutschland, 1943–1955* (München, 1967), pp. 209ff., *Militärgeschichte seit 1945: Aspekte der deutschen Wiederbewaffnung bis 1955*, ed. MGFA (Boppard, 1975), and MGFA, ed., *Anfänge westdeutscher Sicherheitspolitik 1945–1956: Von der Kapitulation bis zum Pleven Plan* (München, 1982), vol. 1. Even before the Federal Republic came into existence, Adenauer had sought military advice from a handful of former officers. Outstanding among them was Generalleutnant a.D. Dr. Hans Speidel, a protégé of Generaloberst Ludwig Beck, the army chief of staff, who resigned over the Czech crisis of 1938 and died in the aftermath of the Twentieth of July 1944; Speidel later became Rommel's chief of staff in France. At a meeting with Speidel in December 1948, Adenauer asked him to prepare a memorandum on the security problems of the western zones of occupation. Speidel's studies from the era 1948–50 are reprinted in Hans Speidel, *Aus unserer Zeit: Erinnerungen* (Frankfurt a.M., 1977), pp. 454–96. See especially the chapters "Die Sicherheit Europas," pp. 454–65, "Gedanken zur Sicherung Westeuropas," pp. 468–71, and "Gedanken über die Frage der äusseren Sicherheit der Bundesrepublik Deutschland," pp. 477–96.

[12] For the first of Schwerin's studies of May 1950, see: BA/MA, Bw 9/3106, "Gerhard Graf von Schwerin, 'Gedankenbeitrag für den Aufbau einer mobilen Bundesgendarmerie,'" 29 May 1950. Schwerin's idea was to create a federal police force that might in turn form the cadre for a future army. In late July 1950, the allied high commissioners vetoed this approach, prompting Adenauer to seek additional military advice from the group around Speidel. See Schwerin's comments of 1974 on these developments in *Aspekte der deutschen Wiederbewaffnung*, pp. 56ff.

[13] In an often repeated phrase, Kielmansegg said in a June 1984 interview that he was the "Grandfather of *Innere Führung*." He takes credit for having coined the term and for having brought the key reformers to the government in the period between 1951 and 1955. For over thirty-five years, he played a major role in the life

nauer directed Schwerin to bring together a group of former Wehrmacht officers, including several associated with the resistance, who had been advising Adenauer on defense issues in recent months. In the strict legal sense, such a gathering was unconstitutional; the allies could punish the participants with life imprisonment for engaging in secret military preparations. With this possibility much on their minds, the group met in great secrecy at the Abbey Himmerod in the Eifel Mountains for four days in October 1950. Kielmansegg acted as secretary for the overall assembly at Himmerod. From the minutes of the meetings of various subcommittees, he consolidated the group's opinions on political, operational, logistical and territorial aspects of the new force into a single paper.[14] The final product of the meeting was a document that eventually bore the title: "Memorandum on the Formation of a German Contingent for the Defense of Western Europe within the Framework of an International Fighting Force."[15] The finished memorandum was intended both as a planning document for the new armed forces and as a basis for negotiations with the western allies. The text, not declassified in full until the mid-1970s, has since become known as the "Himmerod Memorandum" or, as Schwerin himself described it twenty-five years later, the "Magna Carta of the Bundeswehr."[16]

---

of the armed forces. See his "Gedanken zur Führung der Streitkräfte," in *Beiträge zur Konfliktforschung* 4 (1984): 5–34.

[14] Interview with General Johann Adolf Graf von Kielmansegg, June 1984. Unless otherwise cited, the discussion of the Himmerod memorandum is from Norbert Wiggershaus and Hans-Jürgen Rautenberg, " 'Die Himmeroder Denkschrift' von Oktober 1950: Politische und militärische Überlegungen für einen Beitrag der Bundesrepublik Deutschland zur Westeuropäischen Verteidigung," *Militärgeschichtliche Mitteilungen* 21 (1977): 135ff., reprinted by Militärgeschichtliches Forschungsamt (MGFA) (Karlsruhe, 1985). Further citations refer to the 1985 reprint.

[15] BA/MA, Bw 9/3119, "Denkschrift des militärischen Expertenausschusses über die Aufstellung eines Deutschen Kontingents im Rahmen einer übernationalen Streitmacht zur Verteidigung Westeuropas von 9 Oktober 1950," reprinted in Hans-Jürgen Rautenberg and Norbert Wiggershaus, *Die Himmeroder Denkschrift: Politische und militärische Überlegungen für einen Beitrag der Bundesrepublik Deutschland zur Westeuropäischen Verteidigung*, 2d ed. (Karlsruhe, 1985), pp. 36ff. This document included many points contained in a memorandum of 7 August 1950 by Speidel, Hermann Foertsch, and Heusinger (reprinted in Speidel, *Aus Unserer Zeit*, pp. 477–96), which was presented to Adenauer and formed the basis for further planning and policy.

[16] Militärgeschichtliches Forschungsamt (MGFA), ed., *Militärgeschichte seit 1945: Aspekte der deutschen Wiederbewaffnung bis 1955* (Boppard, 1975), p. 142. This tran-

The authors addressed the ethical, political, strategical, operational, and logistical issues facing the future West German soldier, setting them out with considerable prescience and brevity.[17] The memorandum began with a brief discussion of the difficult conditions of West German security, culminating in the call for complete political sovereignty for the Federal Republic as well as total equality for the future West Germans forces within a supranational coalition. "A 'Second Class Soldier,' " wrote the military experts, "would never offer up the necessary moral strength" for the future army.[18] On the strategical and operational levels, the authors proposed the creation of twelve armored divisions under the command of six corps headquarters. These units would be integrated with the western allies as a mobile-enveloping force, deployed as near to the interzonal border as operations would allow. The German contingent was also to include a tactical air arm and a coastal defense navy. With this proposed structure of forces, the Germans boldly contradicted then-current NATO plans that anticipated an American-French-British withdrawal behind the Rhine and the possible use of allied-trained German guerrillas in areas overrun by the Russians. The military experts strongly opposed this use of Germans as irregulars and "auxiliaries," because, "neither the German people, nor the German topography nor the ground cover are suited to this kind of warfare."[19] The West German insistence upon military equality and an allied forward defense of Central Europe have remained prominent features of NATO strategy ever since.[20]

---

script of a forum on West German rearmament held by the MGFA in May 1974 includes the contributions of both historians and participants in the events.

[17] For criticism of the Himmerod memorandum written in the shadow of the intermediate nuclear forces deployments, see the useful, but by no means original, essay by Mathias Jopp, "Zur Entstehungsgeschichte der deutschen Sicherheitsproblematik: Politische Interessen und militärische Planung bei der Integration der Bundeswehr in das NATO Bündnis," in *Unsere Bundeswehr: Zum 25jährigen Bestehen einer umstritten Institution*, ed. Reiner Steinweg (Frankfurt, 1981), pp. 15ff.

[18] Rautenberg and Wiggershaus, *Himmeroder Denkschrift*, p. 37.

[19] Ibid.

[20] For the strategic planning of NATO and its impact on West Germany, see the fully documented and informative work of Christian Greiner, "Die Alliierten Militärstrategischen Planungen zur Verteidigung Westeuropas, 1947–1950," in *Anfänge westdeutscher Sicherheitspolitik 1945–1956: Von der Kapitulation bis zum Pleven Plan*, ed. MGFA (München, 1982), pp. 119ff. On the political, strategic, and operational dilemmas of the Bundeswehr, especially as a result of deployment of nuclear weapons, see Mark Cioc, "Pax Atomica: The Nuclear Defense Debate in West Germany

IN ADDITION to strategical and operational concerns, the authors of the memorandum confronted the relationship of the new army to European and West German politics and society. This analysis indirectly raised the question of the cult of military tradition, although the officers did not confront the details of the maintenance of tradition itself in anything more than general terms.[21] This portion of the document contained both traditionalist and reformist sentiments, which often stood in contradiction to one another. In their analysis of civil-military issues that included an outline for reform of the inner structure of the new army, the experts were responding to what they characterized as the general condemnation of the professional soldier since the end of the war.[22] The authors insisted that before the creation of the new army could begin in earnest, the representatives of the western allies would have to stop the "defamation" of the German soldier and "rehabilitate" him by means of a public declaration. The West German government should offer a "declaration of honor" to former professional soldiers as well as provide social welfare for all those connected with both past and future armies.

Although the Himmerod memorandum stated that the new soldier "must affirm with inner conviction the democratic statecraft and way

during the Adenauer Era," Ph.d. diss., University of California, Berkeley, 1986; William Geffen, "The Role of the Military in West German Defense Policy Making," Ph.D. diss., University of Denver, 1971; Julian Lider, *Problems of Military Policy in the Konrad Adenauer Era, 1949–1966* (Stockholm, 1984); and the contemporary, highly readable, and revealing work of Hans Speier, *German Rearmament and Atomic War: The Views of the German Military and Political Leaders* (Evanston, 1957); Catherine McArdle Kelleher, *Germany and the Politics of Nuclear Weapons* (New York, 1975); *Verteidigung im Bündnis: Planung, Aufbau, und Bewährung der Bundeswehr, 1950–1972*, ed. MGFA (München, 1975); Manfred Messerschmidt, Christian Greiner et al., "West Germany's Strategic Position and her Role in Defense Policy as seen by the German Military, 1945–1949," in *Power in Europe?: Great Britain, France, Italy and Germany in a Postwar World, 1945–1950*, ed. Josef Becker et al. (Berlin/New York, 1986); Stanley Kanarowski, *The German Army and NATO Strategy* (Washington, D.C., 1982); David N. Schwartz, *NATO's Nuclear Dilemmas* (Washington, D.C., 1983); William Park, *Defending the West: A History of NATO* (Brighton, 1986).

[21] The memorandum of Speidel, Heusinger, and Foertsch to Adenauer of 7 August 1950 included the statement that the future German contingent should avoid "false ideas of 'tradition,' internal militarism, and old–fashioned *Kommiss*." The Himmerod memorandum, however, whose authors included the above, contained no direct reference to the maintenance of tradition.

[22] Rautenberg and Wiggershaus, *Himmeroder Denkschrift*, p. 53.

of life" of West Germany, in 1950 there existed no constitutional means for fitting the new army into the democratic order of the Federal Republic.[23] The authors skirted this problem in the document by saying, maladroitly, that the state-of-emergency provisions of the Basic Law should enable the chancellor to provide a legal basis for the German military contingent; at some later date, those responsible would draft the needed military legislation.[24] Nor did the experts seem to have a concrete idea of how to reconcile the professional military with the nascent West German democracy, other than to call for an end to the "defamation" of the army as well as seeking the "consent of the opposition and labor unions" in defense policy. These political and legal pressures, however, diminished in the face of the war scare that followed the outbreak of fighting in Korea. It caused tensions to run high in Europe during the early fall of 1950. The experts addressed such specific military issues as the chain of command of the future German contingent, as well as its operational organization and equipment—practical matters that they knew best as staff officers and that needed to be decided urgently.

The memorandum's statements on the supreme leadership and the chain of command also revealed a combination of old and new, demonstrating the presence of traditional and reformist conceptions side by side in the planning for the German contingent. In contrast to the Reichswehr and Wehrmacht, the supreme military leadership of the new force would be unified, an idea the men at Himmerod drew from the experience of the lost war.[25] No longer would there be separate chiefs of staff for army, navy, and air force. Individual branches would be subordinated to a single officer who would in turn answer directly to the federal president as commander-in-chief. The military experts did not act alone in this issue; Theodor Heuss himself had endorsed such a relationship. This proposal was, however, reminiscent of the arrangement between the kaiser and his armed forces, the Reich pres-

[23] Rautenberg and Wiggershaus, *Himmeroder Denkschrift*, p. 53.

[24] Ibid., p. 55.

[25] See diagram of proposed political and command structures, BA/MA, Bw 9/3119, "Anlage, Vorschlag für die Spitzengliederung im Frieden," in Rautenberg and Wiggershaus, *Himmeroder Denkschrift*, p. 26; also see the earlier proposal by an officer associated with the planning, BA/MA Bw 2/918, "Oberstleutnant a.D. Ernst Ferber, 'Vorschläge zur Gliederung und Organisation des Kommandos einer Deutschen Bundeswehrmacht,' " 1 October 1950.

ident and the Reichswehr, and Hitler and the Wehrmacht, arousing concern that West German soldiers might evade civilian control if they answered only to the president of the Federal Republic. Later organizers of the army, conscious of previous struggles by parliament to control the military in the past, discarded this proposed relationship. Instead, the founders of the new army adopted an arrangement in the mid-1950s that made the minister of defense responsible to parliament as commander of the armed forces in peacetime. During crisis or war, however, the chancellor would assume command of the armed forces. But such a solution, intended to assure civilian control of the military, lay in the future. The passages on civil-military questions do not reveal a willingness on the part of the military experts at Himmerod to subordinate the new army fully to civilian control, or more specifically, to the authority of parliament within the constitution of the Federal Republic. These reforms were only put forward after the war scare of 1950–51 had passed. More than a few statements in the memorandum indicated a traditional insistence on the part of certain professional soldiers that state and society adapt themselves to the primacy of military requirements and the "ethos of national defense."[26]

Nevertheless, the memorandum contained many proposals that recognized the new political and social realities in the Atlantic world and the necessity for reform. While the suggested relationship between the new army and the head of state recalled the past, the section of the Himmerod memorandum on the "inner structure" of the German contingent showed the willingness of the experts to follow a new path. The profoundly altered circumstances of postwar Europe combined with the need to form a new army within a European framework required the creation of "something fundamentally new, without any borrowing from the forms of the old Wehrmacht."[27] The authors, however, recognized the difficulties of personnel and organization that they would face in instituting such a reform. "It is important at the outset that the spirit and principles of the internal new beginning are set down for the duration, and that they remain in force despite eventual change in the organization."[28] Politically suitable per-

[26] Rautenberg and Wiggershaus, *Himmeroder Denkschrift*, pp. 37–38.
[27] Ibid., p. 53.   [28] Ibid.

sonnel were central to any program of military reform. Taking up the initiative of a handful of critical former officers in the years after the war, the Himmerod group proposed a "self-cleansing" of the future officer corps to exclude former Nazis and those with antidemocratic attitudes. This step would bolster public confidence in the new army at home and abroad as well as enhance "the inner cohesion of the troops." The selection of the officer corps, however, would have to avoid the political naiveté of denazification, whose procedures were at once unduly rigid and easily manipulated, so that many true Nazis were able to save themselves, while many innocent people were punished.

The planners at Himmerod had to consider the effects of military tradition in Germany and Europe. Conscious of the need to overcome national military traditions in an integrated army, they insisted on a general commitment in the ranks to the ideal of European unity. They imagined that the future army would become a "school of Europe." The new force would have to adopt its name and symbols accordingly. By promoting a European image of history in the systematic political education of its soldiers, the new army would foster European unity. German recruits were to become convinced citizens as well as soldiers of an integrated Europe. But the desirability of a European ideal notwithstanding, the Himmerod group recognized that national interest would still play a role in the inner structure of the army. As part of an integrated force, the German contingent would nonetheless have to take account of the "military experiences and feelings of the German people." The German defense contribution must find a compromise between the need for a "new conception of military life," and for "less rigid forms," while still respecting the wishes of many Germans "for a more traditional image of the soldier in society."[29]

With the political fate of the Reichswehr in mind, the officers at Himmerod warned against the future army's becoming a "state within a state."[30] The soldier was to be integrated into society—he was no longer to feel himself as a warrior exalted above civilians. The education and training of the ranks would include instruction in political affairs and international law. Despite the conflicts of conscience

[29] Ibid.   [30] Ibid.

caused by the attempt on Hitler's life on the Twentieth of July 1944, the officers wanted to reestablish an oath, or at least a "ceremonial obligation" to either the federal president or the constitution. Soldiers were to swear an oath both to the new German democracy and to a united Europe. While the future soldier would enjoy as many civil rights as possible in uniform, military service would restrict his franchise on the local level. He could neither join political parties and labor unions nor hold political meetings in the barracks. The German contingent was to be founded upon the traditional principles of command and obedience, although the future soldier could never allow these traditions to become an alibi for criminal behavior as they had in the Third Reich. Orders that would result in crimes against humanity or in a violation of international law were to be forbidden. The future soldier would have the right to make complaints in the ranks as well as to address his problems directly to the security committee of the federal parliament.

The experts described each of these proposed reforms with only a few lines in the memorandum. They recognized that the proposals would require more elaboration; a committee was to be formed immediately to carry on this work. The group was to probe more deeply into such issues as future military legislation, the oath, the duties of the soldier, military justice, the process for making complaints, and the social welfare of soldiers. This recognition that more attention needed to be paid to the inner structure of the armed forces accorded with the need, stated elsewhere in the document, for further steps to be taken in the realms of strategy, operations, the structure of forces, and logistics. The experts foresaw that the new army could not take to the field until well into 1952.

The section of the memorandum on the inner structure of the German contingent, which the group had taken on voluntarily, without any outside direction,[31] contained in rough outline many of the elements that were eventually to become a part of the concept of *Innere Führung*. For the first time in the prehistory of the Bundeswehr, the concept appeared that advocates of reform later described as the "citizen in uniform," a term that signified a willingness to refashion the public image and the self-image of the German soldier. The Him-

---

[31] Interview with General Johann Adolf Graf von Kielmansegg, February 1986.

merod group plainly saw that the Federal Republic could not simply resurrect the Wehrmacht, and it recognized that the new army must distance itself from the disastrous errors of the past. But the creation of an alternative army faced enormous political, social, and psychological difficulties. The men who were going to build the inner structure of the new army, and who sought to create "something fundamentally new," borrowed terms from the past to describe their intention. For instance, the rubric (*inneres Gefüge*) under which the officers listed the requirements for the new "inner structure" was a category they had taken over from the Wehrmacht, symbolizing in itself the dilemma of discontinuity and continuity in the new army.[32] Elsewhere in the memorandum the authors demanded an "energetic struggle against elements undermining democracy in West German society," joined with "internal protective measures for the work of rearmament" and a "systematic national enlightenment and education" for the necessity of defense.[33] Such language recalled the era of 1933 and before.

Statements resonant of an undemocratic past also pointed to the potential for conflict between reform and reaction in the ranks of the officer corps. Contemporaries realized that this weakness could threaten the new army the same way it had the old. Such political divisions had loomed large in the experience of those gathered at Himmerod, among whom were Generals Friedo von Senger und Etterlin, Hermann Foertsch, Hans Röttiger, Adolf Heusinger, Hans Speidel, and Admiral Friedrich Ruge.[34] Nearly all of these men had become officers in Wilhelmine Germany and later served in both the Reichswehr and Wehrmacht. The majority had experienced the crisis in the officer corps in 1918–19, when the collapse of the dynasties robbed the soldier of the subject of his oath. Among the younger men

[32] The term predates the Nazi period; one can find discussions of the "inner cohesion" of an army in military references of the late nineteenth century. But in the course of the early 1950s, the term came to be identified with the ideological aspects of the Wehrmacht in National Socialism. On this latter question, see Manfred Messerschmidt, *Die Wehrmacht im NS Staat* (Hamburg, 1969), p. 307.

[33] Rautenberg and Wiggershaus, *Himmeroder Denkschrift*, pp. 37–38, 53–55.

[34] This analysis is indebted to Oberstleutnant Dr. Helmuth Schubert of the Zentrum Innere Führung, Koblenz, for his insights into the generational dilemmas of the officer corps. Detlef Bald, among others, also discusses this problem in his excellent *Generalstabsausbildung in der Demokratie: Die Führungsakademie der Bundeswehr zwischen Tradtionalismus und Reform* (Koblenz, 1984), pp. 26ff.

at Himmerod were two general staff officers, Colonel Graf von Kielmansegg and Major Graf von Baudissin. Commissioned in the 1920s, they had witnessed the fissure in generations and ideology in the officer corps that helped foster the alliance between many professional soldiers and the Nazis.

A similar difference in generations and political outlooks seems to have existed on a lesser scale among the authors of the memorandum's section on the inner structure, among whom were Foertsch and Baudissin. Foertsch had been closely associated with ideological training in the Wehrmacht and was the author of numerous writings espousing the union of Nazi and military ideals.[35] He later served as a leading field commander during the war and was apparently involved in the brutalities of the German operations in the Balkans. The Personnel Screening Board—the body instituted by parliament in the mid-1950s as an outgrowth of the proposal at Himmerod for the self-cleansing of the officer corps—refused Foertsch a commission in the Bundeswehr,[36] although his younger brother Friedrich Foertsch enjoyed a successful career in the new army culminating in his tour as chief of staff of the Bundeswehr from April 1961 to December 1963. The other chief author of the inner structure, Baudissin, became well known over the next decade as an outspoken advocate of military reform in West Germany.

After the meeting at Himmerod, Kielmansegg presented Schwerin with the memorandum from the conference. Schwerin added his own comments to the document, including his judgment on the proposals for the inner structure.[37] His insightful lines marked the beginning of

---

[35] See Foertsch's widely read work of the Nazi period: Hermann Foertsch, *Der Offizier der deutschen Wehrmacht. Eine Pflichtenlehre* (Berlin, 1940).

[36] Wiggershaus, "Zum Problem," p. 60.

[37] BA/MA Bw 9/3119, "Stellungnahme des Grafen von Schwerin zur Denkschrift des militärischen Experten Ausschusses vom 28. Oktober 1950," reprinted in Rautenberg and Wiggershaus, *Himmeroder Denkschrift*, pp. 58–60. Both the Himmerod memorandum and the commentary by Schwerin eventually reached Adenauer's office in the first week of November, after Schwerin had been forced to resign in the political confusion surrounding these first secret steps toward the planning of a new army. Although certain historians have doubted the significance of the memorandum because Adenauer did not initial it, and hence he may not have read it, the paper has enduring importance for its reflection of the thinking of the men who built up the armed forces over the next two decades. See the discussion of this point in Rautenberg and Wiggershaus, *Himmeroder Denkschrift*, pp. 31–33, and in MGFA, ed., *Aspekte der deutschen Wiederbewaffnung*, pp. 119ff.

an official controversy about military reform that has endured into the late 1980s. "In my opinion," Schwerin responded, "the chapter on the 'inner structure' does not think through the issue in its full depth."[38] He recognized the urgent need for reforms, but he warned that the present circumstances of crisis would preclude "an organic, long term build-up, carried out from the bottom up. . . . One will be forced," he continued, "to use numerous, indispensable specialists, necessary for a fast build-up, but who will nonetheless attempt to raise the army as a kind of restoration of the past."[39] Recognizing this danger, Schwerin wrote that one must immediately begin the "difficult assignment" of finding a "successful synthesis" between reform and restoration. The union of the German inner structure with that of the western allies might be one way out of this problem, but Schwerin wrote that such a step required "thorough and precisely thought-out preparation." The founders of the new army, present at its conception in the Eifel mountains during the height of the cold war, recognized the political and psychological dimensions of the task before them.

THE HIMMEROD memorandum outlined the major issues that were to divide proponents of military reform during the build-up and consolidation of the West German military over the next twenty years. Granted the uncertainties of this new beginning, the memorandum symbolized a compromise between military efficiency and the need for political change. As long as the anxiety endured in West Germany about further communist expansion, this compromise remained acceptable to most West Germans, yet this compromise has also led several critics to hold Adenauer and the group at Himmerod responsible for the reappearance of many practices of the Wehrmacht in the Bundeswehr.[40] Such critics have argued that, by allowing officers of the Reichswehr/Wehrmacht to build up the new army, the Federal Republic missed an opportunity to break fully with the past and to create an army appropriate to a democracy.

This criticism is unfair in light of the practical constraints at the

---

[38] Rautenberg and Wiggershaus, *Himmeroder Denkschrift*, p. 60.
[39] Ibid.
[40] Detlef Bald, "Von der Wehrmacht zur Bundeswehr: Kontinuität und Neubeginn," in *Sozialgeschichte der Bundesrepublik Deutschland: Beiträge zum Kontinuitätsproblem*, ed. Werner Conze and M. R. Lepsius (Stuttgart, 1983), p. 397.

time. Adenauer had no real alternative in the fall of 1950 other than to make use of the expertise of officers who seemed prepared to serve the democratic idea. The Himmerod compromise between reform and military necessity made the new force possible within the political and social atmosphere of the cold war. This compromise was in turn part of a wider process of coming to grips with the past in the Federal Republic of the 1950s, which reflected the popular backlash against denazification, reeducation, and the Nuremberg trials. The memory of these postwar events and the West Germans' desire to distance themselves from the blunders of the occupiers circumscribed the freedom of Adenauer's government. Given the political limitations on West German sovereignty at the time—especially the insistence of the United States on a quick West German contribution to European defense—such a solution was the best one could hope for. Key members of the Himmerod group later became the shapers of reform policy in the Bundeswehr. Despite the tension in the document between the old and the new, and the apparent confusion among the authors as to the details of the reform process, the memorandum drafted in October 1950 marks the advent of reform in the Bundeswehr. This enterprise soon shifted from the Eifel mountains to the shores of the Rhine, where the work on the new army continued in Bonn over the next eighteen months.

3. The European Army and the *Dienststelle* *Blank*: Problems and Personalities

IN JANUARY 1951 the Korean War was going badly for the United Nations forces. Western Europe experienced a "great fear" about a coming world war.[1] The French, British, and American high commissioners for Germany and the federal German government engaged in conversations that lasted from early January to June 1951 concerning the West German contribution to European security.[2] Soon after these talks began in the High Commission—located in the fortress-like hotel atop the Petersberg across the Rhine from Bonn and called "Monte Veto" by many—the French invited the West Germans to join the negotiations in Paris on Pleven's proposal for a European army.[3] This enterprise eventually became known as the European De-

[1] Michael Howard uses this phrase in *Western Security* to describe the political situation in Europe during the summer of 1948, but it applies to the turn of the year 1950–51 as well, especially from the West German perspective. See Michael Howard, "Introduction," in *Western Security: The Formative Years, European and Atlantic Defense 1947–1953*, ed. Olav Riste (Oslo, 1985), p. 14

[2] For the U.S. diplomatic exchange on these negotiations, see *Foreign Relations of the United States (FRUS), 1951, European Security and the German Question* (Washington, 1981), vol. 3, pt. 1, pp. 990–1047; the broader negotiations within NATO on the German defense contribution, as seen from a United States perspective, can be found on pages 755–1047. In addition to the general list of works on the European Defense Community cited in fn. 47 in chapter 1, see Wilhelm Meier-Dörnberg, "Politische und militärische Faktoren bei der Planung des deutschen Verteidigungbeitrages im Rahmen der EVG," in *Entmilitarisierung und Aufrüstung in Mitteleuropa 1945–1956, Vorträge zur Militärgeschichte*, ed. MGFA (Bonn, 1983).

[3] The general record group for the West German contingent for European defense in the *Bundesarchiv-Militärarchiv* is Bw/9, "Deutsche Dienststellen zur Vorbereitung der Europäischen Verteidigungsgemeinschaft." Selected West German documents that provide a useful overview of key problems are in BA/MA Bw 9/2002, "Entwurf II Pl 'Vortragsnotiz für den Herrn Bundeskanzler: Zeit- und Arbeitsplan der Dienststelle Blank,' " 18 May 1951; BA/MA Bw 9/1520, "Kurt Fett, Der militärische Chefdelegierte, B.B. Nr. 49/53/geh 'Übersicht über die Arbeiten des Militär Ausschusses,' Paris 14. Februar 1953"; BA/MA Bw 9/1224, "II/1/2 959–14–01 Graf Kielmansegg, 'Ist ein deutscher Wehrbeitrag im Rahmen der EVG einer Nationalarmee innerhalb einer Koalition vorzuziehen?' " 2 March 1953; BA/MA Bw 9/717, "Uberblick über Arbeitsprogramm der Dienststelle Blank," 10 December 1953;

fense Community. These developments led to the recruitment of a growing number of military experts into a branch of Adenauer's Chancellery to prepare for the establishment of a German military contingent. Many of the proposals that had been put forward at Himmerod were adapted to the changing political and military demands of the allies, which had developed over the years from a German force allied with the great powers to a German contingent in a European army and then changed back to a German national army in NATO. The negotiations for the EDC, delayed by politics on both sides of the Atlantic, lasted for three-and-a-half years and ended in failure. Advocates of European integration invested a great deal of faith and labor in the design of this future supranational army, which seemed to the framers of West German and American policy as if it would simultaneously anchor the Federal Republic in the West and provide for the defense of Europe.

As time passed, the debate inspired by these negotiations, linked with the end of the occupation and the details of how the Federal German Republic could contribute to Western defense, became one of the chief issues in the political life of the Federal Republic. Perhaps the most vexing of the problems to be taken up was what the officers at Himmerod and elsewhere called the "honor of the soldier." This issue, inextricably bound up with the maintenance of military tradition, had to be faced immediately. Events compelled the founders of the army to face it before they could address many other details of their work. The first attempts to resolve the dilemma of the soldier's honor affected policy choices regarding the maintenance of tradition over the next thirty years. As with so many other aspects of planning, the problem was exacerbated by time pressures in the shifting international conditions surrounding Federal German armament.

As AMERICAN and British advisers pushed the Federal Republic to arm itself, a handful of officers in Bonn proceeded with the design for the new military during the first months of 1951. It was a period of

---

a summary of the political, social, and ethical issues of the West German contingent is BA/MA, Bw 9/1224, "Bundeskanzleramt, Der Beauftragte des Bundeskanzlers für die mit der Vermehrung der allierten Truppen zusammenhängenden Fragen 'Der europäische Soldat deutscher Nationalität'" (ca. 1954). See also Hans-Erich Volkmann and Walter Schwengler, eds., *Die Europäische Verteidigungsgemeinschaft: Stand und Probleme der Forschung* (Boppard, 1985).

international crisis, political confusion, and personal resentments. The unhealed wounds of the war—visible in bomb-damaged cities and in the faces of the millions of displaced persons and newly released POWs—dominated these months. Added to the international burdens of the worsening cold war, of Germany's limited sovereignty, and of the political divisions between the occupiers were the domestic opposition of key political groups to emerging security policy, and the common man's bitterness that he might have to bear arms again. These problems—many foreseen by the experts at Himmerod—made the task of the military planners especially difficult. Nevertheless, it was the enduring schism in the officer corps that placed the greatest political and psychological burdens on the professional soldiers on Adenauer's staff. The handful of former Wehrmacht officers in the Bonn government aroused the anger of former commanders and comrades. In the years since 1945, such officers had been labeled war criminals and Nazi lickspittles. In response to a renewed need for their services, many of these professional soldiers, like the men at Himmerod, called for a halt to the "defamation" of their profession. The rapid growth of veterans organizations and traditions associations in West German life gave further weight to this demand on the Adenauer government.[4]

[4] These organizations included, among others, the large-scale *Bund versorgungsberechtigter Wehrmachtsangehöriger, Verband deutscher Soldaten, Kyffhäuserbund, Stahlhelm, Bund der Frontsoldaten,* and *Hilfsgemeinschaft auf Gegenseitigkeit* (HIAG, the Waffen-SS organization) as well a multitude of such unit traditions associations as *Traditionsgemeinschaft "Grossdeutschland," Kameradschaftsbund* der 116. Panzer-Division, and *Verband ehemaliger Angehöriger des Deutschen Afrikakorps,* three of the hundreds that quickly came into existence after 1948. A list of these groups can be found in the yearly editions of the *Deutscher Soldaten Kalender/Deutsches Soldatenjahrbuch.* See the brief discussion of veterans in the Federal Republic in Hans-Adolf Jacobsen, "Zur Rolle der öffentlichen Meinung bei der Debatte um die Wiederbewaffnung 1950–51," in *Militärgeschichte seit 1945: Aspekte der deutschen Wiederbewaffnung bis 1955,* ed. MGFA (Boppard, 1975), pp. 86–89. The most comprehensive treatment of this issue before the early 1950s is Georg Meyer, "Zur Situation der deutschen militärischen Führungsschicht im Vorfeld des westdeutschen Verteidigungbeitrages, 1945–1950/1," in *Anfänge westdeutscher Sicherheitspolitik 1945–1956: Von der Kapitulation bis zum Pleven Plan,* ed. MGFA (München, 1982), pp. 577–735. Also see the selected files on relations between the *Dienststelle Blank* and the veterans organizations in BA/MA, Bw 2/1307; Bw 2/ 1257, and Bw 2/1256, as well as the work of Hans Speier, *German Rearmament and Atomic War: The Views of the German Military and Political Leaders* (Evanston, 1957), pp. 18–150; David Clay Large, "Reckoning without the Past: The HIAG of the Waffen SS and the Politics

These calls for the rehabilitation of the soldier might have appeared as nothing more than brazen acts of Nazi self-justification, but they arose from more complex motives; certainly some of the men who made this demand were neo-Nazis or unreeducated nationalists trying to take advantage of the sea changes taking place in international power politics, but not all of them were guilty of this kind of opportunism. A large fraction of professional German soldiers had dismissed the evidence of the Nuremberg trials and the reeducators as nothing more than victor's justice. Certain of these former soldiers were guilty of a self-induced amnesia that made them unable to admit their own role in the barbarities of the war. Other veterans failed to see that the soldiers of the Third Reich might be linked to the genocidal atrocities that had been central to the regime. There were also veterans who had been wholly innocent. Nearly all veterans active in public life regarded their years of military service as a time of morally valid self-sacrifice and honorable comradeship. Their distinction between the goals of the regime and those of its soldiers strikes many observers of the late twentieth century as morally repugnant. But such efforts at differentiation were widespread in the early 1950s. In fact, many figures in public life outside of the veterans organizations made similar distinctions, not solely to excuse recent crimes. In defense of some of these innocent and poorly informed veterans, one can say that there was an absence of historical literature in West Germany on the immediate past. The occupation forces had forbidden research and publication on military affairs from 1945 until 1950. The general attempt by historians to interpret the Nazi regime and its horrors was just getting underway as rearmament took hold. Many Germans failed to comprehend the full institutional extent of Nazi crimes and the role the military played in them until decades after the end of the war. Such gaps in knowledge tended to reinforce popular skepticism about assertions of criminal behavior in the Wehrmacht. As a result of all these circumstances, quite a few former officers of the time, stripped of their prestige and livelihood, reacted with bitterness to the sudden shift toward armament at the end of 1950.

of Rehabilitation in the Bonn Republic, 1950–1961," *The Journal of Modern History*, 59, 1 (March 1987): 79–113; and Dr. Krafft Freiherr Schenck zu Schweinsberg, "Die Soldatenverbände in der Bundesrepublik," in *Studien zur politischen und gesellschaftlichen Situation der Bundeswehr*, ed. Georg Picht, 3 vols. (Berlin, 1965) 1: 96–177.

A number of veterans who answered the call to arms said that they would not put on a uniform again until thousands of their comrades behind bars were released from German and foreign prisons.[5] Professional officers critical of Adenauer's security policy demanded that the government give them pensions and care for their families before it bought new tanks and aircraft.[6] The occupiers had ordered the pensions of hundreds of thousands of veterans cut, arousing many of them against the government. Numerous former soldiers regarded the men who joined the government as opportunists, guilty of sacrificing soldierly comradeship and honor in a self-serving effort to advance themselves in the new army.[7] In the view of their critics, the men at work in Bonn were little more than mercenaries in the pay of the occupiers, whose goal was the mobilization of German cannon fodder. Such antagonisms among professional soldiers did not augur well for the new army. The presence of unreconstructed veterans at odds with the government struck many observers as reminiscent of the civil-military tensions that had obtained during the Weimar Republic. Leading political figures worried that history could repeat itself. The mass of veterans might rally to the banner of an antidemocratic movement before the young republic could consolidate itself.

The man who eventually bore the chief responsibility for solving the problem of the soldier's honor was Schwerin's successor as security adviser, Theodor Blank. He confessed in a conversation of late 1950 with Kielmansegg that the most difficult task before the founders of the new army would be to restore the soldiers' prestige, which denazification, reeducation, and the popular backlash against the professional military had diminished. The Bonn government, acting on the suggestions of the experts at Himmerod, would simultaneously have to rehabilitate the professional soldier while reforming the political conception of his place in state and society.[8]

---

[5] The problem of the ongoing execution of war criminals in 1950 is described in the memoirs of Charles Thayer, a State Department official and political adviser to John J. McCloy, in his *Unquiet Germans* (New York, 1957); also see *FRUS, 1951*, vol. 3, pt. 1, pp. 392–459, as well as Meyer, "Situation," pp. 613–31.

[6] Meyer, "Situation," pp. 635–51.

[7] Interviews with General Ulrich de Maizière, April and June 1984, and with Major General Werner Ranck, May 1984.

[8] Interview with General Johann Adolf Graf von Kielmansegg, September 1985.

As negotiations continued on the Petersberg,[9] Speidel and Heusinger prevailed upon the representatives of the High Commission to ask leading personalities in the West to publicly revise their judgment about the collective guilt of the German military.[10] The generals suggested that western leaders should distinguish between the criminal acts of individual soldiers or entire units and the bearing of the Wehrmacht as a whole. The former were damnable, but the latter were undeserving of the charge of collective guilt. Such a distinction was necessary to win political and psychological support for European defense among veterans in West Germany. The members of the High Commission reacted sympathetically, but nothing further was done until the last weeks of January.

In late January 1951, General Dwight D. Eisenhower, recently designated Supreme Allied Commander Europe (SACEUR), the top general of NATO, traveled through West Germany. He came to look at his future command and to build "spirals of confidence" in Atlantic defense.[11] His visit prompted Speidel and Heusinger to action.[12] Eisenhower's dual role as military commander of NATO and former supreme commander of the allied forces gave him enormous public authority. Statements in his book, *Crusade in Europe*, about the moral culpability of German soldiers had been important for German hearts and minds. The book especially rankled public opinion in the Federal Republic as the move toward the establishment of the new army got underway. Speidel, acting on his own and without support from his civilian superiors across the river, went up the Petersberg to the U.S. High Commission. He successfully convinced the Deputy Commissioner, Major General George P. Hays, that Eisenhower should publicly rehabilitate the "honor of the German soldier."[13] Speidel, Heu-

---

[9] Rautenberg and Wiggershaus, *Himmeroder Denkschrift*, pp. 11ff.; and Gerhard Wettig, *Entmilitarisierung und Wiederbewaffnung in Deutschland, 1943–1955* (München, 1967), pp. 400–01.

[10] Wettig, *Entmilitarisierung*, pp. 400–10; Meyer, "Situation," pp. 674ff.

[11] On the motivations for making this trip within the context of U.S. military political thinking, see Samuel F. Wells, "The First Cold War Buildup: Europe in United States Strategy and Policy, 1950–3," in *Western Security: The Formative Years, European and Atlantic Defense*, ed. Olav Riste (Oslo/Bergen, 1985), pp. 181–97, as well as the message traffic during the Eisenhower visit in *FRUS, 1951*, vol. 3, pt. 1, pp. 392–459.

[12] Wettig, *Entmilitarisierung*, p. 401.

[13] These events are interpreted in Wettig, *Entmilitarisierung*, pp. 400–01; Thayer,

singer, and representatives of the U.S. High Commission worked out the draft text. Eisenhower signed the document at Bad Homburg, near Frankfurt, on 22 January 1951 after meeting privately with the two German generals, in attendance at a larger reception with government and party figures. Eisenhower's statement began by disavowing his belief of 1945 "that the Wehrmacht, and especially the German officer corps, had been identical with Hitler and his exponents of the rule of force." This conviction, he now admitted, had been in error, for ". . . the German soldier had fought bravely and honorably for his home-land."[14] Speidel and Heusinger insisted that Eisenhower's statement remain confidential, out of fear that it might encourage the antidem-ocratic right. Speidel and Heusinger then apparently distributed the text privately to leading officers in the hope of overcoming their op-position to rearmament. A second text from Eisenhower, published soon after the first but without a statement of pardon, asserted that "there is a real difference between the regular German soldier and officer and Hitler and his criminal group. . . . For my part," Eisen-hower continued, "I do not believe that the German soldier as such has lost his honor. The fact that certain individuals committed in war dishonorable and despicable acts reflects on the individuals concerned and not on the great majority of German soldiers and officers."[15]

Eisenhower's statement, a result of German initiative, typified the attempt of former officers of the Wehrmacht to distance themselves from the atrocities of the recent past while upholding the ideals and traditions of the professional soldier. The line drawn between the guilt of a number of war criminals and the mass of German soldiers "who had fought bravely and honorably" signified a political and hu-man compromise. Subsequent generations have damned this bargain for obscuring the institutional guilt of the Wehrmacht in the Nazi state, but this solution, essentially identical to the one offered in the Himmerod document, was the only one politically acceptable to most West Germans, as long as the combined effects of the cold war and of the public aversion to denazification and reeducation held sway in the

---

Unquiet Germans, pp. 232ff. A description of the meeting in Bad Homburg by U.S. High Commissioner John J. McCloy to Secretary of State Dean Acheson is con-tained in *FRUS, 1951*, vol. 3, pt. 1, pp. 445–47.

[14] Cited in Wettig, *Entmilitarisierung*, p. 401.

[15] *FRUS, 1951*, vol. 3, pt. 1, p. 447, and Wettig, *Entmilitarisierung*, p. 401.

Federal Republic, that is, until the late 1960s. Political and psychological conditions were used to justify the choice of allied and West German leaders making this distinction in favor of the institution of the professional officer. The federal government, worried about an impending war and eager to use the new army to get West Germany back into the ranks of the powers, needed the support of career soldiers and could only gain it with such a change of policy. By means of such compromises, the makers of policy tried to resolve the controversies that existed about the role of the Wehrmacht in National Socialism, but this compromise became the object of intense disagreement. The knotted issues of the Wehrmacht, National Socialism, and the honor of the German soldier arose continually within the new army. This complex soon emerged as the central question of policy regarding the maintenance of military tradition, one which demanded a response from a succession of civilian and military leaders. As important as this issue was, however, it existed within a larger complex of interconnected psychological, political, social, and material problems that tended to make the burdens of the soldierly past still heavier upon the new army. For the combination of these problems seemed as if they would nullify all attempts to reform the army.

THE CREATION of a military organization poses difficult tasks even in the best of circumstances. The West German planners, at work under very unfavorable international and domestic conditions, confronted a vicious circle of too little time, political uncertainty, shortage of personnel, technological confusion, and legal obstacles.[16] These problems made certain that not a single soldier put on a uniform or picked up a rifle until years after the Himmerod meeting. For the first

[16] These problems are well described by three leading participants, Kurt Fett, "Die Grundlagen der militärischen Planungen," in MFGA, ed., *Aspekte der deutschen Wiederbewaffnung*, pp. 169–200; Hanz Tänzler, "Vorbereitende Planung für die Innere Führung," pp. 201–23 in the same collection; and Ulrich de Maizière, "Zur Planung und Vorbereitung eines westdeutschen Verteidigungbeitrages: ein Beitrag aus der Sicht eines Mitarbeiters der Dienststelle Blank," in *Entmilitarisierung und Aufrüstung in Mitteleuropa, 1945–1956, Vorträge zur Militärgeschichte*, ed. MGFA (Bonn, 1983). Also see Dietrich Genschel, *Wehrreform und Reaktion: Die Vorbereitung der Inneren Führung* (Hamburg, 1972), pp. 72–236, and Hans-Jürgen Rautenberg, "Zur Standortbestimmung für künftige deutsche Streitkräfte," in *Anfänge westdeutscher Sicherheitspolitik*, ed. MGFA, especially pp. 811–13.

decade-and-a-half of the life of the new military, the planners grappled with a variety of "Catch–22" situations far more vexing than those described in Joseph Heller's novel about the U.S. Army Air Forces of World War II. Initial concepts and planning for the army fell victim to changing political realities, which in turn were then overtaken by a combination of new political, legal, and technological problems. The confusion born of hurried beginnings and sudden halts, against which Schwerin had warned at the time of Himmerod, frustrated the smooth establishment of the new army and hampered the consolidation of the reforms of the inner structure until the 1970s.

At first, everything went very rapidly in the months after October 1950. The kind of force conceived at Himmerod and worked out initially with the allies on the Petersberg was to be "a mobilization army stamped out of the ground."[17] In effect, the German contingent would have been a *levée en masse*, responding to Major General Hays's alarm that the third world war was at hand. Wehrmacht veterans, many unemployed or still unadjusted to civilian life, would have filled the ranks of this army. The German contingent of 1951 was to be an army of young men: the noncommissioned officers and the company grade officers were in their twenties, while the senior staff and general officers were in their mid-forties to mid-fifties. Although this mobilization army never came into existence, its officers and NCOs would have been young and professionally self-confident men, convinced of the operational and tactical lessons they had learned from the last war. Once in uniform again, these men would not easily have accepted the liberal democratic society of postwar Germany.

There was then a real danger in having the West Germans establish their armed forces too quickly.[18] One can argue that had the army been created within a year after Himmerod, rather than in 1956–57, the policymakers might have produced an institution that lived outside the constitutional framework of the Federal Republic and one

---

[17] Hans-Peter Schwarz, *Die Ära Adenauer: Gründerjahre der Republik, 1949–1957*, vol. 2 in *Geschichte der Bundesrepublik Deutschland*, 5 vols. (Wiesbaden, 1981), p. 287; for details of this planned German force from the U.S. perspective, see *FRUS, 1951*, vol. 3, pt. 1, pp. 990–1047, and Stanley M. Kanarowski, *The German Army and NATO Strategy* (Washington, D.C., 1982), pp. 41–43.

[18] This analysis is indebted to Oberstleutnant Dr. Helmuth Schubert, Zentrum Innere Führung, Koblenz, as well as to Rautenberg, "Zur Standortbestimmung," pp. 811ff., and Hans-Peter Schwarz, *Die Ära Adenauer*, p. 287.

that failed to introduce into military life the ideals of the citizen embodied in the Basic Law.[19] Within a successful EDC, the new army might have become either a denazified revival of the Wehrmacht, dominated by an apolitical military functionalism, or an army derived from the military practices and traditions of the Western European powers, especially those of the French. Under these circumstances, any attempt at progressive reforms to prevent the new military's becoming a state within a state would probably have failed.

During 1951, however, the American effort to raise German levies in mass as part of the United States's commitment to NATO ran into French opposition as well as political doubts in the United States and West Germany. The organizers of the new army in Bonn shifted to low gear. Work now crawled forward within the confines of international agreements and the layers of domestic debate on rearmament. Foreign observers believed that the West Germans were dragging their heels on western defense; in fact, they wanted to avoid overeager moves toward the new army without first receiving the international go-ahead and achieving domestic consensus. This delay gave the Bonn government time for reflection and debate. During this period, which lasted five years, the political leadership and their military advisers began an intense exchange about the role of the soldier and of the state that grew out of the first proposals for military reform. But the political imperative to avoid taking concrete steps handicapped the planners in hundreds of ways. On the one hand, they had to perform a miracle of military planning in the conception and execution of a new force integrated into a supranational entity, while on the other hand, they had to dampen widespread fears that they were sowing the dragon's teeth of the old army of aggression.

Enduring memories of Seeckt's army of the 1920s accompanied the planning for the new German soldier. Antimilitary cartoonists of the time depicted the organizers of the new army as look-alikes of Hans von Seeckt, complete with monocles and dueling scars. These figures populated cartoons in which they welcomed Adolf Hitler back from

---

[19] Although the new military was officially founded around the turn of the year 1955–56, the majority of troop units did not come into existence until a year later. See the discussion in chapter 9 of this volume as well as *Verteidigung im Bündnis: Planung, Aufbau und Bewährung der Bundeswehr, 1950–1972*, ed. MGFA (München, 1975), pp. 131–41.

the pit of hell and prepared to resume the war that had ended in 1945. Members of the Adenauer government also recalled the covert efforts of the "black Reichswehr" to break the Versailles treaty on a vast scale by its secret staffs schools, arms plants, and exercise areas. Spokesmen for the West German government, conscious of this anxiety both at home and abroad, repeatedly said that their own armament would adhere to the letter of the law and that they would avoid taking measures beyond those specified on paper until the right moment.[20] This injunction remained in effect from the beginning of 1951 until mid-1955, when the Treaties of Paris went into effect. Only after the West German organizers had redrafted the West German contingent for the EDC into a West German national force did the western allies agree on the international basis for the armament of the Federal Republic. This international delay in turn postponed the parliamentary debate in Bonn on the legal position of the West German soldier until 1957.

The planners, although respectful of the primacy of politics, repeatedly pointed out to the makers of policy the need to take the first practical steps. The organizers were all too aware that delays and uncoordinated measures would paralyze the new army.[21] Over the years, the men in Bonn drafted out the steps of armament in thousands of memoranda and diagrams, all the while nagged by the doubt that the new army might never get off the ground. An early memorandum from the Petersberg negotiations of the first half of 1951 described such plans as a series of "immediate measures," which built upon many of the basic suggestions of Himmerod. These steps would precede the raising of troops and would depend upon the all-important step of parliament enacting the military amendments to the Basic Law.[22]

[20] The high commissioners insisted in the Petersberg negotiations that the West Germans avoid the secret rearmament of the Reichswehr, see *FRUS, 1951*, vol. 3, pt. 1, pp. 990ff.

[21] See BA/MA, Bw 9/717, "Überblick über Arbeitsprogramm der Dienststelle Blank," 10 December 1953, p. 12; interviews with Brigadier General Heinz Karst, March and July 1984; with Professor Wolf Graf von Baudissin, May 1984; and with General Ulrich de Maizière, April and June 1984. See also de Maizière's "Zur Planung und Vorbereitung eines westdeutschen Verteidigungsbeitrages: Ein Beitrag aus der Sicht eines Mitarbeiters der Dienststelle Blank," in *Entmilitarisierung und Aufrüstung in Mitteleuropa*, ed. MGFA (Bonn, 1983), pp. 8off.

[22] BA/MA Bw 9/2002, "Entwurf II P 1 'Vortragsnotiz für den Herrn Blank: Zeit- und Arbeitsprogramm der Dienststelle Blank, Blatt IV: Sofortmassnahmen,' " 18 May 1951. Also see the discussion of these issues in *FRUS, 1951*, vol. 3, pt. 1, pp.

Only with the legal basis in place could the planners of the new army take the next steps. These first measures included equipping the minister of defense and leading government officers with the necessary administrative authority; the creation of a military personnel replacement organization and its staffs; the acquisition of the necessary barracks; the establishment of a support and supply organization as well as the purchasing of needed arms, munitions, vehicles, and clothing; and the recruiting of the first staffs of such maneuver echelons of combat troops as divisions and regiments, as well as the mustering of the cadres of the troop-training units. Over the years the planners prepared hundreds of such memoranda, without receiving a response of money or personnel from either Adenauer's Chancellery or parliament. Succeeding military officials again suggested that the federal border guards—the federal police force created in 1950–51—might serve as a training ground for NCOs, while barracks could be put in shape, uniforms ordered, personnel selected, and equipment inspected.[23]

Adenauer deferred these measures until it was nearly too late. He could ill afford to arouse French political anxieties about the rebirth of German army power or to deepen the fears of international and domestic critics about the rebirth of the Reichswehr. The combination of international and domestic opposition in the years before the Paris treaties went into effect might well have stymied his push toward sovereignty and the western integration of the Federal Republic. Until West Germany at last gained its sovereignty, the planners had no choice but to adhere to the primacy of politics set down by the federal German government. They could only carry out their plans once the western occupiers had removed the last fetters of occupation and allowed West Germany to formally rejoin the ranks of the national powers.

After this step, four-and-a-half years after Himmerod, the machin-

---

990ff., especially pp. 993–96; Fett, "Die Grundlagen," pp. 169–223; Heinz Brill, *Das Problem einer Wehrpolitischen Alternative für Deutschland: Die Auseinandersetzung um die wehrpolitischen Alternativvorschläge des Obersten Bogislaw von Bonin (1952–1955)*, Ph.D. diss., Göttingen, 1977, pp. 40–78, especially pp. 55–58.

[23] Ulrich de Maizière, "Zur Planung und Vorbereitung eines westdeutschens Verteidigungsbeitrages: Ein Beitrag aus der Sicht eines Mitarbeiters der Dienststelle Blank," in *Entmilitarisierung und Aufrüstung in Mitteleuropa 1945–1956*, ed. MGFA (Bonn, 1983).

ery of the new army that had fitfully inched forward since 1951 now had to lurch ahead rapidly. The planners in Bonn had originally calculated that they would need eighteen months after parliament had passed the military legislation before the first troop units could be raised. It would take four more years to bring the army up to its full strength of twelve divisions. In May 1955, however, the incipient détente between the East and West made Adenauer afraid that the allies might return to the 1945 spirit of Potsdam, redraw the map of Europe, and shift the balance of power, all without any say from his government. Adenauer needed the full weight of sovereignty, especially that of his army. He threw out earlier plans for the build-up and rushed ahead before the great powers could partition Europe yet again.[24] The West German military now had three-and-a-half years to build up a force that had previously required about six years. The quick start of 1950, which had been succeeded by renewed stops and starts from 1951 to 1954, was followed by a spasm in 1955–56. Coming after all the confusion and false starts, this final rush disrupted the spirit and equilibrium of the army. These conditions represented anything but the "organic long-term build-up from the bottom up" that Schwerin had insisted upon in October 1950 as essential for the success of the reforms.

The delays and confusions on both the international and domestic levels during the years from 1950 to 1956 had a significant impact on the everyday life of the planning staff. Chief among these problems was a lack of skilled personnel.[25] Fearful that the employment of too many military planners would call to mind the black Reichswehr, the Adenauer government kept military staffing to an absolute minimum. A single individual might easily have overseen administrative areas that today occupy dozens if not hundreds of people in the Ministry of Defense.[26] The constant shifts from one military-political concept of armament to another led to intense overwork, as individuals had to tear up their plans and began afresh time and again. Planners often

[24] These events from Adenauer's perspective are described in Hans-Peter Schwarz, *Die Ära Adenauer, 1949–1957*, pp. 287–302; Rautenberg, "Zur Standortbestimmung," pp. 811–15; also see Johannes Fischer, "Militärpolitische Lage und militärische Planung bei Aufstellungsbeginn der Bundeswehr," in *Militärgeschichte: Probleme-Thesen-Wege*, ed. Manfred Messerschmidt (Stuttgart, 1982), pp. 452–77.

[25] Rautenberg, "Zur Standortbestimmung," p. 812.

[26] See the statistics in Fett, "Die Grundlagen," pp. 175–80.

prepared the outlines for needed programs only to find that the absence of further staff and political authority prevented these efforts from being realized until the allies and the federal government approved. A lack of qualified personnel later plagued the army as a whole. The need for skilled noncommissioned officers and company and field grade officers—the heart of an army—remained a constant problem. As the years passed, the mass of wartime officers and NCOs grew steadily older; men who would have answered the call to arms in 1951 drifted out of reach by 1955–56. Many veteran officers, especially those trained for the general staff, found well-paid jobs in business and the professions. These men were naturally reluctant to jeopardize their new careers to join the armed forces just as the West German economy was expanding rapidly. Once approval finally came for the new army, the planners found that only the very last of the wartime classes of trained officers and NCOs remained available. Changes in strategy, operations, and technology since 1945 had also limited the usefulness of their wartime experience.

The lack of material support for planning made the absence of personnel worse still. As one participant observed years later, his labor began with nothing more than "a pencil and a piece of paper."[27] The raw material of the military bureaucracy—the personnel files, the tables of organization and equipment, and the manuals of regulations and procedures of the old armies—had either been destroyed as part of demilitarization or had been seized by the allies. The historical analysis of the missions and functions of the Wehrmacht, prepared in hundreds of studies under General Franz Halder for the U.S. forces, was still classified and only came into German hands decades later.[28] These handicaps compelled certain planners, for instance, to rely on

[27] De Maizière, "Zur Planung und Vorbereitung eines westdeutschen Verteidigungsbeitrages," p. 82. These difficult circumstances are described in Rautenberg, "Zur Standortbestimmung," pp. 811–14.

[28] For more on this study, see Charles B. Burdick, "Vom Schwert zur Feder: deutsche Kriegsgefangene im Dienst der Vorbereitung der amerikanischen Kriegsgeschichtsschreibung über den Zweiten Weltkrieg. Die organisatorische Entwicklung der Operational History (German) Section," in *Militärgeschichtliche Mitteilungen* 2 (1971): 69–80. See also Christian Greiner, " 'Operational History (German) Section' und 'Naval Historical Team': Deutsches militärstrategisches Denken im Dienst der amerikanischen Streitkräfte von 1946 bis 1950," in *Militärgeschichte: Probleme-Thesen-Wege*, ed. Manfred Messerschmidt (Stuttgart, 1982), pp. 409–35.

memory to reconstruct the tables of organization of infantry divisions during their negotiations with the allies.

And yet in spite of these handicaps, which undermined the material basis for the reforms even before the first soldier joined the ranks, the work was dominated by a sense of ferment and innovation, fondly remembered by the participants years later. They believed that they had a chance to create something new within an altered political setting, and they were proud of this opportunity, despite the many crucial political problems that faced them. The absence of bureaucratic barriers made possible by the small staff, and the close associations between its sections, led to an intense contact that is rare in an established organization. As the years passed, however, factions emerged in the Emerkeil barracks in Bonn, the main site for Adenauer's shadow defense ministry. Disagreements among the military planners reflected the natural tendency in a bureaucracy toward fractiousness as well as different conceptions about the shape of the new army.

THE ENTERPRISE of planning the new army rested in the hands of what seems, by today's bloated standards, to be a very small group of men. Their experiences and beliefs had a profound impact on the character of the effort. The transfer of Kielmansegg, Oster, and Bussche to the new staff in Adenauer's Chancellery established continuity between the proposals for reform drafted at Himmerod and the design of the Bundeswehr.[29] Although the staff planners for the reforms generally went on to positions of authority in the armed forces, they also continued to serve as advisers to those who bore the chief responsibility for the arming of the Federal Republic.

Foremost among those responsible was the chancellor's commissioner on security affairs, the forerunner of the minister of defense during the long period of preparation. Schwerin, the first of these advisers, only served for a short time before leaving office in late October 1950. The circumstances of his departure illustrate the atmosphere of tension and political uncertainty that filled the first months of planning. Not long after the Himmerod meeting, disagreements among the military advisers over the shape of the future army became

---

[29] Interview with General Johann Adolf Graf von Kielmansegg, June 1984; Rautenberg, "Zur Standortbestimmung," p. 785.

public. Schwerin's abrupt resignation came after he was reported to have spoken in a meeting of the possible need for universal military service, a highly unpopular statement given the *ohne mich* mood of the time. It was also taken as a sign that officers were again making policy at the expense of civilians. Adenauer took this opportunity to demand Schwerin's resignation, symbolizing the chancellor's will to assert civilian control over the military. Although the talk about conscription was the immediate cause for the firing, there had been tension between Schwerin and Adenauer and friction with his fellow officers, among them Hans Speidel and Reinhard Gehlen, the Wehrmacht staff expert on the Russian military employed by the Americans after the war, who eventually became chief of West German intelligence. Critics of the former armor officer asserted that Schwerin was too closely identified with the British occupation forces. Germans in the recently created federal government, while eager not to offend public opinion abroad, also wanted to distance themselves from the orbit of the western powers. This atmosphere apparently hurt Schwerin's political durability.[30] Moreover, he had initially been brought into Adenauer's Chancellery to prepare a national police force—later the federal border guards—a requirement now superseded by the need to plan for a West German contribution to a European army. The new task of preparing the political basis for this enterprise required extraordinary political and diplomatic skills on the part of the security adviser, if Adenauer was to overcome the domestic and international obstacles to rearmament.

In light of all these developments, the chancellor appointed Theodor Blank, a CDU parliamentary deputy and trade union chief, to be his new security adviser. The position bore the impressive title: "Commissioner of the Chancellor for Questions Relating to the Augmentation of Allied Troops"—a name in keeping with the uncertain

[30] For more on Schwerin, see Roland G. Förster "Innenpolitische Aspekte der Sicherheit Westdeutschlands, 1947–1950," in *Anfänge westdeutscher Sicherheitspolitik 1945–1956: Von der Kapitulation bis zum Pleven Plan*, ed. MGFA, vol. 1 (München, 1982), pp. 456ff. On the problem of the connection of government figures with the western powers, see Hans Speier, *From the Ashes of Disgrace: A Journal From Germany, 1945–1955* (Amherst, 1981), especially pp. 149–58, which contains a discussion between Speier and Schwerin of 1955 about the influence of Reinhard Gehlen on General Adolf Heusinger and the selection of personnel for the West German defense effort.

status of the task of national security, given the occupation statutes. With this choice, Adenauer carefully underscored his desire that the new army be integrated into the society and the state. Blank's appointment also signified the hope of the government to win over those in German society who had opposed the earlier military institutions. A former reserve officer, Blank was also a trade unionist, a practicing Catholic, and a parliamentarian. This symbolic combination of social groups in the person of the shadow defense minister contrasted markedly with the stereotype of the arrogant and dashing military chiefs of the past. Vice Chancellor Franz Blücher saw the appointment of Blank as a defense of democratic government against a revival of militarism. With his parliamentary experience, Blank could assure the cooperation of the Bundestag in military affairs, while his labor credentials would help to reconcile workers with the professional military.

The chancellor's security adviser would also have to prove himself a skilled diplomat to gain equal status for the Federal Republic among the western allies. An anecdote from his first negotiations with the high commissioners illustrates this prowess.[31] After the first formal talks in the Petersberg hotel in January 1951, Blank and his group of military advisers emerged from the entrance of the building to drive to Bonn. The West German vehicles, however, were nowhere to be seen among the automobiles of the Americans, British, and French. Blank turned to the French official accompanying him and asked in a direct tone: "Where is my automobile?" The Frenchman responded meekly that it was around the corner in the parking space assigned to Germans. "I want to tell you something," Blank answered. "Today I am going to walk to my car, but if it's not standing here in front of the door next time, I won't be back."

The Adenauer government agreed that the future soldier should be subordinate to civilian control as never before in German history. The reordering of the soldier's place in society symbolized within the executive branch the most dramatic break of the Bonn government with the Prussian-German military past—it was perhaps the principal lesson learned from the German catastrophe. The self-image of the Ger-

[31] Interview with General Johann Adolf Graf von Kielmansegg, June 1984.

man soldier, so long one of the first man in the state, would have to conform to this new political and social reality.

The reconstruction of the inner structure of the army was only one of Blank's tasks, but it assumed early prominence in relation to the outside world and its judgment of German rearmament. After the public accepted that the Federal Republic would be armed, that structure became the outstanding issue in the discussions.[32] Blank saw his overall assignment as making a "radical break with the militarism of the past,"[33] by subordinating the new armed forces to parliamentary control, finally fulfilling the liberal hopes for the soldier and the state in German history. As Blank described his task in an address to parliament in June 1955, "the young German democracy, though still in the Nazi shadow, must create new soldiers without having yet won the full faith of the West German people."[34] The key to this dilemma would be a "democratic people's army,"[35] whose "German citizens in uniform" would enjoy the right to vote and freedom of expression. This ideal of the *Staatsbürger in Uniform* became the catch phrase of reform and a subject of much controversy and misunderstanding.

Blank proved an energetic advocate of military reform in public, although certain of his subordinates and outside observers in the press subsequently criticized him harshly. In the eyes of his detractors, he had not been sufficiently forceful in the execution of the reforms once the army was actually established.[36] But it seems to be the case that Adenauer's security adviser did pursue the issue of reform with energy and passion. He asserted that the ideas for reforms had been his, and

[32] Wiggershaus, "Zum Problem," p. 10; Genschel, *Wehrreform und Reaktion*, pp. 27ff. Genschel comes to very different conclusions about Blank's attitudes to the reforms than either Rautenberg or Wiggershaus. He places considerable emphasis on Blank's neglect of measures to consolidate the reforms in 1955–56, while Blank was under enormous political pressure to raise the troops at breakneck speed.

[33] BA/MA, Bw 2/1302, "Erklärung von Januar 1952," August 1952, cited in Wiggershaus, "Zum Problem," p. 10.

[34] Deutscher Bundestag, *Stenographische Berichte*, Bd. 26, 92. Sitzung, 27 June 1955, p. 5214.

[35] *Bulletin des Presse- und Informationsamtes der Bundesregierung*, 28 November 1955, "Theodor Blank: Für eine demokratische Volksarmee."

[36] See "Niederschrift eines Interviews von Frl. Diane Tridoux mit Wolf Graf von Baudissin, am 5. Mai 1980 im Institut für Friedensforschung und Sicherheitspolitik, Universität Hamburg," pp. 4ff., in the possession of the author; Gerd Schmückle, *Ohne Pauken und Trompeten: Erinnerungen an Krieg und Frieden* (Stuttgart, 1982), pp. 134–64.

that they had been fully formed in his own mind by October 1950.[37] At other times, Blank boldly made the comparison between his own task and that of Scharnhorst and Gneisenau, fostering the widespread tendency among spokesmen for the new army to equate the creation of the new West German military with the era of Prussian reform.

Blank, as an advocate of reform, eagerly addressed issues of everyday barracks life that were revealed in a popular work of the time, Hans Hellmut Kirst's novel, *08/15*, which depicted relations between officers, NCOs, and soldiers of the Wehrmacht in a very unflattering light. In the Federal Republic of the early 1950s, the negative example of such sadistic types as Kirst's martinet Sergeant Platzek dominated the popular image of military life. This misconception seemed pervasive, despite the fact that, at the front, officers, NCOs, and soldiers had often lived in kinship totally different from the conditions in rear areas. Indeed, as the years passed, the Wehrmacht had gone a long way toward abolishing many of the reprehensible aspects of everyday military life, much as Ludendorff had done in the reforms made after 1917. The senselessness of the *Kommiss*—the pointless marching, repetitious drills, excessive punishments, and endless cleaning of latrines—had caused public resentment and satire long before the Nazis came to power, and it became a chief object of reform in the new West German military.

The planners recognized that the citizens of the Federal Republic, especially those skeptical of rearmament, would never tolerate the rebirth of the arbitrary militarist spirit identified with the barracks square of the old army. These officials were especially concerned that antimilitary attitudes might deeply affect future recruits. To mitigate this problem, Blank assured audiences that there would be no one like Erich Maria Remarque's martinet Sergeant Himmelstoss in the new armed forces. "Whoever is unable," Blank said, "as an officer, NCO or reserve officer to impart his military skills and knowledge to recruits without treating them as free citizens will have no place with us."[38] Blank also intended to dress his soldiers simply, without braids and ribbons, sparing them the ceremonies and rituals too reminiscent

[37] Wiggershaus, "Zum Problem," p. 12.
[38] Archiv des Presse- und Informationsamtes der Bundesregierung. Biographisches Archiv. Pressenkonferenzen und Interviews, *Rede vor Bonner Studenten*, 16 June 1950, p. 19, cited in Wiggershaus, "Zum Problem," pp. 12–13.

of the past. Unnecessary emphasis on uniforms and externals was "a burden in an age in which the technological progress of armies and modern weapons placed ever greater demands on the soldier's abilities."[39] What the future forces needed, Blank maintained, "was not the *Pathos* of parades and military pageants, but the sobriety with which one does the most essential thing without too many big words."[40] This was a sentiment widely shared by many in West Germany in the early 1950s.

SUBORDINATE to the federal Chancellery, Blank's office enjoyed a special, though exposed, status under the leadership of career civil servants from Adenauer's staff. These men were soon joined by a number of general staff officers—several from the Himmerod group—who served alongside the civilians in a sometimes uneasy partnership. It was in this agency, together with its legislative and academic advisers and counterparts, that the most important events in the building of the army's inner structure and in the debate on military tradition took place. The initial shape of the office that was to be the foundation of the new army gradually underwent a change in character and style with the addition of several former officers to Blank's staff, as the work increased during the period from 1950 to 1952. The office grew in size during 1952 with an influx of more military men and it began to resemble the Ministry of Defense that it finally became in 1955. Most prominent among the career civil servants in the *Dienststelle Blank* was Ernst Wirmer, from the federal Chancellery, the brother of Joseph Wirmer, whom the Nazi People's Court had condemned to death in the wake of the Twentieth of July 1944, the attempt on Hitler's life. The astute choice of both civilian and military personalities connected with the resistance reflected Adenauer's skill at heading off criticism of rearmament at home and abroad.[41] It was also a result of the way the government selected personnel in the early stages, since a handful of leading members of the resistance in power often suggested their friends and acquaintances

---

[39] *Bulletin des Presse- und Informationamtes der Bundesregierung*, 24 November 1952, "Theodor Blank: Für eine demokratische Volksarmee," cited in Wiggershaus, "Zum Problem," p. 13.
[40] Wiggershaus, "Zum Problem," p. 13.
[41] Rautenberg, "Zur Standortbestimmung," p. 786.

for the task of military planning.[42] There also existed a kind of fraternity of staff officers in the *Amt Blank*. German general staff officers had long formed an elite, whose members tended to know each other. Former general staff officers with extensive experience and a willingness to serve the Bonn republic formed a desirable addition to the office. For instance, a newly hired former general staff officer might suggest an acquaintance with whom he had trained and served during the war. These suggestions were in many cases the only basis for the planners' judgments, because the officer efficiency reports of the Wehrmacht, which normally would have provided backgrounds on officers' past service, were in western hands. The criteria for selection also included the officer's behavior in captivity and his later adjustment to civil life. And while these men ultimately had to be acceptable to the western allies within the framework of an international army, it does not seem as if the western high commissioners vetoed the selection of the staff for the *Amt Blank* in any direct or substantial way.[43]

[42] Interviews with General Johann Adolf Graf von Kielmansegg, June 1984, and with General Ulrich de Maizière, April and June 1984. See Hans-Jürgen Rautenberg, "Stationen aus einem Soldatenleben," in *Ulrich de Maizière, Stationen eines Soldatenlebens*, ed. Lothar Domröse (Herford, 1982), pp. 125–32. See also Georg Meyer, "Zur Frage der personellen Auswahl bei der Vorbereitung eines westdeutschen Verteidgungbeitrages, 1950–1956," in *Das Deutsche Offizierkorps 1860–1960* (Boppard, 1980), pp. 351–65; Georg Meyer, "Situation," pp. 657ff.; and Rautenberg, "Zur Standortbestimmung," pp. 785ff. On the long duration of self-recruitment in the German officer corps and its persistence in the first years of the new West German military, see Detlef Bald, *Der Deutsche Offizier: Sozial und Bildungsgeschichte des deutschen Offizierkorps im 20. Jahrhundert* (München, 1982), especially pp. 43–61, and his *Vom Kaiserheer zur Bundeswehr, Sozialstruktur des Militärs: Politik der Rekrutierung von Offizieren und Unteroffizieren* (Frankfurt a.M., 1981), especially pp. 29–34.

[43] On the issue of direct and indirect U.S. influence in military planning, see Speier, *From the Ashes*, pp. 149–58 and 225–26. There existed a kind of German-American military cooperation among the Deputy U.S. High Commissioner Major General George P. Hays and Speidel, Heusinger, and Kielmansegg. Outstanding in this connection is what appears to be the constant West German taking of the initiative in the negotiations. At the outset of planning, Speidel had passed certain of his military memoranda to the U.S. Army through Truman Smith, the former U.S. military attaché to Berlin in the late 1930s; see Hans-Peter Schwarz, *Adenauer: Der Aufstieg, 1876–1952* (Stuttgart, 1986), p. 756. In October 1950 Hays had examined the list of names for the Himmerod meeting without raising objections. Also see the reports of Hays to the secretary of state on the Petersberg negotiations from January to June 1951 in *FRUS, 1951*, vol. 3, pt. 1, pp. 990ff. A letter from Hays to Blank, in BA/MA Bw 9/2002, "Abschrift, Übersetzung, Major General Hays an Blank, 28 April 1951," indicates a willingness to cooperate in certain

A prominent example of this use of an "old boy network" was the recruitment by Kielmansegg of Lieutenant Colonel Ulrich de Maizière for the *Dienststelle Blank* in 1951.[44] De Maizière had been recognized as a brilliant general staff officer who fought on the eastern front for most of the war and during its last days served as army staff liaison to the *Führerbunker*. After his release from allied captivity, de Maizière owned the music section of a Hannover book shop. Summoned to Bonn, he had to readjust quickly to military life. He was immediately sent to the EDC negotiations in Paris as a military adviser to the West German delegation. His considerable staff experience and his never having served on the Western Front between 1940 to 1945 made him an ideal choice for the position. In addition, Hans Speidel, Rommel's chief of staff, became the ranking officer at the Paris negotiations, while Adolf Heusinger took over the Bonn military-political staff (*Unterabteilung II*) in the *Dienststelle Blank*. Kielmansegg became, in his own words, Heusinger's "boy Friday" and was often assisted by de Maizière in dealing with the most pressing issues of policy facing the office.

There were many such problems at hand, including the organization and functions of the Bonn and Paris staffs. The make-up and missions of these two bodies were complex and subject to the pressures of the strained civil-military relationship in the young Federal Republic.[45] The former general staff officers in the Adenauer government worked in an organization that had been consciously staffed with civilians to preclude the rebirth of a traditional general staff spirit. This internal division of powers was reflected in the organizational chart of the shadow defense ministry. It consisted of roughly three main parts: a civilian section made up of career civil servants devoted to administrative and personnel tasks under Wirmer; a military planning section under Heusinger that embraced a multitude of military-political and operational assignments that resembled those of the old general staff; and a legal affairs section with career jurists un-

"democratic" aspects of the German defense contribution, but this offer of U.S. help apparently did not lead to any exchanges beyond the end of 1951. See Rautenberg, "Zur Standortbestimmung," p. 797.

[44] Interview with General Johann Adolf Graf von Kielmansegg, June 1984.

[45] See Genschel, *Wehrreform und Reaktion*, pp. 72–103.

der Eberhard Barth. Separate sections for military bases and facilities and for procurement were later added.

There existed a further separation of traditional staff responsibilities in the organization under Blank. The officials in the Adenauer government recognized that the administration of military personnel and military justice were two autonomous preserves of soldiers that must now be in civilian hands. This decision led to occasional conflicts between certain officers and civil servants, but in spite of the intense controversy, it is the arrangement that has endured in the West German military.[46] The structure and organizational tables of the military-political staff, its chain of command, and its control over specific staff sections and desks were all at times also the causes of bitter disagreement. Although such strife is common to any large organization, these disputes intruded into public view often during the years 1950 to 1956 and suggested a division between reformers and traditionalists on Blank's staff.

These difficulties aside, the worst organizational problem confronting Blank—indeed facing the whole army for much of its first fifteen years—was a chronic shortage of personnel.[47] The need to divide available staff between Bonn and Paris made this situation worse during the first years. The lack of staff hampered all aspects of the planning task, forcing members of the organization to cover several areas simultaneously, often at the expense of vital projects.[48] There was also a constant need to speak to the public as well as to adjudicate with the allies on hundreds of questions connected with the new army. The result was that the planners were spread too thin to deal with problems arising within the staff itself. This state of affairs had a particularly destructive effect on the efficacy of the reforms, for while the men on the staff responsible for reform promoted these ideas in pub-

[46] For the evolution of the West German armed forces administration, see Klaus Hornung, *Staat und Armee: Studien zur Befehls- und Kommandogewalt und zum politisch-militärischen Verhältnis in der Bundesrepublik Deutschland* (Mainz, 1975), and Hubert Reinfried, *Streitkräfte und Bundeswehrverwaltung* (Regensburg, 1979).

[47] See Fett, "Die Grundlagen," p. 175; Genschel, *Wehrreform und Reaktion*, pp. 104–21; Rautenberg, "Zur Standortbestimmung," pp. 811–12; and Speier, *From the Ashes*, pp. 297ff.

[48] For an example of many such complaints, see "II/1/Gr. 1(alt II/2/1) 'Monatsbericht (1.6.–30.6. 1955),' " 27 June 1955, consulted by the writer.

lic, they seemingly neglected to win the hearts and minds of many of their fellow officers.[49]

To the casual observer, the social backgrounds of the officers at work for Blank seemed to be little different from those of their counterparts in the era before 1939. As of September 1952, there were 174 former professional officers in the *Amt Blank*. Of these, 142 were Lutheran and 134 were from northern Germany. Only forty officers were from southern Germany, of whom thirty-two were Catholic. Ninety-eight officers had belonged to the previous general staff or had served in subordinate troop staffs—the majority of these, however, were the products of the rapid general staff training begun in war and not from the prewar two-year course. Thus, as a generalization, one can say that the first military planners in the *Amt Blank* tended to be northern German, Lutheran officers reared in the tradition of the Prussian-German general staff.[50] Yet it was precisely these officers who also planned and eventually carried out the military reforms. And it was generally these same officers who also established the policy for the West German armed forces on military tradition.

[49] Interview with Professor Wolf Graf von Baudissin, May 1984.

[50] Hans-Jürgen Rautenberg, "Zur historischen Entwicklung der Militärreform und des Konzepts der Inneren Führung," in *Innere Führung in Staat, Armee und Gesellschaft*, ed. Hubertus Zubert (Regensburg, 1981), pp. 98–99.

4. Count Baudissin and an Army without Pathos

THE INITIAL WORK on the military reforms in Bonn, dominated by the mobilization atmosphere of the Petersberg negotiations, grew out of the need to define anew the legal basis of civil-military relations. The military organizers would have to protect the future soldier against the misuse of state power, a step that soon became a political precondition for the armament of the Federal Republic. The men at work on the German contingent would have to reorder the relationships between superiors and subordinates while assuring the political status of all soldiers as equal citizens. This effort was to be an important aspect of the future military legislation. The amendments to the law arose in the course of the Petersberg negotiations as the measure that must precede all others for forming the new armed forces. In the process of deciding that issue, the founders of the army eventually had to come to find their own policy toward military tradition.

Because of the connection in timing between the negotiations with the high commissioners and the start of planning for military reform in the *Amt Blank* in March 1951, one might easily conclude in retrospect that the impulse to reorder the new military originated with the western allies and that they directed the execution of the reforms. The opposite, however, was almost certainly the case; that is, the West Germans chose to reform their army for domestic and international reasons of their own. This effort, in fact, took place despite the skepticism of the western allies and, at times, against their open resistance.[1]

---

[1] Interviews with Generals Kielmansegg, de Maizière, and Karst, March-July 1984; Kurt Fett, "Die Grundlagen der militärischen Planungen," in *Aspekte der deutschen Wiederbewaffnung*, ed. MGFA, pp. 169ff.; and Heinz Brill, *Das Problem einer Wehrpolitischen Alternative für Deutschland: Die Auseinandersetzung um die wehrpolitischen Alternativvorschläge des Obersten Bogislaw von Bonin (1952–1955)*, Ph.D. diss. Göttingen, 1977.

The Himmerod memorandum and the Petersberg negotiations reveal the initiative of the founders toward reform. Major General Hays, eager for German troops and having himself directed no such reform, wrote in February 1951 of Blank's position on reform that "we welcome the German statement that the appropriate measures will be taken to assure the appointment of officers who will maintain democratic ideals."[2] In the course of the Petersberg conversations, the high commissioners appeared to be convinced that the West Germans would fulfill their promise. A few weeks after Hays wrote of his approval of the German actions, Blank sought further advice from the American on the development of an army in a "democratic atmosphere according to healthy democratic principles." In response, Hays had his staff summarize for Blank the democratic principles underlying the U.S. Army: an officer corps recruited from all social groups, adequate pay and benefits, military justice based on civil and international law, and the recognition of individual rights as set down in the Constitution. But Hays confessed that he knew little about the development of the inner structure of the German military and demurred from insisting that the West Germans emulate the United States. "I do not know," Hays offered, "whether it would be sensible from the German standpoint to assume the American system in all respects." This German-American cooperation on the question of the army's inner structure went no farther than the exchange of a handful of studies between the experts of the respective staffs and it had ended by the fall of 1951.[3] In these first months of negotiations, the Americans and the British seemed to have cared most about the operational details of a rapid build-up of German combat power—an emphasis that endured over the years and helped to undermine the basis for real military reform.

In the wake of Adenauer's promises of reform, of the Himmerod meeting, and of the Petersberg negotiations, Colonel Kurt Fett, the first chief of the planning section in the *Amt Blank*, took the initial

---

[2] *FRUS, 1951*, vol. 3, pt. 1, p. 1004.

[3] Hans-Jürgen Rautenberg, "Zur Standortbestimmung für künftige deutsche Streitkräfte," in *Anfänge westdeutscher Sicherheitspolitik 1945–1956: Von der Kapitulation bis zum Pleven Plan*, ed. MGFA (München, 1982), 1: 796–97. See correspondence in BA/MA, Bw 9/502 cited in Rautenberg, "Zur Standortbestimmung," p. 797, and in BA/MA Bw 9/2002, "Hays an Blank, Abschrift, 3. Ausfertigung, Geheim, 28. April 1951."

steps toward this goal of reform in March 1951. He directed Kielman-segg, Oster, and Bussche to prepare a study on the legal position of the soldier in society in the past and future. This first project came to nothing, however, until Baudissin joined the office in May 1951. A comrade from Potsdam and from Infantry Regiment No. 9 in the 1930s, Bussche had encouraged Baudissin to attend the meeting at Himmerod. Bussche's favorable impression of Baudissin led Kielman-segg to invite him to Bonn a few months later, where Baudissin be-came head of the *Wehrwesen* section of the staff. His new office was to help draft the military legislation and plan the inner structure of the German contingent.[4]

One can certainly wonder which experiences in his past made Bau-dissin such an advocate of reform. In the years after the creation of the Bundeswehr, he often described in public his horror at the humil-iations of basic training and the barracks square in the Reichswehr of the 1920s. He had also been skeptical about the maintenance of tra-dition in the ranks. Having served as a young officer in what certainly was the most tradition-conscious regiment in the Reichswehr, Bau-dissin once went to a dinner filled with veterans from the old guards regiments. When a toast was offered to the Emperor William, he re-acted by leaving the room. Reflecting on his experiences years later, he asserted that he had a "certain suspicion" about the cult of tradition of the old armies, made up of practices that struck him as sympto-matic of the "extraterritoriality of the Reichswehr" in the first German republic.[5] "The maintenance of tradition ordered from above . . . was at best a means of control and 'advertising.' . . . The officers of the regiment, who often transferred from one company in the regiment with one set of lineage and honors to another, could not take it very seriously."[6]

[4] Interviews with Professor Wolf Graf von Baudissin, May 1984, and with Gen-eral Johann Adolf Graf von Kielmansegg, June 1984. See also "Niederschrift eines Interviews von Frl. Diane Tridoux mit Wolf Graf von Baudissin, am 5. Mai 1980 im Institut für Friedensforschung und Sicherheitspolitik, Universität Hamburg," pp. 1–4. Some of Baudissin's first staff studies on the reforms are contained in BA/ MA, Bw 9/2002 and are interpreted in detail in Rautenberg, "Zur Standort-bestimmung," pp. 786–87 and 817–18.

[5] Interview with Professor Wolf Graf von Baudissin, May 1984.

[6] See 1982 interview with Baudissin cited in Wolfgang Paul, *Das Potsdamer Infan-terie Regiment 9, 1918–1945*, 2 vols. (Osnabrück, 1985), 1: 69.

Baudissin's skeptical statements about the maintenance of tradition do not jibe with the accusations of his outspoken opponents from the 1950s and 1960s. They claimed that he had been an exceptionally aristocratic officer in Infantry Regiment No. 9 and that his bearing had been anything but democratic. Nevertheless, as a regimental adjutant in Potsdam for a number of years, he was responsible for innovations in unit personnel and training there. There he experimented with practices on a small scale that later emerged in the *Innere Führung* of the Bundeswehr. He tried to orient training exercises toward the mission and he arranged for monthly visits of outside experts from government and other realms to the officers club, where soldiers and civilians discussed issues of the day.[7]

In 1942, Baudissin was captured in North Africa. His years behind British and Australian barbed wire gave him the opportunity to contemplate the problem of the military, politics, and society and fostered his intellectual and political transformation. He combined political reflection with an intense devotion to Pietism. After his return to Germany from captivity in Australia, social work became his greatest interest.

Baudissin's work on the new staff of mid-1951 could draw on no earlier studies among his colleagues on the inner structure of the army or on military legislation. Nor did he receive any explicit guidance from his superiors, other than the broad advice that is customary in German staff practice. As the basis for his work, he used the proposals he had helped draft at Himmerod and the earlier directive from Fett. Supplemented with insights from Baudissin's experience in labor relations in the Ruhr before his return to military life, the Himmerod and Fett documents were the basis for the conception of *Innere Führung* that became so closely linked with Baudissin in the public mind.[8] The activities of Baudissin and his colleagues expanded after the war

[7] Paul, *Potsdamer Regiment*, 1: 69–70.

[8] "Befragung Baudissin, MGFA, 28. Februar 1969," cited in Rautenberg, "Zur Standortbestimmung," p. 786; Tridoux interview, pp. 1–4; and interview with Professor Wolf Graf von Baudissin, May 1984. Among the first studies by Baudissin are BA/MA Bw 9/2002, "II Pl/4 964–02a 'Notiz: Vorgesetzenverhältnisse' 1. Juni 1951" and "II Pl/4 964–12 'Wehrgesetz: "Politik in der Wehrmacht" ' 4. Juni 1951." Also see the discussion of the latter by Lieutenant Colonel Ernst Ferber, BA/MA Bw 9/2002, "II Pl/2 'Ausarbeitung II Pl/4 "Politik in der Wehrmacht" vom 4.6.1951,' " 6 June 1951.

scare of 1950–51 had passed and the domestic and international wrangling over the EDC set in.[9] This hiatus allowed time to reflect and debate about the reforms.

Until his departure from the Ministry of Defense in 1958, Baudissin bore primary responsibility on the staff for questions of military tradition, and he became chief spokesman on the subject, especially in the civilian world. Captain Heinz Karst, who joined the office months later, eventually emerged as perhaps the most popular author and speaker on this question before the troops. Baudissin and his contemporaries always understood the issue of the maintenance of tradition to be an integral part of the question of inner structure. But this tradition only became a special aspect of planning and debate late in his tenure in the ministry, during the troop build-up of 1956–58. In spite of the apparent prominence of the maintenance of tradition as a later subject of political and historical discussion in the Federal Republic, the military staff devoted relatively little attention to it as a separate issue until soldiers began to join the army in growing numbers. Prior to 1956, the maintenance of tradition was an implicit but ill-defined problem in relation to a variety of separate aspects of the inner structure handled by Baudissin's staff in the *Amt Blank*.[10] The discussion of military tradition among key framers of policy began slowly and hesitantly after 1951. In this debate, the members of the staff and their advisers clearly came to see the conflicting political and historical aspects of the dilemma, a process of recognition that began in the co-

---

[9] His colleagues included at the outset the former general staff colonels Ernst Ferber, Joachim Freyer, Heinz Hükelheim, and the jurist Dr. Rudolf Binapfel. They were joined in mid-1952 by Major Hans Tänzler and by Captain Heinz Karst, who became Baudissin's deputy in 1955 and his ideological opponent thereafter. These staff officers cooperated on the reforms with others in the *Dienststelle Blank*, of course, notably the legal division under Eberhard Barth. A full account of the vagaries of the *inneres Gefüge* staff is in Dietrich Genschel, *Wehrreform und Reaktion: Die Vorbereitung der Inneren Führung 1951–1956* (Hamburg, 1972); Rautenberg covers much of the same material in a historical narrative in his "Zur Standortbestimmung," pp. 739–879.

[10] See BA/MA, Bw 9/1248, "II/3 11, Merkblätter, Richtlinien, und Grundfragen des 'inneren Gefüges' die erarbeitet sein müssen, bis die Lehrstäbe zusammentreten," 5 September 1952; BA/MA, Bw 9/1.291, "Anforderungen von II Pl Bonn zum Ausschuss 'Innere Führung,' " 9 February 1953; and BA/MA, Bw 9/717, "II/IG, Orientierung über die wichtigsten Unterlagen, die das Referat 'Inneres Gefüge' beim Zusammentritt des Lehrstabes erarbeitet haben muss," 9 December 1953.

operation of staff officers and civilian advisers during the year 1952–1953.

As BEFITTED the task, the nature of the work in the *Dienststelle Blank* was itself new.[11] This planning for the West German soldier, characterized by a high degree of civilian participation, broke with past general staff tradition (Hitler's interference in the later stages of the war notwithstanding). Strictly speaking, of course, until 1955, *all* the planners were civilians, whether they were former general staff officers, civil servants, or academics. Before 1945, military planning had been the jealously guarded preserve of an elite group of officers laboring behind closed doors and usually at cross-purposes with civilians. In contrast, the laying of the foundations for the inner structure of the West German contribution to European defense generally took place in the full view and with the active participation of members of parliament and the public. Several factors contributed to this situation: parliamentary insistence on subordinating the armed forces to civilian control, the shortage of personnel in the *Dienststelle Blank*, and the desire to win public confidence and to integrate the armed forces into society. The appearance of members of the *Dienststelle* before interested groups led to a continuous and fruitful exchange in the years between 1951 and 1955. In the process, the first detailed discussions about military tradition took place within a greater debate over military reforms.[12]

These seminars were supplemented by the hiring of experts from the professional world as consultants to write studies on social, polit-

---

[11] See Hans Christian Greiner, "Die Dienststelle Blank: Regierungspraxis bei der Vorbereitung des Deutschen Verteidgungbeitrages von 1950–1955," *Militärgeschichtliche Mitteilungen* 1 (1975): 99–124; Fett, "Die Grundlagen," pp. 169ff.; and Rautenberg, "Zur Standortbestimmung," pp. 811ff.

[12] BA/MA Bw 2/982, "Vortrag Heusingers auf einer Informationstagung für Mitarbeiter der ADK [Arbeitsgemeinschaft demokratischer Kreise] aus den Soldaten und Traditionsverbänden am 6. November 1954" and "Interview Blanks mit Hans Wendt, Nordwestdeutscher Rundfunk, 9. November 1952," both cited in Norbert Wiggershaus, "Zum Problem der Tradition im Vorfeld eines westdeutschen Verteidigungsbeitrages," unpublished manuscript, 1983, p. 15; Rautenberg, "Zur Standortbestimmung," pp. 798ff.; Hans-Adolf Jacobsen, "Zur Rolle der öffentlichen Meinung bei der Debatte um die deutsche Wiederbewaffnung," in *Aspekte der deutschen Wiederbewaffnung*, ed. MGFA (Boppard, 1975); interviews with Brigadier General Heinz Karst, April and July 1984, and with Professor Wolf Graf von Baudissin, May 1984.

ical, and psychological aspects of the new army.[13] The combination of the seminars and the studies sponsored by the government helped to compensate for the shortage of personnel in the *Amt Blank* and was comparable to the trend in the U.S. military of the time to employ civilian experts, as in the case of the RAND Corporation created by the U.S. Air Force. The seminars provided a forum for professional officers and experts to debate a variety of issues connected with the future army as well as to demonstrate to key groups in society the new spirit of civil-military cooperation that was to be embodied therein. Seminars were held on such topics as education in the armed forces, the legal implications of the new army, and the challenges of dealing with West Germany's young men. The government would invite leading academic experts to these conferences, many of whom became consultants to the military. The transcripts of these meetings with experts and the studies contracted for by the *Amt Blank* gave impetus to the planning and provided the opinions of key groups. These seminars and their importance are described in greater detail in the account of the Hermannsburg and Siegburg meetings that follows. This practice of advice and consultation between military staff and civilian experts was institutionalized after the creation of the Bundeswehr in the Council for Questions of *Innere Führung* (*Beirat für Fragen der Inneren Führung*), and it formed a significant influence in the official exchange concerning the military tradition.[14]

Other social institutions also participated in the planning task and quickly assumed a prominent role in military-political affairs. The Catholic and Protestant evangelical academies, set up in the aftermath of the war as sites for discussing political issues between different social groups, played an important role in the interchange between rep-

[13] BA/MA, Bw 9/482, "Weisung Fett vom 8.3.1951," cited in Rautenberg, "Zur Standortbestimmung," p. 788. A series of these studies was prepared, including among other topics: "the military concept of honor"; "*Heimat*, fatherland, and Europe"; "oath and obligation"; "military leadership, authority in modern, technical armed forces"; "tradition and progress—the meaning of military heritage for the build-up of new armed forces." See BA/MA Bw 2/4026, "Programm der Gutachten," cited in Wiggershaus, "Zum Problem," p. 16.

[14] ZIF/ZUA, 0.2.2., "Bundesminister für Verteidigung (BMVg), Führungsstab der Bundeswehr (Fü B) I 4, Aktenzeichen (Az) 35–10, 'Erlass über die Bildung eines Beirates für Fragen der Inneren Führung,' " 30 June 1958; "BMVg, Fü B I 4, Az. 35–10 'Generalinspekteur an Inspekteur Heer, usw.,' " 18 July 1958.

resentatives of the *Dienststelle Blank* and the outside world.[15] The academies were part of a religious awakening that came to many officers in the wake of the defeat. It was not uncommon for professional officers to study theology after their release from captivity and then to enter the academies; they formed personal links between many former professional soldiers who had recently joined the government and those in the evangelical academies. The role of the churches in shaping the debate on rearmament was also decisive in official eyes, and members of the government were eager to win over clerical opponents to the new army. The academies were an ideal site for such an exchange between soldiers and civilians, a function that they still retain today.

It was before a group of veterans at the Hermannsburg Academy in December 1951 that for the first time Baudissin presented his ideas in public, only six months after his arrival at the *Amt Blank*.[16] Baudissin's comments are striking for their early and consistent emphasis on the political, social, and ethical conditions for the West German contribution to European defense; on the altered quality of German life within the course of history; and on the soldier's role in the ideological confrontation of the postwar world. These were themes that Baudissin repeated and expanded upon for years afterward, assumptions and ideas about the soldier, society, and the value of military tradition that underlay the policy he later helped to establish. Significantly, however, military tradition as a distinct theme was absent in Baudissin's first public statement. His comments touched on almost all aspects of military tradition as it was understood before 1945, but he treated them negatively without expressly mentioning them.

In Baudissin's judgment as he expressed it at Hermannsburg, the catastrophe of recent German history called into question all existing

[15] For examples of the seminars and speaking engagements that were given between the *Dienststelle Blank* and the evangelical academies, see the correspondence between Ulrich de Maizière and certain members of these institutions in BA/MA, Bw 9/214. Also see Hans Speier, *From the Ashes of Disgrace* (Amherst, 1981), pp. 218–19, 268.

[16] For Baudissin's judgment of the importance of this speech, see the Tridoux interview. The text itself is reprinted in Wolf Graf von Baudissin, *Soldat für den Frieden: Entwürfe für eine zeitgemässe Bundeswehr* (München, 1969), pp. 23ff. The discussion of these issues in the *Dienststelle Blank* during the second half of 1951 is in BA/MA, Bw 9/2002 and interpreted by Rautenberg, "Zur Standortbestimmung," pp. 811ff.

values about the state, the individual, and, particularly, the existence of soldiers. The future West German soldier must capitalize on the "grace of the zero point" and fashion something new with the chance offered by this fresh start. The positing of historical discontinuity after 1945—the basis for Baudissin's ideas and those of many others—was to be the foundation of the new inner structure of the army.

Baudissin described the transformed political and social conditions in which the future soldier would serve. The "state of civil war dividing Germany," a phrase often used to characterize the division of the former Reich between East and West, set stark limits on the future soldier, who would serve in a supranational army with former opponents and who might be compelled to fight against family members from the eastern zones of occupation. As Baudissin told his audiences many times during the early and mid-1950s, one of the chief motivations for military reform arose from the special need to prepare German soldiers psychologically for the ideological struggles of the cold war. "Spiritual armament" as a basis for military effectiveness went hand in hand with the requirement to integrate the soldier into the democratic state.

The European soldier of German nationality would be drawn from the ranks of young people whom Baudissin described as having ceased to believe in the lofty, nationalist ideals that had brought their fathers and grandfathers to the colors. The German catastrophe and reeducation had left this generation bitterly disappointed and suspicious of all values passed down to them.[17] Baudissin and his audience faced a "departure from previous history"; it would be criminal to attempt a restoration of the past, yet it would also be a mistake to throw overboard all things from before. The task confronting the new German soldier, then, was one of reform, an enterprise that must conform to the new individual, to the society, and to the government of the Federal Republic. Although Baudissin demanded in later years that the reforms produce a greater democratizing effect in West German society, his original and often repeated characterization of the

[17] Baudissin's judgment of young Germans based upon his personal experience was for him an important motivation for the reforms. For more on this official view of West German youth, see Albert Huth, "Die seelische Lage der heutigen Jugend," in *Schicksalsfragen der Gegenwart: Handbuch historisch-politischer Bildung*, 6 vols., ed. BMVg (Tübingen, 1957), 2: 227–55.

task as a conservative reform best describes the real nature of the undertaking.[18]

Baudissin went on to define the purpose of the future soldier. Above all he must by his existence act to deter war, since the nature of organized violence between states had grown so frightful that war for political aims seemed increasingly impossible. The advocacy of deterrence at the basis of Baudissin's "image of war" was the subject of growing international political and military debate in the 1950s and it soon became the common property of many prominent military thinkers throughout the western world. It also became the essence of the self-image of the Bundeswehr, much as it did for the armed forces in the United States of the 1950s. Baudissin also recognized that the public emphasis upon deterrence in the self-image of the armed forces set limits on what was valid in military tradition. In this sense, he was well ahead of his German and allied military contemporaries. The operational doctrine for the use of nuclear weapons in the defense of Europe was by no means clear in late 1951.[19]

The future army would also have an important educational role in society. Baudissin hoped that the armed forces would win young people for a united Europe and "lead them to the new state [the Federal Republic]." Such purposes reflected his self-proclaimed kinship with the Prussian reformers of the early nineteenth century and their belief that the army should make the subjects of the sovereign into citizens of the nation. The new army would be a school of Europe. In this demand, which echoed a similar idea in the Himmerod memorandum, Baudissin revealed his bonds to the old armies, but he was surely no blinkered advocate of the anti-Catholic and antisocialist "school of the nation" concept that had been prevalent in the late nineteenth and early twentieth centuries.

[18] Hans-Jürgen Rautenberg, "Aspekte zur Entwicklung der Traditionsfrage in der Aufbauphase der Bundeswehr," in *Tradition als Last*, ed. Klaus M. Kodalle (Köln, 1981), pp. 104–05. That this greater democratizing process did not take place perhaps as quickly or in the manner that Baudissin had hoped explains his disenchantment in the 1980s with *Innere Führung*. Interview with Professor Wolf Graf von Baudissin, May 1984.

[19] See Christian Greiner, "Nordatlantische Bündnisstrategie und deutscher Verteidigungsbeitrag von 1954–1957," in *Entmilitarisierung und Aufrüstung in Mitteleuropa, 1945–1956, Vorträge zur Militärgeschichte*, ed. MGFA (Bonn, 1983), pp. 116–43, and Christian Greiner, "Konrad Adenauer—Aufbau der Bundeswehr für Souveränität und Westintegration," *Truppenpraxis* 1 (January/February 1986): 61–66.

In his Hermannsburg address, Baudissin also spoke at length about the reform of daily barracks life and of his intention to banish practices that treated soldiers as mere objects. These highly visible changes in everyday routines came to occupy such a prominent role in the public discussion of the reforms because they affected those things most Germans most recalled about their military service—the caprices of NCOs, the deadening atmosphere of the barracks, and the parade grounds as immortalized by Remarque and Kirst.

For instance, Baudissin proposed that the European soldier of German nationality would have to salute only his own immediate superior officer. He would be spared the constant saluting that offered many NCOs and officers the chance to reprimand soldiers for a sloppy salute. Off duty, he would be able to have a private life, free of martinet NCOs. On duty, intense and realistic field training carried out in small groups would replace the endless drill on the parade ground. The new armed forces would foster the inner cohesion of such small wartime fighting units as crews of aircraft, armored fighting vehicles, and U- and E-boats. Capitalizing on the positive military experiences of the last war, soldiers would fight out of a sense of common purpose rather than blind obedience. Finally, and perhaps most important, the future soldier would have the right to vote, signifying that he was indeed a "citizen in uniform," with civic duties, in contrast to the exclusivist social and political ethos of the German soldier before 1933.

Baudissin's first important public statement on the reforms was followed by scores of others in the 1950s and 1960s, which earned him an impressive reputation in West Germany and abroad as a soldier intellectual. From the remove of thirty-five years, however, the observer who compares Baudissin's speech at Hermannsburg to the reforming ideas of Guibert, of Prussia in 1806, of German liberals before 1848, and of the Social Democrats of the early twentieth century will find little that is strikingly new.[20] The Prussian reformers had advanced similar ideas within the context of their time. Scharnhorst spoke of *Bürger in Waffen* filled with a liberal spirit, an image of the soldier that was later carried forward by such men of the *Vormärz* as Karl von

---

[20] Wiggershaus, "Zum Problem," p. 60. For a brief discussion of Guibert, see Hew Strachan, *European Armies and the Conduct of War* (London, 1983), pp. 25–27. For an overview on the literature on military reform in Germany before 1945, see Karl Demeter, *Das Deutsche Offizierkorps* (Frankfurt, 1962), p. 160.

Rotteck. The French socialist Jean Jaurès, in his tract *L'armée nouvelle*, advocated reforms in favor of the citizen soldier, as did his German Social Democratic brethren before 1914.[21]

Although Baudissin's proposals had their antecedents in European history, as he often admitted, his thoughtful manner, his eloquence, and the energy with which he presented his ideas in public demonstrated to many skeptical yet influential people that German staff officers could revive the humanistic tradition of Scharnhorst, Gneisenau, Boyen, and Clausewitz.[22] Although during the years between 1951 and 1958, Baudissin served on the staff as a *Referent* (expert in charge) with other specialists who shared responsibility for aspects of the reforms, he quickly became the *Chef der Inneren Führung* with international stature.[23]

His growing reputation as the father of the reforms also made a number of enemies for Baudissin. Concentrated in the veterans groups and traditions associations and writing in the *Deutsche Soldatenzeitung*, Baudissin's critics adhered to the virtues of the old armies and were blind to the political necessity for change in the early 1950s.[24] Their response to the reforms was "everything that is good is not new, and everything that is new is not good." Baudissin came to personify everything that these men disliked about the reordering of military

[21] Jean Jaurès, *Die Neue Armee* (Jena, 1913). Jaurès's ideas were championed in the late 1950s by Bundespräsident Theodor Heuss in a much-reprinted speech given before the *Führungsakademie der Bundeswehr*. See Theodor Heuss, *Soldatentum in unserer Zeit* (Tübingen, 1959), pp. 16–17.
[22] Interviews with Admiral Friedrich Ruge, April 1984, and with Major General Dr. Eberhard Wagemann, March and June 1984.
[23] The reforms were often mentioned in contemporary U.S. accounts of West Germany. See Charles Thayer, *The Unquiet Germans* (New York, 1957); Hans Speier, *German Rearmament and Atomic War: The Views of the German Military and Political Leaders* (Evanston, 1957); and Gordon A. Craig, "Germany and NATO: The Rearmament Debate, 1950–8," in *NATO and American Security*, ed. Klaus Knorr (Princeton, 1959).
[24] For a list of these veterans organizations in 1953, see *Der deutsche Soldatenkalender 1953* (München, n.d.), pp. 120–33. Among the many periodicals of the soldiers and traditions associations were: *Soldat im Volk, Die Neue Wehrmacht, Der Notweg, Der Stahlhelm, Alte Kameraden, Der Luftwaffenring, Der Deutsche Soldat, Die Neue Feuerwehr, Der Freiwillige,* and *Wiking Ruf.* The *Deutsche Soldatenzeitung* and *Der Stahlhelm* tended to be most critical of the military reforms. The journals *Wehrkunde* and *Wehrwissenschaftliche-Rundschau* were more scholarly and distanced in their treatment of political and military issues.

life.[25] Emphasis upon military reform struck them as merely a new episode of the political reeducation recently practiced by the American occupiers and of the condemnations heaped upon the professional military by the Nuremberg tribunals.[26] For the growing number of his opponents in the years after 1952–53, Baudissin was little more than a charlatan, ignorant of the face of battle, who tendentiously denied his own aristocratic values and background to capitalize on the spirit of the times.[27]

THE APPEARANCES made by members of the *Dienststelle Blank* in public and the progress of negotiations in Paris prompted others to speak out on the inner structure of the future European army.[28] In late 1951, Adelbert Weinstein, a former staff officer who had become a correspondent for the *Frankfurter Allgemeine Zeitung*, published a series of essays entitled *Army without Pathos*.[29] Weinstein was a critic of rearmament and became a spokesman for many thoughtful former soldiers afraid that the West Germans become the mercenaries of the western allies.[30] His widely read book proved a skeptical, but still con-

[25] BA/MA Bw 9/2527–1, "Tagebuch, Unterabteilung II, 4.8.1952" contains Baudissin's estimate of the opposition to the reforms. The most trenchant early critic was Werner Picht—see his *Vom Wesen des Krieges und vom Kriegswesen der Deutschen* (Stuttgart, 1952) and his *Wiederbewaffnung* (Pfullingen, 1954). For a synopsis of the early criticisms, see Franz Albrecht Klausenitzer, "Die Diskussion um die Innere Führung: Zum Verhältnis von Bundeswehr und Öffentlichkeit," in *Studien zur politischen und gesellschaftlichen Situation der Bundeswehr*, ed. Georg Picht, 2d ed., 3 vols. (Berlin, 1966), 2: 159–244.

[26] A discussion of the reforms among former professional soldiers and representatives of the *Dienststelle Blank* can be found in the 1953–59 issues of *Wehrkunde*, the journal of the *Gesellschaft für Wehrkunde*, which received subsidies from the Adenauer government. See especially Heinz Karst, "Werner Pichts 'Wiederbewaffnung,'" *Wehrkunde* (December 1954): 427ff., and Picht's reply, Werner Picht, "Wo liegt die Divergenz? eine Erwiderung," *Wehrkunde* (February 1955): 60ff. The journal published numerous articles on the subject that represented the different positions on the reforms and did so in a less polemical manner than was the case in the wider press.

[27] Gerd Schmückle, *Ohne Pauken und Trompeten: Erinnerungen an Krieg und Frieden* (Stuttgart, 1982), pp. 121–22.

[28] A collection of early newspaper articles on this activity during the period 1951 to 1953 is in BA/MA Bw 1/15838, "Inneres Gefüge, Allgemeines," n.d.

[29] Adelbert Weinstein, *Armee ohne Pathos: die deutsche Wiederbewaffnung im Urteil ehemaliger Soldaten* (Bonn, 1951). See Rautenberg, "Zur Standortbestimmung," pp. 787ff., on the genesis of this book.

[30] Until his departure from the *Frankfurter Allgemeiner Zeitung* in 1982, Weinstein was the leading commentator on military affairs in the Federal Republic.

100

Clockwise from upper left: JOHANN ADOLF COUNT KIELMANSEGG, staff member of the *Dienststelle Blank* and later Commander of Allied Forces Central Europe in NATO. ADOLF HEUSINGER, chief of the military section of the *Dienststelle Blank*, and later Chief of Staff (*Generalinspekteur*) of the Bundeswehr. (Shown here as a general.) THEODOR BLANK, Security Adviser to Chancellor Adenauer, 1950–1955, Federal Minister of Defense, 1955–1956. WOLF COUNT BAUDISSIN, staff member of the *Dienststelle Blank*, chief staff expert for the "inner structure." (Shown here as a colonel.)

101

structive attempt to address many of the political, social, and ethical issues of rearmament, with the title of the volume setting the tone of Weinstein's argument.

The portion of *Army Without Pathos* on the inner structure of the armed forces was the transcript of a conversation between Weinstein and a group of former officers, among whom was Hellmuth Heye, a CDU parliamentarian and later parliamentary commissioner. The participants in the discussion were anxious that the Federal Republic avoid the political and social errors that the military had committed in the first republic. Just as political exigencies had allowed the anti-republican inner structure of the military to survive in the 1920s, the haste to rearm in the 1950s could well lead to a return to old traditions, a state of affairs that was strengthening the *ohne mich* movement. To overcome these doubts, the new armed forces must banish from their ranks the military pathos and the *Kommiss* spirit of the past, a demand that spoke against the maintenance of military tradition in nearly all of its forms, as practiced by the Reichswehr and Wehrmacht.

As Baudissin had also argued, the book said that the European army must take account of the altered political and social circumstances of Europe in the 1950s. The frenzied appeal to the emotions that had begun with conscription during the war of liberation had resonated too long in German life. Since the early nineteenth century, the soldier's craft had grown increasingly deadly and sober. This contrast between military pathos and the face of battle had assumed grotesque proportions in the wars of the twentieth century. The drum fire of propaganda in the Third Reich about the heroism of the front contrasted sharply with the true nature of war. Every day soldiers did their tasks with stolid determination, despite the overwhelming odds against them. This same spirit should fill the new soldiers, men who would be possessed of a responsibility for self and of a joy in doing their job. Gone would be the hundreds of hours that soldiers wasted in the minute regimentation of the *Kommiss*—ordering their clothing lockers, cleaning the barracks, and marching on the parade ground.

Weinstein's discussion partners generally agreed that the future forces must reduce the old emphasis on symbols and ceremonies. Public display of military pomp served only to mask the true nature of warfare. The rapture-producing elements of military tradition were not only useless but also damaging. Symbols and ceremonies foreign to popular taste should be discarded. In the Weimar Republic, many soldiers had advocated doing away with the parade march; now it should be abolished. The new soldier should adopt uniforms on the model of the Anglo-American battle dress—the "Ike jacket" commonly associated in the popular imagination with the well-fed American GI-occupier laden with cigarettes and chocolate.[31]

There was another problem that was not so easily solved. The victorious allies had forbidden the wearing of all orders and decorations, a practice made permanent with the demilitarization control statutes. Some German soldiers had traded their Iron Crosses for Hershey bars; others had simply tossed them into a ditch. As the prospect of rearmament arose in the early 1950s, those who had quietly put theirs away demanded the right to wear their decorations again. Since nearly every award of the Third Reich bore the swastika in some form, there was a bitter public debate about the wearing of these decorations. The compromise solution—that the medals might be allowed in a denazified form without the swastika—provoked anger. Many veterans responded that if they were not allowed to wear their decorations in the form awarded, they would not wear them at all.[32]

Within the setting of a European army, Weinstein's colleagues realized that this West German desire to free military life of its needless decorations and pomp might come into conflict with future allies unwilling to do the same. This situation seemed particularly true of the Americans. In the late 1940s and early 1950s, the U.S. Army had seemed to many Germans like a true army without pathos. Now, however, the members of Weinstein's discussion group saw the

---

[31] Of course the adoption of the victor's uniform is common enough in history. After Prussia's victories of 1864–71, the U.S. Army introduced a Prussian-style spiked helmet and tunic in the 1880s in imitation of the uniform of the Prussian-German armies of the wars of unification. Conversely, the Reichswehr uniform of the 1920s and 1930s was influenced by the U.S. Army uniform of the time. For a discussion of this issue from the 1950s, see *Handbuch Innere Führung: Hilfen zur Klärung der Begriffe*, ed. Bundesministerium für Verteidigung (BMVg), Führungsstab der Bundeswehr (Fü B) I 6 (Bonn, 1957), pp. 53ff. For a recent, fuller treatment, see Hans-Peter Stein, *Symbole und Zeremoniell in deutschen Streitkräften* (Bonn, 1984), pp. 107–25.

[32] For the official attempt to resolve the issue, see BA/MA, Bw 9/1254, "II 1/2, Az 979–18–01, Blank an das Bundespräsidialamt, 'Wiederzulassung des Tragens der Kriegsauszeichnungen,' " July 1953, which was again put before the Bundestag in 1957 with the *Gesetz über Titel, Orden und Ehrenzeichen vom 26. Juli 1957*.

Americans introduce more parades and rituals into the ranks, reducing their value as a model for the future European army.[33]

The demands for change voiced in *Armee ohne Pathos* were supported by many influential public leaders and social groups within the Federal Republic. Weinstein's work was widely read and quoted. The ideas put forth in the book were taken up by many in the political parties, the churches, the youth organizations, and the trade unions with whom the *Dienststelle Blank* cooperated in the years that followed. The acceptance of the ideal of an army without pathos reflected a consensus among leaders in West German society that the new army must be different from the Wehrmacht and that the errors of the Weimar Republic must not be repeated. This attitude was the basis for a bipartisan and constructive responsibility for the spirit of the new army, nicely summed up by Fritz Erler in 1957. Commenting on the effort by some in the SPD to deny the government money for the new armed forces, he said: "On no account can the army become the property of the government or even of the governing parties. . . . The army belongs to the whole nation."[34] There was a general belief in the need for reform, but once the responsible parties—both in the military and society—tried to determine its specifics, differences of opinion became obvious. This phenomenon was especially evident in the establishment of the policy on military tradition.[35]

[33] The relatively poor showing of U.S. soldiers in Korea also fostered doubts about the value of the inner structure of the U.S. military. See BA/MA, Bw 9/797, "II/IG, Gutachter Tagung in Siegburg am 28. und 29. April 1953," p. 25.

[34] Fritz Erler, "Heer und Staat in der Bundesrepublik," in *Schicksalsfragen der Gegenwart*, ed. BMVg, 6 vols., 3: 232–33.

[35] For a detailed survey of the attitudes of key social groups in the Federal Republic to the inner structure of the new army, see Wiggershaus, "Zum Problem," pp. 1–55, which is based upon the approach of Hans Herzfeld, "Die Bundeswehr und das Problem der Tradition," in *Studien zur politischen und gesellschaftlichen Situation der Bundeswehr*, ed. Georg Picht, 3 vols. (Berlin 1965), 1: 51–95.

5. The Meeting at Siegburg and the *Discipline Générale*: "What Should Be Handed Down?"

THE EUROPEAN Defense Community (EDC) negotiations in Paris in late 1951 and early 1952 stimulated a growing public discussion in West Germany about the spirit of the European soldier of German nationality, as the general effort to create the new army gave way to specific measures. The diplomatic representatives from France, the Federal Republic, the BENELUX states, and Italy signed a treaty on 27 May 1952 regarding the supranational force, whose details of command, operational and territorial organization, logistics, and inner structure were to be decided by the delegations at the interim committee.[1] The details of the structure of the army gradually emerged from the negotiations. The EDC was to be an international force under NATO command in wartime. Each country's contingent would be divided into air, sea, and land forces, with a standard form of military organization, training, and equipment. The Commissariat, the highest central organization of the EDC, would include a joint staff. At echelons above division (or *groupement* as they were officially called), the staffs and organizations would be jointly manned by the partner states, while the divisions and their support units would remain national.

The West German ground forces were to include twelve divisions comprising 310,000 men, including attached staffs, combat support units, schools, and training facilities. The main combat power of the

[1] For an overview of the EDC negotiations as of May 1952, see the summary prepared by Kielmansegg for Adenauer in BA/MA Bw 9/218, "Bundeskanzleramt, Der Beauftragte des Bundeskanzlers für die mit der Vermehrung der alliierten Truppen zusammenhängenden Fragen, 'Zusammenfassender Bericht über das Vertragswerk zur Gründung einer Europäischen Verteidigungsgemeinschaft,' " 11 May 1952. Also see Hans-Erich Volkmann and Walter Schwengler, eds., *Die Europäische Verteidigungsgemeinschaft: Stand und Probleme der Forschung* (Boppard, 1985).

West German contingent would be concentrated in armored and armored infantry divisions of thirteen thousand men each. A tactical air force would be organized with squadrons or wings of thirty-six to seventy-five aircraft as the primary air units under national command, again with equivalent staffs and support organizations. The command structure above the squadron level would be international. A total of 1,350 aircraft and eighty-five thousand men would make up the West German air contingent for the EDC. Finally, German units in a coastal defense navy would operate in Western European waters. The structure of the German forces, based on the Himmerod proposals, conformed with contemporary NATO planning that called for a build-up of European conventional combat power to meet the Soviet advantage in ground forces. At the same time that the EDC negotiators agreed on this composition of forces in early 1952, the Federal Republic pledged not to produce nuclear, biological, or chemical weapons.

Issues of arms were not the least of the problems on the table in Paris. The delegations approached the enterprise of creating a European army with their own national interests. The dilemma of how best to defend Europe within the supranational framework while still preserving the rights and privileges of the allies hampered the talks, as did political pressures in France and Germany against the EDC. The French sought to limit the resurgence of German power, while the representatives of the Bonn government labored to address German interests in the face of this opposition. Specifically, controversies arose over the operational concept of defense on German territory and the deployment of allied units in the Federal Republic, as well as about the inner structure of the new army.[2]

As these negotiations gained momentum during late 1952, a crisis

[2] These international frictions are reflected in the diary entries of Unterabteilung II/1 for 1952–53 in BA/MA Bw 9/2527–1; Kurt Fett, "Die Grundlagen der militärischen Planungen," in *Aspekte der deutschen Wiederbewaffnung*, ed. MGFA, pp. 169–200; Hans-Jürgen Rautenberg, "Zur Standortbestimmung für künftige deutsche Streitkräfte," in *Anfänge westdeutscher Sicherheitspolitik 1945–1956: Von der Kapitulation bis zum Pleven Plan*, ed. MGFA, vol. 1 (München, 1982), pp. 864ff. For some of the West German concerns in late 1952, see the files of the *Amt Blank* for testimony given before the parliamentary security committee, BA/MA Bw 9/714, "Entwurf eines Berichtes über die politischen und militärischen Bestimmungen des EVG Vertrages und deren Auswirkungen," n.d. [ca. November 1952].

in the *Amt Blank* developed concerning the head of the planning section of the military-political staff, former Colonel Bogislaw von
Bonin. The scandal seemed to pit old-line militarists against enlight-
ened advocates of reform and it rekindled public fears about the spirit
of the future army. Bonin, a recent arrival in Bonn, was renowned
among his fellow officers as "embodying the spirit of Potsdam."[3] A
veteran of Potsdam's crack 4th Mounted Regiment of the 1920s,
he had earned a wartime reputation as a man of extraordinary courage. He showed special talents as a general staff officer at the front
and on the operations staff of the army. As the war went on, however,
he grew disillusioned with the regime. He had allowed German forces
to withdraw from Poland in 1944, defying the Führer's senseless orders to stand fast. The Gestapo responded by throwing him into a
concentration camp, from which he later escaped.[4] The scandal arose
when Bonin tried to standardize the organizational structures of the
Paris and Bonn staffs in October 1952.[5] The changes would have subordinated Baudissin's section to Bonin in the chain of command. The
tone of Bonin's directive struck Bussche, the public relations chief, as
being particularly militaristic. The group around Baudissin and
Bussche feared that Bonin was trying to suffocate the democratic reforms. In response, Bussche and his deputy, Dr. Konrad von Kraske,

[3] Moritz Faber du Faur, *Macht und Ohnmacht: Erinnerungen eines alten Offiziers*
(Stuttgart, 1953), p. 182.

[4] On Bonin, see two works by Hans Speier: *German Rearmament and Atomic
War: The Views of the German Military and Political Leaders* (Evanston, 1957), pp.
75–83, and *From the Ashes of Disgrace: A Journal From Germany, 1945–1955* (Amherst,
1981), p. 289. Also see the extensive work of Heinz Brill: *Bogislaw von Bonin, Opposition gegen Adenauers Sicherheitspolitik: eine Dokumentation*, ed. Heinz Brill (Hamburg, 1976); idem, "Bogislaw von Bonins Konflikt mit der Sektion 'Innere Führung,' " *Wehrwissenschaftliche Rundschau* 4 (1976): 121–25; idem, "Das Problem einer
wehrpolitischen Alternative für Deutschland: die Auseinandersetzung um die
wehrpolitischen Alternativvorschläge des Obersten Bogislaw von Bonin," Ph.D.
diss. Göttingen, 1977; and Heinz Brill, *Bogislaw von Bonin im Spannungsfeld
zwischen Wiederbewaffnung-Westintegration-Wiedervereinigung* (Baden-Baden,
1987). Besides arguing for the soundness of Bonin's advocacy of a forward defense
with light antitank forces, Brill suggests the role played by allied opposition to the
reforms. Proponents of alternative defense in the Federal Republic of the 1980s
have revived some of Bonin's ideas of strategy and operations.

[5] BA/MA, Bw 9/2527–1, "Dienststelle Blank, Tagebuch, Unterabteilung II/1
7.X.1952, 10.X.1952, 12.XI.1952"; Dietrich Genschel, *Wehrreform und Reaktion: Die
Vorbereitung der Inneren Führung 1951–1956* (Hamburg, 1972), pp. 141–44; and Brill,
"Das Problem einer wehrpolitischen Alternative für Deutschland," pp. 43–71.

threatened to resign if Bonin did not go. Once the "fraternal feud in the *Amt Blank*" broke in the press, it provoked public concern that the planners might yet fall prey to the carmine-red-striped demigods of the past. Despite the public outcry, Heusinger regarded Bonin as an exceptional officer, indispensable to the work of his staff. This incident symbolized the challenges involved in finding a middle path between the poles of operational necessity and of civil-military cooperation in a pluralistic society.

Bonin was valuable to Heusinger in part because of the respect he enjoyed among many former officers, something that seems to have been less true of Baudissin. Heusinger convinced Blank that Bonin must be retained, whereupon Bussche had no choice but to resign. Heusinger defended his decision with the statement that differences of opinion were necessary in the new military, although he did admit that certain aspects of the scandal had been regrettable. The departure of Bussche from the staff incorrectly nurtured suspicions that the *Amt Blank* was being increasingly divided between reactionaries and reformers, a typology that remained in press accounts of the new German army for decades thereafter. Bonin was indeed a soldier who placed purely military concerns first, and he was skeptical of Baudissin, but he soon isolated himself within the staff and undermined his own influence by his continued disagreements over NATO strategy. However, Bonin's example of an officer attempting to influence policy on his own was not repeated within the new military.

As a result of the Bonin incident, Heusinger with Kielmansegg's encouragement worked out a compromise staff arrangement that placed Baudissin's section directly beneath him. An *Innere Führung* committee, made up of representatives of various staff sections, including the "inner structure" group, met generally under the chairmanship of Ulrich de Maizière.[6] The *Innere Führung* committee was the key forum for working out many details of the reforms in the period between 1953 and 1955. For example, much of Baudissin's effort focused on the legal position of the soldier in society, the determining

---

[6] Interviews with General Ulrich de Maizière, April and June 1984, and with General Johann Adolf Graf von Kielmansegg, June 1984. The transcripts of the first meetings of the *Innere Führung* committee are contained in BA/MA, Bw 9/ 1291, "Ausschuss Innere Führung, 'Kurzprotokoll über die 1. Sitzung des Ausschusses am Mittwoch, den 4. Februar 1953, 1500 Uhr,' " 6 February 1953.

of which required close cooperation with the organization's jurists to transform proposals into acceptable legal language. The *Innere Führung* committee gave overall direction to such cooperation and set priorities for work done in support of the Paris negotiations and for the presentation of laws to parliament. Interestingly enough, military tradition as a distinct theme was considered by the committee only once in the first years of its existence, and then only in a brief discussion about the questionable value of military music in modern warfare. Instead, the gradual process of seeking a new meaning for the military tradition first arose in meetings with academic expert advisers to the new army.

DURING the planning of the legal aspects of the European Defense Community, a number of figures who later became influential in effecting the establishment of policy on military tradition first addressed the problem and speculated about solutions to it. These first discussions deserve a thorough retelling, both because of their initial impact and to counteract the general ignorance about the origins of a policy that still dominates the debate in the Federal Republic on the maintenance of this tradition thirty years later. The policy on military tradition that was in effect until the mid-1960s began to take shape in the early 1950s. Discussions of the time reveal a remarkable continuity in thinking over a decade and a half. They highlight the differing points of view on the issue and demonstrate the important interplay between officers and academics. The participants in these exchanges defined the nature of the problem and confronted the political and social limits on policy, adopting a cautious attitude toward the maintenance of military tradition. Outstanding in all these discussions is the struggle to define terms and to reach a consensus about the valid aspects of the traditions of the past. The planners of the new army anticipated many of the difficulties in the reform of the tradition that befell the Bundeswehr in the late 1950s and 1960s.

WORK ON the new army during 1952–53 centered on two areas of the inner structure: the military amendments to the West German Basic Law destined for parliament, and a European code of military justice under negotiation in Paris, the so-called *discipline générale*. The planning for *Innere Führung* and the military tradition essentially grew out of these considerations.[7] The *discipline générale* had far greater importance than its title suggested. After the West Germans first offered their proposals for the army's inner structure at the Paris negotiations, they learned to their disappointment that the French translated *inneres Gefüge* as *discipline générale*. This and many other terms of the French military conflicted with West German ideas on military reform.[8] These misunderstandings signified the apparent unwillingness of the western allies to embrace Federal German concepts. In contrast to former German regulations on military justice, the draft EDC *discipline générale* was much broader in scope, setting out the details of military ceremonies, the method for making complaints, the relationship between the ranks, and the rights of command. Interestingly enough, these issues more or less corresponded to the headings of the traditional Prussian-German articles of war and the soldier's code, suggesting that despite the promise of the new, there still existed a link to the old. The members of the *Dienststelle Blank* and their advisers recognized this connection with the past in their discussions of the Paris negotiations.

The most notable instances of this official exchange took place at a series of meetings at the Federal Finance School in Siegburg, which began in 1952 and continued throughout the period of planning.[9] As part of this effort, the *Amt Blank* held several meetings with its civilian advisers in the spring of 1953 to seek advice for the Paris negotiations

[7] See selected documents from 1952 in BA/MA Bw 9/1248, "I Pɪ/W/Gɪ/3 'Arbeitsprogramm des Referates Inneres Gefüge für Juli und August,' " 7 July 1952; Bw 9/1460, "I Pɪ W/Gɪ/3 'Weisung für die Verhandlungen über die Discipline Générale in der Gruppe ɪ der Abteilung Personalwesen,' " 22 July 1952.

[8] Fett, "Die Grundlagen," p. 179.

[9] Among the most important transcripts, see BA/MA Bw 2/1267, "Protokoll, Arbeitstagung 'inneres Gefüge,' Akademische Bundesfinanzschule Siegburg, 19.–21. April 1952," and BA/MA Bw 9/797, "II/IG, Gutachter Tagung in Siegburg 28.–29. April 1953." The meeting of April 1952 contained presentations and discussions on such themes as "Das Wesen der Europa-Armee" by Professor Dr. Erich Weniger, "Offizier und Wehrverfassung" by Professor Bohnenkamp, and "Die soziologische Struktur der jungen Generation" by Professor Dr. Schelsky. The discussion of the *Referat* by Weniger sparked a brief exchange on military tradition, noteworthy for the query of one of the participants: "What really is military tradition?" See BA/MA, Bw 9/1267, "Siegburger Tagung, 1952," p. 47. For more on Weniger, see Hans-Jürgen Rautenberg, "Zur Standortbestimmung für künftige deutsche Streitkräfte," in *Anfänge westdeutscher Sicherheitspolitik 1945–1956: Von der Kapitulation bis zum Pleven Plan*, ed. MGFA (München, 1982), ɪ: 837.

on the *discipline générale*. With Baudissin presiding, a group from Blank's staff met with certain academics at Siegburg to examine the draft documents from the negotiations paragraph by paragraph, modifying the language and debating the meaning of terms within the political and social setting of a European army. As its model, the group used the 1934 version of the "Duties of a German Soldier" of the Reichswehr, whose clarity of style and simplicity of form were compared to the new draft regulations, while its political content served as a contrast to the reform concept.[10]

In his opening comments at Siegburg, Baudissin introduced the concept of reform in broad outlines, much as he had done at Hermannsburg, and he asked his academic colleagues to redefine such words as discipline, obedience, responsibility, comradeship, and feeling of community, terms fraught with negative meanings for many young Germans. A stylistically maladroit product of the French delegation, the draft *discipline générale* reflected an understanding of these terms in conflict with the West German ideas of reform.[11] The conference soon became a general attempt to set the "limits of military obedience" in the shadow of the Nuremberg verdicts.[12] While Baudissin touched only briefly on military tradition itself at the start of the conference, the two days of discussion ended, interestingly enough, with a general exchange on tradition that summarized the problem and revealed the obstacles that the new forces would face in treating it. This discussion seems to have had a decisive impact on Baudissin's thinking and upon the policy he helped to shape.[13]

Baudissin's comments on tradition should be prefaced with statements made in the 1980s by two of his contemporaries. A colleague of

[10] While the conference took place in Siegburg, the *Dienststelle* had another meeting on the *inneres Gefüge* with the *Arbeitsgemeinschaft demokratischer Kreise*—a group of politically active, reform-minded former officers including Hellmuth Heye—in Bad Godesberg. See BA/MA Bw 9/1324, "Besprechung zwischen Vertretern der Arbeitsgemeinschaft demokratischer Kreise und der Dienststelle Blank," 27.–28. April 1953. The ADK was regarded by the SPD as a group of reactionaries.

[11] BA/MA, Bw 9/797, "Siegburger Tagung, 1953," pp. 2–3. In this connection, Brill's suggestions concerning the resistance of the allies to the reforms is noteworthy, but the limited availability of the sources in the years from 1983 to 1986 precluded any final answer.

[12] The transcript of the meeting at Siegburg in BA/MA, Bw 9/797 is nearly 190 pages long, and space precludes an exhaustive description of the entire conference.

[13] BA/MA, Bw 9/797, "Siegburger Tagung, 1953," pp. 17–18, 152–87.

Baudissin's in the *Amt Blank*, who later rose to very high rank, observed that Baudissin was a "philosopher of ideals," inclined to think in "absolute categories of human behavior." Another ranking officer who was also a contemporary in *Amt Blank* made a similar observation about Baudissin: "he sees only the mind, neither the soul nor the body." This logical tendency, combined with his penchant for a rather academic style of German, won respect for Baudissin from those skeptical of rearmament, but it disgusted many troupiers because of his academic, intellectual tone. His ideas on military tradition were at the same time extraordinary for his emphasis on the contents rather than the externals of tradition, and yet they were conventional because of his references to Prussian history and the ideals of Frederick II, Stein, and Marwitz.

Mindful of the overemphasis on antiquarian symbolism in the Reichswehr, Baudissin spoke in his opening address of the diminishing value of military tradition as a "possible integrator" of the soldier in society. The problem of military tradition was made worse by the unwillingness of West Germans to think historically. The best tradition, in Baudissin's view, was "an attitude of taking the well-being of other people more seriously than either one's self or an abstract idea." Frederick II had followed this tradition at the Battle of Leuthen, when he allowed those troops to ride home who had doubts about the upcoming assault. Baudissin suggested that advocates of military tradition also had to place "content over form and future before the past."[14]

One can infer a great deal from these short comments. Couched in the style for which he became known, Baudissin's brief observations contained the essential features of his fundamentally skeptical attitude toward tradition. During the next five years, he expanded these ideas in a series of talks on the subject. The old maintenance of tradition practiced in the Reichswehr/Wehrmacht stood in the way of ideas for reform. This vulgar concept of military tradition, practiced with great effect by the Nazis, had to give way to the rediscovery of earlier examples of behavior in war that were worth emulating, particularly examples of men whom Baudissin later described as "conspirators of

[14] "Siegburger Tagung, 1953," pp. 17–18. The text of Baudissin's speech is also reprinted in Wolf Graf von Baudissin, *Soldat für den Frieden: Entwürfe für eine zeitgemässe Bundeswehr* (München, 1969), pp. 140–51.

conscience." These candid statements about military tradition were made in front of a group of academics, not before professional soldiers. The group at Siegburg was made up of like-minded scholars and experts on the law and education with whom Baudissin felt a close personal affinity. Although military tradition was an issue of interest to many thoughtful members of society because of its implications for the soldier's self-image, Baudissin's skepticism about the theme was bound to disturb professional soldiers, who tended to select from the past personalities and examples suited solely to the requirements of battle.

AN EXCHANGE the next day on "camaraderie" prompted a further discussion of military tradition in West Germany and the European army. The passage of the *discipline générale* studied by the group spoke of the spirit of comradeship "rooted in tradition" that constantly renewed itself in military life and in the camaraderie between the branches of the services.[15] One of the participants asked whether this use of the term simply meant "military tradition" or referred to a broader "western heritage" of common values and beliefs that now was to be defended by a European army.[16] When another participant responded that the French probably understood the phrase to mean military tradition symbolized by "the Marseillaise, grand ceremonies, and resounding fanfares," Baudissin asked whether the members of the conference could offer some better alternative. This suggestion prompted a colleague to propose that there should be an explanation of tradition in a supplementary regulation to the *discipline générale* that made a distinction from the past use of the term. Otherwise, "Sergeant XY would get the idea: we'll do things as we did, according to tradition, just like it says there [in the book]." Baudissin agreed by noting that one would have to reexamine the meaning of all words in the future regulations. The term tradition would have to be scrutinized to find some guide for the permanent staff who would eventually handle the issue.[17] This recognition of the need to explain tradition was the forerunner of later official definitions of military tradition in the *Handbuch Innere Führung* of 1957 and the traditions decree

---

[15] "Siegburger Tagung, 1953," p. 152.
[16] Ibid., p. 153.   [17] Ibid.

(*Traditionserlass*) of 1965. The civilian academic advisers to the planners, many of whom continued to work with the ministry after 1955–56 and participated in the writing of the *Traditionserlass*, saw that even in a European army, widely held concepts of military tradition in both the Federal Republic and Western Europe would interfere with the West German military reform.

After the discussion turned briefly to the meaning of *esprit de corps*, an issue with only tangential importance for tradition, Baudissin again asked the group to take up "the dynamite of tradition" and to specify "what should we hand down?" (*was für uns zu tradieren ist*) or, in other words, "what could one put in the regulation under [the heading of] tradition."[18] It was perhaps no coincidence that Baudissin made this request immediately after Heusinger, the head of the military-political staff and Baudissin's superior, arrived from Bonn to join the meeting. Although a significant difference of opinion on this issue between Baudissin and Heusinger was not evident in 1953, the handling of military tradition did lead to disagreements between the two men in later years, apparently with adverse consequences for Baudissin's career. Possibly for that reason, Baudissin chose to take up the discourse with Heusinger backed by the added authority of his scholarly advisers.[19]

In response, Professor Wilhelm Rothacker rather naively offered that the regulation state that "one should derive strength from the noblest traditions of the past." The use of superlative "noblest" would effect the necessary choice of examples from history.[20] Professor Hans Bohnenkamp, later influential in formulating policy on the military tradition of the Bundeswehr as the speaker of the *Beirat für Fragen der Inneren Führung* and co-author of the *Traditionserlass*, described the essential dilemma as an unreflected choice of examples from history. "What," Bohnenkamp asked, "really are 'noble' traditions?" It was insufficient to say that these traditions were simply the memory of great achievements, things, and characters in the past. Rather, once

---

[18] Ibid., p. 163.

[19] Ulrich Simon argues in his *Die Integration der Bundeswehr in die Gesellschaft: Das Ringen um die Innere Führung* (Hamburg, 1980) against any overly simplistic positing of "reformer" and "traditionalist" camps in the Bundeswehr. Interviews with Professor Wolf Graf von Baudissin, May 1984; with General Johann Adolf Graf von Kielmansegg, June 1984; Speier, *Ashes*, pp. 297ff.

[20] "Siegburger Tagung, 1953," p. 163.

made, the appeal to tradition demonstrated that an unbroken "subject of tradition" no longer existed. Tradition had already gone through a sieve of conscious judgment and choice. Human beings, Bohnen-kamp observed, lived with all kinds of traditions—things, forms, and practices that are handed down—but that people were unconscious of as being traditions until they were broken. Tradition was unbroken as long as it was there, without one's having to make it expressly clear as being a thing of tradition. The moment that one referred to tradi-tion, one had already selected and made a judgment of value. Since the German people were divided in their opinion of what constituted a "living tradition" in the present, such appeals to the past were fun-damentally problematic. The choice of traditions for the European army would have to unite people, not separate them.

Bohnenkamp continued with a prescient observation that was only appreciated much later in the years of reflection and debate before the Bundeswehr leadership gave an answer to the question of its tradi-tion. Such a selection from the past "could not take place in the form of a catalogue that described what we can take from tradition and what we cannot." Rather, the contents of worthy traditions should exist in the regulations of the new forces, without a conscious attempt to legitimate the present through an appeal to tradition. Bohnen-kamp's recognition of the tendency among participants in the debate to draw up their own lists of valid and invalid traditions underscored the artificiality of selecting from the past, a dilemma that has not be-come any easier with the passage of time.

In the ensuing discussion, others warned that the use of the term tradition would not "ignite" the younger generation, particularly those in universities. The founders of the new armed forces should follow the advice of Federal President Theodor Heuss to "create tra-dition." Returning to the earlier theme of Europe uniting against a common foe, Professor Hartmann suggested that the soldiers of the EDC should derive their concept of discipline and obedience from the "the old Greek tradition of regarding the soldierly estate as a great form of human common purpose, and understanding it as one of the essential common tasks."[21] The participants in the discussion then sug-gested that the combination of the two ideas, the need to create tra-

[21] Ibid., p. 171.

dition and the heritage of European resistance to a common enemy, would enable them to speak in the *discipline générale* and its regulations of "creating a European tradition."[22]

Although he agreed with these ideas in principle, Baudissin expressed his own reservations about military tradition, doubts that he had formed in part from his experiences with young Germans.[23] "With tradition as the justification for a solution," he observed, "we immediately create two camps, particularly in conversations between people of different generations." He promised to follow closely Bohnenkamp's advice to "speak as little as possible about tradition," in other words, to minimize the legitimation of the new through an appeal to tradition. In the fateful question of military obedience, however, Baudissin believed that the new forces would have to unearth "a good, but long forgotten and buried Prussian tradition [of moral choice], since Prussian military history certainly knows more 'conspirators of conscience' than any other." Nevertheless, one would have to be careful how one phrased such a statement in the new regulations.[24]

The members of the discussion returned to "noble traditions" and a "European tradition," without, however, reaching any final formula. Although there was general agreement about the need to mention some form of European tradition, Baudissin doubted whether "noble" was the best adjective to describe the heritage to be selected for the new forces, a feeling shared by others in the group. Why not, Baudissin suggested, simply use the phrase "good traditions," a formulation that the others agreed would avoid the propagandistic associations of "noble traditions."

The Siegburg conference ended with a short address by Heusinger that was notable for his candid recognition of the connection between personnel, the inner structure, and military tradition in the new army. The struggle at Siegburg to define terms, Heusinger suggested, symbolized the difficulty of planning for the European forces and the effort to create a new spirit in which the new army would grow. This planning would not end soon, but would prove to be a historical development of long duration, a comment indicative of the attitude of

[22] Ibid., p. 172.
[23] Interview with Professor Wolf Graf von Baudissin, May 1984.
[24] "Siegburger Tagung, 1953," pp. 173–74.

caution and patience that marked Heusinger's leadership. He thanked fate ". . . that Baudissin has come to me" and that he had shown himself to be "the one who struggled with these things; consumed himself in this problem; disturbed people, and tenaciously kept the battle going." Heusinger reminded his audience of the struggle faced by the German delegation in Paris. The Bonn proposals for reform were completely incomprehensible to the allies, compelling the delegation under General Speidel to labor for hours at the conference table about the meaning of words. If the reforms were not incorporated in the European regulations, then Heusinger promised his audience that West Germany would institutionalize them in national ones.

This statement underscores one of the key dilemmas of German civil-military relations in the twentieth century: the widely held belief that the inner structure of German military life was inherently more reactionary than those of the other European forces, and that had the Germans adopted western examples of military behavior, the outcome of history might have been different. Although the EDC broke up for reasons of power politics, it is worth noting that the West German attempts to reform the political and legal position of the European soldier in society encountered resistance from the allies, who above all wanted an immediate German contribution made to western defense and were unwilling to accept the progressive ideas embodied in the German reforms.[25] There was growing official West German disillusionment in the wake of Korea with the value of the U.S. armed forces as a model, and the Western European armies scarcely offered the West Germans an inner structure that fulfilled the political and social requirements of military reform in the Federal Republic.

Introducing his comments on tradition, Heusinger recalled his time as a young "taboo lieutenant commissioned in wartime" in the Reichswehr of the 1920s.[26] Not burdened with pre-1914 ideas, the generation of young officers commissioned in battle tried vainly to intro-

---

[25] See documents in BA/MA Bw 9/1248; Bw 9/1460; Fett, "Die Grundlagen," pp. 178–79; Hans Tänzler, "Vorbereitende Planung für die 'Innere Führung,'" in *Aspekte der deutschen Wiederbewaffnung*, ed. MGFA, p. 201; Brill, "Das Problem einer wehrpolitischen Alternative für Deutschland," p. 98.

[26] These ideas are developed in Adolf Heusinger, *Befehl im Widerstreit* (Tübingen, 1950).

duce reforms in the postwar ranks, but they were "flattened" by the older generation of officers. The chief cause of this failure, Heusinger thought, was the narrow attempt to solve the problem within the military itself, without the help of other members of society: the young officers "did not go at it by digging deep enough with these things, [but] saw them too superficially. . . ."

Overall, Heusinger cautioned his audience against the use of the word tradition. The Siegburg discussion had shown that one must add the modifier of "good traditions" to prevent the "wrong ideas": "As Baudissin said, when this word tradition is simply used in conversation, one often experiences that the spirits part at that moment, because one person sees something that, God help us, cannot come back, and the others see things as they have been here [at Siegburg]."[27]

This struggle to define terms in the regulations, Heusinger suggested, was really an attempt to make a connection with these *gute Traditionen*. Such an enterprise should further European unity, highlight the broader historical heritage of the West, and place military tradition within this greater whole. French and German soldiers could then overcome the difficulties caused by the differences in their traditions, which had been intensified over the past fifteen years. Heusinger pointed to the battlefields of North Africa as an example of the common European tradition of "chivalry" as it obtained among the Anglo-German opponents.

Recalling in his final words his experiences in the Reichswehr, Heusinger warned his audience of the dangers inherent in the eight-year pause in the German military craft and of its likely effect on the young people who would join the forces. The future officers and NCOs would face the task—for which they were essentially unprepared—of training new soldiers in peacetime. "The young officer corps of first and second lieutenants is wholly missing; the young NCO corps is totally missing." Furthermore, the field grade officers had little peacetime training experience, since most of them had attained their rank in war. Although Heusinger saw that this *tabula rasa* in military personnel would allow the Germans a new start, it was also dangerous. Any staff officer could recognize that the absence of peacetime military experience and skills in the men from whom the young recruits

---

[27] "Siegburger Tagung, 1953," pp. 181–87.

would receive their first impressions of the new army would produce an explosive situation when combined with the hectic rush to raise new troops. "If it doesn't work," he said, "and there are major accidents, then there will be mistakes that will have a serious effect." The recreation of the German army in 1921–22 and the vast increase of the Wehrmacht after 1934–35 must certainly have been on Heusinger's mind.[28]

THE SIEGBURG meeting of April 1953 was representative of the scores of conferences between soldiers and civilian advisers in the planning of the new German army. The importance of this exchange for the maintenance of tradition in the Bundeswehr appears fairly obvious when one considers that these conferences represented an important phase in the shaping of policy. The meeting prompted high-ranking officers and academics to reflect on the issues in what seems to have been a forthright way. There existed lines of continuity in the makers of policy and in the choices they eventually adopted from the early 1950s to the late 1970s. The members of the Siegburg discussion confronted the limits of psychology, society, and politics in their attempt to answer Baudissin's question of "what should we hand down." The exchanges between Baudissin, Bohnenkamp, and Heusinger revealed three different but not mutually exclusive views on the issue. All present agreed that a fundamental break with the past was necessary, but the practical details of such a move remained unclear within the context of a European army and within West German society. Both Baudissin and Heusinger recognized the need for caution in solving the problem, although Baudissin tended to be more skeptical. He seemed willing to take a more activist approach than his superior. In the process, he often referred to Prussian history, tending to undermine his insistence that the new army was *sui generis*, unconnected to the past. Rothacker's seemingly innocent wish to preserve noble traditions moved Bohnenkamp to speak about tradition as a thing in itself, an insight that Bohnenkamp later introduced into policy. Three of the notable men at Siegburg—Baudissin, Heusinger, and Bohnenkamp—foresaw that the military leadership would even-

[28] Unfortunately, this prophecy proved all too true in the late 1950s and early 1960s with incidents like the one at Nagold in 1963 and in the scandal over *Wehrbeauftragter* Helmuth Heye's report in *Quick* in 1964, described in Chapter 13.

119

tually have to make a statement about military tradition. Although they demurred from giving an answer in 1953, after the creation of the Bundeswehr they directly shaped such policy well into the 1960s. Indirectly, their influence endured into the 1980s. The question of "what should we hand down" to the new army came to puzzle a growing number of people in West Germany as time passed. Soon after the Siegburg meeting, the federal parliament, watchful of any threat to democracy from its soldiers, attempted to find its own answer.

6. The Bundestag Security Committee
Takes Up the Issue

THE CENTER of gravity of the design of the army's inner structure gradually shifted away from the officially sponsored seminars toward the chambers of parliament, as the *Amt Blank* incorporated the ideas of the academic experts into proposed reforms. During
the first stages of the EDC negotiations in late 1951 and early 1952, the
Amt Blank had been reluctant to brief parliament on the specifics of
reform, a hesitancy that aroused anger among legislators and critics
of rearmament.[1] Legislators worried aloud that Blank was a weakling
whom the former officers in his staff were manipulating into policies
beyond the control of parliament. The refusal of the Adenauer government to share details of the future soldier with the legislators because of the Paris negotiations worsened fears that the European
army might yet become a cover for a new military state within a state.
By the summer of 1953, however, this hesitation in the executive
branch gave way to close cooperation. Members of parliament devoted greater attention to the army's inner structure and to the reforms that, after March 1953, were now officially described with the
compact, but somewhat indistinct title of *Innere Führung*.[2] A strong

[1] Werner Picht, "Wo liegt die Divergenz? eine Erwiderung," *Wehrkunde*, February 1955, pp. 6off. See also Norbert Wiggershaus, "Zur Debatte um die Tradition
künftiger Streitkräfte, 1950–1955/56," in *Tradition und Reform in den Aufbaujahren
der Bundeswehr*, ed. MGFA (Herford, 1985), p. 28–29.
[2] Norbert Wiggershaus, "Zum Problem der Tradition im Vorfeld eines westdeutschen Verteidigungsbeitrages," unpublished manuscript, 1983, p. 30. This cooperation is amply reflected in the files in the BA/MA. On the change from the
term *inneres Gefüge* to *Innere Führung*, see BA/MA, Bw 9/2830, "Regelung 'Innere
Führung,' " 10 January 1953, cited in Detlef Bald, *Generalstabsausbildung in der Demokratie: Die Führungsakademie der Bundeswehr zwischen Traditionalismus und Reform* (Koblenz, 1984), p. 29; BA/MA, Bw 9/1520, "Sitzung des Bundestagaus-
schusses für Europäische Sicherheit am 24. Juni 1953," 26 June 1953. The *Amt Blank*
had apparently abandoned the term *inneres Gefüge* as the title of the reforms be-

motivation for this upsurge in activity was the growing realization among West German leaders that the future of the EDC had grown dim and that some form of West German national army was increasingly likely.

In the following years of planning and debate, the Bundestag and the political parties played a decisive role in the creation of the federal armed forces and the foundation of its inner structure. The full account of the contribution of the "parliamentary fathers of the Bundeswehr" remains to be written, as does the history of the political and social aspects of arming the Federal Republic.[3] Nevertheless, some brief comments are appropriate on the role of the legislature in the very lengthy public debate about West German security, military reform, and the maintenance of tradition.

Above all, the parliamentarians in Bonn wanted the army integrated into the new German democracy to prevent the revival of the politically and socially exclusivist armed forces of the past. This desire was surely as great in their hearts and minds as it was among the military planners in Adenauer's executive branch. Stemming directly from the civil-military problems of the Weimar Republic, it dominated all aspects of the legislative discussion of reform and the military tradition. Many parliamentary figures of the 1950s had been active in the Center, Liberal, and Social Democratic parties of the 1920s and they were heirs to an anti-Prussian, south German federalist tradition. They judged the civil-military problems of the Federal Republic through the lenses of their own experiences with the legacy of Prussian militarism in the Reichswehr and the Wehrmacht. Across the political spectrum, from the Social Democrats through the smaller parties of the early 1950s to the CDU/CSU, parliamentarians tried to redress the past failures of liberal forces to subordinate the army to their control. Dr. Richard Jaeger, CSU deputy and member of the parliamentary security committee, summed up this sentiment, drawn from dark historical memory: "Germany had in the past a good army.

---

cause of the popular associations of that term with the ideological aspects of the Wehrmacht.

[3] Some of the key debates through the year 1953 are found in the following: *Stenographische Berichten über die Verhandlungen des deutschen Bundestages und des Bundesrates*, 98. Sitzung, 8 November 1950; 190. Sitzung, 7 February 1952; 191. Sitzung, 8 February 1952; 221. Sitzung, 9 July 1952; 222. Sitzung, 10 July 1952; 240. Sitzung, 3 December 1952; 241. Sitzung, 4 December 1952; and 255. Siztung, 19 March 1953.

Today we doubtless have the start and development of a good democracy. But we in Germany have never had at the same time a good army, a good democracy, and a balanced relationship between the two."[4]

The memory of Weimar led members of the legislative and executive branches to agree on the general goal of civilian control of the military. But West Germans of the early 1950s had enormous problems translating this phrase, borrowed from the English-speaking world, into a smoothly working feature of political life. This problem did not arise from the resistance of the soldiers, but from the novelty of the task and the political uncertainty about its mechanisms and procedures. Adenauer and Blank believed that civilian control meant that the federal government should keep the army firmly in hand, should assure that its top officers accepted Adenauer's policy of western integration, and should carry out the reforms of the inner structure. For the members of parliament, however, civilian control meant that the legislative branch should establish its influence over the new army. It did so in the years between 1952 and 1957.

Despite the vocal objections of the SPD to much of Adenauer's security policy, the Social Democrats eventually took an important lead in the parliamentary effort to guide the development of the new army.[5] The outspoken opposition of many rank-and-file Socialists (SPD) to the rearmament of the Federal Republic might lead some to overlook the less well-known activities of a handful of Socialist experts on military affairs, who emerged in this unaccustomed role in the early 1950s. They made an enormous contribution to the success of Federal German civil-military relations through their work on the political basis of the new army. Kurt Schumacher set an example for such men as Fritz Erler, Carlo Schmid, Wilhelm Mellies, Hans Mer-

---

[4] Deutscher Bundestag, *Verhandlungen, Stenographische Berichte*, 93. Sitzung, 28 June 1955, p. 5228.

[5] On the SPD and the armament of the Federal Republic, see Udo F. Löwke, *Für den Fall, dass . . . Die Haltung der SPD zur Wehrfrage 1949–1955* (Hannover, 1969); Ulrich Buczylowski, *Kurt Schumacher und die deutsche Frage: Sicherheitspolitik und strategische Offensivkonzeption von August 1950 bis September 1951* (Stuttgart, 1973); Hartmut Soell, *Fritz Erler, eine politische Biographie*, 2 vols. (Berlin/Bonn Bad Godesberg, 1976); Martin Kempe, *SPD und Bundeswehr: Studien zum militärisch-industriellen Komplex* (Köln, 1973); David Clay Large, "Reckoning without the Past: The HIAG of the Waffen SS and the Politics of Rehabilitation in the Bonn Republic, 1950–1961," *The Journal of Modern History* 59, 1 (March 1987): 79–113.

ten, Helmut Schmidt, Karl Wienand, and Friedrich Beermann. They did not wish to repeat the failure of Social Democracy in the 1920s to reach out to the Reichswehr; this time they wanted to play a constructive role in the defense of Germany. This willingness mirrored the desire of the men at Himmerod to include the opposition parties in security policy. Heusinger and Kielmansegg had informed Schumacher early on about the details of military planning. They found the Socialist leader to be an advocate of a strong army—with as many divisions as possible—deployed for offensive operations toward the Elbe river. The SPD, as Speidel reported to Blank after a conversation with Schmid in October 1952, "had decided to avoid the 'mistake of Weimar' of standing aside with the future armed force. A German military would have to be the concern of all the people."[6] If this mutual cooperation had not existed, the nature of the establishment of the West German military might have turned out much differently.

The call to reconcile socialism with the military in the years after Schumacher's death in 1952 was made perhaps most effectively by Fritz Erler and Carlo Schmid.[7] Although they bitterly criticized the threat to German unity posed by Adenauer's military integration of the Federal Republic into the West, the Socialist defense experts worked cooperatively with members of Adenauer's government for the integration of the new army into West German society. In fact, certain of the military architects of the inner structure found the Socialists to be more sympathetic and informed allies than the parliamentarians of the CDU/CSU. As the debate about the reforms continued from 1952 to 1957, Erler and Schmid championed such important innovations in the inner structure as the division of supreme command between the branches of government (legislative in peacetime and executive in war); the establishment of a parliamentary security committee with sweeping investigative powers; the institutionalization of the defense minister's special relationship to parliament; the appointment of a parliamentary commissioner to oversee the inner structure of the army; and the establishment of a personnel selection board to fill the first senior ranks.

---

[6] BA/MA, Bw 9/713, "Speidel an Blank," 5 October 1952.

[7] A summary of Erler's ideas is to be found in Fritz Erler, "Heer und Staat in der Bundesrepublik," in *Schicksalsfragen der Gegenwart: Handbuch historisch-politischer Bildung*, 6 vols. ed. BMVg (Tübingen, 1958), 3: 223–56. On Schmid, see Carlo Schmid, *Erinnerungen* (Bern, München, Wien, 1979), pp. 490ff.

This Socialist work on the inner structure benefited civil-military relations within the Federal Republic. It helped to form the basis for the political consensus on the military that existed from the late 1950s until the early 1980s—one of the true success stories of the Federal Republic. Erler and Schmid's concept of a loyal opposition on defense also made sense in party political terms. It engaged the SPD in a constructive role in defense policy at a time when many of its members otherwise deeply opposed Adenauer's concept of West German and Atlantic security. Such involvement also helped to make the SPD acceptable in political circles that habitually mistrusted the Socialists. Erler and Schmid tried to overcome the customary antipathy of German Socialists toward soldiers by warning of the danger of a "CDU Army," whose conservative officer corps would owe their allegiance to Adenauer alone.

In contrast to the experience of Weimar, however, the differences between the parties on many aspects of military affairs were more apparent than real during the five years of debate and reflection. Although Socialists and Christian Democrats strongly disagreed about the foreign political conditions for arming the Federal Republic (and the bitter debate about nuclear strategy from 1955 to 1958 approached the level of Weimar parliamentary struggles), the SPD advocates of parliamentary control found willing partners for military reform in the CDU/CSU. There existed in Christian Democratic ranks a strong aversion to past abuses of military power—Socialists and Catholics alike had been persecuted in the Borussian school of the nation of the old army. Leading CDU/CSU parliamentarians recognized that they could not establish the new army without, or with the opposition of, the Social Democrats.

The Christian Democratic parliamentarians had first taken up the question of security affairs in 1951–52 with the formation of a parliamentary working group under Franz-Josef Strauss. Richard Jaeger oversaw questions of military reform and the spirit of the new army in this group, and like Erler, he became a proponent of military reform in the years that followed.[8] He warned the parliament in early

[8] Jaeger's ideas are summarized in Richard Jaeger, "Heer und Staat in der Bundesrepublik," in *Schicksalsfragen der Gegenwart: Handbuch historisch-politischer Bildung*, 6 vols. ed. BMVg (Tübingen, 1958), 3: 195–222; idem, *Soldat und Bürger—Armee und Staat: Probleme einer demokratischen Wehrverfassung*, 3d ed. (Köln, 1963).

1952 that in the haste to rearm, West Germany might inadvertently return to outdated and unwanted military traditions. "The inner structure of the German forces is a political precondition for rearmament," said the spokesman of the CDU/CSU on the inner structure. "We could not be responsible for again subjecting Germany's youth to the barracks square that for the most part we all experienced—I lived it for six years."[9]

The Free Democrats of the early and mid-1950s were the party most alive to the old cult of military tradition.[10] Liberals often praised the ideal of unique soldierly virtues in debates about the reforms and they resisted the attempts of the Adenauer government to banish traditional militaria from the new army. The party also later pushed for the federal president to assume the supreme command of the military. This is not to say, however, that the liberals were in some sense antidemocratic in their policies on reform and the maintenance of tradition; indeed, despite some criticism about the specifics of the reform, there was a general willingness among them to accept the principle of military reform and to subordinate the military fully to the will of parliament. Although the party counted some notable former soldiers among its members (and perhaps a disturbing number of former Nazis), one of the most famous career officers, General a.D. Hasso von Manteuffel, took an active part in the debate about the spirit of the new army. His record in these exchanges shows him to have been anything but a blinkered traditionalist.[11] Erich Mende, a highly decorated veteran and the party's other defense spokesman, shared with Manteuffel an intense interest in reforming the army.

THE Security Committee of the Bundestag was the site of a constant exchange on *Innere Führung* in the years between 1952 and 1956, where the parliamentarians discussed many aspects of the reforms in prepa-

---

[9] Deutscher Bundestag, *Stenographische Berichte*, 191. Sitzung, 8 February 1952, p. 8177.

[10] Dietrich Wagner, *FDP und Wiederbewaffnung: die wehrpolitische Orientierung der Liberalen in der Bundesrepublik Deutschland, 1949–1955* (Boppard, 1978), pp. 145–54; H. R. Schulz, "Tradition und Fortschritt," in *Armee gegen den Krieg*, ed. Wolfram von Raven (Stuttgart, 1966), pp. 123ff.

[11] "II/1/2–931–05, 'Bericht des Abgeordneten Gen. d.Pz.Tr. a.D. v. Manteuffel über Teilgebiete der Inneren Führung,' " 1 October 1954, consulted by the writer.

ration for the general debate on the new army in the Bundestag.[12] This exchange in the security committee further shaped the concept of tradition in the new forces, giving guidance to the planners that later made itself felt in the policy of the Bundeswehr. All of the political parties worked constructively and enthusiastically; the contributions of Fritz Erler and Carlo Schmid, both members of the SPD, were particularly noteworthy.[13]

As part of this growing exchange between parliament and the *Dienststelle Blank*, Heusinger gave a lengthy summary on the planned reforms to a meeting of the security committee on 10 June 1953, chaired by Fritz Erler, the deputy head of the committee.[14] Heusinger's presentation began with an allusion to the loss of tradition, resonant of Baudissin: "everywhere one can find a search for new forms, everywhere [there is] an insecurity . . . [because] of a loss of spiritual bases upon which mankind has built . . . at least [there is] an uncertainty about which of these can be regarded as right for the future."[15]

[12] This was an organization with many ponderous names: *Sonderausschuss zur Mitberatung des EVG Vertrages und der damit zusammenhängenden Fragen*, later *Ausschuss für Fragen der europäischen Sicherheit*, and finally *Ausschuss für Verteidigung*. One agenda for the discussion in the EVG Ausschuss is in BA/MA, Bw 9/716, "Rundschreiben Strauss," 25 June 1953. Also see H. J. Berg, *Der Verteidigungsausschuss des Deutschen Bundestages: Kontrollorgan zwischen Macht und Ohnmacht* (München, 1982).

[13] Among the many issues discussed before the *Sicherheitsausschuss* were the code of military justice, the military ombudsman in the ranks, the organization of members of the armed forces in a labor union, the name of the new forces after the end of the EDC (Bundeswehr versus Wehrmacht), the takeover into the new military of former members of the Waffen-SS, and the volunteers law, part of the larger set of legislation that provided the legal basis for rearmament. The record of testimony by members of the *Diensttelle Blank* before the committee tends to undermine Ulrich Simon's contention in *Die Integration* (pp. 91, 106) that the representatives were glad to have in the person of Baudissin a means to overcome opposition to new forces from organized labor, youth groups, and the churches; that is to say, that they liked him as a salesman, but that they never really understood or liked what he was selling. The record contained in the BA/MA files seems to disprove the assertion that they did not understand the concept of *Innere Führung*. For an updated version of this claim against all opponents of the reforms, real and otherwise, see the somewhat ahistorical essay by Bernd C. Hesslein, "Innere Führung— der unerfüllte Auftrag der Bundeswehr," in *Im Dienst für Frieden und Sicherheit— Festschrift für Wolf Graf von Baudissin*, ed. Dieter S. Lutz (Baden-Baden, 1985).

[14] BA/MA, Bw 9/716, "Stenographisches Protokoll der 34. Sitzung des Ausschusses für Fragen der europäischen Sicherheit am 10. Juni 1953." Heusinger gave this same address on other occasions when asked to speak on the reforms.

[15] Ibid., p. 3.

Beyond this allusion to the problem of tradition, however, Heusinger's *tour d'horizon* of *Innere Führung* avoided military tradition as an explicit theme, and struck a more cautious note in contrast to his comments at Siegburg a few weeks before. As concerned the relationship with the past, the policy of the new forces would be: ". . . [to] do away with the obsolete and carry over the good old things into the new troops." While the future soldier would study the negative experiences of recent history to prevent a repeat of disaster, Heusinger suggested that one could not simply say that everything in the old army had been bad. In fact, many things had been excellent and there would certainly be a connection with them in the new forces. Beyond these allusions to military tradition—and they were really no more than that—Heusinger offered a summary of the West German ideas for the *discipline générale* that concentrated on the reforms of military justice, training, and education that would secure the future soldier's legal rights and protect him against inhuman treatment. These reforms would ensure that the young man who joined the future army would be "a free person, a good citizen, and an effective soldier."

Heusinger's introduction to *Innere Führung* was the start of a systematic examination of the reforms by the security committee over the next several months.[16] Baudissin appeared before the group to describe in detail the work of his staff in the *Dienststelle Blank*.[17] Of the thirty-five regulations on the *inneres Gefüge* to be written by Baudissin's staff in cooperation with civilian experts, none would deal expressly with the maintenance of tradition.[18] This absence of an explicit proposed regulation in the shadow defense ministry notwithstanding, the members of the security committee soon recognized that military tradition was an issue that required attention. The suggested outline for the discussion in detail of *Innere Führung*, submitted to the *Dienststelle Blank* in July 1953 by committee chair Franz-Josef Strauss, included the "Value or Worthlessness of Military Tradition" as the subject for one of several meetings on the reforms.[19]

---

[16] BA/MA, Bw 9/716, "Rundschreiben Strauss."

[17] "39. Sitzung des Ausschusses für europäische Sicherheit 14. Juli 1953," reprinted in Wolf Graf von Baudissin, *Soldat für den Frieden: Entwürfe für eine zeitgemässe Bundeswehr* (München, 1969), pp. 151–55.

[18] Hans-Jürgen Rautenberg, "Aspekte zur Entwicklung der Traditionsfrage in der Aufbauphase der Bundeswehr," in *Tradition als Last*, ed. Klaus M. Kodalle (Köln, 1981), p. 140.

[19] "Rundschreiben Strauss." Strauss became minister of defense after the political difficulties of raising the Bundeswehr claimed Theodor Blank in 1956. Strauss in

Once they took up the issue, the parliamentarians and their military counterparts were of one mind that a democratic and European-oriented spirit should fill the new army. But beyond agreement on this self-evident formula, the discussion in the committee on the value of military tradition seems to have been plagued by the same uncertainties in defining terms that befell the men at Siegburg.[20] The group agreed that "[in recent history] tradition had been broken."[21] The summary of the meeting continued:

Intellectual judgments of a time and proven practical necessities, which stand out beyond the needs of the moment, should be taken over with scrutiny. All traditions should be considered for their value. The army's world of ideas and spiritual bases should not differ from the people's general ideas. Traditions of a mechanical, formal, and sentimental character are to be rejected. Outcome of the discussion: Prevent the spiritual exclusivity of the army. The state must clearly circumscribe the function of the army. Parliament's concern [for this issue] should be expressed in an attentive personnel policy.[22]

This was the parliamentarians' attempt to answer Baudissin's question. One can safely say that it was the description of an answer, but not the answer itself. Such general definitions of the problem, to which most could subscribe yet still hold very different ideas about the substance of a valid tradition, were tolerable before the army came into existence, but they would cease to be enough as soon as the soldiers themselves began to ask about their heritage. Nonetheless, this statement on tradition must have seemed adequate to the members of the committee, for in subsequent legislative analyses of *Innere Führung*, military tradition no longer appeared as a separate theme, but was subdivided among such topics as ceremonial obligations, barracks life, and military pageantry.

THE WORK between the legislators and the military staff on *Innere Führung* continued into 1954 after the formation of a new parliament and the reelection of the Adenauer government. The Bundestag began to debate the first amendments to the German Basic Law that

---

turn fell victim to scandal in 1962 after the publication in *Spiegel* of classified documents on the NATO commandpost exercise FALLEX.

[20] Wiggershaus, "Zum Problem," p. 32.

[21] BA/MA, Bw 9/720, "II/IG, Entwurf, 'Arbeit des Sicherheitsausschusses in der 1. Legislaturperiode auf dem Gebiet der "Inneren Führung," ' " 27 November 1953.

[22] Ibid.

would furnish the legal basis for the new army, as politics finally doomed the European Defense Community in late August 1954. This combination of domestic and international events increased the political importance of the reforms in West Germany and for the Atlantic world.

The French National Assembly, smarting from the debacle in Indochina and uncertain about the political effects of increased U.S. reliance on tactical nuclear weapons on the central front of NATO, refused to consider the ratification of the EDC treaty on 30 August 1954 and dealt the death blow to the international army.[23] Undeterred by this setback, the West German and Atlantic proponents of a German contribution to Atlantic defense pressed forward with the Paris treaties that in May 1955 made the Federal Republic a sovereign state with its own army.

The emergence of the Bundeswehr as a defensive army integrated into both German society and the Atlantic alliance—a force without complete control over its own troops in wartime—symbolized the return of West Germany to the ranks of the powers a little more than ten years after the end of the war. This development also marked the permanent division of the former Reich between East and West. The prospect of German soldiers commanded by Wehrmacht veterans free of the control mechanisms of the EDC renewed anxieties that a West German national army would incubate a spirit of militarism, or, as Erich Weniger later wrote, allow a haven for "an inner immigration from democracy," much as the Wehrmacht had provided for some Germans escaping from Nazism.[24] These developments prompted renewed and increased public attention to the reforms of the military and compounded the political and intellectual difficulties faced by the group at work on them.[25]

[23] See Edward Fursdon, *The European Defense Community: A History* (London, 1980), pp. 266–99; Raymond Aron and Daniel Lerner, *France Defeats EDC* (New York, 1957). See also Hans-Erich Volkmann and Walter Schwengler, eds., *Die Europäische Verteidigungsgemeinschaft: Stand und Probleme der Forschung* (Boppard, 1985).

[24] Erich Weniger, "Die Gefährdung der Freiheit durch Ihre Verteidiger," in *Schicksalsfragen der Gegenwart: Handbuch politisch-historischer Bildung*, 6 vols., ed. BMVg (Tübingen, 1959), 4: 349–81.

[25] This development, for instance, is obvious in the issues of *Wehrkunde* in the years 1954 to 1956.

Within this atmosphere of fresh concern over the inner structure of a West German army, the maintenance of military tradition arose as a theme of debate in the security committee only very briefly in the fall of 1954. The discussion there revealed a continuity between legislative viewpoints held during the EDC debate and those held after its demise; that is to say, the shift to a national army does not appear to have worked any immediate and dramatic transformations in the parliamentary judgment of military tradition. The issue seems to have remained peripheral, with all concerned inclined to define tradition negatively.

This state of affairs was reflected in Baudissin's testimony on 6 September 1954 before the subcommittee on military ceremonies, a presentation that included the position of the *Dienststelle Blank* on such issues as military bearing, uniforms, parades, the grand tattoo, the posting of the guard, military music, and flags. Baudissin's speech sparked a lively exchange that ended with the firm conclusion that all forms of military ceremonies were antiquated and obsolete.[26]

The group agreed that the only legitimate display of troops in public was one that revealed their worth in battle. There should be no more parades and reviews as in the old armies, since they did not conform to the sobriety of the present day. Parades impeded the training regimen, increased the tendency toward barracks-square drill, and gave civilians no indication of the military efficiency of the troops. In the future, the troops should borrow from the Swiss practice of parading before the local population while moving to and from maneuvers. Sunday open house at the *Kaserne* would also be a welcome chance for people to see their soldiers.

Mindful of the Nazi emphasis on militaristic and pseudo-militaristic rituals in daily life, the legislators insisted on eliminating the use of soldiers in public ceremonies. The future member of the West German army was not to be "human decoration for state holidays," but should have the day off to take part as a private citizen. The use of the grand tattoo had assumed grotesque proportions before 1945, and should be returned to its original meaning and used only by troops in the field. There should be only one guard regiment in the capital,

---

[26] "II/2/1 'Vermerk über die Sitzung des Unterausschusses III (Paul) des Sicherheitsausschusses des Bundestages am 6.9.1954,'" 8 September 1954, consulted by the writer.

complete with military band, which would be used purely for representative purposes. The committee recommended that no additional bands be created, since they wasted money and had no real military tasks. Sentries on guard were to be free of representational chores. The committee thought it ridiculous to have the "guards march up and down in front of Buckingham Palace like marionettes," while civilians behind the fence actually protected the queen.

In future, regimental and unit flags of all kinds were to be done away with, save for utilitarian vehicle pennants, free of the mythical importance attached to old unit flags and standards. The committee considered the soldier's uniform in the same spirit of iconoclasm, acting against the cult of the uniform in the Third Reich.[27] The colorful tunic of the old walking-out dress was to be replaced with an identical uniform for army and air force with as few insignia as possible—an idea that had actually been considered during the war. As often as possible, the new soldiers should receive permission to wear civilian clothes. Turning the idea of the *Staatsbürger* in uniform on its head, the committee suggested that once the young soldier had completed half of his service, the army should give him a new civilian suit, since many soldiers did not own a good one or would have outgrown their old one.[28]

The security committee as a whole took up the issue of military ceremonies at the end of November 1954.[29] The meeting sparked a lengthy and interesting debate on the maintenance of tradition, which, while it essentially supported the conclusions of the subcommittee's report, nonetheless highlighted the need for self-representation in the new armed forces.

Kielmansegg opened the meeting by informing the members that

[27] Early in the EDC planning, the staff had done away with the field-gray army uniform, the old M–1935/42 steel helmet, and the "dice shaker" (*Knobelbecher*) marching boots of the Wehrmacht. As Kielmansegg observed in an interview in 1984, the Danes and the Dutch were not to get the visual impression that the new army was a reincarnation of the SS, which, like the army of the Wehrmacht, had worn field-gray during the war.

[28] This insistence on a generous permission to wear civilian clothes was a break with the customs of the Wehrmacht, but not with the prewar armed SS, which had required its recruits to keep a civilian suit.

[29] "Bericht über die Sitzungen des Ausschusses für Fragen der europäischen Sicherheit des Deutschen Bundestages am 30. November und 1. Dezember 1954," 1 December 1954, consulted by the writer.

with the EDC treaty now gone, the *Dienststelle Blank* no longer planned to create a special guard regiment, but would probably rotate individual companies to Bonn for representational duty from units elsewhere. The parliamentary deputies of the SPD, Gustav Höhne and Ulrich Merten, responded that such a guard regiment would be unproductive and a "pure waste of time." This statement prompted SPD Deputy Carlo Schmid to plead for what he believed was the special need for a republic to represent itself. The state, Schmid replied, should show its troops to the people, as was done in all countries abroad. In response, Deputy Mellies supported Schmid's belief that the young republic should demonstrate its armed forces to the outside world, but should do so with simulated battle exercises of armor and air units, instead of parades and troop reviews.[30]

Others on the committee were anxious that, given the mentality of the Germans, any demonstration of military power would provoke suspicions of militarism. Again Schmid reminded the group of the positive side of symbols and ceremonies: ". . . the military is serious enough. One should easily include a theatrical element . . . to symbolize the cooperation between people, state, and armed forces."[31]

The discussion turned to the future of the grand tattoo. Deputy Merten of the SPD rejected it with the observation that the armed forces of today should have nothing more to do with sentimentalities.[32] In response, Hellmuth Heye seconded Schmid's advocacy of symbols by warning against "our German beastly seriousness," which made them unloved abroad. One should loosen things up, Heye offered, especially because the public wanted it that way. Schmid continued by saying that the armed forces had to have symbols, since the people should see the military as being more than an "armed labor

---

[30] Baudissin became an advocate of this practice, see ZIF/ZUA, 0.2.1.0., "II/1/Gr.1, Graf Baudissin, 'Bericht über die Reise in die USA vom 30. Juni bis 29. August 1955,' " 14 September 1955, pp. 16–17. This is an extraordinarily revealing document of Baudissin's impressions of the United States, its military, and the interrelationship between West German reform and U.S. military tradition. It further highlights the fact that the discussion of German military tradition had to take place in an international context.

[31] "Bericht über die Sitzungen des Ausschusses für Fragen der europäischen Sicherheit des Deutschen Bundestages am 30. November und 1. Dezember 1954," p. 2.

[32] Ibid.

service."[33] This reference was surely a criticism of Baudissin and those who wanted to denude the forces of all ribbons and braid. That it was made by one of the great leaders of the postwar Socialists is all the more noteworthy.

Such symbols, Schmid offered, would help bind the soldier closer to democracy and to the state. In this spirit, he suggested that the forces should provide the future regiments with the black-red-gold national flag as a regimental standard. Again speaking out against military pathos, Merten responded that regimental flags were senseless under modern conditions. The memories of the struggle in the Weimar Republic over the colors of the national flag may have played a role in Schmid's thinking. Even the Reichswehr had not had its own unit flags; they were reintroduced by the Wehrmacht in 1935. Interestingly enough, the Bundeswehr followed the advice of Merten and others by not introducing unit standards in 1955–56. The armed forces only did so in 1964, after the proliferation of local *Traditionspflege* had assumed embarrassing proportions, especially in the case of unofficial unit flags of all shapes and varieties.[34]

THE DISCUSSION in the security committee of 1953–54 reflected the prevailing desire among many participants in the building of the inner structure to create an *Army Without Pathos*, one whose military pomp would be reduced to an absolute minimum. The hyperinflation of military symbols and ceremonies in the past and the mythic role they had played in the Third Reich made this desire understandable within the attitudes of the early 1950s. This concern was especially justified as the military planners reflected on the visual impact of West German soldiers abroad and on the unhappy memories they might arouse.

But Schmid's singleminded insistence that the young republic should bind its citizen soldiers through a certain symbolism proved a

---

[33] Ibid.

[34] For an instance of this at times amusing phenomenon, see ZIF/ZUA, 3.1.3.2., "Notiz, 'Tradition—Fahnen und Standarten—eigenmächtige Beschaffung,' " ca. October 1962, a commentary on the announcement in the October 1962 issue of *Die Bundeswehr* (the journal of the *Bundeswehrverband*) about a regimental commander bestowing on his own artillery unit its own standard. One of these self-bestowed flags is described in E. O. Schneider, "Die Fahne der Panzerjäger Unteroffizier Lehrkompanie," in *Zeitschrift für Heereskunde* nos. 39–40 (1975–76), pp. 75–76, 78.

justified demand once the Bundeswehr was raised, however isolated his standpoint was in the mid-1950s. Later in the parliamentary debate about the spirit of the Bundeswehr, Schmid demanded that the West German people respect the positive role of pathos, suggesting that he and his colleagues could not build the new republic upon principles alone, but would have to create it from historical examples as well.[35]

In a similar vein, while the ceremonies issue was being prepared for debate in September 1954, a staff officer of the *Dienststelle Blank* warned in a memorandum that if the public debut of the new West German soldiers contrasted too strongly with popular expectations, the mass of the German people would be skeptical about these forces. Although the author of the memorandum personally supported the intention of the planners to reduce military pomp, he correctly observed that these plans were not being made in a vacuum. The new army had to meet public expectations of what a soldier should be with a minimum of military symbols and ceremonies. If the new forces ignored this need, there would be backlash in the ranks. The troops themselves would return to outdated forms in reaction to negative comments from the local population.

[35] Wiggershaus, "Zum Problem," p. 28.

7. The Personnel Screening Boards:
The Twentieth of July 1944

THE PROBLEM of finding a valid military heritage in the years of preparation for the Bundeswehr revealed itself most strikingly in the selection of its first officers. The participants in the arming of the Federal Republic realized from the start that they must select the leaders of the future army with great care. In its brief attempt of 1953–54 to define military tradition, the security committee suggested that parliament should express its concern for the issue by means of an attentive personnel policy. Years earlier, the officers at Himmerod had recognized the need to commission only former soldiers spiritually and politically open to the new republic.[1] The men at Himmerod had proposed a review board to examine future applicants for the officer corps—an organization reminiscent of the military reorganization commission in the era of Prussian reform. From the very beginning, the issues of future personnel and the military tradition became inextricably linked. The effort to frame policies for selecting future officers also led to a long and interesting debate among the founders of the army on the importance of the 20 July 1944 attempt on Hitler's life, the results of which have had a particularly lasting effect upon the Bundeswehr.

In the *Dienststelle Blank* anxiety about the political reliability and personal quality of the future officers remained high during the planning phase. The defense officials and parliamentarians wanted to avoid such scandals as had recently beset the Foreign Office.[2] Although beginning in August 1950, a parliamentary subcommittee had vetted the selection of diplomatic personnel, this watchdog group

---

[1] Genschel, *Wehrreform*, pp. 205–16; Norbert Wiggershaus and Hans-Jürgen Rautenberg, *Die Himmeroder Denkschrift von Oktober 1950: Politische und Militärische Überlegungen für einen Beitrag der Bundesrepublik Deutschland zur Westeuropäischen Verteidigung*, 2d ed. (Karlsruhe, 1985), p. 3.

[2] Meyer, "Personelle Auswahl," in *Offizierkorps*, pp. 363–64.

consisted of career foreign service officials, with the exception of one man who had belonged to the Catholic Center Party. They had restored to service a number of officials whose Nazi pasts had subsequently come to light. An investigative committee of parliament quickly denounced the personnel policies of the Foreign Office, increasing public pressure on those involved in the selection of the future soldiers not to make similar mistakes.[3]

The Himmerod proposal for a selection board was resurrected in the *Amt Blank* at first by Ernst Ferber and later by Wirmer's personnel and administrative staff.[4] At first the body was to be composed solely of officers, but this idea was dropped when officials realized that it would appear too much like a traditional military tribunal of honor. By the end of 1952, after Blank had briefed the security committee on the proposed policy for the selection of personnel, the plans were modified so that the examiners would be either civilians or former military officers not interested in a commission in the new military. This board would examine all applicants for commissions as majors and above, as well as prepare the decisions for the federal cabinet on all appointments to the rank of colonel and general. Such outside

---

[3] On the subject of continuity in the German administration and civil service, see Theodor Eschenburg, "Der bürokratische Rückhalt," in *Die Zweite Republik: 25 Jahre Bundesrepublik Deutschland—eine Bilanz*, ed. Richard Löwenthal and Hans-Peter Schwarz (Stuttgart, 1974), pp. 64–94.

[4] BA/MA, Bw 9/505, "Ministerialdirigent Wirmer, Vermerk, Anordnung einer 'Gutachtergruppe militärisches Personal,'" 26 February 1952; Bw 9/505, "I Pl/2, Vermerk, Grundsätzliche Fragen auf dem Personalgebiet, die zur Entscheidung heranstehen," 9 April 1952. See also Phillip Freiherr von Boeselager in *Aspekte*, pp. 212–16; Georg Meyer, "Zur Frage der personellen Auswahl bei der Vorbereitung eines westdeutschen Verteidigungbeitrages 1950–56," in *Das deutsche Offizierkorps 1860–1960*, ed. Hanns Hubert Hoffmann (Boppard, 1980), pp. 351–65; Reinhard Stumpf, "Die Wiederverwendung von Generalen und die Neubildung militärischer Eliten in Deutschland und Österreich nach 1945," in *Militärgeschichte: Probleme—These—Wege*, ed. Manfred Messerschmidt (Stuttgart, 1982), pp. 478–97. See also Genschel, *Wehrreform*, p. 206; Hans-Jürgen Rautenberg, "Zur Standortbestimmung für künftige deutsche Streitkräfte," in *Anfänge westdeutscher Sicherheitspolitik 1945–1956: Von der Kapitulation bis zum Pleven Plan*, ed. MGFA, vol. 1 (München, 1982), pp. 788–95; Hans-Adolf Jacobsen, "Zur Rolle der öffentlichen Meinung bei der Debatte um die deutsche Wiederbewaffnung," in *Aspekte der deutschen Wiederbewaffnung*, ed. MGFA (Boppard, 1975); Victor Renner, "Der Personalgutachterausschuss," *Politische Studien*, December 1955; John Sutton, "The Personnel Screening Committee and Parliamentary Control of the West German Armed Forces," *Journal of Central European Affairs* 19 (1959–60); Eric Waldman, *The Goose Step is Verboten: The German Army Today* (New York, 1964), pp. 52–58.

groups as the churches, youth organizations, trade unions, and political parties would be encouraged to suggest individuals to sit on the committee. The security commissioner promised the parliamentarians that the personnel board would select officers whose intellectual independence and political attitudes would win the trust of democratic forces in the Federal Republic. In response, the security committee energetically supported the plan and took a strong interest in it. The personnel screening board, Fritz Erler told parliament in 1954, would assure "that the future force would not become the army of a single political party or coalition; rather, it would assure that the future personnel would be chosen not merely for their technical expertise but also according to their qualities of character as well as their unconditional reliability and loyalty to the democratic system."[5] This advocacy was symbolized by the special law in parliament of 1955 that set up the Personnel Screening Board (*Personalgutachterausschuss* or PGA) and by the requirement that the legislature confirm its members. The further work of the organization, however, was not to be under the purview of parliament nor of any other branch of government.

As was often true in relation to the emergence of the Bundeswehr, events soon compelled the creators of the force to change their initial plans. The flood of applications forced a division of the task between two organizations—the PGA and the *Annahmeorganisation* (Acceptance Organization). The PGA confined itself to the ranks of colonel and general, while the *Annahmeorganisation* took care of the rest. The standards for acceptance in the *Annahmeorganisation* were to be set down by the PGA—a requirement that later fell victim to the crush of time and paperwork.[6] Of the two organizations, the *Annahmeorganisation* faced by far the greater task. It had to examine the applications of over two hundred thousand volunteers—twenty-five thousand in its first six months alone.

INTENSE public attention soon focused on the PGA during 1955. As Ulrich de Maizière characterized it years later, the PGA was an organization with extraordinary powers, independent of all other agencies

---

[5] Deutscher Bundestag, *Stenographische Berichte*, 17. Sitzung, 26 February 1954, p. 563.
[6] Genschel, *Wehrreform*, p. 211; interview with Brigadier General Harald Freiherr von Uslar-Gleichen, May 1984.

of government.[7] It set its own agenda, deliberated in secret, and with-held all sources of information from those it examined. Its decisions were final. And its charter empowered it to scrutinize the leading members of the *Dienststelle Blank*. Although the creators of the PGA and *Annahmeorganisation* could easily agree that these powers were justified by the need to select future military officers with care, the criteria the boards would employ were less apparent. The *Dienststelle Blank* had put on a special seminar at Bad Tönnisstein in September 1954 to lay the foundation for the work of the PGA.[8] The twenty-five participants at Bad Tönnisstein came from all walks of life, principally from the ranks of civil servants, the professions, and former officers. Much of the meeting was taken up with an exchange on Baudissin's presentation on the future soldier and *Innere Führung*.[9]

The discussion at the conference emphasized the parallels between the ideas generating *Innere Führung* and those that prevailed in modern labor-management relations. The group agreed that future officers would have to be educated in a spirit of partnership and civic courage. The reappearance of Seeckt's military tradition in the ranks might undermine this enterprise, but the group nonetheless insisted that one would still have to try to preserve what was valuable from the past. Veterans and traditions associations that were keeping alive the old concept of military tradition posed the greatest danger to the realization of the reforms. The participants concluded that the entire question of military tradition should remain in the background while the troops were raised and while the units developed their own tra-ditions, a conclusion that foreshadowed the policy the Bundeswehr leadership soon adopted.[10] This position was summed up by Heusing-er's statement, "do not touch it—let the new German army grow its own traditions."[11] It seems likely that this attitude of reserve toward

---

[7] Ulrich de Maizière, "Zur Planung und Vorbereitung eines westdeutschen Ver-teidigungsbeitrages: ein Beitrag aus der Sicht eines Mitarbeiters der Dienststelle Blank," in *Entmilitarisierung und Aufrüstung in Mitteleuropa 1945–1956, Vorträge zur Militärgeschichte*, ed. MGFA (Bonn, 1983), pp. 90–91.

[8] Deutscher Bundestag, 3. Wahlperiode, Drucksache 109, *Tätigkeitsbericht des Personalgutachterausschusses für die Streitkräfte, 16. 12. 1957 mit Anlage 3 (Richtlinien für die Prüfung der persönlichen Eignung der Soldaten von Oberstleutnant-einschliess-lich-an abwärts)*, pp. 6–7; Genschel, *Wehrreform*, p. 208.

[9] Genschel, *Wehrreform*, p. 208.

[10] Ibid.

[11] BA/MA, IV V Min, Bl 2–2/593, "Tagungsbericht Bad Tönnisstein, 16/17 Sep-

military tradition and the anxiety about the impact of the veterans and traditions organizations on the new forces became codified in the criteria for the selection of officers, further intensifying the problem of military tradition once the PGA and *Annahmeorganisation* took up their work in late 1955.

The guidelines for the examiners of the PGA demanded from applicants for senior ranks that they "[have a] view of the valid values of tradition and a sober realization of the outdated."[12] The guidelines further required that the future colonels and generals should have gained the historical insight "that the priority of the military way of thinking over the political had contributed to the misfortune of the German people."[13] Although the authors of the guidelines spoke of a valid tradition, they failed to include specific criteria to measure or specify such a tradition.[14] These rather abstract demands for historical reflection were eclipsed, however, by a final, more concrete demand that went to the very core of the tradition dilemma: the requirement to make a statement on the Twentieth of July 1944 attempt on Hitler's life. This event bulked large in the emerging policy of the West German armed forces in relation to military tradition.

THE ORIGINAL impetus to include the Twentieth of July in the selection criteria for future soldiers dated from the first public discussions of the new army and its inner structure. As momentum for the European army grew in late 1951, the Institute for the Advancement of Public Affairs—among the first of the several organizations that cooperated with the *Dienststelle Blank*—held a seminar in Weinheim/Bergstrasse near Heidelberg on "The Citizen and National Defense in Democratic Germany." Among the participants at this important meeting under the chairmanship of the director of the institute, Theo-

---

tember 1954," cited in Rautenberg, "Aspekte," p. 143. Of the group assembled at Bad Tönnisstein, seventeen later became members of the PGA and of these, a handful had regularly taken part in other *Dienststelle Blank* seminars.

[12] BA/MA, IV V Min(Bl) 164/1–35, "Richtlinien von 23 Oktober 1955" cited in Rautenberg, "Aspekte," p. 144; Deutscher Bundestag, 3. Wahlperiode, Drucksache 109, *Tätigkeitsbericht des Personalgutachterausschusses für die Streitkräfte, 16. 12. 1957 mit Anlage 3 (Richtlinien für die Prüfung der persönlichen Eignung der Soldaten von Oberstleutnant-einschliesslich-an abwärts)*, pp. 24–25.

[13] *Tätigkeitsbericht*, p. 25.

[14] Rautenberg, "Aspekte," p. 144.

dor Steltzer, were Blank, Wirmer, experts in international law from the foreign ministry and the Chancellery, trade union leaders, representatives of commerce, editors and journalists, as well as members of the opposition like Fritz Erler and figures connected with the resistance, including Bussche and Annelore Leber, widow of the murdered Socialist resistance leader, Julius Leber.[15]

In its draft report to the greater assembly, a subcommittee had taken up the question of manning the future army, which led to the problem of the Twentieth of July 1944. The subcommittee had suggested that the new army must carefully select officers of all grades, men who would have the necessary "human maturity," "political judgment," and professional ability to avoid the drillmaster attitude of the old armies. An important means to determine if an applicant possessed such judgment and ability would be his attitude toward the past.[16] "A criterion," the members of the subcommittee suggested, "for the presence of these qualities would be the recognition of the moral meaning of the Twentieth of July resistance." The group then broadened this statement to include "the liberal resistance against the National Socialist rule of force"—a phrase that included the members of the resistance outside the armed forces.

Once the general group had addressed these suggestions from the subcommittee, the men and women at Weinheim went on to debate nearly all aspects of making the resistance to Hitler a foundation stone of the new inner structure—many of which have remained lively subjects for debate ever since. Skeptics of the proposal asked how, in practical terms, would one actually honor the Twentieth of July and the larger resistance without this problem becoming a thing of mere "lip service" and *Persilscheine*. Advocates of the demand responded that the recognition of the resistance would be the result of "an inner struggle, from which the overall attitude of the applicant would be visible."

---

[15] Rautenberg, "Standortbestimmung," p. 800.
[16] BA/MA, Bw 9/221, "Auszugweise Abschrift aus 'Bürger und Landesverteidigung'—Bericht einer Tagung, Seite 64/5, Das Problem des 20. Juli," n.d.; Deutsche Gesellschaft für Auswärtige Politik, Archiv, 215 F, "Tagungsprotokoll vom 8./9.12.1951," cited in Rautenberg, "Standortbestimmung," pp. 799f. See the Weinheim transcript cited in *Bürger und Landesverteidigung: Bericht einer Arbeitstagung*, ed. Institut zur Förderung öffentlicher Angelegenheiten (Frankfurt, 1952), pp. 64–67.

In response, an officer who had been involved with the military resistance warned against the requirement to recognize the opponents to Hitler. Many soldiers, he offered, had known fully the illegalities of the Nazi system but had refrained from breaking their oaths because they regarded "the duty of obedience out of moral motives as the highest good." The Twentieth of July was such a difficult psychological and moral problem for soldiers that the new army could not allow the issue to become "a cliff around which one had somehow to sail."

Other members stressed that this requirement should not become an *ex post facto* confession of guilt from those who had not resisted. Instead, the applicant in looking back would simply have to see the moral motives of the resistance fighters. This assertion notwithstanding, skeptics of the proposal again warned that the use of the Twentieth of July as "a political test question . . . contained explosives for the inner structure, as well as for the obedience and discipline of the future force." Such a conclusion moved yet another member of the group to respond that the new army would place a "time bomb in its ranks" if an applicant for a position of leadership had "not come to grips" with the problem before he entered service again.

Such objections notwithstanding, the Weinheim group concluded their report with a renewed emphasis on the Twentieth of July. After the assembly had changed the word "recognition" to "respect," the final passage of the report read: "*A criterion for the presence of these qualities will be the respect for the moral meaning of the liberal resistance against an illegal system of force—a resistance that, for example, was to be found in the attempted coup of 20 July 1944.*"[17] This statement proved to be an important one, for once the selection of officers began four years after Weinheim, the examiners of applicant officers for high grades did indeed use the issue of the Twentieth of July as a criterion to gauge the overall attitude of the applicant.

Although the group at Weinheim succeeded after some debate in adopting a position on the resistance to Hitler, during the years before 1955 the *Dienststelle Blank* proved very cautious in its treatment of the Twentieth of July. The staff, conscious of the declaration at Weinheim, recognized the importance of the issue, describing it in a mem-

[17] *Bürger und Landesverteidigung: Bericht einer Arbeitstagung*, ed. Institut zur Förderung öffentlicher Angelegenheiten (Frankfurt, 1952), p. 67.

orandum of September 1952 as a "basic problem in need of clarification both in, and by, the office. Discussion should include all staff. List of basic questions: the image of the future soldier; which type of commander for peace and war; position on the Twentieth of July; war criminals; . . . and what are we defending in Europe?"[18]

This call within the staff for an official statement, however, did not lead to a final answer, despite the fact that members of the press often asked Theodor Blank for just such a position. Sensitive to press reports of disagreements in his staff on the issue and to the public criticism that he employed only "breakers of oaths," Blank answered a radio reporter in November 1952 that each man had to decide the issue of the *Attentat* for himself, and that choice had to be respected.[19] This was a response that again got taken up by participants on the debate on tradition and it was repeated in the subsequent official discussion for years thereafter. This answer by Blank also symbolized a compromise on the military resistance that became, as Hans Speier observed at the time, the basis of the political and spiritual agreement for rearmament.[20] "It was possible to serve Germany in the last war by opposing Hitler as well as by fighting the enemy, the implication being that both resistance to Hitler and lack of resistance were justified."[21] Blank's answer to a radio interview in 1952 notwithstanding, the *Dienststelle Blank* never formulated an official position on the resistance, a clear reflection of the difficulties of steering a course between practical necessities and ethical dictates.[22]

Perhaps one reason that the officials in the *Amt Blank* hesitated to

[18] BA/MA, Bw 9/1248, "II/3/11 'Merkblätter, Richtlinien und Grundfragen des "Inneren Gefüges" die erarbeitet sein müssen, bis die Lehrstäbe zusammentreten,' " 5 September 1952.

[19] "Wortlaut des Interviews, das der Bundestagabgeordnete Theodor Blank dem Vertreter des Nordwestdeutschen Rundfunks Hans Wendt am 9. November 1952 gewährt hat," Presse- und Informationsamt der Bundesregierung, 9 November 1952, p. 7, consulted by the author. See the correspondence prompted by the Wendt-Blank interview in BA/MA, Bw 9/221, "Generaladmiral Hansen an Blank," 13 November 1952; "Notiz, Graf Kielmansegg an von dem Bussche," 23 November 1952, and the draft response by Bussche with the suggestion that Baudissin prepare a standard answer to the issue: "Axel von dem Bussche. II/9 'Vermerk für Graf Kielmansegg-Brief des General-Admirals Boehm an Herrn Blank, meine Stellungnahme,' " 27 November 1952.

[20] Hans Speier, *German Rearmament and Atomic War: The Views of the German Military and Political Leaders* (Evanston, 1957), p. 31.

[21] Ibid.

[22] Wiggershaus, "Zum Problem," pp. 84–89.

favor the event officially came on 20 July 1954. Otto John, a noted survivor of the 20 July 1944 plot from the circle around Wilhelm Canaris and now head of the West German domestic intelligence service (*Bundesamt für Verfassungsschutz*), defected to East Berlin immediately after attending a ceremony in honor of the anti-Hitler resistance. Once in East Berlin, he warned of a neo-Nazi revival in the Federal Republic. His comments seemed to have been directed against intelligence officials in the *Amt Blank* and the Gehlen Organization, the latter headed by the later chief of the Federal Intelligence Service, Reinhard Gehlen. Such comments carried enormous weight among critics of Adenauer's government, for John's responsibilities included combat against the radical right threat in West Germany. His defection also stirred a controversy about the political wisdom of honoring the conspiracy against Hitler.[23]

These events notwithstanding, the PGA was separate from the *Amt Blank* and free to act as it chose, although the PGA included much of the 1951 Weinheim resolution on the resistance in its guidelines. In many cases, the wording of the requirement for the PGA was nearly identical to that of Weinheim. The passage on the attempted coup began with the statement that soldiers should be "bound by eternal ethical dictates."[24] With a consciousness of an "eternal responsibility," the future soldier was to respect the rights of those around him as well as their religious and political beliefs. The guidelines continued: "With such an outlook, the future soldier must acknowledge the decision of conscience by the men of the Twentieth of July 1944. He should combine this [recognition] with respect for them and for the many other soldiers, who, with a feeling of duty, staked their lives to the end."[25]

This requirement was lent greater weight by the presence on the committee of figures connected with the Twentieth of July such as Fabian von Schlabrendorff, a leading survivor of the plot, and Annelore Leber. Before the committee, an applicant had to show the ex-

[23] Hans-Peter Schwarz, *Die Ära Adenauer, 1949–1957*, in *Geschichte der Bundesrepublik Deutschland*, ed. Karl-Dietrich Bracher et al., pp. 236–39.

[24] *Tätigkeitsbericht*, p. 24, also excerpted in *Handbuch Innere Führung: Hilfen zur Klärung der Begriffe*, Bundesministerium für Verteidigung (BMVg), ed. Führungsstab der Bundeswehr (Fü B) I 6 (Bonn, 1957), p. 81.

[25] Ibid.

aminers an understanding for the motives of the conspirators, without necessarily proclaiming his own support for them.[26] The members of the board would ask of the future officer: "How would you explain the Twentieth of July to your men?" or "Can you understand the motives of the men of the Twentieth of July?" As first laid down at Weinheim, the answer to the question would help the committee to judge the applicant's attitude to the new forces.[27]

The questions regarding the Twentieth of July were less troublesome for those who had spent the past ten years in the West, where they had witnessed the political consolidation of the Federal Republic. But the issue proved especially difficult for the many who had had little opportunity to reflect on recent history, particularly refugees from the eastern zones of occupation and recently released prisoners of war from the Soviet Union.[28] The question regarding the Twentieth of July provoked an amusing, biting parody among those in West German society critical of the PGA's work: "Screening Committee's question—'How do you feel about the Twentieth of July?' Officer candidate's answer—'Oh, I guess I could just as well come on the nineteenth.' "[29] In reality, of course, such humor was a symptom of the public displeasure with the reforms, particularly among veterans groups.

The independence of will in the PGA surprised many and provoked greater criticism about its secrecy and the apparent willfulness of its process of selection. The PGA refused to transfer into the Bun-

[26] Wiggershaus, "Zum Problem," p. 88; interview with Brigadier General a.D. Harald Freiherr von Uslar-Gleichen, May 1984.

[27] Interviews with Brigadier General Harald Freiherr von Uslar-Gleichen; with General Ulrich de Maizière, April and June, 1984; with General Johann Adolf Graf von Kielmansegg, June 1984.

[28] Interviews with Brigadier General Harald Freiherr von Uslar-Gleichen, May 1984, and with Major General Werner Ranck, May 1984.

[29] David Clay Large, " 'A Gift to the Future?': The Anti-Nazi Resistance Movement and West German Rearmament," *German Studies Review* 7, 3 (October 1984): 522. Although Large's essay is highly readable, he has overlooked a large number of sources. His work should be compared to the publications of the MGFA to give a more complete picture. See especially Norbert Wiggershaus, "Zur Bedeutung und Nachwirkung des militärischen Widerstandes in der Bundesrepublik Deutschland und in der Bundeswehr," in *Der militärische Widerstand gegen Hitler und das NS Regime 1933–1945: Vorträge zur Militärgeschichte*, ed. MGFA (Bonn, 1984), pp. 501–28, and Gerd R. Ueberschär, "Gegner des Nationalsozialismus 1933–45," *Militärgeschichtliche Mitteilungen* 35, 1 (1984): 141–96.

deswehr four leading officials of the *Amt Blank*, among them former Colonel Kurt Fett, the first chief of the military planners in the *Dienststelle Blank* and senior officer in the planning staff for the Paris EDC negotiations. He had returned to Bonn as chief military planner after Bonin openly began to question the strategic concept of the Bundeswehr.[30] The selection board apparently took umbrage at Fett's promotion within the operations staff of the Wehrmacht after his superior's removal in the wake of the Twentieth of July.

Although Fett reacted to the decision with silence, one of his colleagues whom the examiners also rejected, former Colonel Werner Bergengruen, answered the rejection by taking out a newspaper ad: "Former general staff officer with ministerial service (rejected by Personal Screening Committee), 47 years old, representative appearance, business experience, negotiator abroad, seeks position in industry."[31] Bergengruen's job search sparked a lively exchange in the Bundestag, moving Erler to say that his unseemly action demonstrated how unfit he was for service. The incident, in Erler's opinion, further underscored the need for an independent selection committee.[32] Fett and Bergengruen were not alone in failing to pass the tests of the PGA. By the end of 1957, the committee had reviewed six hundred applications. Of these, it recommended to the federal cabinet the acceptance of 468 into the forces; another fourteen were taken with reservations (*mit Beschränkungen beurteilt*) and fifty-three were turned down. Some forty-seven officers withdrew voluntarily after they had applied.[33]

The critics of the PGA, most of whom were also Baudissin's opponents in the press and in the veterans groups, assaulted the committee for what they described as its revival of the abuses of the denazification proceedings and the defamation of the soldierly calling. It

---

[30] Interviews with General Johann Adolf Graf von Kielmansegg, June 1984, and with General Ulrich de Maizière, April and June 1984. Limitations of space preclude a full discussion of Bonin's operational ideas. For more on Bonin's dramatic departure from power, see Heinz Brill, "Das Problem einer wehrpolitischen Alternative für Deutschland: die Auseinandersetzung um die wehrpolitischen Alternativvorschläge des Obersten Bogislaw von Bonin," Ph.D. diss. Göttingen, 1977, and Speier, *German Rearmament and Atomic War*, pp. 75–83.

[31] Meyer, "Personelle Auswahl," in *Offizierkorps*, p. 365.

[32] Ibid.

[33] *Tätigkeitsbericht*, pp. 13ff. See also Boeselager, *Aspekte*, pp. 212–16.

was unbearable that of the thirty members on the board, only a third were professional soldiers, the rest civilians—including *eine brave Hausfrau*. This state of affairs prompted the recently released former Grand Admiral Dönitz to exclaim that the PGA would render the ethos of the future naval officer corps identical to that of a housewife.[34] Such outbursts were characteristic of the worsening relations between the veterans and traditions organizations and the *Dienststelle Blank*/Ministry of Defense.[35]

INVESTED with renewed political importance by the guidelines used by the PGA, the Twentieth of July continued to constitute a major question for the self-image of the Bundeswehr and for the military tradition its leaders sought to form. The founders of the Bundeswehr, in their advocacy of military resistance to Nazism (albeit tempered with the statement that those who fought bravely at the front were no less honorable), were clearly ahead of the West German public of the 1950s, which only slowly accepted the moral and political example of the anti-Nazi conspirators. In addition, this selection within the West German armed forces of the military resistance reflected a greater tendency among the leadership of the Federal Republic of the cold war era to legitimate the young state through an exemplification of the conservative resistance to Hitler.[36] Often this choice of valid historical examples took place at the expense of other social groups, particularly the workers, thus provoking controversy not only among many veterans organizations on the right but among leftist groups as well.

As the West German military leadership tentatively offered an answer to the question of how to choose a valid heritage in the mid-1950s, the moral example of the anti-Hitler resistance became an outstanding feature in the military tradition Baudissin sought to foster as chief staff officer for *Innere Führung* during the period between 1955 and 1958.

[34] Herzfeld, "Tradition," pp. 60–61.
[35] See Schenck zu Schweinsberg, "Soldatenverbände," in *Studien*, pp. 137–40, and Wiggershaus, "Zum Problem," pp. 44–49.
[36] Gerd Ueberschär, "Gegner des Nationalsozialismus 1933–1945," *Militärgeschichtliche Mitteilungen* 35, 1 (1984): 141.

8. Count Baudissin's Answer: The First Courses at Sonthofen, Cologne, and Koblenz

A S THE PROCESS of planning for the Bundeswehr belatedly gave way to the first practical steps to raise the troops in the spring and summer of 1955, Count Baudissin formulated an answer to his own question of 1953 at Siegburg on what traditions should be carried over into the new German army.[1] This answer emerged in a series of speeches and writings presented in the years 1955–56, and it was given even greater detail in 1957–58.[2] These presentations certainly bore the

[1] ZIF/ZUA, 0.4.4.4.8., "Kommandeur, Schule der Bundeswehr für Innere Führung [Ulrich de Maizière] G–3, Az 35–05–14 'Probleme bei Planung und Vorbereitung des deutschen Verteidigungbeitrages,' " 5 November 1960, p. 10. See also Claus Freiherr von Rosen, "Tradition als Last: Probleme mit dem Traditionsangebot der 'Gruppe Inneres Gefüge' (1951–1958) im Leitbild 'Staatsbürger in Uniform' für die Tradition der Bundeswehr," in *Tradition als Last*, ed. Klaus M. Kodalle (Köln, 1981), pp. 169ff.

[2] See "Reform oder Restauration im Programm der deutschen Wiederbewaffnung," Bad Boll, January 1955, a tape transcript and speech notes reprinted in part in Rosen, "Tradition als Last," pp. 169ff.; Count Wolf Baudissin, "The New German Army," *Foreign Affairs* 34, 1 (October 1955): 6ff.; Wolf Graf von Baudissin, "Soldatische Tradition und ihre Bedeutung in der Gegenwart," *Wehrkunde*, September 1956, pp. 430ff. Also reprinted in *Handbuch Innere Führung: Hilfen zur Klärung der Begriffe*, ed. Bundesministerium für Verteidigung (BMVg), Führungsstab der Bundeswehr (Fü B) I 6 (Bonn, 1957), pp. 47ff., and in Wolf Graf von Baudissin, *Soldat für den Frieden: Entwürfe für eine zeitgemässe Bundeswehr* (München, 1969), pp. 79ff.; ZIF/ZUA, 0.4.4.4.2., "Graf Baudissin, 'Die Bedeutung der Reformen aus der Zeit deutscher Erhebung für die Gegenwart,' " 17 December 1957, reprinted in edited form in *Wehrkunde*, February 1958, pp. 81ff., and in Wolf Graf von Baudissin, *Soldat für den Frieden*, pp. 86ff.; ZIF/ZUA, 0.2.1.0, "Graf Baudissin, 'Gedanken zum 20. Juli,' " ca. 1956/7, reprinted in *Handbuch Innere Führung*, pp. 79ff.; BA/MA, Bw 2/3958, "Heeresoffizierschule II (Husum), Vortrag Major Dr. Herrmann über 'Tradition und Fortschritt in Theorie und Praxis' am 15.11. 1957, handschriftliche Notizen über Stellungnahme Graf Baudissins während der anschliessenden Diskussion," cited in Norbert Wiggershaus, "Zum Problem der Tradition im Vorfeld eines westdeutschen Verteidigungsbeitrages," unpublished manuscript, 1983, p. 18; ZIF/ZUA, 0.2.1., "Schule der Bundeswehr für Innere Führung, 'Stichwörter des Vortrages von Oberst Graf Baudissin zum Thema Tradition,' Koblenz-Pfaffendorf," 10 June 1958. The evolution of Baudis-

148

imprint of the meetings at Siegburg, Weinheim, and Bad Tönnisstein, but they also revealed the opposition of the enemies of reform during the latter stages of the planning and the first years of the new army. Baudissin's new definition of tradition was also an answer to his critics.

As a reflection of his own heartfelt beliefs and experiences, and in response to those whom he viewed as traditionalists, he chose the men of the Twentieth of July and the Prussian reformers as exemplars for the formation of tradition in the new army.[3] This kind of choice was a fundamental part of his effort to prevent the Bundeswehr from making a direct connection through the maintenance of traditions and conventions with the Wehrmacht and the Reichswehr. The selection of the military resistance to Hitler as an ideal was Baudissin's reaction to pressures from the outside to revive the old *Traditionspflege*.[4] In lieu of more binding statements or guidance from senior officers in the leadership, his statements were the de facto policy of the new German army on military tradition. In the years from 1955 to 1957, Baudissin's position existed in an uneasy tension with Heusinger's advice to "let the German army grow its own traditions."

BEGINNING with his address on "Reform and Reaction" at Bad Boll in January 1955, which as Claus Freiherr von Rosen has observed prefigured his later presentations, Baudissin described the dangers of appealing to tradition in the new army.[5] In the spirit of Siegburg, he warned his audience against the dangers of oversimplification.[6] Although many people believed that tradition was "a definite prescription for here and now," Baudissin suggested that this certainty vanished as soon as one began to examine things more closely. Prussian

---

sin's thinking on tradition while he was the principal staff officer responsible for *Innere Führung* is contained in these works. For a complete list of Baudissin's speeches and writings as ministry staff chief for *Innere Führung*, see his *Soldat für den Frieden*, pp. 321–27.

[3] Interview with Professor Wolf Graf von Baudissin, May 1984. See also Speier, *Ashes*, pp. 299–300.

[4] Interviews with Professor Wolf Graf von Baudissin, May 1984, and with Brigadier General Heinz Karst, July 1984. The role of the Twentieth of July in the selection criteria of the personnel boards rendered the event increasingly important for the self-image of the armed forces.

[5] Rosen, "Tradition als Last," p. 169.

[6] Ibid.

history, for instance, revealed a "constant struggle of opposing attitudes." He asked his audience to "think of such conspirators of conscience as Marwitz, the Prince von Homburg, and Beck. Think of those who believed that their special honor was the unreserved fulfillment and execution of an order. Think of those who were always without tradition but did so much for Prussia . . . or think of . . . Scharnhorst, who demanded the congruence of the political and military order." Seen this way, Baudissin suggested, tradition "was always a bundle of attitudes that calls the individual and his times to decide for one of the lines [of tradition]."[7]

This juxtaposition of examples from Prussian history underscored the dilemma of arriving at a clear policy on tradition in the new military. In fact, his selection of episodes revealed how tradition and the historical record often conflict, despite the fact that participants in the debate regularly threw them together. Baudissin apparently believed that a policy on tradition should include a gallery of ancestors that would allow soldiers to choose their own ideal of tradition based upon their own outlook.

Turning from this rather general—but no less incisive—description of the problem of tradition to its effects upon rearmament and military reform, Baudissin exhorted his listeners to make a common front against those who, for whatever reason, were unwilling to adjust to the altered conditions of the present. Both the stridency of his tone and the contents of his warning are noteworthy, because they reveal his recognition of the internal and external threats to the reforms as well as the need to convince the audience of the intention of the *Amt Blank* to carry them out.

"If," he continued, "we understand by the term 'restoration' the renaissance of forms and contents [of tradition] that are authoritarian, totalitarian, patriarchal, scornful of human beings, pre-technical, and anti-progressive, then I would describe that as reaction. And one has to do everything against such forces because we stand before the single alternative: either freedom with all consistency or totalitarianism with all consistency."[8] Baudissin's warning was that the reappearance of traditional forms in the new army would drive away young people,

[7] Ibid., pp. 169–70.   [8] Ibid., p. 170.

antagonize the allies, weaken the Atlantic alliance, and strengthen the communists.

Such a conclusion reflected an interesting attempt by Baudissin to link the tradition problem with the ideological confrontation of the cold war. This association was not surprising, since the ideas of *Innere Führung* addressed psychological warfare no less than the integration of the soldier into West German society.[9] In associating the two, he propelled the question of military tradition from the periphery into the center of questions of importance.

WHILE Baudissin's speech at Bad Boll sought to assure his audience of the military reformers' will to make *Innere Führung* work, he must also have been preparing for the long-awaited introduction of the reforms. He chose, in his own words, the "founding assembly of the new German officer corps," a series of seminars and courses for the new leadership on politics, economics, international law, the inner structure, principles of education, and political information.[10] These courses were to be given over a period of several months, before the actual work of forming troop units and their training began, while the new officers were still open to the newness of things and as yet untouched by the grind of events.

Beyond these courses intended for the first months of the new forces, the reformers in the *Innere Führung* staff proposed a school for *Innere Führung* where military and civilian specialists could study aspects of the reforms and present their findings to the services and the public.[11] The school, established in Cologne in 1956, was moved to

[9] The relationship between psychological warfare and military reform in the Bundeswehr has been the subject of two studies, Siegfried Grimm, *"Der Bundesrepublik treu zu dienen": die geistige Rüstung der Bundeswehr* (Düsseldorf, 1970), and Peter Balke, *Politische Erziehung in der Bundeswehr: Anmassung oder Chance?* (Boppard, 1970).

[10] Dietrich Genschel, *Wehrreform und Reaktion: Die Vorbereitung der Inneren Führung 1951–1956* (Hamburg, 1972), p. 217. See also "II/3/11, 'Lehrplan und Organisation des Lehrstabes,' Unterschrift, Baudissin, Bonn," 14.1.1953, cited in Genschel, *Wehrreform*, p. 217; "Stoffplan und Zusammenstellung der Themen für Lehrgang W (Entwurf)," ca. Summer 1954, consulted by the writer.

[11] ZIF/ZUA, 0.2.1.2., "II/2/1 'Aufbau "Schule Innere Führung," ' " 17 May 1955; ZIF/ZUA, 0.2.1.2., "Schule der Bundeswehr für Innere Führung," n.a., n.d. See also the excellent work by Peter E. Wullich, *Die Konzeption der Inneren Führung der Bundeswehr als Grundlage einer Allgemeinen Wehrpädagogik* (Regensburg, 1981), pp. 119–21.

Koblenz in 1957. Next to the ministry itself, it quickly became a main center for the formulation of the policy on military tradition.

Significantly, however, and for Dietrich Genschel a clear sign of Theodor Blank's faintheartedness about the reforms, both the planned introductory courses and the scope of the *Schule der Bundeswehr für Innere Führung* were cut back in the haste to raise troops. What had originally been proposed as an undertaking of several months' time was reduced to a few weeks.[12] In their truncated form, the introductory courses for the Bundeswehr's new officers were held during the late spring and summer of 1956, giving Baudissin and his staff their first chance to introduce the reforms to the group that would be most affected by them.[13]

The official discussion on the location for the seminars was itself a symptom of the historical problems facing the new army. The courses were to take place at a former *Ordensburg* (political leadership school) of the Nazi Party in Sonthofen in Allgäu. Renamed "Ludwig Beck Kaserne" in honor of the general who led the resistance to Hitler in the 1938 Czech crisis and who died in the wake of the Twentieth of July *Attentat*, this choice of locale for the first seminars caused Minister of Defense Theodor Blank to seek the counsel of the Bundestag defense committee. The parliamentarians ultimately agreed with the choice, but the incident reflected the lingering doubts connected with this new beginning.[14]

As part of the presentations on *Innere Führung*, Baudissin gave a talk on "Military Tradition and its Meaning in the Present," a carefully planned speech that may be regarded as his main statement of policy on military tradition in the first years of the Bundeswehr.[15] As he had first done in the Himmerod memorandum, Baudissin called for a radical break with the past. He placed much needed emphasis on the shared traditional values that were being increasingly obscured in the

[12] Genschel, *Wehrreform*, pp. 210–22; interviews with General Ulrich de Maizière, June 1984; with Lieutenant General Carl-Gero von Ilsemann, March 1984; with Brigadier General Heinz Karst, March 1984; with Professor Wolf Graf von Baudissin, May 1984; with General Gerd Schmückle, March 1984.

[13] Genschel, *Wehrreform*, pp. 219–22.

[14] Wiggershaus, "Zum Problem," p. 79.

[15] The title is mentioned in an undated plan for the courses drafted before the summer of 1954, see "Stoffplan und Zusammenstellung der Themen für Lehrgang W (Entwurf)" n.d., p. 3, consulted by the writer. The speech is in note 2, p. 148 of this chapter.

fight over what was valid in the heritage of the past. Analyzing the nature of tradition, he insisted that his audience distinguish between the maintenance of spiritual and ethical values, which he described as traditions, and the preservation of forms and externals, which he described as conventions. All too often, he noted, the two got confused, as most people seemed to concentrate on the externals, rituals, and symbols of military life rather than its underlying ethical principles.

This confusion had been especially true in relation to the new Bundeswehr uniform introduced in 1955–56. Much of the public debate had focused on how the new army had broken with German tradition.[16] The military planners had conformed to the wishes of the parliamentarians in designing the new uniform to symbolize the new beginning for both the man on the street and the allied officer on a NATO staff. Identical for army and air force, the uniform bore no resemblance to that of the Wehrmacht; it consisted of a double-breasted short jacket of dark gray cloth, American-style branch collar insignia, new badges of rank, an American-style helmet, peaked cap, and webbed belt. The West German government apparently approved the new style of uniform because a group of young soldiers had found it attractive. Once the soldiers appeared in public, however, a vocal group in West German society did not. They ridiculed the new tunic as a "monkey jacket" or a "mailman's jacket." This criticism became all the more problematic in 1956, when the East German *Nationale Volksarmee* resurrected the field-gray uniform of the Wehrmacht-Heer almost without change, save for the absence of Nazi insignia.[17]

In Baudissin's view, however, the importance of military tradition far exceeded the debate about the color and cut of a uniform. Items of uniform were no more than conventions that were routinely replaced. He listed a few examples of outlived conventions in German military history: the effort to retain the lance in the Reichswehr, the

---

[16] An interesting historical discussion of the new uniform is in Werner Hahlweg, "Die neue Silhouette des deutschen Soldaten," in *Wehrwissenschaftliche Rundschau* 6, 3 (March 1956): 142–50. See the response to Hahlweg in Walter Straub, "Die neue Ausgeh-Uniform," in *Wehrwissenschaftliche Rundschau*, 6, 7 (July 1956): 391–95.

[17] See Hans-Peter Stein, *Symbole und Zeremoniell in den deutschen Streitkräften* (Bonn, 1984), pp. 110–12, and Thomas M. Forster, *NVA: Die Armee der Sowjetzone* (Köln, 1965), pp. 143–44, and Oskar Bluth, *Uniform und Tradition* (Berlin, 1956).

153

habit of addressing superiors in the third person ("Does Herr Oberst desire . . . ?"), and Kaiser Wilhelm's penchant for resurrecting Prussian uniforms of the eighteenth century. He reminded his audience of August Bebel, who at the turn of the century had called for the abolition of parade-ground soldiers and for the orientation of all military life solely toward the realities of battle.

The discussion of conventions notwithstanding, the centerpiece of Baudissin's speech was in the spirit of Bohnenkamp's 1953 suggestion at Siegburg to speak of the contents of tradition. Baudissin described the traditional values that should obtain in the Bundeswehr: a desire for peace, humanity, a chivalrous attitude, loyalty, and above all, a sense of moral responsibility for one's fellow man. To make his point, he alluded to historical examples from Prussian-German history: Arndt, Marwitz, Yorck, Scharnhorst, Gneisenau, and Moltke.

The lessons learned from the abuses of the past now dictated that military obedience conform to ethical boundaries. The Prussian reformers had faced the compromise between blind obedience and the need for soldiers to weigh humanitarian and political needs in carrying out their missions. Indeed, contrary to the impression left by the Nuremberg trials and the Anglo-American reeducators, Prussian-German history revealed a surprising degree of freedom in military service, where soldiers had disobeyed orders out of conscience and had acted upon their own judgments in the face of events. Baudissin encouraged his audience to honor these "conspirators of conscience" (*Frondeure aus Gewissenszwang*), who had seen that obedience must respect religious and moral values.

The tradition of these men of conscience had been undermined by the overtechnicalization of the military craft. The Nazis had done all they could to destroy it; the Bundeswehr would have to work hard to revive it. The former chief of the general staff, Ludwig Beck, and his fellow participants in the Twentieth of July had pointed the way for the West German forces to follow.

Again warning his listeners that tradition did not offer any pat formulas for the present, Baudissin ended his comments with a reference to his critics. Reformers and restorationists had always struggled with one another; indeed, this struggle was an ineradicable element of history. Possessed of a spirit of service and a consciousness of a "western tradition" as described at Siegburg, the new soldier should recognize the continuity between his modern calling and the original image of the western soldier: the knight who also embodied the values of the Christian tradition.

Soldiers would have to guard against a tendency to claim tradition for themselves at the expense of other social groups. Such a tradition exhausted itself in formalities and was suited only for the museum. In the ultimate sense, Baudissin concluded, the laws of the Federal Republic embodied the values of "our tradition": the preservation of peace, the defensive nature of the new forces, the imperative of due process of law, the limits of military obedience, and the duty to comradeship and truthfulness.

Baudissin's presentation, which was widely reproduced even into the late 1970s, is remarkable for what it contained, and perhaps even more notable for what it did not. It is the fruit of Baudissin's own experiences and of five years of planning for the new army. He set an enviable moral standard for the new army, illuminated with examples from history, primarily the Prussian reforms and the Twentieth of July. His definition of tradition included ideas and formulations that stemmed from dozens of seminars and meetings with civilian experts and reflected the impact of these events and personalities upon the new army. However skeptical the modern-day observer may have become of both the Prussian reformers and the military resistance to Hitler, Baudissin's honoring of those who had fostered traditions of freedom remains as laudable today as it was thirty years ago.

But these traditions of freedom and human dignity had been overwhelmed by the men who had ultimately decided Germany's fate in the first half of the twentieth century. Baudissin's presentation was an implicit statement that the Wehrmacht was invalid as a source of tradition for the Bundeswehr. The tension between Baudissin's image of the ideal soldier in a democracy and the burden of the recent German past was demonstrated in another of the Sonthofen speeches.

THE TWENTIETH of July *Attentat* was the subject of its own presentation at Sonthofen. Although in later years Baudissin spoke and wrote with eloquence on the military resistance to Hitler, he did not do so at Sonthofen.[18] A fellow staff officer from the ministry, Major

---

[18] See the lists in Baudissin, *Soldat für den Frieden*, pp. 321–27, and in Lutz, *Festschrift für Wolf Graf Baudissin*, pp. 388–90.

155

Dr. Hans-Christian Trentzsch, spoke on the "The Soldier and the Twentieth of July."[19] Trentzsch's speech was later published as the ministry's official statement on the Twentieth of July controversy.[20] It reaffirmed the compromise on the military resistance that had been offered unofficially by Blank years earlier. It honored the ethical motivations of both those who had participated in the resistance and those who had done their duty as they saw it and continued to fight at the front. And, if one can make a further generalization that applies equally to the entire issue of military tradition in the 1950s and 1960s, the presentation was an interesting manifestation of German inwardness in the context of rearmament in its emphasis upon the individual's need to judge history for himself.

At the outset, Trentzsch acknowledged the difficulties of honoring the military resistance in the Germany of the zero hour and of the occupation. The Nazi damnation of the conspirators as a clique of ambitious and ruthless officers had echoed long after war's end. An account of Winston Churchill's words of praise for the men of the Twentieth of July, spoken in the House of Commons in 1946, was banned in the western zones of occupied Germany as part of a general prohibition of news of military affairs. In the confusion of the immediate postwar world, there was little or no information in Germany to overcome the general condemnation of the conspirators that followed the bomb blast, a vacuum that allowed the majority of Germans to avoid any individual moral encounter with the problem.[21]

Now, however, reflection on the Twentieth of July offered the soldier the opportunity to increase his sense of individual responsibility by addressing the ethical issues of resistance, as the personnel boards were requiring of applicants to the officer corps. In retrospect, the assassination attempt had taken place in exceptional circumstances that demanded an extraordinary act of rebellion. Sensitive to recent criticisms about the official honoring of the event, Trentzsch re-

---

[19] Hans-Christian Trentzsch, *Der Soldat und der 20. Juli* (Darmstadt, n.d.).

[20] BA/MA BV 3/8119, "Ergebnisbericht über Unterabteilungsleiter Besprechung am 2. Juli 1956," cited in Wiggershaus, "Zum Problem," p. 19; interviews with General Ulrich de Maizière, April and June 1984. Although the presentation may have been regarded as an official statement, the Twentieth of July did not become the subject of an official order of the day (*Tagesbefehl*) until 1959. See the discussion of the Twentieth of July in the writing of the traditions decree in chs. 10–13 below.

[21] Trentzsch, *Der Soldat und der 20. Juli*, pp. 7–10.

minded his audience that in a democracy that protected the rights of the citizen, armed rebellion would be unnecessary. The legacy of the Twentieth of July set no norm for resistance, but it compelled the soldier to examine his own ideas about individual responsibility, the oath, and military obedience. He observed, however, that ". . . the judgment on the Twentieth of July cannot be dictated to the soldier by anybody. [Each person] has to go his own way and find his own decision, and he will find it when he honestly struggles with the problem."[22] The decisive criterion, however, had been offered by Henning von Tresckow: "the ethical value of a person first begins where he is ready to give his life for his beliefs."[23]

Given the strong popular disdain for the military conspirators, Trentzsch's presentation symbolized the growing determination of the reformers to place the men of the Twentieth of July in the valid tradition of the new army. But the speech was also an attempt to qualify the *Attentat* at Rastenburg so that it could not become the justification for resistance of all kinds in the Bundeswehr. Or, as Baudissin observed, the honoring of the men of the Twentieth of July was neither "an undermining of the combat effectiveness of the Bundeswehr nor a threat to the Federal Republic."[24]

Although the Sonthofen courses did not live up to the *Innere Führung* staff's original hopes, they were nonetheless decisive in the evolution of an official policy on military tradition.[25] The presentations at Sonthofen were later edited and published with other material in the *Handbuch Innere Führung* (1957), a work that in the absence of any subsequent official publication remained the standard text on the reforms until the early 1970s. Provided as "aids for the explanation of ideas," the handbook was not an official regulation with binding force on officers and men, but an anthology of readings for the officer's *Bildung*. The intention was apparently to make the intellectual exchange of the planning phase available in a book issued informally to all officers.

As commendable as this intention may have been, however, modern bureaucratic life, especially in the military, is dominated by regu-

---

[22] Ibid. p. 32   [23] Ibid.
[24] ZIF/ZUA, 0.2.1.0., "Graf Baudissin, 'Gedanken zum 20. Juli,'" ca. 1957, reprinted in modified form in *Handbuch Innere Führung*, pp. 83–85.
[25] Genschel, *Wehrreform*, pp. 217–20.

lations. In the first years of the new army, soldiers in search of a catalogue of valid military traditions would reach for the *Handbuch Innere
Führung*. Unaware of the particulars of the debate, they would be
disappointed not to find in it a regulation. Many officers observed
privately that they would never look at the book at all. This confusion
made necessary both the traditions decree, published in 1965, and the
regulation on *Innere Führung* itself that finally appeared in 1972.[26]

ONCE the Sonthofen courses had ended, the *Schule der Bundeswehr
für Innere Führung* in Koblenz-Pfaffendorf became the vehicle for
Baudissin to expand his image of a valid military tradition for the new
army. He continued to base this image heavily upon the era of Prussian reform. On 30 October 1957, at a ceremony for the 200th birthday
of Freiherr vom Stein and the 150th anniversary of the signing of the
Nassau decrees, Baudissin gave an informative and revealing speech
at the School for *Innere Führung* on "The Meaning for the Present of
the Reforms from the Era of German Rising," which Claus Freiherr
von Rosen accurately describes as autobiographical.[27]

Baudissin began with words of admiration for Freiherr vom Stein's
great gift, namely that despite his being rooted in an unbroken tradition, he no longer let himself be convinced that these traditional political ideas and social ranks were practical after Prussia had been defeated.[28] Stein had refused to accept things uncritically, an attitude
that led him to regard conventions and externals with mistrust. History and tradition were for him not simply things to be remembered
on holidays. Of greater importance were principles of freedom, law,
honor, and the dignity of the individual. The state, in Stein's view,
should in turn educate its citizens by means of an inner constitution
that embodied these liberal values. By participating in the life of the
state, the citizen would experience these values daily, and thus become
the guardian of them.

---

[26] See *Zentrale Dienstvorschrift 10/1, Hilfen für die Innere Führung*, ed. BMVg
(Bonn, 1972). This issue is discussed in Wullich, *Die Konzeption*, pp. 106–08.

[27] ZIF/ZUA, 0.4.4.4.2., "Graf Baudissin, 'Die Bedeutung der Reformen aus der
Zeit deutscher Erhebung für die Gegenwart': Nach einer Ansprache an der Schule
der Bundeswehr für Innere Führung in Koblenz-Pfaffendorf am 30.10. 1957," also
reprinted in *Wehrkunde*, February 1958, pp. 81–85, and Baudissin, *Soldat für den
Frieden*, pp. 86–94. See also Rosen, "Tradition als Last," p. 172.

[28] ZIF/ZUA, "Reformen," p. 1.

Such ideas, Baudissin argued, had been shared by the other Prussian reformers, all of whom had been driven by their country's political and military debacle to see the fragility of accepted conceptions, standards, and forms. But as Baudissin observed, Prussia's catastrophe did not break the resistance of the *Restaurateure*, who avoided reality and tried to blame the defeat on others, not the least among them the reformers themselves. These traditionalists looked back with enchantment upon a romanticized past. They insisted upon the enduring validity of their apparent experiences, and condemned those who sought other standards and ways of doing things. Although on the face of it, Baudissin was describing the situation that Gneisenau confronted in 1809, his listeners undoubtedly drew parallels with the West German army in 1957, as he surely must have intended.

Reminding his audience of the triumph of the restoration and reformers' fate after 1819, Baudissin recalled that under the protection of the Holy Alliance, the reformers had been branded Jacobins. Gneisenau and Clausewitz were shoved off to unimportant posts; later, as part of the general decline of liberalism in central Europe, those German democrats and liberals who sought to preserve these ideas became enemies of the state.

The course of German military history after the defeat of the reforms had seen the triumph of the "narrow-minded soldier," whose "blind obedience" and overspecialization had isolated him from Germany's changing political and social realities. The result had been the well-drilled, expertly trained soldier who was not only uncivil and apolitical, but who also placed too much emphasis upon training and discipline.

Baudissin warned his audience against the dragooning of historical figures to serve in the present through a gross oversimplification of the past, as both the Nazis and the East Germans had done with the Prussian reformers. This danger aside, there were still qualities in the reformers that were exemplary for the tradition of the new army. The ability of the reformers to "think in context" and to see the impact of their profession upon the state and society was surely a valid quality for the Bundeswehr. Being true to one's principles to the point of nonconformism was another. The determination with which Stein and his contemporaries adhered to the principles of freedom, human rights, and human dignity were the measure of an "ethical rootedness," which was, in Baudissin's view, even more essential in the ideological confrontations of the present.

PERHAPS more than any other of the addresses Baudissin made before or after, his speech on Stein indicates both his strengths and weaknesses as the architect of much in the *inneres Gefüge* and as the principal spokesman on military tradition in the first years of the Bundeswehr. His emphasis upon Stein's liberal qualities despite being rooted in an aristocratic tradition fit within a laudable heritage of reform from above in German history. *Innere Führung* could well be placed within this continuum of reform from above, since the personalities and the process of building the inner structure in the mid-1950s also seem to fit this pattern.

The statement that one should pursue one's ethical principles to the point of nonconformity can also help to explain Baudissin's own diminishing fortunes in the military leadership of the late 1950s. His personal strengths and weaknesses were bound up in the program of military reform that now had to stand the test of life in the new army. Often attacks on *Innere Führung* were indistinguishable from personal assaults on its leading spokesman. Naturally Baudissin reacted to this development with a stiffening of will, and his ideas on reform seem to have become even more outspoken.

AS THE BUNDESWEHR emerged, the military leadership had slowly come to grips with the need to define military tradition within the greater efforts at reform. At all times, the shadows of Hans von Seeckt, Adolf Hitler, and Roland Freisler loomed over them. *Innere Führung*, like the West German Basic Law and many other political innovations of the Federal Republic, had been the answer of the West German government to the abuses of the recent German past.

The bureaucratic setting of terms about military tradition within the overall program of reform became a kind of dialectic with the troops. The policy characterized by Heusinger's dictum of "wait and see" and Baudissin's emphasis on ideals of tradition that, however laudable, excluded much of the recent military experience of most Germans, would now be tested. The difficult birth of the Bundeswehr completed in 1955–56 was to be followed by a problematical first decade.

This periodization of the new army's recent history appeared in a commentary on military tradition by Wilhelm Ritter von Schramm in October 1959, when the ministry further reflected on the nature of the problem of military tradition.[29] Schramm described the first phase of the new armed forces from 1950 to 1956 as the having been under the *Primat des Politischen* (the primacy of politics). The conception of the reforms had been a necessary response to the political condition of the Federal Republic and to the world situation. The second phase that began with the raising of troops was described as one of "military requirements." After a ten-year hiatus, officers had to adjust to a new image of war and to train soldiers to fight alongside former enemies in a possible nuclear wasteland. Schramm called this period a military restoration or soldierly renaissance. Although Schramm was critical of Baudissin, it was no less true that during the period of "military requirements," the ideas of the reforms had to meet the reality of politics, human expectations, and the latent resistance of many professional soldiers.

Schramm erred, however, in his choice of names for his periodization. The era of "military requirements" was as much under the "primacy of politics" as the conception of the forces had been, perhaps even more so. This putative separation of politics and military requirements was symptomatic of the problems being encountered with the reforms. The armed forces were always to serve eminently political ends. Adenauer regarded the Bundeswehr as the means of assuring West Germany's role in an Atlantic alliance beset with growing difficulties. His NATO allies wanted the new armed forces ready as soon as possible, a political demand that had significant ramifications for the military requirements of the new army.

This growing political friction in the years after 1955–56 doomed both Heusinger's policy of "do not touch, let the traditions grow" and Baudissin's emphasis on the Prussian reformers and the Twentieth of July. Each of these attempts at policy had been a way of dealing with the legacy of the Third Reich and the Wehrmacht without confronting them head on. The new soldiers who put on their intentionally

---

[29] Wilhelm Ritter von Schramm, "Bundeswehr und Tradition: Eine systematische Untersuchung," *Wehrkunde*, October 1959, pp. 505ff.

drab gray uniforms in 1956 soon compelled the leadership to abandon their still-evolving definition of military tradition and to address the recent past directly. The drafting of the ministerial decree on tradition outlined in the next part of this study is a result of this clash between the plans for reform and the actual military restoration.

PART TWO

The Decree on Tradition

9. "Inner Strangulation": The Troops and the Reforms

THE RAISING of the Bundeswehr began in an old stable in the Ermekeil barracks that had become a garage, later dubbed the *Feldherrnhalle* by the men who received their commissions there.[1] It was a curious place for the birth of what would have to be a miracle of military organization. Within three months of being mustered, the first soldiers were supposed to be battle-ready and to form cadres for additional training companies, battalions, and divisions. The planners in the *Amt Blank*/Ministry of Defense developed a plan by the spring of 1955 that foresaw 95,000 men in uniform at the end of the first year, over 270,000 at the end of the second, and a total of 500,000 men at the end of the third year, a pace of rearmament that would eclipse that of the Wehrmacht between 1935 and 1939.[2] The plan was Adenauer's response to political pressure from the allies. The accelerated pace of armament, against which the military planners fruitlessly warned for several years, came after 1955 witnessed considerable uncertainty about the future of West German security. The incipient détente between the great powers, rumors of an American pullback from Europe, the worsening of the anti-French war in Algeria, and West German public debate about defense and nuclear strategy all moved Adenauer to get as many troops in uniform as quickly as possible. He hoped to use the Bundeswehr to strengthen the influence of the Federal Republic in NATO at a time when the United States, France, and the United Kingdom appeared to be scaling back their troop strengths on the

---

[1] Interview with Brigadier General Heinz Karst, July 1984.
[2] BA/MA Bw 9/1310, "Gesamtplanung für die Aufstellung der Streitkräfte und die sich daraus ergebenden wichtigsten Probleme," ca. May 1955; Johannes Fischer, "Militärpolitische Lage und militärische Planung bei Aufstellungsbeginn der Bundeswehr," in *Militärgeschichte Probleme—Thesen—Wege*, ed. MGFA, pp. 472–74; MGFA, *Verteidigung im Bündnis*, pp. 61–66; Fett, "Grundlagen," *Aspekte*, pp. 169ff.

central front because of overseas commitments or in favor of nuclear weapons.[3]

On Scharnhorst's two hundredth birthday, 12 November 1955, a date chosen by the "inner structure" staff to signify the spirit and tradition of the new start, Theodor Blank stood beneath an enormous Iron Cross and awarded the first one hundred and one volunteers of the Bundeswehr their commissions in the garage of the *Ermekeilkaserne*. The promise of reform, Blank said, would now have to be made into a reality.[4] These first soldiers, among whom were Speidel and Heusinger, would have to build the new army while neither glorifying all in the military past of Germany nor damning it totally. The new army, Blank explained, would take nothing from the past without first examining it to see if it was still valid for the present. The reforms of the new army would help fulfill the purpose of soldierly existence—to preserve peace.[5]

MANY OBSTACLES still stood in the way of the reforms, as the men whom Blank had just sworn in well knew. By January 1956, the men of the *Feldherrnhalle* had been joined by the initial group of one thousand volunteers, soon to be followed by five thousand more. They entered an army that had to overcome not only the moral and historical burden of its creation, but also incomplete political, strategic, legal, and material bases for its birth.[6]

The question of the legal status of the West German soldier stood foremost in relation to the future of the new army. As the first soldiers

---

[3] Fischer, "Lage," pp. 453ff. See also *Verteidigung im Bündnis: Planung, Aufbau und Bewährung der Bundeswehr, 1950–1972*, ed. MGFA (München, 1975), p. 83. On the first NATO field and commandpost exercise of the strategy of nuclear massive retaliation, "Carte Blanche," see Mark Cioc, "Pax Atomica: The Nuclear Defense Debate in West Germany during the Adenauer Era," Ph.D. diss., University of California, Berkeley, 1986; Julian Lider, *Problems of Military Policy in the Konrad Adenauer Era, 1949–1966* (Stockholm, 1984); Hans Speier, *German Rearmament and Atomic War: The Views of the German Military and Political Leaders* (Evanston, 1957); and Gordon Craig, "NATO and the German Army," in *NATO and American Security*, ed. William Kaufmann (Princeton, 1956).

[4] "Theodor Blank, Rede anlässlich der Ernennung der ersten Freiwillingen Soldaten am 12. November 1955," reprinted in *Wehrkunde*, December 1955, pp. 522–23.

[5] Ibid.

[6] ZIF/ZUA, 0.4.4.4.8., "Kommandeur, Schule der Bundeswehr für Innere Führung [Ulrich de Maizière] G–3, Az 35–05–14, 'Probleme bei Planung und Vorbereitung des deutschen Verteidigungsbeitrages,' " 5 November 1960.

joined their units, the members of parliament were still debating the military amendments to the Basic Law. This legal uncertainty increased the confusion of an already strained start of the Bundeswehr. Nor did the parliamentary debate about the military legislation soon end—some of the key military laws did not go into effect until 1957. Despite these problems, however, the laws governing the position of the soldier in the state finally provided the Bundeswehr with the political basis upon which to make the reforms into a reality. Just as the *discipline générale* had been the central focus of reform in the stillborn EDC, the military legislation of the years between 1954 and 1957 became the central focus of reform in the first years of the new army. The legislation codified in law the principles of *Innere Führung* and signified a dramatic break with Prussian-German military tradition. In this effort, Jaeger and Erler carried on the cooperation begun in the security committee to pass the reform legislation in a bipartisan spirit. The victory of the legislation passed in the Bundestag assured the support of parliament for the armament of the Federal Republic, but substantial problems remained.

Except for the 26 March 1954 vote in parliament amending the Basic Law to allow the federal government to provide for the defense of the republic, the new army lacked a legal foundation, even as the men of Ermekeil barracks and the first training companies in Andernach, Nörvenich, and Wilhelshaven put on their uniforms at the turn of the year 1955–56. The ongoing debate on the first piece of additional military legislation, the Volunteers Law, had gotten off to a bad start in late May 1955.[7] The chancellor's eagerness to rush forward with the new army generated the resistance of parliament. Adenauer, anxious about a revival of the spirit of Potsdam among the four powers, wanted to form the first training cadres with a few thousand volunteers by spring of 1956. In late May 1955 he had ordered the drafting of a "lightning" Volunteers Law, which his staff prepared in two days. To parliament, however, a law of only three paragraphs was another example of Adenauer's highhanded approach to foreign policy. The lightning bill threatened to nullify years of parliamentary work on military reform. The legislature turned back the law, describing it as "totalitarian," and forced the redrafting of its provisions. In particular,

---

[7] Hans-Peter Schwarz, *Die Ära Adenauer*, pp. 295ff.

the bipartisan alliance insisted on the institutionalization of the personnel screening committee.

Following the issue of the selection of personnel, the question of supreme command of the armed forces provoked an intense debate. The liberals of the FDP fought to restore the Weimar institution of having the president of the republic retain supreme command, but this effort was defeated by the larger parties. The amendments to the Basic Law made the defense minister commander in chief of the armed forces in peacetime, but answerable to the Bundestag. The *Generalinspekteur*, the chief of staff of the West German armed forces, is the equivalent in the U.S. military of the chairman of the joint chiefs in rank but not in influence, because the *Generalinspekteur* acts principally in an advisory function. The minister of defense was to occupy the highest position in the chain of command, deciding matters of military personnel and administration.[8]

The changes to the Basic Law also provided for alternative service for conscientious objectors; forbade women from serving in the armed forces; guaranteed the basic rights of soldiers during their period of service, while setting certain limits on them; gave the defense committee of the Bundestag special investigative powers; established the post of the parliamentary commissioner (*Wehrbeauftragter*) to oversee the implementation of *Innere Führung* at the unit level; delineated conditions for a "state of defense"; gave the *Bundespräsident* the right to commission officers and NCOs; forbade the creation of a separate military justice system; and established the organization and functions of the civilian military administration that placed in civilian hands many of the administrative tasks of the old uniformed military officials of the Wehrmacht.[9] The law also set limits on the ability of

[8] ZIF/ZUA, o.4.4.4.8., "Maizière, Probleme," p. 4.

[9] This arrangement is complicated and requires some explanation. In contrast to the U.S. Department of Defense, where soldiers and civilians serve side by side and in many instances at the upper levels, civilians write the efficiency ratings [report cards] of officers, the command and administrative organization of the Bundeswehr is separated into military and civilian structures. For instance, while the commander of a *Verteidigungsbezirk*—a defense headquarters area equivalent to a division that may embrace a government district of two or more counties—has the combat and combat support units under him, the administration of the bases and facilities of these units, as well as many liaison functions with the local government, are in the hands of the local civilian mobilization and garrison administration of-

soldiers to hold office while in uniform and established that the rights and powers available for an internal emergency would require amendments to the Basic Law.[10]

These amendments and additions to the constitution were supplemented by the soldier's law, the most important piece of military legislation, which went into effect on 1 April 1956. Among other things, it provided the new armed forces with their name, over the objections of critics, who thought that Bundeswehr sounded too much like *Feuerwehr* (fire brigade). It set down as never before the duties and rights of the West German soldier, implementing much of the German work on the *discipline générale*.[11]

In response to the focus on the Twentieth of July, the soldiers' law required that draftees participate in a ceremonial obligation—not an oath-taking—to the armed forces, while career soldiers were to swear an oath. Baudissin's staff had been against the revival of the oath because of the conflict of conscience inherent in the idea of absolute obedience, which had become overwhelming during the Nazi era.[12]

---

ficials. This arrangement was understood as part of the division of power that dominated the writing of the defense legislation.

[10] ZIF/ZUA, 0.4.4.4.8., "Maizière, Probleme."

[11] The basic rights of the soldier included: the obligation to mutual loyalty between soldier and state, the assurance that the soldier enjoyed the rights of all citizens, except as limited by his service; the preservation of human dignity; the free expression of personality; the protection of his physical person; equality before the law; freedom of belief; freedom of religion; free expression of his opinions; active and passive franchise; and the right to legal protection.

[12] See ZIF/ZUA, 0.2.1.0., "IVB, Graf Baudissin, 'Vereidigung einer Unterabteilung am 24. September 1956,' " 24 September 1956. Space precludes a fuller discussion of this issue, which was heavily connected with the subject of the Twentieth of July and was the object of intense debate. See the files in ZIF/ZUA, 1.1.6, "Schule der Bundeswehr für Innere Führung 'Auszüge aus dem Protokoll des Bundestages vom 6. März 1956 (132. Sitzung) zur Frage des Eides' "; ZIF/ZUA, 1.1.6, "Der Bundesminister für Verteidigung-Staatssekretär 'Richtlinien für Vereidigung vom September 1956,' " 8 August 1956; Norbert Wiggershaus, "Zum Problem der Tradition im Vorfeld eines westdeutschen Verteidigungsbeitrages," unpublished manuscript, 1983; Hans-Jürgen Rautenberg, "Zur Standortbestimmung für künftige deutsche Streitkräfte," in *Anfänge westdeutscher Sicherheitspolitik 1945–1956: Von der Kapitulation bis zum Pleven Plan*, ed. MGFA (München, 1982), 1: 824–28; DOKZENTBw, Nr. U 6671, Hauptmann G.W. von Gravenitz, "Die Bedeutung des Eides für den Soldaten. Die Diskussion des Eides im Bereich der Evangelischen Militärseelsorge seit 1945" (Führungsakademie der Bundeswehr, Abteilung Luftwaffe, 30 September 1978); DOKZENTBw, Nr. S 2794, Hauptmann D. Speidel, "Eid und feierliches Gelöbnis in unserer säkularisierten Gesellschaft" (Führungsakademie der Bundeswehr, Abteilung Heer, 1 October 1970). Once General Ulrich

Apparently the career civil servants in the *Dienststelle Blank* insisted on it, however, because civil servants had always sworn an oath. Further military legislation included the code of military justice, another outgrowth of the *discipline générale* debates, and the conscription law. The question of conscription had been a major source of the SPD opposition to rearmament, and the debate on the Period of Service Law in July 1956 brought this controversy to a climax with the institution of a draft army.

Years later, both Baudissin and Ulrich de Maizière described as decisive the importance of the military laws for the realization of *Innere Führung*.[13] Perhaps more than any other single event or set of events, these laws simultaneously broke with the traditions of the past and acted to foster what have become the Bundeswehr's own traditions, particularly the institution of the office of parliamentary defense commissioner.[14] The idea for the parliamentary commissioner began with SPD deputy Paul, who in 1954 prompted members of the *Sicherheitsausschuss* (Security Committee) in cooperation with Ulrich de Maizière to investigate the soldier's ombudsman in Sweden, which became the model for the West German institution. The military laws embodied the years of planning, discussion, and draft regulations that had dominated the preparation for the new army. The legislation symbolized a political victory for reform, but one that would remain hollow until the new officers and NCOs could fill it with life.

WHILE the laws consolidated *Innere Führung* at the national level of civil-military relations, they also contributed to its misunderstanding in the ranks, and in some instances tended to increase resistance to it. If the need to redefine the legal status of the soldier had helped to give birth to *Innere Führung*, the reform concept did not begin and end as

---

de Maizière became *Generalinspekteur*, the ministry considered doing away with the oath. See ZIF/ZUA, 1.1.6., "BMVg, Fü S I 4, Az 30–08–10–01, 'Ersatz für das feierliche Gelöbnis: Ausarbeitung von Merksätzen und Unterrichtshilfen,' " 6 September 1970.

[13] Interviews with Professor Wolf Graf von Baudissin, May 1984, and with General Ulrich de Maizière, April and June 1984. See Ulrich de Maizière, "Der Wehrbeauftragte, die Innere Führung und die Soldaten," *Europäische Wehrkunde-Wehrwissenschaftliche Rundschau*, May 1984, pp. 289–93.

[14] For the best scholarly treatment of the *Wehrbeauftragter*, see Wolfgang Vogt, *Militär und Demokratie: Funktionen und Konflikte der Institution des Wehrbeauftragten* (Hamburg, 1972), especially the bibliography, pp. 333–54.

a code of military justice, although many thought so. Even as loosely defined as it was in 1956, *Innere Führung* embraced the self-image and spirit of the armed forces, things less susceptible to regulation than vulnerable to the soldiers' spiritual and physical conditions. These conditions were poor in late 1956.[15] The fundamentals of the soldier's personal existence—his pay, health insurance, and benefits for his family—were were still being debated in the parliament.[16] The short-age of NCOs and company grade officers, foreseen by Heusinger in 1953, robbed military life at the unit level of its equilibrium. Young officer candidates in the streets of Hamburg were surrounded by mobs and jeered, and in other German towns men in uniform were greeted at best with a glum indifference. The new soldier's weapons were hand-me-downs from the NATO allies and complaints about American-made weapons were widespread. In many cases, the equip-ment did indeed compare unfavorably with that of the Wehrmacht: American armored vehicles of the 1950s still used gasoline engines that were less safe than diesel engines, and U.S. machine guns were neither as quick-firing nor as reliable as older German models. German firms, however, balked at the prospect of making guns again. Thoroughly demilitarized, reeducated, and busy with peaceful products, German industry was slow to invest the enormous sums needed to manufac-ture arms. Industrialists were also afraid of the political cost—after all, some of industry's most notable representatives had ended up in the docket next to the Nazi *Prominenz*, civil servants, and generals. Given the problems of material support, the army's first winter re-minded many of the campaign in Russia. The soldiers' clothing and housing were inadequate; there were too few winter uniforms. The many bases and facilities built in the 1930s for the Wehrmacht were filled with NATO allies or domestic relief agencies. The Federal Re-public was not sufficiently equipped to house or train all the troops it was committed to calling up.[17] In fact, the inability of the federal gov-

---

[15] ZIF/ZUA, o.4.4.4.8., "Probleme, Maizière," pp. 7–8. For a firsthand account of the conditions at the first army training base south of Bonn at Andernach, see Gerd Schmückle, *Ohne Pauken und Trompeten: Erinnerungen an Krieg und Frieden* (Stuttgart, 1982), pp. 103ff.

[16] ZIF/ZUA, "Probleme, Maizière," pp. 9–10.

[17] Ironically those old Wehrmacht barracks in U.S. hands, once desired by the new West German army, later became an object of some dissatisfaction for the Americans. While the Bundeswehr built new facilities in the 1950s and 1960s, the

171

ernment to requisition necessary real estate from the various German *Land* governments made the Federal Republic fall behind its promised military timetable to NATO. But perhaps this setback was really for the best, since too few soldiers had joined to fill the new barracks and training areas on hand in mid-1956. The hoped-for number of volunteers had not answered the call to arms, nor had enough members of the federal border guards exchanged their green uniforms for the gray of the Bundeswehr. The build-up of the army seemed to many to be on the verge of collapse.

Already dismayed about their dwindling influence, the proponents of the reforms in the staff wrote of the danger posed by these miserable conditions. In a report on the status of the *Innere Führung* in late 1956, Baudissin warned that neither the material nor the personal basis for the reforms existed among the troops.[18] Soldiers whose quarters, clothing, pay, and benefits were so obviously inadequate were understandably unreceptive to the elevated ideals of *Innere Führung*. The training and education of the troops were hindered by the absence of legal guidelines for military justice and for making complaints. There were too few training aids, regulations, and classrooms. Baudissin concluded that *Innere Führung* had not kept pace with other aspects of rearmament. Neither officers nor men had fully grasped the tasks of the reforms. Troop instructors schooled in the Wehrmacht resurrected the *Kommiss* methods embodied in the 1936 regulations, a symptom of the growing movement in favor of restoration of the drillmaster mentality within in the ranks.[19]

Although in the fall of 1956 the Adenauer government slowed the pace and scale of rearmament, the public support for the Bundeswehr grew after the war scare following the Suez Crisis and the Hungarian

---

United States retained its old real estate, but neglected it. The constant possibility that the United States would withdraw from Germany, the cost of military operations, and the impact of the Vietnam War led the U.S. forces there to put off repairs, so that by the late 1970s, the buildings were in terrible shape. U.S. officers would then complain about the contrast with handsome Bundeswehr facilities, unaware of the circumstances behind it.

[18] BA/MA, N 492/11, "IV B 1831/56 'Zustandsbericht über die Innere Führung,' " 10 November 1956, cited in Peter Wullich, *Die Konzeption der Inneren Führung der Bundeswehr als Grundlage der allgemeinen Wehrpädagogik* (Regensburg, 1981), pp. 134–35.

[19] Ibid., p. 135.

uprising.[20] The difficult physical conditions of the ranks remained, however, strengthening the revival of a drillmaster mentality at the unit level. What had been a phenomenon to be deplored in internal memoranda became the subject of headlines after 3 June 1957, when fifteen paratrooper recruits from the First Airborne Division drowned while crossing the river Iller in Bavaria.[21] The men in the platoon were following an order to cross a river that, according to the recently passed military legislation, they did not need to carry out. For the critics of the Bundeswehr, the Iller tragedy indicated the army's return to blind obedience, putting the lie to five years of promises by the ministry. The conflict between the ministry's reforms and the insistence of troop instructors of the wartime generation on realistic, harsh training undercut the appeal of *Innere Führung*.[22]

As Baudissin's former deputy Lieutenant Colonel Heinz Karst observed in a memorandum of late 1957 at the *Innere Führung* school,[23]

[20] MGFA, *Verteidigung im Bündnis*, pp. 83–84.

[21] MGFA, *Verteidigung im Bündnis*, p. 124. The airborne troops were a constant source of trouble for the *Innere Führung* policymakers in the first decade of the Bundeswehr. Very often, these West German paratrooper instructors had been trained by the U.S. or French armies, which instilled a *Kommiss* spirit in them that *Innere Führung* had sought to exclude.

[22] Again, this was a problem that Heusinger had foreseen at Siegburg. For a reaction to the event at the corps level of command, exhorting commanders to adhere to principles of the reforms, see ZIF/ZUA, 1.1.3.0., "Der Bundesminister für Verteidigung, Kommandostab im Wehrbereich IV (Wehrbereichskommando IV) Abt. G2, Tagebuch Nr. 7452/57, 'Grenzen des Gehorsams,' " 24 June 1957.

[23] "Oberstleutnant Heinz Karst 'Gedanken über Erfahrungen meines Truppenkommandos' Koblenz-Pfaffendorf," 1 October 1957, consulted by the writer. By this time, the famous rift between Baudissin and Karst over the spirit and practice of *Innere Führung* was growing more severe. This memorandum has to be judged in the light of Karst's criticisms of the reforms in practice. Karst gained national attention in the summer of 1955, when he published a memorandum on civil-military relations that was critical of the perceived disadvantages to soldiers, especially regarding pay; see the copy of this document in ZIF/ZUA, 0.2.1.0., "Die Denkschrift Karst," August 1955. Karst was then asked to testify before the *Sicherheitsausschuss*, but was supported by Blank, Heusinger, and Baudissin. Shortly thereafter, Generals Heusinger and Speidel sent a memorandum to Chancellor Adenauer decrying overzealous attempts by civil servants to control all aspects of the military. It received no response. See Hans Speidel, *Aus unserer Zeit: Erinnerungen* (Frankfurt, 1977), pp. 337–39. Karst's rhetorical gifts made him a popular speaker on the reforms before the troops. For a fairly objective synopsis of the feud between Karst and Baudissin, see Ulrich Simon, *Die Integration der Bundeswehr in die Gesellschaft: Das Ringen um die Innere Führung* (Heidelberg, 1980), pp. 28–55. Many of the ideas contained in Karst's 1957 memorandum were later expanded upon in *Tradition im*

many soldiers, NCOs, and officers had begun to dismiss *Innere Führung* as the "soft wave" or "inner strangulation" or "inner bullshit." The troops responded by reviving Wehrmacht conventions as a form of passive resistance.[24] Soldiers began to salute using the Wehrmacht style (but not the Nazi salute!) and resisted the posture for standing at attention borrowed from the U.S. Army. In the old armies, the soldier at attention placed his hands at his side with the fingers outstretched along the seam of the trousers. The command "Fingers on pants seam!" was the equivalent of "attention!" in the U.S. military. In the Bundeswehr, however, soldiers were to make a fist beside their thighs while at attention, as in the U.S. military. Bundeswehr soldiers later described this position in resentful tones as the "peeing stance," the "little paws with a waiter's tip," and the "SPD stance."

Karst warned that the ministry would have to redouble its efforts to promote *Innere Führung* and perhaps consider adopting a different name to describe the reforms because of the negative associations of the term in the ranks. With a vivid image revealing his own literary bent, Karst described the Bundeswehr as being like a man standing upon a deck of moving planks who must read an interesting book while on the verge of nausea. At first he looks at his book; he then casts a glance at the heaving ground beneath him; finally he decides to throw the book away and to seek a firmer footing.[25]

Atomzeitalter, first published as a *Beilage zur Truppenpraxis*, January 1958, and later incorporated in his widely read book of 1964, Heinz Karst, *Das Bild des Soldaten: Versuch eines Umrisses* (Boppard, 1964), pp. 225–58.

[24] Karst, "Erfahrungen," pp. 1–3. This development is interpreted at length in Hans-Peter Stein, *Symbole und Zeremoniell in den deutschen Streitkräften* (Bonn, 1984), pp. 127–284.

[25] Karst, "Erfahrungen," p. 3.

10. Death's Head and St. Hubertus Cross: Unit Lineage and Honors

DURING 1957–58, as new units were created at breakneck speed, a growing number of veterans groups, traditions associations, and Bundeswehr unit commanders requested permission from the Ministry of Defense to restore the system of maintaining unit lineage and honors introduced in 1921 by Seeckt. Companies, squadrons, and batteries of the new Reichswehr had preserved the lineage and honors of regiments of the old armies. This somewhat artificial system became a prominent feature of the inner structure of Reichswehr/Wehrmacht and was closely identified in the popular mind with the ambivalent attitude of the Reichswehr to Weimar democracy.

The calls for a revival of the Reichswehr tradition compelled the leadership of the Bundeswehr "to make good on its promise of a new beginning,"[1] while challenging it to preserve the good will of many former professional soldiers. The request from the veterans groups filled the leadership of the Bundeswehr and their civilian advisers with uneasy memories of the 1920s.[2] The veterans groups and the traditions associations had been a potent antidemocratic force in the Weimar Republic and might become so again.

There were other aspects to the lineage and honors problem that worked against the relaxed policy that the Bundeswehr leadership in relation to military tradition summarized in the phrase, "let it grow." First, the leadership was uneasy about the "*ohne mich*" attitudes

---

[1] Hans-Joachim Harder, "Traditionspflege in der Bundeswehr," unpublished manuscript, 1983, p. 21. The published work is Hans-Joachim Harder, "Traditionspflege in der Bundeswehr, 1956–1972," in *Tradition und Reform in den Aufbaujahren der Bundeswehr*, ed. MGFA (Herford, 1985). Harder's work formed the basis for chapters 10–13 of this volume, although the following chapters include greater detail from the sources and the results of interviews with the participants.

[2] Interviews with Major General Dr. Eberhard Wagemann, March 1984, and with General Ulrich de Maizière, April 1984.

among the West German population and wanted to overcome them through public relations campaigns in local garrisons. A symbolic connection with the lineages and honors of popular old units might well promote good feeling. Secondly, with the new forces neither up to strength nor combat-ready, the Bundeswehr leadership saw the veterans as a usable reserve of manpower at a time when the cold war was growing more intense. Finally, the usurpation by the East German *Nationale Volksarmee* of many historical personalities and traditions of the Prussian-German armies fed internal official fears of what can only be described as an East-West "tradition gap." This last facet of the problem was compounded by the tens of thousands of politically active displaced persons from the communist east who wanted the unit traditions of their lost homes maintained as well.[3]

THE Armed Forces Staff had to respond to these pressures. Interestingly enough, neither Baudissin nor any officer from his staff had a hand in writing this first study on lineage and honors, which helped to set in motion the decree on tradition. Instead, the Armed Forces Staff gave the task to Colonel Dr. Hans Meier-Welcker, an early member of *Dienststelle Blank*, soon to be chief of the military history staff in Lanegau (later Military History Research Office in Freiburg im Breisgau) and the biographer of Seeckt.[4] Meier-Welcker addressed the question of unit *Traditionspflege* in a staff paper of October 1957.[5] Together with a handful of other officers and civilians, Meier-Welcker was influential in formulating the traditions policy that began to emerge in the late 1950s and early 1960s.[6]

[3] Bundesministerium für gesamtdeutsche Fragen, ed., *Die politische Armee der Sowjetzone in den Jahren 1955–1958* (Bonn, 1959); ZIF/ZUA, 3.3.2.8.2., "Schule der Bundeswehr für Innere Führung, I. Entwurf 'Fragenkatalog zum Inneren Gefüge der NVA,' " 12 October 1959. For a later example of this interesting dilemma, see ZIF/ZUA, 3.3.2.8.2., "Fü B VII 6 Az 31–60–15–00, Tgb. Nr. 259, 'Deutschland-Bild der jungen NVA Offiziere,' " 23 February 1965. On the DDR, see Gerhard Zazworka, *Soldatenehre* (Berlin, 1957); *Die fortschrittlichen militärischen Traditionen des deutschen Volkes* (Berlin, 1957); Wolfgang Döhnert and Manfred Seifert, *Söldner oder Soldat* (Berlin, 1956); Oskar Bluth, *Uniform und Tradition* (Berlin, 1956); and Walter Rehm, "Militärtraditionen in der DDR," in *DDR und die Tradition*, ed. Jens Hacker and Horst Roegner Francke (Heidelberg, 1981).
[4] Hans Meier-Welcker, *Seeckt* (Frankfurt, 1967).
[5] Hans Meier-Welcker, "Die Pflege der Tradition in der Bundeswehr," ca. October 1957, consulted by the writer. Also cited in Harder, "Traditionspflege," as BA/MA, Bw 2/4939, "Chef des Stabes (Ch.d.S.), Fü S, Az 35–08–07," 25 October 1957.
[6] As future head of the MGFA, Meier-Welcker was to be the staff historian,

In his paper, he recognized the general desire of former and active soldiers for the preservation of unit traditions, a wish shared by many civilians in garrison towns of the Bundeswehr. To meet these wishes, however, the leadership of the armed forces would have to reconcile diverse points of view. The system of military tradition "must beneficially affect the spirit of the Bundeswehr," while still corresponding to Germany's present political and international situation.[7] This balanced maintenance of tradition must "help the old soldiers to have a positive attitude toward the Bundeswehr," while at the same time it should not "provoke the public, but win their approval."[8] In striking this balance, the Bundeswehr would have to bring forth the soldierly values of the past "while bridging the gaps" in Germany's military past. The maintenance of tradition was to make use of historical military achievements for the education of soldiers. This task was to be the responsibility of the unit commanders.

In addressing the transfer of lineages and honors from units of the old armies to the new army, Meier-Welcker suggested that for the time being the division of Germany precluded former units from central and eastern Germany from awarding their lineages and honors to Bundeswehr units. The technical problems of such a move were overwhelming. The old regiments were gone; the personal continuity that existed in regiments where father, son, brother, and uncle had served was no longer possible. New kinds of weapons and tactical organizations made a connection difficult, as did the enormous number of units in the peacetime army of pre-1914, the army of 1921–39, and the army of 1939–45, which in no way corresponded to the smaller Bundeswehr.

Although Meier-Welcker did not mention them, two additional political arguments related to the communist east spoke against the takeover of lineages and honors as well: public anxiety about military revanchism, and the fear that the transfer of unit traditions from the communist zones to the new units would signal an acceptance of the

---

which probably explains his involvement in this instead of Baudissin's. The *Unterabteilung IV B* [as the *inneres Gefüge* staff was called; it later became *Fü B I*] was working on a draft statement for commanders on tradition in addition to having just published the *Handbuch Innere Führung* in September 1957. The book can be regarded as the official position, even if it was not published as a guideline or a decree. Interview with Professor Wolf Graf von Baudissin, May 1984.

[7] Meier-Welcker, "Pflege," p. 1.

[8] Ibid.

status quo.[9] Nonetheless, Meier-Welcker suggested that the traditions associations of units from central and eastern Germany could have an informal "charter relationship" with a Bundeswehr unit. The takeover of lineage and honors from the Waffen-SS and units with such politically charged names as "Hermann Göring" and "Feldherrnhalle" was out of the question. However, individuals from these units might be welcomed in a charter relationship with the new army, if they joined the larger veterans organizations like the *Verband deutscher Soldaten*, the *Kyffhäuserbund*, or the *Ordensgemeinschaften*.

The strength of Meier-Welcker's plan lay in his suggestion that the Bundeswehr leadership pursue a locally oriented course in its revival of lineages and honors, concentrating on the local continuities between old and new units in the garrison communities. Traditions could then develop by themselves in a natural way. "Tradition has everything for itself in a specific garrison: the memory of the population, [and] the [presence of] buildings and monuments."[10] Meier-Welcker also suggested that units could establish relations with the veterans on a territorial basis through the bond of a common branch tradition. For instance, a Bundeswehr infantry unit could invite all infantry veterans in the area to its functions, including those outside established traditions or veterans organizations, thereby limiting the influence of these groups.

The Chief of Staff of the Bundeswehr, General Adolf Heusinger, still as cautious on the issue of military tradition as he was in 1953–54, agreed completely with Meier-Welcker's conclusions. Heusinger asked him to prepare a plan for linking the traditions of former units in garrison towns with Bundeswehr units now in those towns. He did note, however, that the time for a final decision on unit lineage and honors lay perhaps a year ahead.[11] As the task was given to Meier-

[9] Interviews with Professor Wolf Graf von Baudissin, May 1984; with General Ulrich de Maizière, March 1984; and with Major General Dr. Eberhard Wagemann, June 1984.

[10] Meier-Welcker, "Pflege," p. 3.

[11] ZIF/ZUA, 3.1.2.2., "Fü B Bw B, Az 35–08–07 'Vermerk, Traditionspflege,' " 10 January 1958; ZIF/ZUA, 3.1.2.2., "Generalinspekteur Heusinger an Oberst Dr. Meier-Welcker, 'Traditionspflege,' " 13 January 1958. The comment by Baudissin's staff on this paper is in ZIF/ZUA, 3.1.2.2., "Fü B Bw B1, Az 35–08–07 'Stellungnahme zur Pflege der Tradition in der Bundeswehr,' " 8 November 1957.

Welcker, he was to draw up a plan to include the units in Bundeswehr garrisons until 1914, after 1918, and up to 1933.

Baudissin's staff agreed with Meier-Welcker's territorial solution, in part because it argued against the takeover of specific lineages and honors. Baudissin's staff also suggested an additional chapter on the meaning and contents of tradition to be added to the directive on lineage and honors to prevent the traditions question from developing in an unfavorable direction. Despite such support from Baudissin's group, Meier-Welcker's concept of tradition really seems to have incorporated very few of Baudissin's ideas. Rather, Meier-Welcker seems to have equated lineages and honors with tradition and insisted that tradition serve an educational purpose. These concepts were notable features of the old Reichswehr/Wehrmacht *Traditionspflege*.

WHILE the Armed Forces Staff pondered the issue, the forces took advantage of the absence of guidance from above and moved on their own. As is so often the case in a bureaucracy, events outpaced the ability of staff specialists to plan for them. The requests from the veterans were overtaken by the initiatives of local commanders, eager to improve the sagging morale of their new troops, who acted on their own in dealing with local veterans organizations.[12]

In one instance of February 1958, the *Panzer* Battalion 2 in Hemer, Westphalia took part in the two hundredth anniversary of the Blücher Hussars with an honor guard at the celebrations of the veterans association. The Bundeswehr unit ceremonially assumed the lineage and honors of the three Hussar regiments of the imperial period (among them the Death's Head Hussars of Danzig) and the traditions of the Reichswehr/Wehrmacht Cavalry Regiment 5 of Stolp in Pomerania, a unit that had maintained the lineage and honors of the "Death's Head Hussars" in the 1920s and early 1930s. For political reasons, the Bundeswehr commander and the veterans of the Blücher Hussars agreed on the phrase "guardianship" to describe the event.[13]

---

[12] For an example of this local maintenance of tradition, see "Panzeraufklärer— Husaren von Heute" in *Deutsches Soldatenjahrbuch 1963: Elfter deutscher Soldatenkalender*, ed. Helmut Damerau (München, 1963), pp. 128–29.

[13] ZIF/ZUA, 3.1.2.2., "Schreiben, Kommandeur, Panzerbataillon (PzBtl) 2 an Befehlshaber, Kommando Territoriale Verteidigung (KTV)," 17 March 1958.

In an explanation to his higher headquarters, the commander of the unit wrote that he had been a member of Cavalry Regiment 5 in the mid-1930s, where he had served as a lieutenant. Many of the members of his battalion were from the eastern territories of the former Reich, because there was a high percentage of displaced persons from central and eastern Germany in the Bundeswehr. The commander believed that his self-initiated maintenance of tradition was a proper way to keep alive memories of the imperial and Reichswehr garrisons of Danzig and Stolp. More important, the troops had reacted positively to the new lineage and honors. To further raise the *esprit de corps*, he asked permission from his higher headquarters to rename the *Panzer-kaserne* in Hemer in honor of Marshal Blücher.[14]

At the same time, Baudissin himself visited the unit. In a conversation with the officers in the club, he pointed to the crests on the wall that recalled the garrisons of Danzig and Stolp. To highlight the possible political difficulties of these seemingly innocent decorations, Baudissin asked the officers how they would have reacted on seeing similar crests in a Polish officers club in 1937. It would no doubt have struck Germans of the time as an expression of Polish designs on the Free City. Plainly, the effort of the Bundeswehr to "keep alive the memory of the lost eastern territories" could easily be misinterpreted by its critics as military revanchism.[15]

In a similar incident, the staff of the military headquarters for Hesse, Rhineland-Palatinate, and Saarland (*Wehrbereichskommando IV*) learned from the *Kasseler Tageszeitung* that Infantry Regiment 42 had taken over the unit insignia of Jäger Battalion 3 of the Reichswehr Infantry Regiment 15: the elk's head with the St. Hubertus cross that signified all German hunters, a popular and widespread symbol. The elite Jäger units of woodsmen armed with accurate weapons from Electoral Hesse in the seventeenth century had been among the first Jäger troops in Germany. Eager to make this connection with the local heritage, the commander had already mounted the crest on the gate of his headquarters.[16]

---

[14] Ibid.

[15] Interview with Professor Wolf Graf von Baudissin, May 1984.

[16] ZIF/ZUA, 3.1.2.2., "Wehrbereichskommando IV (Mainz), Chef des Stabes an Fü B über Kommando Territoriale Verteidigung," 17 March 1958; "Hirschgeweih und Hubertuskreuz: Anstecknadel für junge Reservisten," in *Hessische Nachrichten*

THE *Innere Führung* staff realized that the policy of "let it grow" was fostering a proliferation of local initiatives, which required intervention, preferably in the form Meier-Welcker's territorial solution of a few months earlier.[17] In response, on 16 June 1958 Heusinger issued the following directive to the staffs of services and territorial defense:

1. An assumption of the traditions of old units by units of the Bundeswehr may not take place without the express permission of the Ministry of Defense.

2. Wishes among troops for the assumption of traditions, and similar requests from the veterans organizations are in every case to be directed to the Ministry of Defense.

3. For the time being, a thoroughgoing reserve is to be practiced in this question.[18]

Heusinger's caution reflected his belief that the question of lineage honors could only be addressed once the build-up of the armed forces had slowed. His directive was also tied to ongoing plans in the ministry for some kind of transfer of the old lineage and honors, to be directed from above.

These events coincided with a growing official exchange on the nature of tradition during 1958, as well as with Baudissin's departure from the ministry to take command of a brigade headquartered at Göttingen.[19] In a discussion with Heusinger some weeks before leaving Bonn, Baudissin presented the ideas of his staff on the question of military tradition. He left with the impression that Heusinger was "evasive . . . and seems to believe that the [traditions] question can

---

12 March 1958; "Grenadiere bald unter dem Hubertuskreuz," in *Kasseler Tageszeitung* 12 March 1958.

[17] ZIF/ZUA, 3.1.2.2., "Fü B I 3, Az 35–08–07, an Leiter Fü B I 'Traditionspflege in der Bundeswehr, Übernahme von Traditionstruppenteilen,' " 8 April 1958.

[18] ZIF/ZUA, 3.1.2.2., "Entwurf, Weisung, 'Traditionspflege' vom Generalinspekteur der Bundeswehr an Führung Heer, Luftwaffe, Marine Territoriale Verteidigung, und Inspektion Sanitätswesen," 12 June 1958.

[19] For the first time, the command staff published an article on the subject in the ministry's political education magazine for the ranks. See "Die Truppe fragt: Wie steht die Bundeswehr zur deutschen soldatischen Tradition?" in *Information für die Truppe*, 2 March 1958, pp. 49–51. For a speech by Heusinger at Locuum in March 1958, see the reprint in "Von Himmerod bis Andernach: Dokumente zur Entstehungsgeschichte der Bundeswehr," in *Schriftenreihe Innere Führung*, ed. BMVg (Bonn, 1985), pp. 160–65.

better be resolved without me."[20] Despite Baudissin's departure from the *Innere Führung* staff, his Siegburg colleagues in the recently formed Council for Questions of *Innere Führung*, Hans Bohnenkamp and Erich Weniger, took up lineage and honors in an ad hoc subcommittee upon the request of the ministry. This group produced several position papers on military tradition during 1958 and 1959 that were very much in the spirit of the Siegburg meetings.[21] The council assumed a central role in making the policy on military tradition, which it has maintained up to the present.

Worried that the assumption of lineage and honors would open the door to those whom the PGA had tried to exclude, the members of the council refused to accept such a transfer. Many of these units had "glorified bloody battles without sufficient criticism," in cases where better and more responsible leadership could have avoided such losses. Alluding to the recent public debate on the introduction of nuclear weapons into the Bundeswehr, the members of the subcommittee wrote that in an era of such weapons, this transfer of lineage and honors would give an "almost frivolous image" to the troops about the responsibility for life and about the lethality of warfare.

In response to the often-made claim that the Bundeswehr must help to integrate former soldiers into West German society and win them for the new forces, members of the council countered that the traditions associations could not be equated with the former soldiers of the Wehrmacht, nor were they the main reservoir of recruits for the Bundeswehr. In most cases, the traditions associations represented one specific generation and its kind of thinking. The troops of the Bundeswehr could no longer "reeducate" these old soldiers; they had

---

[20] Entry from Wolf Graf von Baudissin's personal diary, 3 May 1958, cited in Claus Freiherr von Rosen, "Tradition als Last: Probleme mit dem Traditionsangebot der 'Gruppe Inneres Gefüge' (1951–1958) im Leitbild 'Staatsbürger in Uniform' für die Tradition der Bundeswehr," in *Tradition als Last*, ed. Klaus M. Kodalle (Köln, 1981), p. 177. For the state of his thinking at the time of his departure, see ZIF/ZUA, 3.1.2.2., "Schule der Bundeswehr für Innere Führung, 'Stichwörter des Vortrages von Oberst Graf von Baudissin zum Thema: Tradition,' " 10 June 1958; ZIF/ZUA, 0.2.1., "Oberst Graf von Baudissin, 'Abschiedsansprache in Bonn am 30. 6. 1958,' " n.d.

[21] See "Gutachten des Unterausschusses des Beirates für Fragen der Inneren Führung, Zur Neubegründung von Traditionsverhältnissen," 11 December 1958; "Beirat für Fragen der Inneren Führung, Gutachten zur Neubegründung der Traditionsverhältnissen," 5 March 1959, both consulted by the writer.

enough to do with just educating themselves. The members of the council nonetheless endorsed the territorial and branch-oriented solution to the transfer problem.

The debate on tradition between the service staffs and the institutions responsible for implementing *Innere Führung* revealed other conflicting aspects of the problem. In June 1958, the personnel officers (G1, S1, and A1) who oversaw *Innere Führung* in their commands met in Bonn/Duisdorf for a personnel officers conference and a command post planning exercise or "war game." Among the tasks of the war game was a problem on tradition. The G1/A1 officers agreed that in the next twelve months they would be swamped with details of traditions transfers, in addition to the myriad other tasks of raising troop units. The whole issue should be put off for another year.[22]

At the same time, another of the groups charged with thinking about military tradition, the *Innere Führung* school in Koblenz, had offered a seminar on the issue.[23] The specialist on tradition on the *Innere Führung* staff in the ministry, Major Schütz, spoke to a group of commanders as part of this seminar.[24] The discussion of military tradition quickly took a prominent place in the school's work. The staff in Koblenz collected opinions on lineage and honors; generally they found that the honoring of the Prussian reformers and the men of the Twentieth of July provoked antagonism and disbelief among many participants. On numerous occasions, the class members demanded to know why the military deeds of the Wehrmacht—that is to say, their own or those of their fathers—were not given their due by the Bundeswehr. For them, a transfer of lineage and honors was both desirable and natural.[25]

By the end of 1958, the army staff had finally prepared a detailed plan for the transfer of the lineage and honors of the army of 1939 to

[22] ZIF/ZUA, 3.1.2.2., "Fü B I 3, Notiz für Leiter, Fü B I, 'Tradition,' " 3 November 1958.

[23] ZIF/ZUA, 3.1.2.2., "Fü B I, Fü B I 3 Az: 35–08–07 an Schule der Bundeswehr für Innere Führung, 'Seminar Tradition' beim IX. Kommandeurlehrgang," 3 October 1958. An example of this kind of seminar is to be found in ZIF/ZUA, 3.1.2.2., "Schule der Bundeswehr für Innere Führung, Lehrgruppe I 'Soldatische Tradition' Major i.G. von Ilsemann," 15 August 1959.

[24] Major Heinz Karst, Hans-Adolf Jacobsen, and Major Carl-Gero von Ilsemann were among the early lecturers on the subject at the Koblenz school.

[25] Interviews with Lieutenant General Carl-Gero von Ilsemann, June 1984, and with Brigadier General Heinz Karst, July 1984.

the army planned for 1961. Nevertheless, Heusinger directed that ". . . the transfer by the Bundeswehr of individual lineage and honors of former units of the Wehrmacht after 1933 cannot be considered at this time." All subsequent requests for these transfers were to be postponed until further arrangements had been made by the Bundeswehr staff.[26]

These "further arrangements" involved a ministerial decree on tradition that had its official start in 1957 under Baudissin, but which had roots going all the way back to Weinheim, Siegburg, and Bad Tönnisstein. The leadership of the armed forces now concentrated on producing a general decree that would address a full range of issues concerning tradition. The writing of the decree continued until the summer of 1965. This delay of several years allowed the proliferation of local traditions to go on unchecked, even against the directives of higher headquarters. In relation to this major issue of the inner structure with great symbolic value, the Bundeswehr staff in the years of further discussion stood by its early decision not to transfer lineage and honors. The Armed Forces Staff acceded to the wishes of its civilian advisers, prohibiting the restoration of a Reichswehr convention, despite the contrary demands from active duty and retired soldiers and from the population of local garrisons. Ultimately, the technical problems were simply too great for such a transfer. In arriving at such a policy, however, the Bundeswehr underscored its own discontinuity as part of its general effort of reform.[27]

[26] ZIF/ZUA, 3.1.2.2., "BMVg, Fü B I 4, Az 35–08–07, an alle Kommandeure und Chefs selbstständiger Einheiten," 17 December 1958. The Army Staff's memorandum is in ZIF/ZUA, 3.1.2.2., "Fü H I 3, Az 35–08–07 an Fü B I 'Übernahme von Traditionen,' " 4 October 1958.

[27] Harder, "Traditionspflege," p. 26.

11. Early Drafts of the Decree: The Role of Theodor Heuss and the Council on *Innere Führung*

THE DECISION in the Ministry of Defense to issue a decree on military tradition went against the desires and beliefs of many in West German society. To them, it seemed that such a decree would be nothing more than a typically bureaucratic and authoritarian example of the overregulation of German life. As one high-ranking officer observed looking back on this choice from the perspective of the mid-1980s, "One really has to be a German to decree in writing what tradition must be."[1] Contemporary participants in the official discussion of the problem protested that the ministry should allow the Bundeswehr to form its own traditions without interference from above, unconsciously echoing Heusinger's earlier observation of 1954 at Bad Tönnisstein. However, by 1959 recent difficulties with lineage and honors and the constant scrutiny from the outside world—the editor of *Spiegel*, Rudolf Augstein, wanted to do an article on the subject—forced the ministry to abandon its policy of "let it grow" and to assume an active role in resolving the problem.

The tone of the ministry's work was set by Theodor Heuss's speech at the *Führungsakademie* (Command and General Staff College) in Hamburg on 12 March 1959.[2] In his well-received and widely publicized presentation in praise of the new army, Heuss recalled the controversy of 1956 over the uniform of the Bundeswehr, and in an ironic tone, he condemned the superficial aspects of military conventions: "Keep away from me the merely decorative!" Warning that caution was necessary in the transfer of lineage and honors, Heuss observed that the serious nature of modern war precluded the Bundeswehr

[1] Letter from General Gerd Schmückle to the writer, April 1986.
[2] Theodor Heuss, *Soldatentum in unserer Zeit* (Tübingen, 1959).

from becoming an "association for the telling of outdated fairy-tales."[3] Instead he encouraged the new forces to make a spiritual connection with the men of the Twentieth of July and to form its own traditions.

Much like Baudissin's ideas on tradition in content, although delivered in a more conversational manner, Heuss's comments were laudable proposals from an individual of great moral authority. The ministry's authors included these remarks in their work, but the drafting of a decree was considerably more difficult than the writing of a speech. Again, as had happened in the planning phases for the new forces, the ministry brought into the decision-making process a wide variety of advisers, many of whom were veterans of the inner structure debates. This move was a calculated effort to prevent eventual criticism by appealing to the authority of a number of experts.[4] The first drafts of the decree included position papers from both the Council on *Innere Führung* and the Military History Office as well as from prominent members of the educated middle class and the legislative branch. In early 1959, the SPD parliamentary deputy from Hamburg, Helmut Schmidt, asked the Ministry of Defense to involve the defense committee of the Bundestag in the preparation of the decree. Heusinger agreed, and the defense committee joined in the review of all drafts to be presented to the minister of defense. Although a noteworthy feature of the process within the Bundeswehr involved the cooperation of many groups on civil-military issues, the many viewpoints—and the inevitable conflicts—contributed greatly to the nearly eight years it took to publish the final decree.[5]

THE DOCUMENT would finally have to answer the question, first posed at Siegburg, of what should be handed down from the past to the new army. It would have to be an enduring answer, because a ministerial decree bore far greater weight than did all previous pronouncements on the subject. Many in the staff already recognized the dangers of such a statement. At the high point of the first ministerial work on the traditions decree in early 1959, while the first coordinating draft of the paper was making the rounds of the service chiefs, the

[3] Ibid., p. 19.
[4] Hans-Joachim Harder, "Traditionspflege in der Bundeswehr," unpublished manuscript, 1983, p. 28.
[5] Interview with Major General Dr. Eberhard Wagemann, June 1984.

specialists of the navy staff warned that there was no reason at the moment to bring out a decree on tradition. The naval leadership feared that the ministry would arrive at a decree in a haphazard way without sufficient reflection.[6]

The Bundesmarine had actually been the first of the services to confront the problem of tradition, when events seemed to warn that the new navy of the 1950s might become a center of controversy because of its heritage. The self-image of the navy that emerged from defeat after 1945 contrasted strongly with that of 1918. The navy had neither caused the Second World War through its existence nor hastened the defeat through mutiny. The professional naval officer corps looked proudly on its achievements in battle, especially in submarine warfare. Fatefully enough, however, the naval leadership had also failed to participate in the resistance to Hitler, and the Führer had named Admiral Karl Dönitz as his successor just before the end of the war. The verdicts at Nuremberg against Erich Raeder and Dönitz disturbed the surviving naval leadership for many years.

These issues had come to a head in early 1956 as the first sailors put on their uniforms. In the first address before the naval training company in Wilhelmshaven, Kapitän zur See Karl Adolf Zenker, chief naval planner in the *Dienststelle Blank*, had defended the military record of Raeder and Dönitz. He somewhat dramatically revealed to his audience that he had sought Raeder's blessing to serve the Federal Republic.[7] Once news of the speech reached the public, Zenker's comments prompted a debate in the Bundestag on military tradition and the future of the soldier in the Federal Republic. Saying that the military needed good traditions, Carlo Schmid demanded that the new navy distance itself from "Hitler's helpers." The Bundeswehr, in Schmid's view, should foster a tradition of "humanity and human dignity," as exemplified by Scharnhorst, Clausewitz, Graf Spee, the men of the Twentieth of July, and Martin Niemöller.

These recent events were clearly on the mind of the first Chief of

---

[6] The staff comment suggested that Heuss's speech be used as a statement of policy. ZIF/ZUA, 3.1.2.2., "Inspekteur Marine an GenInsp Bundeswehr," 18 March 1959; interview with Admiral Friedrich Ruge, April 1984.

[7] Deutscher Bundestag, *Stenographische Berichte*, 140. Sitzung, 18 April 1956, pp. 7207–08. Norbert Wiggershaus, "Zum Problem der Tradition im Vorfeld eines westdeutschen Verteidigungsbeitrages," unpublished manuscript, 1983, pp. 23–24.

Staff of the Navy, Vice Admiral Friedrich Ruge, when he spoke of naval tradition in a letter to commanders written in early 1957.[8] A veteran of four German navies in his lifetime, Ruge recalled vividly the destructive political effects of the maintenance of imperial traditions in the 1920s. Nevertheless, he also believed in the importance of history and naval tradition for the self-image of the Bundesmarine. In his letter to the commanders, Ruge pointed out that tradition was a moral term that included all the virtues and values that had proven themselves enduring through generations. These traditions had been forged in the fire of history, obliterating what was worthless and leaving behind the remainder as a "hard currency that each new generation finds worth having." Symbols were the means for tradition to become "visible and binding." Persons, things, and names serve as symbols for the navy, but Ruge also warned against their danger by drawing an image from the seafarer's world: "Symbols are like lighthouses to determine one's position and to set course. If they are distant, one can safely sail towards them; if they are close, one will avoid going aground only with great difficulty."[9]

RUGE'S LETTER on tradition was the first official guidance of its kind in the West German armed forces, but it addressed only the navy—the service that seemed the least tainted by its past, despite its failure to participate in the resistance to Hitler. Although Ruge's letter contained interesting insights, it left untouched several difficult ethical issues of the recent past that confronted the armed forces as a whole. In composing the ministerial traditions decree, the staff had to face these issues. The two most noteworthy were the legacy of the Twentieth of July plot and the relationship of tradition to history in regard to the self-image of the Bundeswehr.

Baudissin's honoring of the men of the Twentieth of July in the first years of the new army had been a bold attempt to resolve the dilemma of command and obedience—of the oath and the right to resistance—that the Nazis and the war had left behind. The Weinheim

---

[8] ZIF/ZUA, 3.1.2.2., "Kommandeur Brief Nr. 3/1957, BMVg VII A 3," 27 February 1957. Interview with Admiral Friedrich Ruge, April 1984. See Friedrich Ruge, *In vier Marinen, Lebenserinnerungen als Beitrag zur Zeitgeschichte* (München, 1979).

[9] ZIF/ZUA, 3.1.2.2., "Kommandeur Brief Nr. 3/1957, BMVg VII A 3," 27 February 1957.

requirements and the PGA had invested this chapter of the recent past with great importance. Heuss's appeal to the new forces in 1959 to make a connection with the spirit of the military resistance to Hitler, as well as the earlier importance of the Twentieth of July in the PGA and the Sonthofen courses, required the ministry to take a position on the military resistance as part of the decree. Such a statement would have to go beyond Baudissin's speeches and writings or Hans Christian Trentzsch's Sonthofen piece. The scope of the exchanges among the staff included some thirty separate draft proposals from the specialists in the ministry.[10] The struggle to find a common formula on this issue significantly delayed the formulation of the decree. The basis for all these drafts was a position paper from the Council on *Innere Führung*.

As they had since the start of the discussion of the inner structure at Weinheim in 1951 and Bad Tönnisstein in 1954, the civilian academic advisers to the armed forces chose the resistance to Hitler as a major feature of the military heritage they considered valid and worthy to be emulated. In its position paper of March 1959, the members of the Council for *Innere Führung* strongly advocated making the Twentieth of July a principal source of tradition for the Bundeswehr.[11] The members of the council paraphrased the guidelines from the PGA: "the touchstone of whether the Bundeswehr can develop its own traditions from itself" lay in its ability spiritually to come to terms with the Twentieth of July and to appreciate its historical meaning. The military resistance would give the Bundeswehr the model of great soldiers, who "placed the call of their troubled conscience above obedience to an unworthy authority."[12]

In addressing the problem of honoring the majority of soldiers who fought to the end, the council had this to say:

Undeniably, great military achievements—even those of the last war—form a memory that should be included in the heritage now being developed. Great deeds were done again and again, especially against superior forces and under a bad supreme command. Pride in these cannot lead to a blurred depiction of wartime events, and still less to a political justifica-

[10] Harder, "Traditionspflege," p. 13.
[11] "Beirat für Fragen der Inneren Führung, 'Gutachten zur Neubegründung der Traditionsverhältnissen,' " 5 March 1959, consulted by the writer.
[12] Ibid., p. 3

tion of the last war. With such critical distinction, it should be possible to take up those experiences where responsible officers upheld and developed free forms of leadership and command despite attempts from above to limit these through a lack of trust. [Worthy of the tradition of the Bundeswehr] were types of command where the relationship of trust between superior and subordinate, and officer and soldier took on new forms.[13]

Major Schütz, on the *Innere Führung* educational staff in the ministry, repeated the essence of these ideas in his first draft of the decree on tradition for Heusinger. But he added an important revision, obviously drawn from Trentzsch's speech at Sonthofen, that the honoring of the participants in the Twentieth of July "does not discriminate against those, who from their point of view or conception of responsibility, took another path of obedience out of honest conviction."[14]

As is usually the case, the draft decree underwent more changes on the way up the chain of command. These revisions altered the interpretation of the Twentieth of July yet again. Major Schütz's draft received a single but important addition from the ministry *Innere Führung* staff section chief, Colonel von Wangenheim, who underlined "*ein Prüfstein*" (a touchstone) to mean one of several. This underlining pushed the balance of the draft in favor of the necessity of obedience.[15]

This first ministerial answer to the tradition question was ill-fated. The attempted balance between resistance and obedience in the draft decree won the blessings of neither side. The Chief of the Armed Forces Staff, Major General Cordt von Hobe, commented that the decree was intelligently laid out but "foreign to the troops."[16] Heusinger ultimately refused to sign the document once it reached his desk, but not before he suggested deleting the passage "the pride in these [military accomplishments] should not lead to a political justification of the Second World War." In contrast, Heusinger insisted on

---

[13] Ibid.
[14] ZIF/ZUA, 3.1.2.2., "Handschriftlicher Entwurf, Traditionserlass (Fü B I 3, Major Schütz)," 6 March 1959, p. 4. For more on Major Schütz's ideas on the maintenance of tradition at this time, see "Fü B I 3, 'Tradition, Traditionsbildung und Traditionspflege in der Bundeswehr,' " March 1959, consulted by the writer.
[15] Harder, "Traditionspflege," p. 15.
[16] ZIF/ZUA, 3.1.2.2., "Vermerk, Chef des Stabes, Fü B," 9 March 1959.

an increased emphasis on the need for recognizing those who had taken "another path of obedience."[17]

Despite this initial failure in the first half of 1959, the work on the traditions decree continued among the staff. The military leadership soon had an opportunity to follow the injunction of President Heuss to make an example of the military resistance. On 20 July 1959, the fifteenth anniversary of the attempt on Hitler's life, Heusinger issued an order of the day drafted by Gerd Schmückle and Wolfram von Raven that commemorated the event as a "bright spot in Germany's darkest time."[18] The soldiers of the Bundeswehr stood "in honor before the sacrifice of those men, whose consciences were called [to act] by their knowledge. They are the best witnesses against the collective guilt of the German people. Their attitude and spirit are an example to us all."[19]

This statement was the first on the military resistance that had the imprimatur of the highest-ranking officer in West Germany, finally fulfilling the demands for such guidance that dated from the early 1950s. The wording of the order also clearly reflected the ongoing debate within the ministry regarding the traditions decree on the issues of resistance and obedience. The passage describing those "whose consciences were called by their knowledge" sought to distinguish between members of the Wehrmacht in positions of authority who might have had an overview of the political situation and the mass of soldiers who were ignorant of events. In effect, then, while the Bundeswehr made heroes of Stauffenberg and his co-conspirators, the soldiers at the front, who could not know the full extent of Nazi crimes, had been justified in fighting on in a spirit of duty and self-sacrifice.

[17] ZIF/ZUA, 3.1.2.2., "Fü B I, Leiter, 'Vermerk bei Vorlage Traditionserlass am 11. März 1959,' " 13 March 1959. Further details about the outcome of this version of the decree are in "Fü B I Ltr. Az 35–08–07 an Generalinspekteur, Erlass 'Traditionsbildung und Traditionspflege in der Bundeswehr,' " 9 April 1959; "Fü B I 4, 'Zeittafel Traditionserlass,' " 21 March 1959, both documents consulted by the writer.
[18] ZIF/ZUA, 0.4.7.1.2., "GenInsp Bw, Fü B I 6, Az 35–20–17–50, 'Zum 15. Jahrestag des 20. Juli,' " 20 July 1959. Letter from Gerd Schmückle to the writer, April 1986.
[19] ZIF/ZUA, 0.4.7.1.2., "GenInsp Bw, Fü B I 6, Az 35–20–17–50, 'Zum 15. Jahrestag des 20. Juli,' " 20 July 1959. The use of this guidance in 1959 contrasts to the celebration of the event in 1958. *Information für die Truppe* had reprinted an excerpt from Heusinger's *Befehl im Widerstreit*, see "Zum 20. Juli," *Information für die Truppe*, 10, 1958, pp. 425–28.

Although in the years after 1945 many Germans deftly used their ignorance of events as an excuse for Nazi atrocities—and the generation of 1968 bitterly attacked such distinctions as historically unpalatable—this differentiation between a politically informed leadership and a less-aware rank and file was nonetheless a necessary one to draw at the time.[20] As long as the armed forces included many former officers and NCOs from the Reichswehr and Wehrmacht, the leadership had little choice but to accommodate their pasts without completely damning it, as denazification and reeducation had done in the immediate aftermath of the war.[21] By signing the July 1959 order of the day, Heusinger had in fact publicly underscored his own knowledge of the misdeeds of the Nazi political leadership, since in July 1944 he had been chief of the army operations staff present at Rastenburg and was among the "better informed."

During the 1960s, the officially sanctioned honoring of the Twentieth of July came into its own in the ranks of the Bundeswehr, even though opinion polls still revealed widespread public antipathy to the event. The yearly celebration of the *Attentat* at the unit level assumed considerable importance for the self-image of the armed forces and it proved popular among the younger soldiers. After 1961, it became common practice to name facilities of the Bundeswehr in honor of the men of the resistance and for commanders of units of all sizes to commemorate members of the conspiracy in small presentations.[22] These speeches often linked the *Attentat* at Rastenburg and the 17 June 1953 revolt against the East German communist regime. Each had been an "uprising of conscience" against a totalitarian rule afflicting the German people. Of course, this spiritual connection was well

[20] Interviews with General Ulrich de Maizière, June 1984; with General Johann Adolf Graf von Kielmansegg, June 1984; with Colonel Dr. Norbert Wiggershaus, July 1984; and with Lieutenant Colonel Dr. Helmuth Schubert, July 1984.

[21] For an interesting discussion of the change in popular attitudes about the Nazi past in the course of the late 1950s and early 1960s, see Hans-Peter Schwarz, *Die Ära Adenauer: Epochenwechsel 1957–1963*, vol. 3 in *Geschichte der Bundesrepublik Deutschland*, ed. Karl-Dietrich Bracher, 5 vols. (Stuttgart, 1983), pp. 204–15.

[22] "Appell am 20. Juli," *Information für die Truppe*, 8, 1961, pp. 491–97; DOK-ZENTBw, Nr. R6359, Hauptmann Heinz Schumann, "Der deutsche Widerstand gegen die NS Diktatur in den Informationsschriften der Bundeswehr zur politischen Bildung," Führungsakademie der Bundeswehr, Generalstabs/Admiralstabs Lehrgang, 6 October 1978; Siegfried Grimm, *"Der Bundesrepublik treu zu dienen"*: *die geistige Rüstung der Bundeswehr* (Düsseldorf, 1970), pp. 179–81.

suited to the atmosphere of the cold war and reflected the prevailing interpretations of totalitarianism in political science and history.

This development had an unintended effect abroad. The growing acceptance of the Twentieth of July in the Bundeswehr unsettled West Germany's French allies. As the Algerian war reached its bloody climax in 1961–62, a group of terrorist French officers appealed to the tradition of the military conspiracy against Hitler to lend historical authority to their resistance against Algerian independence under Charles De Gaulle.[23] This turn of events demonstrated that West Germans had to deal with their maintenance of tradition within an international context that was no less intractable than the domestic one. The further problems of military tradition revealed themselves in the attempt of historians associated with the ministry to sketch out an official image of history for the Bundeswehr.

[23] Jesco von Puttkammer, "Von Zossen nach Bonn: eine Bilanz der deutschen Wiederbewaffnung," *Bestandaufnahme: eine deutsche Bilanz, 1962*, ed. Hans Werner Richter (München, 1962), pp. 93–105.

12. The Search for Franz-Josef Strauss's Image of History

PROBLEMS of lineage and honors and of the Twentieth of July were two prominent aspects of military tradition that had to be resolved in the traditions decree. In their final sense, however, they were a part of a greater debate on the interplay of tradition and history. During 1961–62, the specialists addressed this connection in an interesting exchange between the Bundeswehr staff and the leading academics preparing the decree.

When an early version of the decree reached the desk of Minister of Defense Franz-Josef Strauss, he found fault with the absence of specific events and personalities in the draft as well as its failure to offer an overall historical conception. Later efforts also aroused his displeasure. "I cannot bring myself to sign such a draft," Strauss wrote. "If it is not possible to put forth a better and more satisfactory version, then I would prefer the tradition of the Bundeswehr develop on its own instead of signing this draft decree and subjecting it to the general public criticism [that would follow]."[1]

Referring to complaints that *Innere Führung* was too vaguely defined at the troop level, Minister Strauss insisted on a greater clarity of historical examples in future drafts of the decree. He directed that these include a compact and usable "image of history." This missing image of history and other deficiencies in the drafting of the decree prompted Strauss to include several individuals outside of the ministry in the project. Added to the group were Brigadier General Ulrich de Maizière, commander of the *Innere Führung* School; Professor Dr. Gerhard Möbus, chief of the Research Staff of the *Innere Führung* School; and Colonel Dr. Hans Meier-Welcker of the military history staff. Strauss also listed a handful of notable academics and publicists who should be invited to join the work: Gerhard Ritter, Percy Ernst

[1] ZIF/ZUA, 3.1.2.2., "Vermerk, Minister Strauss," 4 April 1961, pp. 1–2.

194

Schramm, Reinhard Höhn, Max Braubach, and Walter Görlitz. These established historians had published important accounts of the military and politics in the 1950s and 1960s. Absent from this list was Baudissin, who was leaving his brigade at Göttingen to go to the NATO staff of Allied Forces Central Europe in Fontainebleau, where in the normal course of work he would not necessarily be involved with the decree.[2]

COLONEL Meier-Welcker's discourse with the historians expanded in conversation and correspondence to include Werner Conze and Hans-Günter Zmarzlik. Meier-Welcker and his civilian colleagues tried to differentiate between history and tradition, but they failed to agree on a valid image of history for the Bundeswehr's use. In his reply to the ministry, Meier-Welcker made important observations about the nature of tradition, much in contrast to his earlier paper of 1957.[3] As a scholarly discipline, history could be of little help to military tradition. He elaborated on this point at some length:

According to its essence, tradition is unchanging, continuous, naively free of problems and exclusively positive in its statement. In order to eliminate the discrepancy between historical reality and tradition-bound conceptions, the image of history is adapted and idealized to the dominant ideas of the moment. The person who believes in tradition takes from the old and antiquated ideas as much as he likes; he is thus conservative. In addition, however, he imposes his ideas and those of his time on the past. In this way, he receives an unbroken picture of "authentic" soldierhood, "authentic" comradeship and "authentic" soldierly virtues. . . . But the word history has a double meaning. History . . . is full of problems and criticism. History tries to grasp events and personalities in their contemporary reality. It seeks to comprehend problems in their own time, neither as symbols nor as spiritual and moral values. It does not support tradition; rather, it destroys the simple unity of its ideals. History and historical consciousness, on the one side, and traditional consciousness, on the other, lie at two different levels. Each has its own purpose and

---

[2] Many of the Bundeswehr officers with whom this writer spoke said that service in NATO staffs is regarded as a kind of exile from the Bundeswehr itself.

[3] ZIF/ZUA, 3.1.2.2., "MGFA I, Az 35–08–07, an BMVg Fü B I mit Anlage 'Grundgedanken zur Bearbeitung des Traditionserlasses,'" 16 November 1961; ZIF/ZUA, 3.1.2.2., "Fü B, Fü B I 3, Az 35–08–07, an Minister über Staatssekretär," n.d.

value. If one places them in relation to one another, then they contradict each other.[4]

Meier-Welcker observed that the decree was the first attempt in German military history to prepare an overall directive on tradition in the armed forces. In the past, military leaders had often decreed that tradition was to be respected, but the symbols and the values were generally known. The *Kriegsherr* had only to remind the soldiers of them. The military sense of tradition had always been there, so that a specific decree upon which to base tradition had been unnecessary. After the catastrophe of recent history had called all values and symbols into question, there was little agreement of any kind about tradition in West Germany. This lack of consensus contrasted with the outward unity of opinion on military tradition in Seeckt's Reichswehr. An arbitrary choice of examples from the past to support policy was a political act, not a historical one. If a historian prepared an image of history that corresponded to the nature of tradition, then it could only be regarded as a forgery of history.

Meier-Welcker concluded that tradition was ever-present and was always renewing itself, since no human being could exist without it. One could not reject tradition, one had to use it. The Bundeswehr, however, had to separate itself from old traditions that had nothing more to give to the new army. One need not quarrel with the historical values of these older traditions, which applied to another army at another time. The values of the present must be the sole measure of the spiritual direction of the Bundeswehr; only they could guide the choice of what was worthy of tradition.[5]

The exchange of ideas underscored the difficulties of the Bundeswehr in combining tradition and history. Without exception, Meier-Welcker wrote, the historians rejected the idea that the traditions decree could be based on any "briefly outlined image of history." In general, however, the academics agreed with the overall idea of the decree, although there were dissenting voices.

The others were invited to respond to Meier-Welcker's memorandum. Professor Percy Ernst Schramm wrote to register his doubts: "I would go further than [your] solid memorandum which I immedi-

[4] Meier-Welcker, "Grundgedanken," pp. 2–3.
[5] Ibid., p. 9.

ately read with great attention. I am actually shocked that such a decree is planned!" Convinced that it was too soon for such a measure, Schramm believed that all artificial attempts to found tradition would inevitably alienate people; instead, one should allow tradition to grow of its own accord. Professor Werner Conze, on the other hand, commented: "I find your memorandum outstanding; [I] am critical and must warn, however, against any panicky attempts. But I encourage the formation of a modern and appropriate tradition with the understanding that tradition is neither 'grown' in place nor made artificially. Rather it can and should be guided, awakened, and planted through many sensible deliberations."[6]

Finally, Professor Gerhard Ritter made perhaps the most insightful comments on the nature of history and tradition. "Nevertheless, political integration and an effective historical tradition form themselves only where a struggle has ended in victory."[7] Obviously this situation did not apply to the Bundeswehr. He warned against an overemphasis on the negative aspects of history, since these posed a potential threat to the political integration of the soldier in society.

One may not regard the question of tradition and history solely from the standpoint of a historian. Historical thinking rightly defends itself against falsifying history for a specific political purpose. . . . But without an image of history that leads to a clear, precise, I don't mind if simplified, but in any event tangible conception of the past, the formation of an otherwise indispensable tradition will be impossible.[8]

An image of history that was reduced to myth was dangerous, but Ritter advised that one should not place the great achievements and values of the past in too critical a light, as this practice would "destroy contemporary self-confidence." Conscious of the limitations on the new forces, Ritter suggested to Meier-Welcker that the new army find

[6] "Schreiben, P. E. Schramm, Historisches Seminar der Universität Göttingen an Oberst Dr. Meier-Welcker," 15 November 1961; "Schreiben, Dr. Werner Conze, Hegelhausen/Heidelberg an Oberst Dr. Hans Meier-Welcker," 1 January 1962, p. 1. Both documents consulted by the writer.

[7] "Schreiben, Professor Dr. Gerhard Ritter, Universität Freiburg an Oberst i.G. Dr. Meier-Welcker," 4 December 1961. The published version of this letter is in Klaus Schwabe and Rolf Reichardt, eds., *Gerhard Ritter: Ein politischer Historiker in seinen Briefen* (Boppard, 1984), pp. 559–61. Original document consulted by the writer.

[8] Ibid.

a middle path between history and tradition, one which preserved historical memories "without erecting monuments to heroes or covering up unpleasant truths."

Ritter's observations neatly summed up the dilemma facing the Bundeswehr. The disasters of German history compelled the leaders of the West German armed forces to examine the past, a demand that worked against the formation of a tradition free of problems. Other countries in the twentieth century seemed quite willing to select the best from their pasts and ignore their failures, or to idealize their defeats into victories. Despite the fundamental validity of Ritter's comments, any attempt by the Bundeswehr to interpret its history in perhaps a less harsh light would be interpreted by its critics as an act of restoration.

WHEN Meier-Welcker's paper reached the ministry, the Bundeswehr Chief of Staff, Friedrich Foertsch, recognized the "fundamental soundness of the historians' viewpoints," but was more inclined to agree with the opinion of his Chief of Staff, Major General Albert Schnez.[9] Commenting on Meier-Welcker's memorandum, Schnez wrote, "Many bright ideas! However, the work could lead to the conclusion that this tired, old Europe no longer believes in itself." Europe, Schnez continued, had placed everything in doubt and had lost faith in itself. When skepticism of this kind made things so problematic, then everything was in doubt. He thought that the fixing of terms in the debate on tradition verged on decadence, although he quickly observed that this comment applied to "our spiritual and intellectual situation" and not to Meier-Welcker.[10]

In his written comment, Schnez asked rhetorically, "are there not some remedies for this tired, old Europe?" He realized that it was nearly impossible to demand a clear, hard, and unbroken soldierly line of thought, but there was a danger that the "pure bourgeois soldier" was falling victim to the general process "of softening up of the epoch and continent." Schnez believed that the traditions decree must find the "essential thing with enduring value in our world." This prescription would include "the forces which have proven themselves as the

<hr/>

[9] "Fü B, Fü B I 3, Minister über Staatssekretär. 'Erlassentwurf über Traditionsbildung und Traditionspflege,'" 3 March 1962, consulted by the writer.
[10] Ibid. Interview with General Albert Schnez, April 1984.

pillars of European and German history in all its peaks and valleys . . . from medieval chivalry to the technical ideal of the *Panzergeist* ('spirit of the armored branch')."[11]

Schnez, although doubtless a conservative, exemplified an attitude within the Bundeswehr all too simply described as reactionary. Frequently identified by outside critics as a saboteur of *Innere Führung*, Schnez nonetheless did point to the need for an image of tradition that included more than negatives. His wish for some positive statement on tradition was reasonable enough, even if it was couched in the phrases almost always employed by the critics of *Innere Führung*. It echoed the apparent widespread opposition to Baudissin's emphasis on the Prussian reformers and on the military resistance to the Nazis.

The continuing work on the decree included other organizations in the *Innere Führung* structure. As head of the *Innere Führung* School, Brigadier General de Maizière rewrote the introduction and first passages to the draft decree that were under consideration in 1961–62. His work was guided by the belief that the decree should include a description of the mission of the armed forces, as well as the insight that the Bundeswehr should form its own traditions, and that this new tradition should be joined with the past. De Maizière also believed that the draft should include criteria for selection of persons and events worthy of the *Bundeswehrtradition*.[12] Nevertheless, de Maizière agreed with the scholars that one could not offer the minister of defense a single, compact image of history as the centerpiece of the directive on tradition.

These requirements emerged in the introduction to the subsequent draft, the fourth separate draft by the staff specialists made after a total of twenty studies and preliminary drafts were done. The new version stated that society was in the grasp of thorough social change; totalitarian forces, especially communism, threatened the Federal Republic; Germany was divided—a part of the German population lived un-

---

[11] "Fü B, Fü B I 3, Minister über Staatssekretär. 'Erlassentwurf über Traditionsbildung und Traditionspflege,'" 3 March 1962, consulted by the writer. Hans-Joachim Harder, "Traditionspflege in der Bundeswehr," unpublished manuscript, 1983, pp. 36–37.

[12] ZIF/ZUA, 3.1.2.2., "INFüSBw, Kdr. Az 35–08–07, Tgb. Nr. 521/62," 22 January 1962; ZIF/ZUA, 3.1.2.2., "Fü B, Fü B I 3, Az 35–08–07, an Minister über Staatssekretär," 3 March 1962.

der the communist rule of force; technological developments had brought about a radical change in the nature of war; and the Federal Republic alone could no longer defend itself.[13]

The draft decree, written in part by de Maizière himself, acknowledged that the Bundeswehr's mission stood in the triad of the "Nation, Europe, and the Atlantic Community." After exhorting soldiers to develop their own traditions, the authors of the decree listed the virtues that were the criteria for a valid tradition. A brief reference to the Twentieth of July concluded: "The tragic events of the Twentieth of July 1944 show the final choices of conscience before which a soldier and his people can be placed."[14] This judgment was a far less ambitious statement than stood in the drafts of 1959. The draft decree also embraced the examples of the Prussian reforms and the "liberal developments in southern German military history" as valid for the tradition of the Bundeswehr.

LIKE ITS predecessor of 1959–60, however, the draft decree of 1962 was stillborn. Perhaps because the draft plainly failed to fulfill Strauss's wishes, Foertsch kept it under wraps for two months before presenting it to Minister Strauss, who downgraded its status from a ministerial decree to a set of ministerial guidelines. When the document was taken to the Bundestag defense committee, the members hinted to the ministry's representatives that the decree should be withdrawn altogether, since there was no hope of it being accepted. The draft decree had failed to give an adequate appreciation of the German soldier in both world wars or to praise the creators of the Bundeswehr.[15]

Eager to save face and avoid a clash with the legislative branch, the ministry withdrew the draft. Minister Strauss then ordered that a parliamentary deputy should participate in the further writing, which prompted one of the ministry staff to write in exasperation: "From

[13] "Der Bundesminister der Verteidigung, Fü B I 3, Az 35–08–07, 'Traditionsbildung und Traditionspflege in der Bundeswehr,' " n.d. [ca. March 1962], consulted by the writer.

[14] Ibid., p. 3.

[15] "Sitzung des Verteidigungsausschusses am 25.10.1962, 9. 30 Uhr-Soldatenbuch und Richtlinien für Tradition," n.d. [ca. October 1962], consulted by the writer; interview with Major General Dr. Eberhard Wagemann, March 1984.

the CDU? From the SPD? From the FDP? Each one wants something different!"[16] This comment was prescient. Another year passed
and the work in the ministry, hindered by the political differences
among the growing circles of the decree's authors, once more failed
to produce a result.

[16] "Handschriftlicher Notiz am Schreiben eines persönlichen Referenten im
Ministerium an Fü B I," n.d. [ca. 26 October 1962], consulted by the writer.

13. Colonel Wagemann Completes the Decree

THE DIFFICULTIES caused by the rapid growth of the Bundeswehr became more glaring as work proceeded in the ministry on the traditions decree. Several scandals drew attention to the weaknesses of the inner structure of the armed forces and cast doubt on the effectiveness of the reforms. The *Spiegel* affair of October 1962, which accelerated the decline of the Adenauer government, had begun with public revelations about NATO's assessment of the limited combat power of the Bundeswehr. This issue, however, was soon overshadowed by the wider scandal that followed the *Spiegel* affair, concerning freedom of press and democratic rights in the Federal Republic. Only a few months later, in mid-1963, news of abuses by training officers and NCOs against paratroop trainees at Nagold near Stuttgart caused an outcry about *Innere Führung* and training in the armed forces.[1] Borrowing practices from U.S. and French paratroops, Bundeswehr trainers subjected recruits to grueling forced marches and other physical abuses. In June 1963, this brutal treatment resulted in the death of a recruit. Added to these practices were accounts of unofficial celebrations in the paratroop training companies of the 1941 invasion of Crete. This misconduct was widely interpreted as a sign of an inner crisis in the Bundeswehr, and it forced a consideration of the issue of military tradition. In the local proliferations of a still-undefined *Bundeswehrtradition*, the soldiers were borrowing customs from the allies inconsistent with the principles of reform. Even though such physical abuses were prohibited by the military legislation and by additional regulations, the search for an elite

[1] "Inspekteur des Heeres, Tgb. Nr. 944/63, An die Kommandeure des Heeres, 'Zwischeninformation über die Vorkommnisse in Nagold,'" 5 December 1963, consulted by the writer; ZIF/ZUA, 2.6.5.4., "'Protokollarische Bemerkungen zu "Nagold" Offiziersausbildung am 16.01.1964,'" 24 January 1964; "Der Bundesminister der Verteidigung, 'Die Vorfälle in der Ausbildungskompanie 6/9 in Nagold,'" 31 January 1964, consulted by the writer.

self-image and tradition at the unit level seemed to be a symptom of greater ills.[2]

The Nagold affair was soon followed in June 1964 by a crisis that drew still greater public attention to the issue. The *Wehrbeauftragter* Hellmuth Heye published a series of articles in the magazine *Quick*, warning of the dangerous inner state of the armed forces.[3] Apparently acting out of frustration over the unwillingness of either the Bundestag or the ministry to respond to his concerns, Heye chose this spectacular method to call attention to the revival of the *Kommiss* in the ranks. Describing his wish to fulfill the promise of the reforms as a pipedream, Heye warned that he could no longer hold back the trend undermining *Innere Führung*. "If we don't turn the rudder around now," Heye wrote, "then the Bundeswehr will develop into the force we did not want. The trend towards a state within a state is unmistakable."[4] The outdated methods of training and the troop leadership at the unit level showed mere lip service to *Innere Führung*. The Bundeswehr was not only failing to create the "citizen in uniform," it was also losing the soldier's trust.

Heye also mentioned tradition. Defending himself against claims that he wanted to extinguish all traditions, he responded that one had to distinguish between proper and false traditions. Tradition was a spiritual thing, as he underscored with the famous quote attributed to Scharnhorst—"It [tradition] means to march at the head of progress"—and could be expressed in such simple things as naming Bundeswehr units after the part of Germany where they were stationed, a tradition of the old armies.

Although Heye's choice of medium to express his concern provoked the censure of parliament and led to a common front of parliamentarians and defense ministry officials against him—contributing

[2] For a further discussion, see Winfried Martini, "Nagold: 'Die wahren Ursachen,'" in *Die Dritte Gewalt* 2 (October 1964): 6–19; Carl-Gero von Ilsemann, "Nagold—die wahren Ursachen: Kritische Anmerkungen zu dem Beitrag von Winfried Martini," in *Die Dritte Gewalt* 3 (February 1964): 1–19.

[3] See Hellmuth Heye, *In Sorge um die Bundeswehr: Sonderdruck wichtiger Quick Berichte* (München, 1964); Ulrich Simon, *Die Integration der Bundeswehr in die Gesellschaft: Das Ringen um die Innere Führung* (Heidelberg, 1980), pp. 62–63; Wolfgang R. Vogt, *Militär und Demokratie Funktionen und Konflikte der Institution des Wehrbeauftragten* (Hamburg, 1972).

[4] Heye, *In Sorge*, pp. 12–13.

to his later resignation—his criticism was especially damning because of his military credentials and his longstanding parliamentary support of the armed forces.[5]

THESE EVENTS calling attention to the army's inner structure made the completion of the traditions decree all the more necessary. In mid-1964, the Army Chief of Staff, Lieutenant General Alfred Zerbel, demanded that the Armed Forces Staff stop the wild *Traditionspflege*, a reasonable call, since the ministry had been promising guidelines since the late 1950s. At this time, Colonel Dr. Eberhard Wagemann took over responsibility for education and training in the ministry, a position that included the drafting of the decree. A veteran of Stalingrad and a student of Erich Weniger after the war, Wagemann brought a combination of military and scholarly experience to the task. Under his direction, the Bundeswehr sought to create more of its own conventions. The forces introduced unit flags and shoulder insignia. Its publications placed a greater emphasis on the traditions of such branches of the service as infantry and artillery, an echo of Meier-Welcker's earlier concept of the late 1950s.[6]

Nevertheless, these measures were secondary to the completion of the decree, the drafting of which remained deadlocked. In a summary for Colonel Wagemann of the obstacles preventing its publication, Dr. Helmut Ibach, a civilian staff expert, observed in October 1964: "the pluralism of the authors writing the decree prohibits a formulation [of tradition] upon which all can agree."[7] In Ibach's view, an army needed tradition for its self-confidence, but that tradition had been broken by the events of the Third Reich and the outcome of the war. As honest as the attempts in the previous drafts had been to bridge this gap, they all had resulted in an artificial effect. In the process, the decree had become an attempt to base the program of reform on historical antecedents, but "without the bending of historical facts,

---

[5] Three years earlier, at the time of the war scare over Berlin, ministry officials had called attention to similar ills; see "Fü B I 4, 'Bericht über die Situation in der Bundeswehr—September 1961,' " 12 September 1961, consulted by the writer.

[6] Interview with Major General Dr. Eberhard Wagemann, June 1984.

[7] ZIF/ZUA, 3.1.2.2., "Dr. habil. Ibach, Fü B I 4, 'Sprechzettel für Oberst i.G. Dr. Wagemann,' " 27 October 1964.

this can scarcely be achieved. One ignores history 'as it was' in favor of history as 'it should have been.' " The goal had led in earlier drafts to an exhaustive depiction of German military history from the Germanic tribes to the present that was "too long for a decree and too short as a history." Moreover, "it was against the essence of historical scholarship to 'decree' an image of history."[8]

Clearly, Wagemann faced many obstacles to the completion of the task, the first of which was reaching an agreement among the political parties. He chose the recently reelected Council on *Innere Führung* under the guidance of Professor Hans Bohnenkamp as an expert, nonpartisan group whose judgment would be acceptable to parliament. Wagemann also recognized that the concept of military tradition put forth by Baudissin was not working. Too many regarded Baudissin's ideas as a denial of the past. This denial had to be replaced by some positive statements about Germany's military tradition.[9]

The new round of work got started in the summer of 1964 with a draft decree prepared by Wagemann's predecessor in the *Innere Führung* staff, Colonel Heinz Karst, who had left Bonn to take command of a brigade at Schwanewede.[10] The recent publication of Karst's *Das Bild des Soldaten*, a highly popular book on the self-image of the Bundeswehr and its soldiers, lent greater importance to his work on the decree. Professor Walter Hubatsch, a member of the *Innere Führung* Council, had submitted a written comment that Wagemann incorporated into his draft of the decree.

Colonel Wagemann sent this new draft to the Council on *Innere Führung* in the summer of 1964. Again the question of the image of history in the Bundeswehr arose. The members of the council echoed earlier protests against adding any officially endorsed version of history, decrying it as an artificial attempt to lay down an interpretation of history that is always in flux. The *Beirat*'s draft did contain many references to military history in its sections on the "principles of tra-

[8] Ibid.

[9] Interviews with Major General Dr. Eberhard Wagemann, March and June 1984.

[10] ZIF/ZUA, 3.1.2.2., "Fü B I, Fü B I 4, Az 35–08–07, an GenInsp über Chef des Stabes Bw," 17 July 1964; interviews with Brigadier General Heinz Karst, March and July 1984.

dition" and the "valid heritage" of German military history. These passages referred to the historical criteria that would enable a young officer to judge an enduring military tradition.[11]

Once the staff had reworked its proposed decree, the council quickly agreed to all passages save one. As had been so often the case, the section of the decree dealing with the military resistance in the Third Reich was the stumbling block. In a passage expressing the virtues of mission-oriented orders (*Auftragstaktik*) and Clausewitz's idea of "freedom in obedience" (*Freiheit im Gehorsam*), a member of Minister of Defense Kai-Uwe von Hassel's staff crossed out the sentence: "Hilter and his paladins were the first to disrespect it [*Freiheit im Gehorsam*]," because as the official noted, "this is so obvious that it does not justify saying it."[12] He apparently wanted to avoid mentioning Hilter's name in the text.[13] In response to the deletion by the minister's staff, the head of the council, Professor Bohnenkamp, insisted that the draft include some mention of the breaking by the Nazis of this liberal tradition of the German armed forces. Bohenkamp eventually worked out a compromise sentence with Wagemann: "The Nazi regime was the first to disrespect it," a formulation that excluded mention of Hitler.[14]

In order to gain the assent of the chief of staff to the change, Wagemann argued in a note that:

the sentence does not contain a polemical accusation. Rather, it is the sole sentence [in the decree] that reminds us of the conflicts to which the entire military leadership was subjected in World War II. One must recall Heusinger's *Befehl im Widerstreit* or the suicide of several generals in the

---

[11] ZIF/ZUA, 3.1.2.2., "Fü B I, Fü B I 4, Az 35–05–00, 'Vermerk für Militärischen Führungsrat (MFR) am 15. Januar 1965,' " n.d.

[12] ZIF/ZUA, 3.1.2.2., "Persönlicher Referent des Ministers, 22514, an Fü B I 'Erlass "Bundeswehr und Tradition," ' " 16 June 1965. For more on *Auftragstaktik*, see Volkmer Regling, "Grundzüge der militärischen Kriegsführung, 1648–1939," in *Handbuch zur deutschen Militärgeschichte, 1648–1939,* ed. MGFA, 6 vols. (München, 1979), 5: 379ff. The term is generally unknown to Americans. See the explanation for this term in the insightful work of Martin van Creveld, *Fighting Power: German and U.S. Army Performance 1939–1945* (Westport, 1982), pp. 36–37.

[13] ZIF/ZUA, 3.1.2.2., "Persönlicher Referent des Ministers, 22514, an Fü B I 'Erlasses "Bundeswehr und Tradition," ' " 16 June 1965; interviews with Major General Dr. Eberhard Wagemann, March and June 1984.

[14] ZIF/ZUA, 3.1.2.2., "Fü B I 4, Az 35–08–07, an GenInsp über Chef des Stabes Bw," 24 June 1965.

war. Without this sentence, the Bundeswehr as the bearer of tradition of the "old army" will not distance itself in its field from the unexpert interference in [military affairs] of the Nazi regime which cost us the war and millions of soldiers. At the same time, the Bundeswehr will miss the opportunity for the future to turn back interference by the political leadership as unprofessional.[15]

Wagemann's appeal won Bundeswehr Chief of Staff Heinz Trettner's blessing, but the latter portions of his comment alluding to civil-military relations in the Nazi period displeased Minister of Defense von Hassel. The minister wrote tersely to Trettner about Wagemann's comment, "Everyone seems to have overlooked this sentence [about unprofessional interference]. If the Staff Officer for Training and Education [Colonel Wagemann] intends to mean the political leadership in the Ministry and the Bundeswehr, then he is to be relieved. I want a report on this immediately."[16] The tone of von Hassel's note betrayed the latent tensions in the Bundeswehr's civil-military relationship in the mid-1960s, while Wagemann's formulation reflected a certain naiveté about the possible reaction of civilians to such a claim regarding outside interference in military affairs.

The controversy only subsided after Trettner assured the minister that Wagemann had meant the reckless interference of a criminal regime in a possible future war, not that of a democratically legitimate government.[17] Hassel had other comments on the decree. He altered the phrase "Prussian-German tradition" to "German military tradition" and described the "Nazi system" rather than the "Nazi regime" as having disregarded the idea of freedom in obedience.[18]

Dismayed at the years taken to draft the decree, and eager to avoid the political pitfalls that had hindered its previous debuts, Hassel acted on the suggestion of his Ministerial State Secretary Gumbel, and informed Dr. Richard Jaeger (CDU), the head of the Bundestag defense committee, that the decree was about to be published and a

[15] Ibid.

[16] ZIF/ZUA, 3.1.2.2., "Fü B I 4 Az 35–08–07 an GenInsp Bw, Handschriftlicher Vermerk des Ministers an GenInsp Bw," 1 July 1965.

[17] ZIF/ZUA, 3.1.2.2., "Generalinspekteur an Herrn Minister: Ihr handschriftlicher Vermerk vom 1. Juli 1965," 7 July 1965; ZIF/ZUA, 3.1.2.2., "Oberst i.G. Dr. Wagemann, Fü B I 4 an Herrn Unterabteilungsleiter Fü B I," 2 July 1965.

[18] ZIF/ZUA, 3.1.2.2., "Originalexemplar des Erlasses, Unterschrift und schriftliche Korrekturen des Minister von Hassels," 1 July 1965.

draft copy would be sent over. This move made the assent of the committee unnecessary. Dr. Jaeger got a copy of the decree on 9 June 1965. The ministry press bureau suggested that the decree be introduced to the public on 20 July 1965, but Hassel refused to wait and signed the decree on 1 July.[19]

As presented to the press shortly after its publication, the decree set out the purposes and educational role of military tradition, the standards for its selection in the present, the essential contents of tradition, and the means and occasions for the maintenance of tradition.[20]

The first part on "principles" began with the statement: "Tradition is the handing down of the valid heritage of the past. The maintenance of tradition is a part of military education. It opens the way to historical examples, experiences, and symbols; it should enable the solider better to understand and to fulfill his mission today and tomorrow."[21]

The first part of the decree contained the standards the Bundeswehr must apply to its valid heritage. The democratic order of the Federal Republic and the Bundeswehr's mission as a draft army "to serve the Federal Republic of Germany loyally and bravely defend its people" were the fundamental measures of all tradition. The soldiers of the Bundeswehr had to recognize the threat against both the state and the individual and meet these with the traditions of a readiness to act, courage, and a willingness to sacrifice. Tradition was not to serve as self-justification, nor allow an escape from critical self-examination. Rather, only those soldiers who had also fulfilled their responsibility as human beings could serve as examples for the present.

Part two on the "valid heritage of German military history" confronted the prejudices against the term tradition and referred to the

---

[19] Interview with Major General Dr. Eberhard Wagemann, June 1984; Hans-Joachim Harder, "Traditionspflege in der Bundeswehr," unpublished manuscript, 1983, p. 43.

[20] ZIF/ZUA, 3.1.2.2., "BMVg Pressereferat 'Mitteilungen an die Presse, Nr. II/86,' " 14 July 1965; the decree itself is ZIF/ZUA, 3.1.2.2., "BMVg Fü B I 4, Az 35–08–07, 'Bundeswehr und Tradition,' " 1 July 1965, published in *Information für die Truppe, Beilage zu Heft 9/1965*, July 1965.

[21] "Bundeswehr und Tradition," *Information für die Truppe, Beilage zu Heft 9/1965*, p. 3.

enduring values of Germany's past. In a passage that later provoked criticism for its archaic style, the authors of the decree observed that "to each person is given his father, mother, hour of birth, fatherland, mother tongue, and his own position in history."[22]

The authors of the decree stated that what today was considered as worthy of tradition had usually begun as a novelty. One had to remain open to new ideas and maintain a lack of prejudice; these were the qualities necessary for a progressive tradition. German military history "contained in peace and war countless soldierly achievements and human accomplishments which deserved to be passed on." But war was not to be justified as an "opportunity for proving one's self," especially in view of the technological development of modern weapons. The opportunity for testing one's self in the present lay in the readiness for battle and the soldierly efficiency that deterred war.

This part of the decree also addressed the problems of nationalism and patriotism. Although recognizing Germany's tragic experiences with nationalism, the decree's authors observed that it still played a positive role in the world. Nonetheless, the Federal Republic was steadily becoming part of supranational entities that provided new opportunities for comradeship and intellectual exchanges with free peoples. The decree also sought to differentiate between love of country and nationalism, saying that the sense of being bound to one's home had gradually increased over time to encompass much of Europe and the Atlantic alliance.

The fulfillment of one's duty had always been among the most important aspects of German soldierhood. It was also one of the bases of personal freedom. The ideals of obedience and fulfillment of duty were embodied in the loyalty of the soldier to his superior—in this case, the Federal Republic. This loyalty was expressed in the oath that bound both soldier and superior to one another.

Paragraph fourteen contained the important statement on the military resistance:

According to German military tradition, the achievement and dignity of the soldier rests to a large degree upon his freedom in obedience. The training for self-discipline, the call for shared responsibility and the kind of command exemplified by mission-oriented tactics (*Auftragstaktik*) gave

[22] Ibid., p. 4.

this freedom ever greater room [to develop]. The National Socialist regime was the first to disregard it.

[The Bundeswehr] must once more tie itself to this freedom in obedience. One's own responsibility in the risk of life, position, and reputation has always given a human dimension to the soldier's obedience. Finally answerable only to their conscience, the soldiers of the resistance proved themselves to the final degree against the injustice and criminality of the national socialist rule of force. Such loyalty to conscience must be preserved in the Bundeswehr.[23]

The decree also contained the statement that the soldier proved himself by acting under the pressures of time in unclear situations. It belonged to German military tradition to judge a soldier's performance more harshly for hesitation than for a mistake made in resolution. Those who had to act could fail quickly, obviously, and with permanent consequences. So long as they acted after careful decision, however, they should be able to face the judgment of those around them.

In the subsequent passages, the authors of the decree called for political thought and responsibility as first expounded in the Prussian reforms of the early nineteenth century. "The value of [the soldier's] service is largely determined by the political aims [he serves]." This insight required all the more that soldiers educate themselves. At the end of this section, there was a list of virtues that again aroused public criticism for sounding like schoolbook platitudes. These virtues included honesty; respect of human rights; tolerance; discipline of intellect, speech, and body; and loyalty to one's conscience. Various symbolic expressions of the unity of German military tradition were offered as well. Those with particular meaning were: the black, red, and gold flag of the Federal Republic that signified the responsibility of the citizen and the striving of all Germans for unity, law, and freedom (also expressed in the *Lied der Deutschen*); the eagle of the German federal coat of arms, "the oldest German symbol of sovereignty and the rule of law"; and the Iron Cross, "the symbolic expression of ethically determined soldierly bravery."

The armed forces could awaken the consciousness of tradition in its soldiers at the swearing of the oath, the presentation of weapons

[23] Ibid., p. 6.

to young soldiers, promotion ceremonies, the playing of the grand tattoo, the celebration of memorial days, and the launching of ships. Military tradition was to be made vital through historical instruction by officers and NCOs with the use of examples. With the permission of the ministry, troop units and barracks could be named for "personalities whose attitude and achievements had been exemplary." Historical artifacts could also be collected to acquaint the young soldiers with tradition, but memorabilia with swastikas could not be shown. Flags of old armies (but not those of the Nazi period) could be displayed at ceremonial events as long as the Bundeswehr unit carried its own unit flag.

Paragraph twenty-six contained the final answer on the matter of lineage and honors: "The traditions of former troop units will not be awarded to units of the Bundeswehr." The authors of the decree then tried to explicate their position to the old soldiers, with the observation that it should be possible to maintain comradely relations without an official carryover of lineage and honors. Bundeswehr units should include in their social activities all former soldiers in the vicinity, both in groups and as individuals. However, the authors stated "it must remain clear that the Bundeswehr distinguishes itself in its political position, its mission, and its structure from the armed forces of earlier periods."[24]

The authors of the decree further specified the drawbacks of the official award of lineage and honors from the old to the new forces. Nonetheless, the final paragraphs of the decree spoke of the Bundeswehr's honoring of the "soldierly achievement and sacrifice" and the need for an exchange of experiences and meetings between old and active soldiers. This would increase mutual respect. Former soldiers could be invited to official functions and celebrations, but ceremonies intended for the maintenance of tradition had to be subordinated to the demands of taste. Finally, the decree included the statement that "all events for the maintenance of tradition were to serve education and further bind the Bundeswehr to its present mission."[25]

SUCH, THEN, was the answer given to the question of what should be handed down to the new army. In its authors' emphasis on the

[24] Ibid., p. 9.   [25] Ibid., p. 10.

contents of tradition, it fulfilled the demand of Siegburg in 1953 to specify more than merely the external and decorative aspects of tradition. It authors avoided the transfer of lineage and honors, but offered an open door to the veterans of the old armies in the manner proposed by Meier-Welcker and others in the mid-1950s. It paid homage to the resistance to Hitler as Baudissin had also done in the first years of the new army, seizing upon the lead of Weinheim, the PGA, and the Council on *Innere Führung*. Its authors had heeded the warnings of their academic advisers by avoiding a catalogue of historical examples.

The decree was a compromise, like many others compelled by the difficult birth of the army. Without precedent in German history, the effort within a modern military bureaucracy to select a valid tradition from the mixed heritage of the past—especially the German past— was a difficult task. Despite the honest and forthright labor that had gone into the decree, it was certain to generate controversy both for what it included and for what it left out. Baudissin's observation at Siegburg in 1953 that the word tradition created two camps was certainly true of the new decree.

14. "What Is a Valid Heritage?" First Reactions to the Decree

THE PUBLIC reaction immediately following the decree's appearance was generally favorable, with many in the press sympathetic to the difficulties the ministry had faced in writing it.[1] The choices to honor the men of the Twentieth of July and to prevent a takeover of lineage and honors won praise from many editorial writers, although certain of the commentaries criticized the decree for the lack of concrete historical examples in the text and, as one writer described it, for its resort to "school-book platitudes."

The criticism of the decree that came from the right wing of West German politics was directed against what they considered the ministry's exclusion of the armed forces of the Third Reich from the valid part of the military heritage. Many veterans of the Waffen-SS were dissatisfied with their treatment in the decree. CSU Deputy Albrecht Schlee, acting for the Waffen-SS veterans organization HIAG in Oberfranken, asked Hassel to alter the decree to allow some form of official relations between Waffen-SS veterans and the Bundeswehr. The calls from Waffen-SS veterans prompted Hassel to remind the public that the Bundeswehr differed fundamentally in its conception and purpose from the earlier armies. In a further discussion of the issue, the ministry spokesmen maintained that while the Bundeswehr had nothing against individual Waffen-SS veterans so long as they were not guilty of crimes, the Bundeswehr could not accept individuals who identified with the Nazi regime. "At the moment where he [former Waffen-SS soldier] expresses the ideas of the SS, he is no longer a soldier."[2]

---

[1] "Bundeswehr und Tradition," in *Vorwärts*, 28 July 1965; "Tradition—nicht nur Bewunderung," in *Rheinische Post*, 16 July 1965; "Traditionspflege," in *Christ und Welt*, 23 July 1965; "Die Pflege der Tradition in der Bundeswehr," in *Neue Zürcher Zeitung*, 17 July 1965; "Richtlinien für die Traditionspflege der Bundeswehr," in *Frankfurter Allgemeine Zeitung*, 16 July 1965.

[2] "Schlee an Hassel: Traditionserlass ändern," in *Bayreuther Tagblatt*, 27 July 1965.

The more left-liberal criticism also focused on the omissions in the decree, interpreting them as the ministry's failure to come to grips with the Nazi past. Serious criticism in the press gained momentum in the fall of 1965, setting the tone for many of the attacks on the decree that followed over the next several years, which lasted well into the 1980s. In October 1965, Bernd Hesslein, Lothar Jansen, and Joachim Fest on the television program *Panorama* criticized the decree's failure to describe which military achievements should be handed down. By taking flight into "vague phrases," the authors had left the choice of examples to the troops. Earlier publications of the Bundeswehr on the Twentieth of July had been more binding. The commentators praised the clarity of examples in the *Handbuch Innere Führung* (1957), while suggesting that the lack of specifics in the decree would leave the new army to its own errors and contradictions, even though Hassel had described the *Handbuch* as being superseded by the decree.[3]

Joachim Fest complained that the ministry's authors had consciously chosen such vague terms as respect, freedom, law, sacrifice, and patriotism in an effort to create a wall of fog. These were no more than the empty shells of words. Nowhere could one find rules of behavior for decisive situations. Repeating Theodor Heuss's warning that tradition was a dangerous word, Fest suggested that the decree's "verbose vagueness" only increased this danger by promoting a misunderstanding of the term.

Hesslein renewed his attack on the decree a month later in a broadcast interview with Baudissin, now a three-star general and deputy chief of staff of Plans, Policy and Operations in the Supreme Headquarters Allied Powers Europe (SHAPE) in Paris.[4] After discussing the fate of the reforms and his concern about them, Baudissin praised the decree for its setting of the measure for a valid tradition and for its recognition of the resistance to Hitler. In response to the question of whether the decree should contain more specifics, Baudissin sug-

[3] ZIF/ZUA, 0.2.1.4., "Kommentarübersicht-DFS Panaorama: Traditionserlass der Bundeswehr, 'In seiner wortreichen Unerheblichkeit fördert er geradezu das Missverständnis,' " 5 October 1965; interview with Major General Dr. Wagemann, June 1984.

[4] ZIF/ZUA, 0.2.1.4., "Setzt sich die Reform durch? Bundeswehr und Tradition—Ein Interview mit General Graf Baudissin," 15 November 1965.

gested that the ministry certainly would have to provide officers with historical examples in a "gallery of ancestors" from which individuals could choose on the basis of their background and outlook.[5] But Baudissin himself refrained from listing these examples by referring to the difficulties of such a historical interpretation in a pluralistic society.

The Hesslein interview with "the father of *Innere Führung*" reflected the fact that by the mid-1960s, Baudissin had effectively lost all contact with forces for the reform of the armed forces. This apparent lack of influence caused dismay among Baudissin's admirers in the press, who nonetheless continued to interview him with regularity during the course of the 1960s. In response to the apparent declining fortunes of the chief reformer and the uncertain fate of the reforms themselves, in January 1965 the city of Hamburg had jointly awarded Kielmansegg, Baudissin, and de Maizière the Freiherr vom Stein Prize in recognition of their achievements with *Innere Führung*.[6]

PUBLIC CRITICISM added to the task faced by the leading commanders and staff officers of the Bundeswehr, who explained the decree to troops, veterans, and civilians during the fall of 1965. A seminar on "Fatherland and Tradition in the view of the Modern Soldier," held at the *Innere Führung* school in Koblenz some weeks after the publication of the decree, revealed the reactions of a part of the officer corps.[7] Describing his experiences with members of the seminar, Captain Koethe of the school's staff recounted that many officers were pleased with the language of the decree and with the latitude that its authors gave to individuals. They were satisfied that the decree's guidelines applied to all the armed forces and allowed for new traditions to develop in the Bundeswehr. Nevertheless, there were critics as well. Upon reading the decree, one replied: "Captain, if you had

---

[5] Ibid., pp. 2–3.

[6] The original text of Baudissin's speech at the February 1965 ceremony is in ZIF/ZUA, 0.2.1.0., "Graf von Baudissin, 'Innere Führung-Versuch einer Reform,'" February 1965. As Baudissin spoke for both Kielmansegg and de Maizière, they edited the text of his speech. The insertions and deletions made in red on the original are an interesting measure of the differences between the men on the issues of reform and tradition as they existed in 1965. Baudissin had sent the draft now in the ZIF/ZUA files to the commander of the *Innere Führung* School.

[7] ZIF/ZUA, 3.1.2.2., "Wilfried Koethe, Korvettenkapitän 'Zum Traditionserlass,'" 28 October 1965.

given me five sheets of blank paper instead of this decree, the success [among the troops] would have been the same."[8] Other critics, relishing the chance to bash the ministry, were less tactful. The decree said nothing; it said too little. After nine years of the Bundeswehr, it was a pretty miserable result. The decree said not one jot more than officers had already been doing in the troops for years—why had it been brought out at all?

Joining the commentators in the press, other officers insisted that the decree should have included a catalogue of the good and the bad, or as Koethe himself suggested, a "poison cabinet." The remainder of the criticism focused on the relationship of the Bundeswehr to the Wehrmacht. "What good are Scharnhorst and Gneisenau," one officer asked, "if, in looking back . . . we soldiers of the Bundeswehr prefer to choose the Wehrmacht from 1933 to 1945. One needs . . . nothing more than that." Further criticism asked, "Why is the Bundeswehr so willing to make an example of the deed and attitude of the men of the Twentieth of July, while at the same time it renounces the tradition of the simple soldier at the front?" Another officer observed: "The publication of this decree strikes me as a really risk-free deed by the ministry. Since there is nothing in the decree, no one can attack it. The ministry is then in fine shape, but we have to go before our troops with this empty pathos. The risk is thrown into our hands." Finally, as yet another officer asked, "what really is 'a valid heritage'—the decree doesn't give any information!" The nearly total misunderstanding of the decree was a constant feature of the debate on tradition in the Bundeswehr.

In part as a response to these objections to the decree, and also because such guidance had already been planned, Wagemann published two documents to explain the decree in October 1965. The first of these two guides to the troops included suggestions for teaching the theme to officers, NCOs, and troops with three examples of instruction that had been tried at the Luftwaffe NCO school at Guerzenich.[9]

Colonel Wagemann suggested in his introduction that it was more important for officers and NCOs to have a clear understanding of

[8] Ibid., p. 1.
[9] "Der Bundesminister der Verteidigung, S I 4 Az 35–08–07, 'Hinweise für die Unterrichtung über den Erlass "Bundeswehr und Tradition," ' " 18 October 1965, consulted by the writer.

tradition and to maintain it properly than to spend a great deal of time lecturing the troops on the subject. The themes for a discussion among officers could include: "Basic statements and difficult questions in the decree"; "Why tradition in the Bundeswehr?"; "Examples for soldiers"; and "How do we maintain tradition?" Furthermore, officers could use the material from the winter essay competition on "Soldiers of the Wehrmacht and their Relationship to Political Power: General Beck, General Freiherr von Fritsch, General Guderian, Fieldmarshall von Kluge, Fieldmarshall von Manstein, Fieldmarshall Rommel, and Colonel Graf Stauffenberg." Wagemann suggested that the discussion address the value of each of these men as a military example. One had to judge them both as human beings and as soldiers. One should foster an understanding of the situation of conflict in which each of them found themselves.[10]

The examples for instruction appended to Wagemann's guide were pedagogical tools to lead the student-soldier through the instruction—"What do you think of when you hear the word tradition?"; "What value does tradition have for people?"; "In which form have you experienced tradition in the Bundeswehr?"—but these aids contained no "gallery of ancestors" as demanded by Baudissin. Wagemann's guidance did include an index of articles from *Information für die Truppe* from 1958 to 1965 with such citations as: "A soldierly example: Colonel Freiherr von Boeselager"; "General Ludwig Beck"; "What does Clausewitz mean for us today?" and "Jewish soldiers in the Air Corps of the First World War."[11] As lengthy as this list was, it could not be described as a list of the Bundeswehr's ancestors with the ministry's imprimatur.

Colonel Wagemann supplemented his internal guidance with an article in *Wehrkunde* intended for a wider audience that addressed much of the recent criticism in the press.[12] Responding to claims that the ministry should have given more historical examples, Wagemann pointed out that the decree had confined itself consciously to identifying those elements of tradition acceptable to the Bundeswehr. It had only judged two specific events: the Nazi regime and the Twentieth of July 1944 *Attentat*. There would have been far greater criticism, Wagemann wrote, had the ministry set down on paper a partic-

---

[10] Ibid., p. 2.   [11] Ibid.
[12] Oberst i.G. Eberhard Wagemann, "Zum Erlass 'Bundeswehr und Tradition,' " in *Wehrkunde*, October 1965, pp. 501–8.

ular interpretation of historical scholarship and then forced the troops to accept it in the form of a decree.

Intentionally or not, Wagemann described the purpose of the decree in a way that accentuated the tendency toward characteristically German self-consciousness in the quest for a valid tradition. He also revealed what can only be described as Wagemann's echoing of Clausewitz, that historical study improves the soldier's powers of the mind. As Wagemann wrote, the measures of tradition in the decree were to help the individual soldier confront history and allow him to make a choice from the "tradition of a valid heritage of the past." In the process, the individual who reflected on events and personalities "would sharpen his conscience and his power of judgment."

Wagemann argued that many critics of the decree were uncomfortable with the freedom allowed by its provisions. Soldiers should also be able to partake of the freedoms they had sworn to defend, including freedom of thought. In the best case, the soldier's ideals of tradition, whether comprised of historical personalities or events, would include only those completely unsullied by the past. But, Wagemann asked, where were they? "Who among us who has survived . . . was at the time free of cowardice and opportunism?" The Bundeswehr traditions decree was not an attempt to gloss over crimes. It could not list the plainly black and white cases of German history, but instead it dealt with the vast number of gray ones, "to which, in case of doubt, we ourselves all belong." This kind of statement is unique to the many years of debate on military tradition in the Federal Republic, and it indicates clearly Wagemann's approach to the issue.

In his concluding remarks, Colonel Wagemann reminded his readers that the decree should be judged by its authors' intentions and not by those of its critics. The decree had not sought to make specific judgments about events or persons. It had not tried to sketch an overall picture of what should be a German tradition. It had not tried to give a different meaning to military service by replacing the Bundeswehr's mission anchored in the law nor had it sought to influence soldiers ideologically.

THE TASK of meeting the criticism of the press was easier than personally going before the veterans to explain the decree. As the senior officer in the new army, Lieutenant General Ulrich de Maizière, the chief of staff of the army, spoke to representatives of the assembled traditions associations of the *Panzer* and *Panzergrenadier* divisions of the old army at the Bundeswehr's armor school at Munster-Lager the day before memorial day on 13 November 1965.[13] Describing his audience years later as "Guderian's children," de Maizière addressed the former commanders and teachers of the present generation of Bundeswehr officers. Under General Guderian in the mid-1930s, many of those at Munster-Lager had built up the German armored branch and gone on to leading command and staff positions during the war. However, the Bundeswehr had refused to name any of its bases or facilities for Guderian because of his role in the Twentieth of July and its aftermath. He became closely identified with those Wehrmacht officers who remained fully loyal to Hitler despite the futility of the lost war.

De Maizière had quickly written the speech on the way to Munster-Lager as an attempt not only to introduce the decree to a skeptical audience but also to demonstrate that the ministry had not slammed the door on the veterans. Reminding his audience that the decree was unprecedented in German history, de Maizière quoted from the ideas of his 1962 draft with the observation that tradition was not history. Tradition, however, did serve education and required making a choice from history. The authors of the document sought to provide the criteria for that choice.

The chief of staff of the army devoted particular attention to the question of unit lineage and honors. Citing examples from his own service as a brigade commander in Hannover, he described the territorial solution to relations with veterans that was nearly identical to Meier-Welcker's ideas of the late 1950s. Bundeswehr garrisons should care for the traditions of all veterans in their vicinity, but none to the exclusion of the others. Had the Bundeswehr made a connection with specific units of the old armies, inevitably some veterans would have been excluded. Also, de Maizière noted, the takeover of lineage and honors from old units of central and eastern Germany would have signaled an acceptance of the territorial status quo, which in 1965 was still an anathema to the CDU government. Ending with a statement that the Bundeswehr must also look to the future, he described the first production since the war of a major German armored fighting vehicle,

[13] ZIF/ZUA, 3.1.2.2., "Bundesministerium der Verteidigung, Inspekteur des Heeres [Ulrich de Maizière], Adjutant 'Rede, gehalten in Munster am Vorabend des Volkstrauertages 1965,' " 29 November 1965.

the Leopard, as *Traditionspflege* of the armored branch and a connection with the Panther and Tiger tanks of the war.

Reflecting on the speech many years later, de Maizière believed that the former tank leaders had accepted what he had said, although perhaps they did not approve of it.[14] The address was very much in keeping with the talent for compromise and consensus that marked de Maizière's career. First advanced in the late 1950s and later promoted by de Maizière, the territorial approach to the veterans was a middle path between a formal transfer of lineage and honors and the radical isolation of the new force from the old soldiers—a political, social, and human impossibility given the bonds between the generations.

The reception of the decree at the troop level is somewhat less easy to characterize. As one high-ranking commander, Lieutenant General Wilhelm Meyer-Detring, commander of I. Corps in Münster, wrote: "Many officers apparently expected both something more and something different from the ministry's traditions decree."[15] Responding to Wagemann's guidance and seizing upon the initiative left to subordinates, Meyer-Detring suggested to his officers that the document compelled the formation of their own judgments. Since many officers had neither the time nor resources for such reflection, Meyer-Detring and his staff prepared some examples to use with the decree, which he was careful to point out were meant neither as a standard formula nor as an order that should replace the individual's "labor of thought."

Meyer-Detring suggested that given the lack of historical knowledge among most soldiers, officers should use symbols to acquaint the troops with tradition. This goal could be reached by asking soldiers to explain the name of the *Kaserne*; by emphasizing the noteworthy deeds of soldiers and NCOs in wartime; by asking a veteran to speak about the "specific behavior demanded of the modern soldier"; and even by toasting the *Bundespräsident* by raising a glass to him on festive occasions.[16]

Surely more important in Meyer-Detring's guidance than the

[14] Interview with General Ulrich de Maizière, June 1984.

[15] "Der Kommandierende General (KG) I. Korps, an alle Generale und Stabsoffiziere des I. Korps, 'Gedanken zum Erlass "Bundeswehr und Tradition," ' " December 1965, consulted by the writer.

[16] Ibid. Meyer-Detring's suggestion should not be overinterpreted, although the federal president still fulfills the symbolic void left by the kaiser.

anachronistic toasts to the federal president were a number of historical topics suggested for the continuing education of officers. Sample themes included: (1) "Valid and invalid heritage of the past: the attitude of the officer corps to the Social Democratic party, 1875–1914"; (2) "The essential differences of the military structure [of Germany] 1807/14, 1862, 1921, 1935 and 1955"; (3) "Self-critical realizations cannot obscure historical realities, even those of outstanding military leaders: Seeckt and Moltke and their relationship to politics, or Guderian's participation in the court of honor after 20 July 1944"; (4) "When did *Auftragstaktik* become a tradition in the German army?"; (5) "Was the political thought of the Prussian reformers vital in the elder and younger Moltke?"; (6) "Moltke—an educated officer as a master of the art of war and language." Doubtless drawn from other instructions in military history, these were sophisticated assignments that were supplemented with an extensive bibliography.[17]

Under the rubric of "wrong ways and difficulties," Meyer-Detring's guidance also included a revealing discussion of the Twentieth of July that highlighted the unresolved problem of this touchstone of the military tradition of the Bundeswehr. The esteem for the men of the Twentieth of July obligated commanders and staff officers to place resistance and obedience in proper relation to one another. It was an insoluble problem to give soldiers the historical knowledge that would enable them to grasp properly the exceptional situation of the year 1944 and to use it for the formation of tradition. At the soldiers' level, "situations of resistance will probably not be found. It is more important to make clear and to demonstrate to him [the soldier], that he can depend in our system not to be placed before such insoluble conflicts, and that, as a rule, military tradition simply is obedience." Moreover, officers could not merely avoid the problem. One had to take the time and trouble to express the relationship between the rule of obedience and the exception of resistance with a number of examples.

Perhaps the best way to understand Meyer-Detring's guidance is to refer to his own later reflections on the issue.[18] In a discussion of the

---

[17] "KG I. Korps, An alle Generale und Stabsoffiziere, 'Quellennachweis,' " January 1966, consulted by the writer.

[18] *Militärgeschichte seit 1945: Aspekte der deutschen Wiederbewaffnung bis 1955*, ed. MGFA (Boppard, 1975), p. 219.

reforms among fellow officers and historians less than a decade later, Meyer-Detring uttered a sentence that summed up the historical dilemma of the Bundeswehr: "I must say quite openly, that when I entered the Bundeswehr as a colonel again, I had a great deal of difficulty digesting all the new things, from fighting an atomic war to *Innere Führung*, so that within a couple of years I could be a convinced interpreter of these things for the larger officer corps. . . . We set up [the army] too quickly." Meyer-Detring's guidance for the traditions decree was plainly a part of his own effort to "digest all the new things," including the many historical contradictions they contained.

PERHAPS the most intriguing reaction to the decree on tradition took place not in the Federal Republic, but in Austria. There the political experience with the maintenance of military tradition had been both similar and different from the German case. Like the army of Second Reich, the Imperial and Royal Army of the Habsburgs had ceased to exist in the wake of defeat. In 1924, the Federal Army of the First Republic, borrowed, in effect, from the Reichswehr the regimental maintenance of tradition practiced under Seeckt; in fact, the uniform of the Bundesheer was very similar to that of the Reichswehr until 1933. Although the Bundesheer was later absorbed into the Wehrmacht in 1938, within the guise of a "Greater German" military tradition, certain aspects of a distinctly Austrian military *Traditionspflege* endured under the Nazis. In the 1950s, the neutral Austrians, like the West Germans, established an army, once they had gained their sovereignty.[19] Although the armament of the Austrian republic sparked far less political debate internationally than did the arming of the Federal Republic, the Austrian military leadership hesitated to make an official statement on the maintenance of tradition until the mid-1960s.

Once the Federal German decree appeared, however, the Austrians took a different course than had the Bundeswehr. On 26 October 1966, the Austrian Minister of Defense, Dr. George Prader, announced that the Austrian army would maintain the traditions of the

[19] Johann Christoph Allmayer-Beck, "Landesverteidigung und Bundesheer," *Österreichische Militärzeitschrift* 10 (1972): 264ff.; Manfred Rauchensteiner, ed., *Das Bundesheer der Zweiten Republik: Eine Dokumentation* (Wien, 1980).

army of the First Republic and the Habsburg Imperial and Royal Army.[20] In effect, then, the Austrians returned to the maintenance of the tradition of the 1920s, complete with Seeckt's traditions companies, after the Bundeswehr had publicly distanced itself from an official assumption of lineage and honors. This explicit Austrian return to tradition was followed a few months later on 17 March 1967 by a decree on the subject from the Austrian ministry of Defense—the document no doubt triggered by the Federal German one. The authors of the Austrian decree outlined the purpose of military tradition in terms similar to those of the West Germans, but they diverged sharply in setting up special tradition units. The relationship of these units with the veterans organizations was further delineated in the text.[21] Although the West German and Austrian armies plainly faced somewhat different problems with regard to the legacy of 1933–45, the coincidence of the issuance of the two documents in the mid-1960s highlights the political impact the Federal German decree on tradition had on it neighbors.

THE DOCUMENT intended as an answer to the question "what should we hand down?" brought the discussion of military tradition to a climax in 1965. In effect, the decree on tradition addressed the problems of the 1950s and of the generation of company and battalion commanders from the Wehrmacht who had joined the Bundeswehr and still made up a major part of its officer corps. During the mid-1950s, Baudissin had sought to answer his own question, but his response did not endure because many soldiers refused to accept the way he had dealt with the Third Reich. The decision in the Adenauer government to create the army instantly, with little regard for practical details, also doomed Baudissin's answer, instead favoring the po-

---

[20] Robert Spiering, "Der Österreichische Traditionserlass," in *Zeitschrift für Heereskunde* 31, 213 (September/October 1967): 136–38. See also the documents and the general discussion in Bundesministerium für Landesverteidigung, Abteilung Bildung und Kultur, Staatsbürgerliche Erziehung, *Traditionspflege im Bundesheer: Allgemeine Einführung* (Wien, 1968).

[21] The reprinted text is in the sources in note 20. Also see Robert Spiering, "Wesen und Wert der Überlieferungspflege," in *Zeitschrift für Heereskunde* 31, 214 (November/December 1967): 164–65; Johann Christoph Allmayer-Beck, "Gedanken zum Problem der Überlieferungspflege," *Österreichische Militärische Zeitschrift* no. 1 (1968): 41–43.

litical effort to enhance the standing of the Federal Republic in the NATO alliance. This choice helped undermine the effectiveness of *Innere Führung* in the first decade-and-a-half of the Bundeswehr. As the 1950s ended, the new soldiers of the Bundeswehr resurrected many features of the cult of tradition practiced by Seeckt. In the wake of this reaction, the military leadership sought to offer a second answer to the question of Siegburg in 1953 in the form of the ministerial decree. This conception of a valid heritage, which consciously avoided being a catalogue of good historical examples, responded to the need for a statement about the past that spoke somewhat more directly to the problem of the Wehrmacht than had Baudissin. In conclusion, one can say that the decree of 1965 reflected the events of the fifteen years from 1950 to 1965, mirroring the attempt at reform in the West German military and the reaction of the rank and file.

By the mid-1960s, however, the Bundeswehr stood on the verge of a period of renewed controversy about its mission and about the military reforms. This turbulence coincided with the coming to grips of West German society with the German past as never before in the short history of the Federal Republic. This process shook the compromise upon which the new army had been built. As a result, the accepted measure of a valid military tradition changed in the Federal Republic, ensuring that the decree on tradition received constant scrutiny. The description of the fate of the decree over the next decade-and-a-half completes the account of the policy developed in the Bundeswehr to digest its past in the first years of its existence.

PART THREE

A New Generation Seeks Its Valid Heritage

15. Transition and Open Conflict, 1966–1972

THE COLD WAR gave birth to the Bundeswehr and sustained it in its first ten years; once the struggle between the United States and Soviet Union reached its climax in the early 1960s and détente took hold later in the decade, the Bundeswehr faced a new series of political and social challenges to its mission. The diminishing tensions between America and Russia coincided with the transformation of statecraft and society in the Federal Republic of the late 1960s and the early 1970s. The outcome of these changes divided West Germans in their attitudes toward international security, the alliance, and their armed forces.[1] As the political and social beliefs of the Adenauer era gave way, these events left their imprint on the military reforms and the maintenance of tradition in the West German military. Any full interpretation of this stage in the history of the Bundeswehr would go beyond the limits of the present study; the brief comments that follow suggest the chief trends in civil-military relations that obtained from the mid-1960s until the early 1980s as they relate to the maintenance of tradition in the Bundeswehr.

What was the essence of this civil-military transformation that surrounded the Bundeswehr? The confrontation between the United States and the Soviet Union had finally convinced most West Germans by the end of the 1950s that Atlantic defense was a reasonable price to pay for the return of West Germany to the community of nations, even if this cost entailed the permanent division of the old

---

[1] See Klaus Hildebrand, *Von Erhard zur Grossen Koalition: 1963–1969*, vol. 4 in *Geschichte der Bundesrepublik Deutschland*, ed. Karl-Dietrich Bracher et al., 5 vols. (Stuttgart, 1984); William Geffen, "The Role of the Military in West German Defense Policy Making," Ph.D. diss., University of Denver, 1971. An excellent introduction to the era from 1966 to 1970 is to be found in the protocol of a meeting held at Zentrum Innere Führung in 1982 to interpret the events of the time, see: "Ausbildungspädagogik: Auf der Suche nach dem Bild des Offiziers: Seminar zu den Thesen der 'Leutnante 1970' und der Ergebnisniederschrift einer Arbeitstagung der 'Hauptleute von Unna,'" in *Texte und Studien des Zentrums Innere Führung*, ed. ZIF (Koblenz, 1984); see also Simon, *Die Integration*, pp. 111–20.

Reich. The antitotalitarian consensus in Federal German politics and society, that is the general rejection of both a Nazi past and a Marxist-Leninist future in favor of an Atlanticist, democratic present, had provided the new army with the political conditions necessary to overcome the problems of its troubled first decade.

The tenth anniversary of the West German army in 1965 was no small accomplishment. The successful integration of the Bundeswehr into West German society contrasted sharply with the political isolation of the Reichswehr in the first republic. By the end of the 1950s, politicians and soldiers had agreed on the shape of national defense in a way that their predecessors in the Weimar Republic had been unable to do thirty years earlier. The maintenance of tradition in the Bundeswehr, despite the cautious policy of "let the traditions grow" and the hesitancy of the ministry in publishing the decree, had been one aspect of this political success story. The answer to the question of which were valid military traditions reflected the grand political compromise worked out in the course of the 1950s. The men of the Bundeswehr accepted the limits on German sovereignty imposed by NATO. Despite the validity of much of Bonin's critique, his defiance of the Atlantic strategic status quo was a solitary episode. During the first decade of the new army, no officer atop an armored car led the troops through the streets of Bonn to encircle the Bundestag at gun point. Soldiers worked for, and assented to, parliamentary controls that ensured the loyalty of the defenders of freedom toward the Bonn democracy. They promised to guarantee the civil rights of the conscripted citizen in uniform, despite many setbacks in reaching this goal. In return, the soldiers, mostly veterans of the Wehrmacht, were not to be completely cut off from the German military past; they could carefully select their traditions and symbols according to their mission and the political order. But soon after the traditions decree had appeared and the tenth anniversary had been celebrated in 1965, things slowly began to go wrong with the grand compromise.[2]

The cold war consensus in Federal German politics and society, beset by events both at home and abroad, began to come apart in the mid-1960s. This gradual process of decline advanced imperceptibly in

[2] This analysis is indebted to Professor Michael Geyer of the University of Chicago, whose thoughtful criticisms have greatly enriched this study.

the late 1960s and early 1970s, then it accelerated at the end of the 1970s. The West German military and the Atlantic alliance struggled with the long-term consequences of this collapse well into the 1980s. The initial phase reached its loud climax as the world went through the political upheavals of the closing years of the 1960s. First came the last hurrah of Baudissin's critics in the ranks of the Bundeswehr. Before these officers retired, they mounted a final assault on the military reforms, just as West German politics saw the revival of radical opposition to liberal democracy from both the left and right. The open conflict of the years 1967 to 1972 about the basic principles of *Innere Führung* marked a caesura in the history of the Bundeswehr, in effect closing the chapter of its development that began with Himmerod.[3]

More significant, however, for the development of the maintenance of tradition in the Bundeswehr in its second and third decades has been the second phase, which followed the late 1960s. One might argue that this period has lasted until the 1980s. Here the opponents of the cold war consensus dominate the political scene, political figures who took to the streets in the extraparliamentary opposition in the late 1960s, manned the left wing of the SPD in the 1970s, and advanced the Greens to political power in the 1980s. These men and women, disillusioned with America as a model because of the social turmoil of the 1960s and the Vietnam War, struck at the twin pillars of Atlantic strategic integration and economic growth upon which the Federal Republic had been built.[4] During the epoch from the late 1960s until the late 1970s, figures on the left, though perhaps divided over other issues, backed away from the defense coalition in West German politics that had supported the Bundeswehr and the Atlantic alliance. After the mid-1970s, they increasingly attacked the cold war compromise that lay at the base of the maintenance of tradition in the

---

[3] General Gerd Schmückle argues for this periodization in Simon, *Die Integration*, pp. 115–16.

[4] G. Langguth, *Die Protestbewegung in der Bundesrepublik Deutschland, 1968–1976* (Köln, 1978); K.A. Otto, *Vom Ostermarsch zur APO: Geschichte der ausserparlamantarischen Opposition in der Bundesrepublik, 1960–1970* (Frankfurt, 1982); Harald Mueller and Thomas Risse-Kappen, "Origins of Estrangement: The Peace Movement and the Changed Image of America in West Germany," *International Security* 12, 1 (1987): 52–88; Willy Brandt, *Begegnungen und Einsichten: Die Jahre 1960–1975* (München, 1978); Arnulf Baring, *Machtwechsel: Die Ära Brandt-Scheel* (Stuttgart, 1983).

Bundeswehr. They looked at the past more critically, and were alto-gether less forgiving of individual guilt in the Third Reich. They re-discovered and adapted the arguments of political figures of the 1950s who had refused to accept the civil-military compromise of West Germany. There was a growing willingness among the critics of the cold war status quo to confront the burden of the Nazis in a direct way.

The highly publicized trial of Adolf Eichmann in the early 1960s went a long way toward breaking the public silence about the Nazi past in West Germany.[5] Prominent in this development was the parliamentary debate of 1965 about the extension of the statute of limitations for Nazi war crimes, which was scheduled to run out that year.[6] The handing down in 1965 of the verdicts in the Auschwitz trials, after several years of hearings, had drawn further worldwide attention to the repulsive details of Nazi genocide, reminding thoughtful Germans that the problem of the Nazi past would not simply fade way.[7] Indeed, as time passed, the significance of the Nazi experience in West German life became greater through a series of episodes.

This critical tendency found its echos in the historical writing of the time, especially in literature on the Third Reich. While German historians of the schools of Fritz Fischer and Hans-Ulrich Wehler sought to reveal the continuity between earlier periods of German history and the Nazi years, scholars of the German army like Manfred Messerschmidt and Klaus-Jürgen Müller pointed to the ideological connections between the Nazis and the military.[8] Their work convincingly suggested that the border between the field-gray and brown spheres of civil-military life under National Socialism had been far less distinct than many had wanted to believe in the early 1950s. These

[5] Hans-Peter Schwarz, *Die Ära Adenauer: Epochenwechsel 1957–1963*, in *Geschichte der Bundesrepublik Deutschland*, ed. Karl-Dietrich Bracher et al., 5 vols. (Stuttgart, 1983) 3:204–15; Rudolf Morsey, *Die Bundesrepublik Deutschland: Entstehung und Entwicklung bis 1969* (München, 1987) pp. 83–87; Anselm Doerring-Manteuffel, *Die Bundesrepublik Deutschland in der Ära Adenauer* (Darmstadt, 1983), p. 183.

[6] For an overview, see Klaus Hildebrand, *Von Erhard zur Grossen Koalition, 1963–1969*, in *Geschichte der Bundesrepublik Deutschland*, ed. Karl-Dietrich Bracher et al., 5 vols. (Stuttgart, 1984), 4: 130–34; Morsey, *Die Bundesrepublik*, pp. 83–87.

[7] J. Weber and P. Steinbach, eds., *Vergangenheitsbewältigung durch Strafverfahren? NS Prozesse in der Bundesrepublik Deutschland* (München, 1984).

[8] Manfred Messerschmidt, *Die Wehrmacht im NS Staat: Zeit der Indoktrination* (Hamburg, 1969); Klaus-Jürgen Müller, *Das Heer und Hitler: Armee und nationalsozialistisches Regime* (Stuttgart, 1969).

scholars argued that certain German officers had willingly cooperated with the Nazis far more than had previously been admitted. There was evidence that units of the Wehrmacht had engaged fully in genocidal massacres, in concert with the SS killing squads during the Eastern campaigns. As these historical truths entered into a wider political discussion, they complicated the policy of the Bundeswehr toward the heritage of the Wehrmacht. The widely accepted assertions made by former officers that Hitler and the Nazis alone were to blame for the crimes of the regime seemed unbelievable to the young protesters of the late 1960s. The distinction that Eisenhower had made in his declaration of honor for the German soldier between the guilt of certain individuals and groups and the enduring integrity of the institution appeared ever less credible. The revisionist scholarship had a growing impact upon the Bundeswehr and its maintenance of tradition in the 1970s and 1980s.

These international and domestic political changes confronted the maintenance of tradition in the Bundeswehr in the period of transition that followed the breakdown of the cold war consensus. Having briefly outlined these two stages, let us return to the transition to consider the rise of internal opposition to *Innere Führung* at the close of the 1960s.

THE YEARS from 1966 to 1972 witnessed an almost continuous public controversy about the political spirit of the Federal German soldier and *Innere Führung*. Advocates of different positions about the soldier and the state of the 1950s brought forward their ideas yet again, but this time they did so with a kind of frenzy unknown a decade earlier. Although the renewed controversy about *Innere Führung* arose in part from causes within the Bundeswehr itself, the vehement debate about military reform was fueled by the stormy international and domestic climate of the Federal Republic and the alliance.[9]

In the realm of international politics, quakes in the alliance in the mid-1960s unsettled the foundations of West German security.[10] The Atlantic alliance faced a renewed crisis that seemed to dwarf such

[9] Interviews with Generals Wagemann, de Maizière, Karst, March–July 1984, with Ulrich Simon, September 1985.

[10] Park, *Defending the West*, pp. 85ff.; Morsey, *Bundesrepublik*, pp. 73–83; Hildebrand, *Von Erhard zur Grossen Koalition*, pp. 170–202.

events of the 1950s as the rearmament debate, the Suez crisis, and the first nuclear deployments. The exigencies of national interest on both sides of the Atlantic undermined NATO. As the Americans turned away from Europe toward Asia, they widened the war in Vietnam and hollowed out U.S. ground and air forces in Europe. During 1966, the United States reduced the number of its troops committed to NATO in West Germany; Senator Mike Mansfield went so far as to introduce a resolution to withdraw U.S. forces from Europe. At the same time, French President Charles De Gaulle announced that France would withdraw from the joint NATO command structure, disrupting the deployment of forces on the central front and robbing it of its territorial depth and its zone of communications. In the midst of these developments, the Americans pushed their European allies away from a strategy of a massive first use of nuclear weapons, which had been institutionalized in alliance planning in the course of the 1950s. Instead, the United States insisted upon a flexible conventional and nuclear response to a Warsaw Pact assault. These moves heightened the existing need for a strategic and operational rethinking of Bundeswehr doctrine. But some believed, in view of the Vietnam War and the *grandeur* of De Gaulle's France, that this revision of NATO doctrine heralded a general U.S. retreat from Europe. The framework within which the West Germans and the allies had created the Bundeswehr appeared to be breaking down.[11]

Forces of change were at work at home, too. By 1966 Germans had grown weary of the founding fathers of the Adenauer era. Although these men had led the Federal Republic to international prestige, political stability, and economic growth, Adenauer's passing from office in 1963 cast a long shadow over his successors. The first chancellor had withdrawn to his garden in Rhöndorf; his successor, Ludwig Erhard, the organizer of the economic miracle, struggled against declining political fortunes within his own party and the ruling CDU/CSU/FDP coalition.[12] The men of the founding generation seemed to be in the

---

[11] On the effect of these developments on the troops, see the transcripts of the Ministerial G1 conferences in ZIF/ZUA, o.2.1.6., BMVg, Fü S I 4 Az 33–07, "Arbeitstagung 1968 G1/A1 Offiziere (Innere Führung)," 6 March 1968; BMVg, Fü S I 3–Az 33–07, "Einführungsreferat, BG Dr. Wagemann, StAL, Fü S I, 'Überblick über aktuelle Fragen aus dem Gebiet der Inneren Führung,' " 30 June 1971.

[12] Hildebrand, *Von Erhard zur Grossen Koalition*, pp. 152–240; Morsey, *Die Bundesrepublik*, pp. 75–93.

autumn of their political careers, overtaken by international and domestic events around them.

Most unsettling of all, recession struck the West German economy in middle of 1966.[13] The economic miracle that had looked as if it would "run on and on," much like that symbol of West German economic strength, the Volkswagen Beetle, seemed to be cracking up. A sharp economic downturn in 1966 aided radical politics, a phenomenon that had been nearly meaningless in the politics of the Federal Republic since the early 1950s. Suddenly, the polemics of the neo-Nazi National Democrats (NPD) against the "System of Bonn" garnered well over 5 percent of the vote in several state elections.[14] The conjuncture of economic distress and radical politics recalled the dissolution of the Weimar Republic. Now that economic prosperity was running out of steam, would democracy endure in West Germany, or would it prove to be nothing more than a mask to be discarded, as it had been in the early 1930s? Despite recent successes in civil-military relations, such fears only worsened longstanding anxieties about the position of the soldier in the West German state.

THESE DEVELOPMENTS in the political and economic spheres serve as background for a series of episodes that challenged the spirit of the Bundeswehr and *Innere Führung*. In August 1966, old tensions within the civil-military structure of the Ministry of Defense broke into the open in the so-called "Crisis of the Generals," the first of several crucial controversies that took place before the beginning of the 1970s.[15]

[13] Hillgruber, *Deutsche Geschichte*, pp. 90–91; Hildebrand, *Von Erhard zur Grossen Koalition*, pp. 202–31; Morsey, *Die Bundesrepublik*, pp. 87–91.

[14] Morsey, *Die Bundesrepublik*, pp. 104–05; Hildebrand, *Von Erhard zur Grossen Koalition*, pp. 371–74; P. Dudek and H. G. Jaschke, *Entstehung und Entwicklung des Rechtsextremismus in der Bundesrepublik*, 2 vols. (Opladen, 1984).

[15] See Ulrich de Maizière, *Führen im Frieden: 20 Jahre Dienst für Bundeswehr und Staat* (München, 1974), pp. 123ff.; MGFA, *Verteidigung im Bündnis*, pp. 186–88; Klaus Hornung, *Staat und Armee: Studien zur Befehls- und Kommandoverhältnis und zum politisch-militärischen Verhältnis in der Bundesrepublik Deutschland* (Mainz, 1975), pp. 215–334; Simon, *Die Integration*, pp. 63–65; William Geffen, "The Role of the Military in West German Defense Policy Making," Ph.D. diss., University of Denver, 1971. A discussion from the 1980s of organizational problems of the West German Ministry of Defense and the position of the Chief of Staff of the Armed Forces is to be found in Catherine Kelleher, "Defense Organization in Germany: A Twice Told Tale," in *Reorganizing America's Defense: Leadership in Peace and War*, ed. Robert J. Art and Samuel P. Huntington (Washington/New York, 1985), pp. 82–107.

On 12 August 1966, the Air Force Chief of Staff, Lieutenant General W. Panitzki, handed in his resignation to Minister von Hassel, followed the next day by that of Armed Forces Chief of Staff General Trettner. Shortly thereafter, Major General Pape, the commanding general of *Wehrbereich III* (the territorial military district encompassing North Rhine Westphalia) resigned in solidarity with Trettner. The resignation of the generals caused a political furor. Commentators worried aloud that these developments signaled the much-feared revolt of the military against the primacy of politics.

The action signified something less than a putsch against the civilian control embodied in the military legislation of the 1950s; rather, the generals acted out of more sober motives, and also Panitzki's motives were different from those of Trettner and Pape. All the resignations reflected longstanding structural defects in the civil-military bureaucracy of the ministry. Since the 1950s, key officers had protested internally against certain bureaucratic ills within the walls of the ministry. The chief evil, in their view, had been the subordinate position of the chief of staff of the Bundeswehr to the civilian undersecretary of defense.[16] Whenever a bureaucratic fight between an officer and a civilian official in the ministry broke out, the latter almost always won, regardless of the merits of the case. Despite attempts within the ministry in 1964 and 1965 to alter the chain of command and to augment the authority of the Bundeswehr chief of staff, the ranking officers found their hands tied by red tape, as several problems crowded in on the military during the summer of 1966.

Most spectacular among these difficulties (and the reason for Panitzki's resignation) were the mysterious crashes of the most glamorous weapon of the Bundeswehr, the Lockheed F–104G fighter bomber. Equipped to carry nuclear bombs (held in U.S. hands in peacetime), this plane helped to further West Germany's claim to equality with British and French nuclear power in Europe. Anxious to save their prized weapon system and to deflect criticism, the air force leadership tried in early 1966 to create a special staff with sweeping powers to clear up the problems with the "Starfighter." The civilian side of the ministry denied the executive authority demanded by

[16] Hornung, *Staat und Armee*, pp. 101ff.; Simon, *Die Integration*, pp. 63–64; MGFA, *Verteidigung im Bündnis*, pp. 186–88.

the air staff. The civilians felt that such a move would violate existing administrative prerogatives as well as the principle of a joint civilian-military staff upon which the Bundeswehr was based. As a result, Panitzki chose to resign.

Another crisis came to a head in the ministry over the question of labor unions in the Bundeswehr. After the enactment of the military legislation, West German soldiers had had the right to join a labor union, the *Bundeswehrverband*, established in 1956. This union, however, had a monopoly in the West German barracks. A public employees union identified with the SPD, *Öffentliche Dienste, Transport und Verkehr* (ÖTV), had protested against the hegemony of the soldiers' union and demanded the right to distribute its own information to men in uniform.

After some debate in the ministry, Under Secretary Gumbel acceded to the wishes of the ÖTV in the so-called "union decree" of 1 August 1966. Trettner, angered by Gumbel's failure to consult with him sufficiently, offered his resignation; he was joined a short time later by the commanding general in North Rhine Westphalia, Major General Pape. The contents of the decree had apparently been less offensive to Trettner than the way in which Gumbel had published it. These events brought the leading advocates of *Innere Führung* into the limelight again. In response to Trettner's actions, Baudissin and Gerd Schmückle joined ÖTV in September in an act of protest against a growing conservative trend among many of the officers and men of the Bundeswehr. Adelbert Weinstein suggested in the *Frankfurter Allgemeine* that Baudissin be summoned from the NATO staff to take over Trettner's job in Bonn. Minister Hassel instead named General Ulrich de Maizière as Trettner's replacement. The new chief of staff received many, but not all, of the increased powers demanded by conservative critics.[17]

Despite anxiety about a plot of the generals, the developments of August 1966 can best be described as symptoms of the bureaucratic wrangling that afflicts nearly all the armies of the world. The tensions created by strong differences of personality between Trettner and Gumbel—combined with the sight of jet aircraft crashing into the German countryside—were at the root of the problems, along with

[17] MGFA, *Verteidigung im Bündnis*, pp. 186–87.

the inclination of certain officers to go public with their protests if circumstances warranted such a drastic step.[18] Even greater difficulties soon followed in the political transition and social upheaval that now swept through the Federal Republic.

THE MALAISE of the Erhard government grew steadily worse as summer turned to fall in 1966. After the Free Democrats deserted the coalition, the Christian Democrats and the Social Democrats formed a Grand Coalition government under Kurt-Georg Kiesinger in December 1966. His chief tasks were to master the economic problems of the Federal Republic and to undertake initiatives toward the Soviet bloc, within the spirit of reduced tensions between America and Russia. If anything, however, the advent of the Grand Coalition government only worsened political and social tensions. "Otto Standard Consumer" (a popular figure from postwar drama and films) was jolted out of the euphoria of sausages and automobile chrome by the Weimar-like specters of international and economic uncertainty as well as by a restive neo-Nazi movement. To some critical West Germans, it no longer seemed possible to oppose the policies of the government within the framework of parliamentary democracy. But the nascent NPD was only the beginning of a radical political opposition to the status quo.

Radicalism on the right was quickly followed by a far more powerful challenge from the left. The latter half of the 1960s saw a global outpouring of protest stretching from Berkeley to Paris, from Berlin to Peking. Following the example of such men as Herbert Marcuse or Mao-Tse Tung, the generation of people under thirty seemed to mount a worldwide siege against the established order. West Germany proved to be no exception to this trend. In the course of the year 1967–68, many young people, infuriated with Socialists Willy Brandt, Herbert Wehner, and Helmut Schmidt for a making common cause with the "reactionary CDU/CSU," deserted the ranks of the SPD, accusing the party of having abandoned the last vestiges of Marxism on its way to becoming a pluralistic national party. These men and women, later known as the "Generation of 1968," took to the streets in the Socialist German Students Confederation (SDS, a group

---

[18] Simon, *Die Integration*, pp. 63–64; Hornung, *Staat und Armee*, pp. 317–33.

that had seceded from the SPD as early as 1960), which in turn formed the basis for the extraparliamentary opposition (APO). The death of a protester during a visit of the shah of Iran to West Berlin in June 1967 galvanized the movement of the new left, whose membership came from a variety of groups from East German apparatchiks of the SED to neutralist-pacifists of the "Eastermarch" antinuclear movement. These groups made a common front against the old cold warriors of the republic.[19]

The spirit of iconoclasm against all traditions that moved these youths was opposed to the "mustiness of a thousand years," and it challenged the Bundeswehr as it did few other institutions of West German life. Critics of state and society assaulted the army as the authoritarian embodiment of everything wrong with the Bonn democracy. The number of men refusing military service rose rapidly; despite the "count me out" mood of the 1950s, only in the late 1960s did a growing number of draftees actually opt for alternate civilian service.[20] In the ranks, NCOs and company grade officers found ever greater resistance to their orders and directives among draftees. Such friction exacerbated civil-military tensions that had festered beneath the surface for years; in turn, conservative forces in West German society and within the Bundeswehr rallied against the challenges from the left.

HANS-GEORG STUDNITZ, a conservative journalist, set the direction for the military's counterattack against the transformation of West German society and politics with a small volume published in

---

[19] Hillgruber, *Deutsche Geschichte*, pp. 94–95; Hildebrand, *Von Erhard zur Grossen Koalition*, pp. 372–83; Morsey, *Die Bundesrepublik*, pp. 102–04; the best work in English on the evolution of antinuclear protest in West Germany is Mark Cioc, *Pax Atomica: The Nuclear Debate in West Germany, 1950–1961* (New York, 1988).

[20] See statistics in DOKZENT Bw RA 1053 "Materialien zur Diskussionsveranstaltung 'Soldat und Gesellschaft,' " ed. BMVg, Informations- und Presse Stab, April 1981, pp. 44–45. On the effect of these developments on the troops, see the transcripts of the Ministerial G1 conferences in ZIF/ZUA, 0.2.1.6., BMVg, Fü S I 4 Az 33–07, "Arbeitstagung 1968 G1/A1 Offiziere (Innere Führung)," 6 March 1968; BMVg, Fü S I 3–Az 33–07, "Einführungsreferat, BG Dr. Wagemann, StAL, Fü S I, 'Überblick über aktuelle Fragen aus dem Gebiet der Inneren Führung,' " 30 June 1971.

late 1967 entitled *Save the Bundeswehr!*[21] The book echoed conservative criticisms of the new army and its reforms that had been making the rounds since the early 1950s. But Studnitz advanced his ideas in a combative style at a time when many West Germans, particularly those on the right, were willing to listen. Studnitz did more than merely rehash old antireform sentiment—he skillfully exposed problems of military life that had long aggravated professional soldiers. The long-term ill effects of the rapid build-up—too few officers and NCOs having too much to do with precious little means to do it—were played against an apparent official indifference and public scorn for the necessities of defense. Studnitz also criticized the bureaucratic style of leadership that rankled professional soldiers. In the view of Studnitz, these conditions were the fault of *Innere Führung*.[22] Only a return to tradition could save the army.

"The Bundeswehr," he wrote, "has become a mirror image of the West German society of consumers," an overly bourgeois entity devoid of social rank.[23] In an army without pathos, "the soldier is denied the luster of the past . . . everything that would strengthen the consciousness of being linked with history is kept from the Bundeswehr."[24] The stress on the Twentieth of July also came under fire: the honoring of the event "placed the soldier before the abyss of history, political anarchy, and military catastrophe . . . it did not lead toward the state, but away from it."[25] The reformers had robbed the symbols of the army of their real meaning: there was no sense of martial glory in the recently awarded unit standards.[26] The relaxed attitude toward a soldier's duty to salute his superiors harmed discipline, for "the obligation to salute is no outdated relic. It strengthens *esprit de corps* and is as necessary in the nuclear age as it was under the Great Elector,"[27] since the "ultimate purpose of military discipline is to prepare the soldier for the encounter with death." He also took aim at two democratic institutions of civil-military peace: the personnel

---

[21] H. G. von Studnitz, *Rettet die Bundeswehr!* (Stuttgart, 1967).

[22] For the impact of the Studnitz book and the Ministerial response, see ZIF/ZUA, o.2.1.3., BMVg, Fü S VII 1 Az o–60–01, "Aktuelles Stichwort Nr.3—Wird Herr Studnitz die Bundeswehr retten?" 5 February 1968; "Freiherr von Wangenheim, Oberst a.D. Wiesbaden, 'Rettet die Bundeswehr von Hans Georg Studnitz,' " Frühjahr, 1968.

[23] Studnitz, *Rettet die Bundeswehr!* p. 158.

[24] Ibid., p. 77.   [25] Ibid., p. 59.   [26] Ibid., p. 71.   [27] Ibid., p. 74.

screening committee and the parliamentary commissioner, who stood for parliament's "mistrust of the military." With these institutions, "the Bundestag undermined the authority of the military in a way that even Hitler was unable to do."[28] He also attacked the decree on tradition as an antitraditions decree.[29]

An army that is separated from the life-giving umbilical cord of tradition is like a woman who is damned to live without love. Within the army, the glowing breath of history meets the life feeling of the present; out of this encounter grows the spirit of the future. The traditions associations of the Wehrmacht, Reichswehr, and Imperial Germany must be brought to the Bundeswehr. The names and symbols of regiments that have covered themselves with glory should be transferred into the Bundeswehr.[30]

Studnitz's book was a hit among professional soldiers. Critics worried that the popularity of the work reflected an antidemocratic groundswell among men in uniform.[31] In fact, this archconservative journalist had tendentiously capitalized on the feelings of professional frustration and social isolation in the officer corps in the late 1960s. Familiar complaints about shortages of company grade officers and NCOs, overwork, and too much red tape had greater resonance than Studnitz's pathos-laden appeal to an antidemocratic military tradition. Yet observers of the West German military found it difficult to make a distinction between symbolic issues on the one hand, and practical problems on the other.

KIESINGER'S Grand Coalition government soon faced another challenge. At issue was the parliamentary vote on the emergency legislation amendments to the Basic Law, a conflict that reached a climax in June 1968.[32] The draft laws superseded the remaining rights of the allies to intervene in crises and war in West Germany, restoring a crucial aspect of sovereignty to the Federal Republic. The laws allowed the government to declare a phased mobilization of civilian agencies and services in crisis and war. Fatefully enough, the amendments also regulated the use of the Bundeswehr in meeting domestic political dis-

---

[28] Ibid., p. 100.   [29] Ibid., p. 70.   [30] Ibid., p. 169.
[31] Simon, *Die Integration*, p. 60.
[32] Hildebrand, *Von Erhard zur Grossen Koalition*, pp. 369–71; Morsey, *Die Bundesrepublik*, pp. 106–07.

turbances.[33] Several weeks before the debate in the legislature, the most violent demonstrations yet swept West Germany, following the assassination attempt on APO leader Rudi Dutschke in early April; at the same time, social and political unrest spread in France and the United States. Critics of the military saw the Kiesinger government preparing the armed forces to put down a civil war. The conjuncture of the Grand Coalition and the new laws seemed to the left like a revival of Hitler's enabling legislation of March 1933.

As passions grew hotter in the last months of 1968, a kind of "counterreformation" stirred within the German army staff (as distinct from the overall Bundeswehr leadership).[34] A growing number of conservative officers argued that the military had to respond to the political and social challenges to their profession. One element of this critique argued for a greater honoring of past symbols, figures, and events. The demand for this more "traditional" maintenance of tradition emerged in a series of episodes within the officer corps during these turbulent years.

Brigadier General Heinz Karst, the most intellectual, reflective, and controversial of the men identified with the counterreformation, played a significant role as chief of training and education in the army staff; he was later bitterly and unfairly criticized for what some perceived as "red-white-and black militarism" in his directives to the army's educational and training staff.[35] "With the departure from the 'fair weather democracy,' " Karst wrote in July 1968 in his series of "Training Comments," "we military superiors are compelled more than before to render an account of where we stand in state and society."[36] He insisted that officers "stand up against the negative tenden-

[33] MGFA, *Verteidigung im Bündnis*, pp. 248–54.

[34] The term is taken from Simon, *Die Integration*, p. 113; by far the best interpretation of these developments is the protocol of a 1982 seminar at Zentrum Innere Führung to assess this development, "Ausbildungspädagogik: Auf der Suche nach dem Bild des Offiziers: Seminar zu den Thesen der 'Leutnante 1970' und der Ergebnisniederschrift einer Arbeitstagung der 'Hauptleute von Unna' " in *Texte und Studien des Zentrums Innere Führung*, ed. ZIF (Koblenz, 1984); also see Simon, *Die Integration*, pp. 111–20.

[35] ZIF/ZUA, 0.2.1.2., Hermann Wessling, "Die Generalität auf dem Wege nach Athen: Der Ungehorsam des 'Erziehungs-Generals Karst,' " Ms. n.d. [ca. June 1969]; also see Simon, *Die Integration*, pp. 41–55 for an intelligent discussion of Karst's ideas.

[36] "General des Erziehungs- und Bildungswesens im Heer, 'Ausbildungsbemerkung 1/68,' " 9 July 1968, consulted by the writer.

cies of the *Zeitgeist.*" In his further directives on army education and training, Karst took up the fight. He criticized current intellectual and social trends, while constantly reminding officers to uphold the authority of their profession, using quotes from Plato and Nietzsche.[37] But Karst did not write solely of things of the spirit; he also fought against the lassitude of peacetime army training. His directives called on subordinates to train soldiers more realistically, preparing them for the requirements of an unsparingly harsh image of war. Certain critics later mistakenly interpreted Karst's directives as an assault on military reform, which they were not; by no means did Karst embrace the one-sided, reactionary views of Studnitz. Rather, he believed that the practice of *Innere Führung* should be adapted to the present and that more stress should be placed on the combat power of the troops. Much of the internal challenge to *Innere Führung* arose from the demands of professional officers to strengthen the fighting power of the Bundeswehr. This trend in the years 1968–70 collided with the ideas of the long-haired cohort of draftees, who entered the ranks with very different ideas about the right of the state to make demands on them.

The counterreformation of the army leadership entered a new, more significant phase in the spring of 1969. On 19 March the Vice Chief of Staff of the Army, Major General Hans Hellmuth Grashey spoke in the Moltke Hall of the Command and General Staff College (*Führungsakademie der Bundeswehr*) in Hamburg-Blankenese to the first two classes of general staff officers trained in the mid-1950s. Grashey's comments were in keeping with his reputation among his admirers as a man of dynamic qualities, destined for a high position of leadership. To others, he was a *Troupier*, a narrow-minded soldier and traditionalist, his thoughts alien to the spirit of reform. Although not intended for the public, the gist of his speech found its way into the *Spiegel* magazine.[38] The vice chief of staff's verbal assault on the institutions of reform was the most spectacular in the history of the Bundeswehr, ushering in months of controversy that coincided with

[37] "General des Erziehungs- und Bildungswesen im Heer, 'Kurzinformation 3/ 68,' " 11 July 1968, consulted by the writer.
[38] Interviews with General Ulrich de Maizière, April 1984; with Major General Dr. Eberhard Wagemann, June 1984; and with Lieutenant General Carl-Gero von Ilsemann, March 1984. The incident is further mentioned in Ulrich de Maizière, *Führen im Frieden: 20 Jahre Dienst für Bundeswehr und Staat* (Bonn, 1974), pp. 139–40.

the fall of the Grand Coalition government. Although many in West Germany shared Grashey's skepticism about the effects of reform upon military efficiency, he was the highest-ranking officer to make these assertions in an official forum. Grashey later chose the path of early retirement, once the furor surrounding his speech had passed.

The vice chief of staff expressed his deep concerns about the state of the army to an audience of general staff officers. The ills of the Bundeswehr were the product of three sources: the bloated civilian armed forces administration in the ministry and subordinate echelons, the parliamentary commissioner (the symbol of parliament's "institutionalized mistrust of the troops"), and the concept of *Innere Führung* itself. Looking forward to better times, however, he predicted that the general staff would regain its former role as the prime mover of military life. His most disturbing assertion was the statement that the program of military reform begun in the early 1950s had been nothing more than a "mask." "What is so new about it?" he asked, referring to *Innere Führung*. It was something that had always existed in the German armed forces, but which the founders had sold as new to win the support of the SPD for rearmament. "But, now one can finally take the mask from one's face and say, 'Well yes, it [*Innere Führung*] has always been there.' " With the Federal Republic under siege from the left and the right and with an incipient breakdown of discipline visible in the ranks, the time had come for the soldiers to cast off the mask of reform.

These were startling words from an officer who had served in the *Amt Blank* and was later chief of staff of the acceptance organization that screened middle-level officers. If Grashey were to be believed, the leadership of the military had consciously duped the Social Democrats and quite a few others in West Germany. His comments constituted a direct attack on his superior, General de Maizière, who was clearly identified with the creation and implementation of the reforms. Immediately following Grashey's speech, Colonel Eberhard Wagemann stood up to contradict Grashey on the spot. He told the audience that Grashey's statements were simply untrue and did not represent the position of the Ministry of Defense. Grashey responded by berating Wagemann in front of the entire assembly.

THE GRASHEY speech marked the beginning of a protracted public debate about *Innere Führung* that spread in concentric circles through

West German politics for the next eighteen months. For no sooner had the uproar surrounding the speech in Hamburg passed than Chancellor Kiesinger made headlines with his own comments about *Innere Führung* to the annual meeting of the Bundeswehr Association in Bad Godesberg on 18 June 1969.[39] While describing the salutary effects of military service on young men, he called the terms citizen in uniform and *Innere Führung* "old clichés," in need of revision. "Often certain terms get worn out over time and lose some of the life they once had," Kiesinger suggested, implying that the concepts of reform belonged more to the 1950s than to the present. Praising the effect that exemplary junior grade officers and NCOs had on the bearing of young draftees, he then observed that one should see the Bundeswehr ". . . as a great 'school of the nation' for our youth." With this maladroit reference to William II's concept of political education in the old army, the chancellor seemed to be signaling to the opponents of *Innere Führung* that they could now "open fire" on the reforms.[40]

The growing controversy surrounding the armed forces in the spring of 1969 moved the ministerial leadership to ponder the effects of current unrest on the military reforms, yet there does not seem to have been any direct link between this effort and Kiesinger's public comments. As General de Maizière observed years later, *Innere Führung* had been the product of the ideological calm and political consensus of the 1950s. The rise of radical political groups and the general restiveness in the ranks compelled Minister of Defense Gerhard Schröder and de Maizière to reconsider aspects of the reforms. When the armed forces chief of staff requested that the service chiefs prepare draft suggestions for possible changes to the inner structure of the military, he made the important provision that such suggestions should conform to the Basic Law; clearly de Maizière was trying to preserve the reforms. In turn, the service heads delegated the task to their staffs. While the air force and navy leadership produced short, bland proposals, those of the army were drastic indeed.[41]

In June 1969 the Army Chief of Staff, General Albert Schnez, gave

---

[39] Kurt-Georg Kiesinger, "Die Aufgaben der Bundeswehr in unserem demokratischen Staat," *Die Bundeswehr: Zeitschrift des Bundeswehrverbandes* 7 (1969): 300–01; for the ensuing controversy, see the series of newspaper clippings in ZIF/ZUA, 0.2.1.1.

[40] Simon, *Die Integration*, p. 105.

[41] Interview with General Ulrich de Maizière, June 1984.

six brigadier generals—among them Karst—the task of writing a study for internal use that would address a variety of problems in a direct manner. Karst worked with the other generals on an early draft of the study, entitled "Thoughts on Improving the Internal Order of the Army," which went through several revisions, with contributions from many authors, before being completed and stamped "secret."[42] In spite of the fact that the document was classified, it was leaked to the press in December 1969. Although the paper became known as the "Schnez Study," critics blamed Karst for having written its most controversial passages.[43]

The study contained specific suggestions for helping the army fulfill its tasks on the battlefield: "The mission of the Bundeswehr is the point of departure for all reflections affecting the army's size, structure, internal order, combat power as well as its integration into the state."[44] But this tendency to highlight the requirements of combat betrayed what seemed to later observers a willingness within the army staff to follow Grashey and ask for the junking of *Innere Führung*. Despite assertions that the principles of *Innere Führung* remained valid, the authors insisted that the reforms must be adapted to the present political and social conditions. These steps should be taken to assure the fighting power of the army in the worst case. "This assignment must be clear to every soldier. He is not there solely to deter, but to fight in case deterrence fails. He can only contribute to deterrence by achieving this fighting power. Therefore, being a soldier is an assignment *sui generis* and not a 'profession like any other.' "[45] This final statement was a direct attack on Baudissin's ideal of the soldier in society.

[42] ZIF/ZUA, 0.2.1.2., "Führungsstab des Heeres, 'Studie: Gedanken zur Verbesserung der inneren Ordnung des Heeres,' " June 1969; "Entstehungsgeschichte der 'Studie des Heeres' Brigadegeneral Heinz Karst," 20 February 1984, consulted by the writer.

[43] The text of the document appeared in public in late-1969 and is reprinted in Klaus Hessler, *Aktuelle Dokumente: Militär-Gehorsam-Meinung, Dokumente zur Diskussion in der Bundeswehr* (Berlin, 1971), pp. 50–91; however, quotations below are from the original in the ZIF/ZUA. It seems fairly plain that Karst did not in fact write the version that aroused the greatest outcry from the public; rather, unknown authors in the Ministry of Defense completed a revised draft long after Karst's contributions were made. Simon, *Die Integration*, pp. 66–67; Karst, "Entstehungsgeschichte."

[44] ZIF/ZUA, 0.2.1.2., "Studie des Heeres," pp. 3–10.

[45] Ibid., p. 4.

The authors outlined a series of bold demands on civil society, including amendments to the Basic Law to strengthen the authority of the military in crisis and war.[46] They demanded greater restrictions on the right of draftees to refuse military service[47] as well as curtailment of the rights of soldiers to make complaints to the parliamentary commissioner.[48] Nor did the army staff ignore the historical image of the military and the maintenance of tradition. The troops were at present "damned to a life without history"; nor did the soldiers have a "true sense of tradition." Echoing the words of Himmerod and the demand for a declaration of honor for the German soldier, the authors wrote that ". . . the political and military leadership must clearly and openly accept the tradition of the German soldier." The image of the Reichswehr and Wehrmacht in the media must be balanced: "historically one-sided depictions of the soldierly past are to be swiftly answered by the Public Affairs Staff of the armed forces as well as with the help of the Military Historical Research Office." The authors stressed that

the danger of a historical void is to be resisted as much as that of a false creation of heroes. The possibilities contained in the traditions decree should be exhausted; this may require that the decree be revised. . . . The means available for the artistic decoration of troop barracks should be better utilized. Military scenes should be emphasized that strengthen the consciousness of tradition. These decisions should rest with those who use the buildings, i.e., with the troops (divisional commander/military district commander).[49]

But it was not the enthusiasm for historical wall paintings that sparked such anger among Schnez's critics, but this concluding passage: "Every attempt to cure symptoms promises as little effective success as the removal of individual deficiencies. Only a reform that has the goal of going after the illness at its roots, at the 'head and limbs' of the Bundeswehr and society, can decisively raise the fighting power of the army."[50]

These were indeed tough words from the army staff. The authors had not only ignored de Maizière's injunction to avoid mention of the Basic Law but ended up sounding like Erich Ludendorff writing about the subordination of society to the requirements of total war. After the full text of the document became public later in the year,

46 Ibid., pp. 28–29.   47 Ibid., pp. 30–31.   48 Ibid., pp. 32–33.
49 Ibid., pp. 51–52.   50 Ibid., p. 67.

many critics suspected that the military counterreformation had goals for the Federal Republic that were similar to those Ludendorff had espoused in the 1920s. Grashey's claim that the reforms had been a mask to dupe the SPD and the demands of the "Schnez Study" for beefed-up fighting power were exacerbated by the publication of an alleged statement by Karst that "Baudissin's concept was on the rocks" because of its internal contradictions and the wish of its creator to establish an "unsoldierly army."[51]

These events came to a head as the election of the SPD/FDP social-liberal coalition under Brandt led to the demise of the Kiesinger government in the fall of 1969. Helmut Schmidt, long a member of the defense committee and a reserve officer, became minister of defense in the Brandt cabinet. Both Schmidt and de Maizière now had to face the growing unrest within the army leadership and the ranks. For the first time since Gustav Noske in the early 1920s, an SPD minister of defense had to confront, in the eyes of some critics, a seemingly rebellious corps of professional officers. Nor was Schmidt's task made any easier by the advent of Brandt's Ostpolitik, which tended to undermine support among draftees for a high state of military preparedness in the Atlantic alliance. This situation brought no joy to many Socialists, who remained enduringly suspicious of what they regarded as a "CDU army." In fact, the new minister actually enjoyed great confidence among many professional soldiers. He had long advocated their interests as the SPD defense expert in parliament; his tenure signified a break with the traditional antagonism between German socialism and the professional soldier. One of Schmidt's first measures was to call Wagemann to Bonn to take over the ministerial staff that oversaw *Innere Führung*.

In the months from late 1969 to 1970, the Schnez study became the manifesto of the internal military challenge to reform; in a certain sense the document retained this role well into the 1980s. The study met with approval and agreement in the ranks of the officer corps.[52] The reasons for its popularity were similar to the appeal of Studnitz's

---

[51] "Not am Mann," *Spiegel*, 16 June 1969, pp. 75ff. General Karst chose early retirement in 1970. While the press commentaries of the time speculated that he had been forced into retirement, in his own words, he chose this step after he learned that he would not receive a divisional command.

[52] Simon, *Die Integration*, p. 67.

book, although it reflected greater seriousness of purpose than the journalist's pamphleteering. The Schnez study greatly escalated the controversy about military reform and shaped the subsequent debate over the next eighteen months. As this debate grew louder, the lower echelons of the officer corps responded with their own ideas.

THE PUBLICATION of the Schnez study prompted a group of young lieutenants in December 1969 to write a critique of the conservative challenge entitled "The Lieutenant 1970."[53] The authors of the nine theses that made up the paper were eight lieutenants at the army's officer school in Hamburg. The paper was to serve as the basis for an upcoming discussion with Baudissin. The lieutenants deplored the ideas of the Schnez study and other conservative statements about the ethos of the officer corps; in particular, they objected to the tendency of the conservatives to abstract soldierly virtues from the rest of society. They dismissed officers who claimed such virtues as bravery, chivalry, and self-sacrifice for its own sake as being unique to soldiers. "I want to be an officer of the Bundeswehr that does something not for itself," but for a greater goal. The officer should carry out his mission in order to "optimize society."[54] The lieutenants referred to military tradition to emphasize their point. The heritage of the Prussian and German officer had been to fulfill his mission for the goal of a greater good, and not simply for the benefit of the mission itself.

The lieutenants further directly criticized the decree on tradition: "I want to be an officer of the Bundeswehr who rejects a tradition that consists solely of epigonic reproduction and dispenses with the creation of something new."[55] The purpose of tradition was neither to keep a heritage nor to pass it on. Speaking in the spirit of the times, the lieutenants defined tradition thus: "Therefore, tradition is for us the utilization of history to produce something new. If we do not create something new, then we have not brought the world any far-

---

[53] ZIF/ZUA, 1.2.1., "Der Leutnant 1970: Arbeitsthesen erstellt von Leutnanten der Heeres Offizier Schule II, Lehrgruppe C für eine Diskussion mit Generalleutnant a.D. Wolf Graf Baudissin am 18.12.1969," n.d. [ca. December 1969]; the text is reprinted in Hessler, *Dokumente*, pp. 92–96; the citations below are from the original in ZIF/ZUA; an account of the drafting of the document by one of the authors, Major i.G. Uthemann, is in *Bild des Offiziers*, pp. 11–22.

[54] ZIF/ZUA, 1.2.1., "Leutnant 1970," p. 1.

[55] Ibid., p. 3.

ther; then we have failed."[56] Such a definition was perhaps less satis-
fying than those of Siegburg and Sonthofen, but the response of the
lieutenants to Schnez underscored the difficulty of upholding the image of military tradition embodied in the 1965 decree. Indeed, once
the document became public in January 1970, Baudissin commented:
"For the first time, active officers have passed me from the left!"[57] Baudissin's pleasure in this development was not shared by many other
regular officers. The nine theses found little support, even among
other junior officers in the ranks. In fact, many company grade officers
seemed to have adhered more closely to the conservative program of
the Schnez study.

The "Lieutenant 1970" document prompted another group of officers to prepare their own commentary on the state of the professional
soldier. In December 1970, thirty company commanders of the 7th
Panzergrenadier Division in Unna near Dortmund drafted a paper re-
sembling the form of "Lieutenant 1970," but the intention of the writers of this document was quite different.[58] The company commanders
had been encouraged by their divisional commander, Major General
Eicke Middeldorf, to produce the draft during a series of meetings;
after much bureaucratic wrangling, the paper was leaked to the press
in March 1971.[59] The document, similar in tone to the Schnez paper,
contained a long list of complaints, but this time they were offered by
young troop commanders in the infantry, armor, and artillery. While
proclaiming their support for democracy and *Innere Führung*, the
captains spoke of inadequate material, political, and legal means to
fulfill their mission. They could no longer uphold discipline and train
troops effectively for war. They were no longer willing to accept the
responsibility for these conditions in front of the troops. Their complaints focused on poor planning, inadequate personnel, too much

[56] Ibid.
[57] "Bundeswehr-Leutnante-Ich will," *Spiegel*, 2 February 1970, p. 34; a collection
of commentaries on the lieutenants' paper is in *Information für die Truppe* 5 (1970):
483–510.
[58] ZIF/ZUA, 6.2.1.3., "Abschrift: Niederschrift der Ergebnisse einer Arbeitstagung von Hauptleuten (Kompanie Chefs), 7. Panzergrenadier Division im Dezember 1970," n.d. [ca. April 1971]; the paper is reprinted in Hessler, *Dokumente*, pp.
115ff. and interpreted in Simon, *Die Integration*, pp. 67–68 and in *Das Bild des Offiziers*, pp. 7ff.
[59] ZIF ed., *Das Bild des Offiziers*, pp. 23–30.

Clockwise from upper left: ULRICH DE MAIZIÈRE, staff member of the *Dienststelle Blank*, head of the *Innere Führung* School and Command and General Staff College, and Chief of Staff of the Bundeswehr. (Shown here as a general.) EBERHARD WAGEMANN, staff officer of the *Innere Führung* and one of the chief authors of the 1965 decree on tradition. Later Commander of the 7th *Panzergrenadier* Division and of the Command and General Staff College. HEINZ KARST, staff member of the *Dienststelle Blank* and Brigadier General in the Bundeswehr as chief of army training and education. HELMUT SCHMIDT, SPD member of the Parliamentary Defense Committee, Minister of Defense and Federal Chancellor.

249

red tape, overwork, and the indifference of the higher echelons of command.

The captains made one observation that epitomizes the internal military challenge to *Innere Führung* in the years 1967 to 1971: "The integration of the soldier into society is judged to be a higher good than his value as a fighting man. The effort to make the self-image of the soldier more civilian obscures that which is specific to the soldier. He is denied the unique image of his profession, this in contrast to all other careers."[60] Soldiers were not merely "military-technical specialists, but fighters."[61] The captains called for the Bundeswehr to place greater emphasis on ceremonies that demonstrated the combat effectiveness of the forces as well as on more public swearings of the oath.

Again, the most damaging portion of the document was its conclusion, where the captains seemed to attack the principle of civilian control. They wrote of their "mistrust in the political and military leadership."[62] In their view, the government of the Federal Republic had consciously downplayed the threat from the Warsaw Pact in order to promote détente and Ostpolitik.[63] The civilian and military leaders also demanded too much of the troops in everyday service. They were responsible for a "permanent overburdening" of the army, the result of planning failures and inadequate personnel, which were the legacy of the 1950s. Finally, the captains accused their superiors of political opportunism. The leadership made organizational and operational decisions in order to curry favor with the leading political parties. In turn, the parties were seeking to gain undue political influence over the army.[64] This "politicization" of the troops contaminated the trust between superiors and subordinates.

After the company chiefs presented their demands (but before the affair broke in the press), de Maizière and Wagemann went to Unna to hear the captains out.[65] The encounter was a stormy one. The company commanders placed demands on de Maizière in a manner not unlike students protesting at a university. The captains spoke of the

[60] ZIF/ZUA, 6.2.1.3.,"Niederschrift, Hauptleuten," p. 6.   [61] Ibid.
[62] Ibid., p. 13.   [63] Ibid.   [64] Ibid., pp. 14–15.
[65] For the reaction of the armed forces chief of staff to the document, see ZIF/ZUA 6.2.1.3., "Der Generalinspekteur der Bundeswehr, Fü S I 5–Az. 35–20–17–02 'Information für Kommandeure: Stellungnahme zur einer Niederschrift aus dem Bereich der 7. Panzergrenadier Division,' " 6 April 1971.

frustration of training soldiers as a hopeless situation. Recalling his final days as general staff liaison to the *Führerbunker* in April 1945, de Maizière responded that a hopeless situation existed when an army had to fight off the armed might of the whole world, while its leading officers had been accused of trying to kill the head of state. The problems of the company commanders in the 7th division were serious, de Maizière offered, but by no means hopeless.

The incident of the "Captains of Unna," as they came to be known during 1971, was the climax of the military challenge to *Innere Führung*; the counterreformation later ebbed away in the course of 1971–72. Generals Grashey and Karst retired from the army during 1970, and Schnez, after Schmidt had defended him before parliament, retired by the end of 1971. The company commanders at Unna had badly overreached themselves by seeming to go against the primacy of politics. Their eagerness for a confrontation and their criticism of the political leadership undercut their political credibility. Nevertheless, they received wide sympathy from their brother officers. More than eight hundred of the nine thousand captains in the Bundeswehr wrote in support of the captains of Unna; of these, 114 captains and general staff officer candidates at the Armed Forces Command and General Staff College in Hamburg, the best captains in the Bundeswehr, were among the first.[66] Nor were these men disciplined because of their writings. Schmidt's answer to them was to hold a series of seminars with company grade officers of all three services to which the thirty captains of Unna were invited. In the course of these discussions with Schmidt, the officers saw that their problems were not necessarily shared by the other branches of the armed forces. Major General Middeldorf, however, was relieved of command for his role in the incident, and Wagemann became the commander of the 7th *Panzergrenadier* Division, further symbolizing the trust he enjoyed among the centrist civilian and military leadership.

IN THE FIRST years of the 1970s, the social-liberal coalition under Defense Minister Helmut Schmidt introduced a number of reforms in the bureaucratic organization of the Ministry of Defense and in the personnel and training of the armed forces. These reforms corrected

[66] Simon, *Die Integration*, p. 68.

251

many of the deficiencies that had long unsettled the everyday life of the troops.[67] One of Schmidt's measures answered the old criticism that the program of reform was ill-defined in the existing regulations, despite the fact that the military legislation, particularly the soldier's law, codified the principles of reform in detail. In 1968, the Undersecretary of Defense, Karl Carstens, had ordered the staff to write a compact and intelligible interpretation of *Innere Führung* that described what it was and how it was to be used. The result of this labor was ready in 1971, whereupon Schmidt ordered it reworked into a regulation, *Zentrale Dienstvorschrift 10/1: Hilfen für die Innere Führung*, which appeared in September 1972.[68] Now at least, one could answer critics who claimed that the soldier had nothing tangible in the gray plastic covers of Bundeswehr field regulations to tell him what *Innere Führung* really meant. Like the drafting of the traditions decree, the regulation had many authors who had worked under the guidance of State Secretary Karl Berkhan and General de Maizière.

The regulation contained a description of the constitutional basis of the armed forces; the new document restated forcefully that the Basic Law was the point of departure for the concept of the "citizen in uniform." The chapters of the regulation that followed described the hierarchical order of the Bundeswehr within a pluralistic society; that is, the idea that the Bundeswehr is an army within a democracy, as opposed to being a "democratic army." The authors included the observation that freedom was not limitless and that compulsion could not be arbitrary. Further chapters described the duties and rights of the soldier as well as his self-image. The heart of the regulation, however, was the "Theses for Superiors" that described the kind of leadership demanded in the Bundeswehr. The document contained appendices with the most important laws, regulations, and decrees on *Innere Führung* (including the 1965 decree on tradition) as well as important statements on *Innere Führung* from a variety of politicians, soldiers, and civilian advisers to the armed forces.[69]

---

[67] MGFA, *Verteidigung im Bündnis*, pp. 253–79; Kelleher, "Defense Organization," pp. 93–96; *Weissbuch 1973/1974: Zur Sicherheit der Bundesrepublik Deutschland und zur Entwicklung der Bundeswehr*, ed. BMVg (Bonn, 1974), pp. 225–34.

[68] Zentrale Dienstvorschrift (ZDv) 10/1, *Hilfen für die Innere Führung*, BMVg, Fü S I, ed. (Bonn, 1972).

[69] ZIF/ZUA, 0.2.1., "Mitteilungen an die Presse, IX/145 'Hilfen für die Innere Führung,' " 14 September 1972.

Commenting two years later on the effects of the new regulation, the authors of the official history of the Bundeswehr suggested that "the publication of ZDv 10/1 . . . probably cleared up many questions [about the reforms] and as a result quiet returned to the troops."[70] But this explanation of the "return of quiet" to the ranks fails to answer the question of why the internal military challenges to *Innere Führung* essentially disappeared in the early 1970s; furthermore, the official history gives us few clues as to why the conservative critique of the maintenance of tradition in the Bundeswehr, made visible in the Schnez study and the claims of the captains of Unna, also subsided in the years after 1972. Three aspects of an explanation present themselves.

First, as General Gerd Schmückle observed in 1976, the collapse of the military counterreformation resulted in part from demographic changes in the officer corps.[71] "The people who believed in 1970 that the moment had come to put their ideas into practice were no longer there a short time later: the Chief of Staff of the Army [Schnez] and the chief ideologue of the time [Karst] as well as several others. As a result the opposing position was gone."[72] In fact, the debate about *Innere Führung* lost much of its vehemence as the army's founding fathers retired and the Bundeswehr came to be officered by men from the "white years"; that is, by those men who had experienced the Third Reich in their youth and who had at most served in the antiaircraft auxiliary or the *Volkssturm* (peoples militia). By 1975, certain general officers in the Bundeswehr were of the class of 1928, while every tenth colonel had been born between 1928 and 1937.[73]

In the second instance, the conditions of everyday military service improved steadily in the 1970s, thus removing one of the principal sources of dissatisfaction among professional soldiers, dating from the early 1950s.[74] The shortage of key company grade officers and troop NCOs was alleviated, while barracks and training facilities were improved. Morale rose as the unbearable workloads that had been

[70] MGFA, *Verteidigung im Bündnis*, p. 269.

[71] Gerd Schmückle, quoted in Simon, *Die Integration*, p. 115.

[72] Ibid.

[73] Simon, *Die Integration*, p. 115; for further statistics and discussion, see Detlef Bald, *Vom Kaiserheer zur Bundeswehr: Sozialstruktur des Militärs: Politik der Rekrutierung von Offizieren und Unteroffizieren* (Frankfurt/Bern, 1981).

[74] Simon, *Die Integration*, p. 116.

imposed on the junior ranks were diminished. Reforms of military education and training, especially in basic training, took hold in the ranks and found wide acceptance among the junior grade officers.[75] The improvements fostered in part by Social Democratic ministers of defense defused the explosive potential that had existed among the lieutenants and captains during the period from 1968 to 1971. This reservoir of frustration about the details of everyday military life had made the younger officers willing adherents of the sentiments expressed in the Schnez study and the manifesto of the captains of Unna.

Finally, beyond improvements in the professional conditions of service in the Bundeswehr, West German society and politics calmed down as the 1970s wore on. The era of the Grand Coalition and the troubles of the late 1960s receded into memory with the energy crisis of the early 1970s and the rise of a terrorist opposition to the Bonn democracy. This transformation had its effects on the spirit of the army as well; the civil-military problems and concerns of the 1950s were now being left behind; civil anxiety about the soldier and the state no longer seemed to be so acute. The sense of isolation that unsettled professional soldiers in the midst of earlier decades of violent protest gave way to a greater tolerance between civilians and men in uniform, although distinct problems of civil-military relations remained beneath the surface because of the less obvious effects of détente and of social-liberal policies.[76]

The conjunction of these three disruptive factors in the stormy months of 1968–69 seemed to give the conservative forces their greatest chance to revise *Innere Führung*; the sense of crisis in the land galvanized the conservatives into action, with some hope of success. The Schnez study and the captains of Unna revealed the desire among some for a maintenance of tradition not unlike that put forward in Studnitz's book of 1967. Officers boldly demanded an image of the German soldier that openly acknowledged those characteristics— physical courage, a spirit of discipline and self-sacrifice in battle—that distinguished him from other servants of the state. In the process,

---

[75] *Weissbuch 1973/74*, pp. 225–34.

[76] This analysis is indebted to Simon, *Die Integration*, pp. 117–19, as well as interviews with Generals Karst, de Maizière, Wagemann, and von Ilsemann, March– July 1984.

they summarily rejected the spirit of compromise embodied in the decree, which implied a kind of symmetry between martial and civilian attitudes that these officers found artificial and unconvincing. Once, however, the conjunction of these three sources of strength for the counterreformation had broken down, the movement lost its momentum.

These events marked the climax of a twenty-year debate on the spirit and self-image of the West German soldier. This exchange grew much softer with the departure from the ranks of the generation of men who had begun their military service in the Reichswehr, went through the trauma of the Wehrmacht, and then built up the Bundeswehr.[77] The ideas and counterideas concerning the spirit of the future soldier of the 1950s—and the definitions of military tradition that resulted from that debate—were now taken up by the generation that had found its political voice in the spring of 1968. The success of the social-liberal coalition in its stewardship of the Bundeswehr in the 1970s, in effect carrying forward to fruition the policy of "not repeating the errors of Weimar," of which Carlo Schmid had spoken in 1952, created a new situation by the mid-1970s. As the era of reduced tensions between the United States and Soviet Union broke down, the social-liberal coalition groped to find its way in the midst of a changing political world. The problem of military tradition re-emerged in West German political life, where it once again provoked controversy about the German past and the position of the soldier in the state.

[77] "Die Entwicklung der Grundsätze der Inneren Führung," in *Information für die Truppe* 12 (1975): 83.

16. The Fate of the Traditions Decree and the Rise and Fall of Its Successors, 1976–1986

IN OCTOBER 1976 Colonel a.D. Hans-Ulrich Rudel—a divebomber ace, the most highly decorated officer of the war, and a notable figure in neo-Nazi politics in the 1950s and early 1960s—attended a meeting of the traditions association of the Immelmann Squadron at the Bremgarten Air Force Base near Freiburg. His appearance at a Bundeswehr facility sparked a revival of public and official discussion of the maintenance of tradition in the Bundeswehr. This new debate, a continuation of the one begun in the 1950s, lasted well into the 1980s. The present chapter offers an overview of these events as a kind of epilogue to previous chapters; its purpose is to show the ramifications of the debate of the 1950s and 1960s in the very recent past, and to place these events in their historical context. This final chapter cannot claim either the historical distance or the full access to sources that has informed the earlier ones. It will identify the chief authors and their texts, as well as relate the ideas and counterideas of the 1970s to those of the 1950s. The treatment will highlight continuities and discontinuities in the debate.

While the strongest criticism of the maintenance of tradition in the late 1960s came from the military counterreformation on the right, from the mid-1970s to the early 1980s, the left mounted a far stronger assault on the policy of the Bundeswehr toward the soldierly past.[1] This later exchange on the maintenance of military tradition and the

---

[1] The literature on the traditions debate of the late 1970s and early 1980s is vast; for an overview, see Lucian Kern and Herbert Kruse, *Die Argumentationsmuster in den Auffassungen gesellschaftlich relevanter Gruppen zur Traditionspflege in der Bundeswehr: Ein Materialbericht*, in *Sozialwissenschaftliches Institut der Bundeswehr: Berichte no. 23* (1981), and DOKZENT Bw PA 2718, Major Dr. K. Buschmann, "Der Traditionsbruch zwischen Bundeswehr und Wehrmacht: Ursachen, Folgerungen, und gegenwärtiger Stand der Diskussion," Thesis, Führungsakademie der Bundeswehr, October 1982.

spirit of the Bundeswehr, although it took place in many social and political groups, was especially intense in the ranks of the ruling Social Democratic party. Since 1969, Social Democratic ministers of defense had overseen the Bundeswehr; the first of these men, Helmut Schmidt, who became chancellor in 1974, was a leading architect of grand strategy in the Atlantic alliance. But the very success of the Social Democrats in security policy bore with it the potential for disintegration, once world tensions had resumed in the late 1970s. Although Rudel's appearance in Bremgarten was the immediate cause of the controversy in the years following 1976, the remote causes are to be found in the international political setting of the time. The breakdown of détente and the widening gulf between the United States and Europe visible in economic policy and NATO strategy in the late 1970s and early 1980s made themselves felt in the Bundeswehr. The maintenance of military tradition was later swept up in this trend as the cold war consensus between the Atlantic allies underwent a period of intense trials. *Traditionspflege* became a touchstone to judge the conflicting attitudes of the Social Democrats toward the state authority of the Federal Republic and its position in the alliance. This development fell roughly into two phases: the first was from 1976 to 1980 and the second was from 1980 to 1982. In 1976–77 critics of the left and center began to attack provisions of the 1965 decree on tradition that allowed for contacts with veterans, using this issue as a means to question the relationship of the Bundeswehr to the Nazi past. In the second interval, the question of military pageantry became the chief issue of debate, after 1980. This exchange of views in the SPD and the downward slide of the social-liberal coalition led the Ministry of Defense to scrap the traditions decree of 1965 in the spring of 1981 and to write another that appeared in late 1982. This second decree in turn became the object of controversy in the years that followed, while the new Christian-liberal coalition ordered the preparation of yet a third document in 1983. Thereafter, the dilemma of the Nazi past in the German-speaking world increasingly became a concern not only of the Bundeswehr but also of the Western alliance, beginning with a series of episodes that took place during 1984–86.

The principal strands of debate about the maintenance of tradition fell chiefly into two categories. The ones most influential on policy were the arguments of critics of the cold war compromise; the counterarguments of the advocates of the status quo embodied in the 1965 decree were less effective; the defense of the cold war maintenance of tradition carried less weight in the late 1970s and early 1980s. The two sides struggled, as they had for twenty-five years, to answer Baudissin's question of 1953 about what values and symbols should be "handed down" to the West German military. And as before, the chief problem remained the relationship of the Bundeswehr to the Wehrmacht and to National Socialism. Now, however, the growing distance from the Nazi past, joined with a far more critical attitude among the younger participants in the debate about the legacy of National Socialism, set this latest crisis apart from those of earlier decades.

The critics of the maintenance of tradition in the Bundeswehr in the first period objected to all symbolic and personal connections with the Wehrmacht. The willingness among makers of policy of the 1950s to allow certain continuities with the old armies gave way to a tendency to isolate the Bundeswehr from the pre-1945 era. The critics of the cold war compromise called for the creation of a *bundeswehreigene Tradition* (tradition drawn solely from the Bundeswehr). This change resulted in part from the ways in which some political figures of the generation of 1968 saw strong continuities in German society across the abyss of 1945; in the eyes of certain outspoken opponents, the continuities of personnel at Himmerod (despite the work of the PGA) had made the Bundeswehr vulnerable to the world of ideas of the Wehrmacht. Recent historical scholarship aided the case of those opposed to the Wehrmacht as a source of tradition in the Bundeswehr.[2] But the debate of the late 1970s and early 1980s, fueled by the emotions of the rising cold war, went much farther than earlier episodes in its criticism of the soldierly heritage of the Bundeswehr.

The critics of the cold war compromise in the second phase, roughly starting in 1980 with a series of violent demonstrations against Bundeswehr ceremonies in public, challenged the values of military symbolism and pageantry in general. In this regard they

---

[2] This argument was offered most effectively by Manfred Messerschmidt in *Das Verhältnis von Wehrmacht und NS Staat und die Frage der Traditionsbildung* in *Aus Politik und Zeitgeschichte: Beilage zur Wochenzeitung das Parlament* 17/1981, 25 April 1981, pp. 11–23, and is summarized in Buschmann, "Der Traditionsbruch zwischen Bundeswehr und Wehrmacht."

echoed those SPD members on the security committee of the early 1950s who had opposed the reintroduction of traditional military pageantry. And they also resembled the authors of the "Lieutenant 1970" thesis who had criticized as undemocratic the emphasis upon soldierly values and symbols being exalted above other groups in society. The critics in the early 1980s argued for the abolition of nearly all military symbolism and pageantry in the ranks, deploring in particular the ceremonial oath swearing and the grand tattoo; these customs they described as being derived from a "pre-democratic past" and hence they were invalid as a source of tradition. Such arguments were in fact a revival of old positions from the 1950s, now advanced by a far broader and more politically outspoken segment of the public.

The critics were answered by the defenders of the cold war compromise, who mainly drew their numbers from the military veterans and traditions associations and the opposition Christian Democratic party. Although there were a number of Bundeswehr officers in this camp, professional soldiers could be found among the opponents of the cold war compromise as well. The defenders of the 1965 decree, oriented mainly toward the requirements of the battlefield, argued for the importance of soldierly virtues and pageantry in the Bundeswehr. The proponents of the status quo were unwilling to divorce the Bundeswehr wholly from pre-1945 soldierly examples and symbols. These men echoed Heusinger's words of the 1953 that not everything in the German military past had been bad. In many cases, one could carefully choose select continuities with previous armies. The advocates of the status quo again brought forward the doubletrack attitude toward soldierly virtues, obedience, and resistance visible in Theodor Blank's radio interview of 1952 and Hans-Christian Trentzsch's explanation of the moral motivations of soldier in the Third Reich, all of which Hans Speier had commented upon at the time.[3] Members of the officer corps and certain CDU parliamentarians emphasized the value of soldierly virtues as things in themselves, choosing to exemplify bravery and self-sacrifice, even among members of the Wehrmacht. But such a position, which seemed nothing more than common sense in the 1950s, was no longer self-evident in the late 1970s. The clash of the two positions emerged in full once Rudel's visit to

---

[3] Speier, *Rearmament*, pp. 30–32.

the air base in South Baden became an object of public discussion. The following pages interpret the evolution of this debate in its two phases from 1976 until the mid-1980s.

THE CONTEXT of the Rudel affair makes little sense without some mention of the details of lineage and honors in the West German air force. In the early 1960s, the West German air force had diverged from the army's example in the question of lineage and honors.[4] While the army had avoided the official award of old unit designations to its tactical echelons, in April 1961 the air force Chief of Staff General Josef Kammhuber, himself a highly decorated pilot of the war, revived certain squadron lineage and honors of the time between 1935 and 1945. The air force had created traditions squadrons after 1935 that were named for such great fliers as Manfred von Richthofen, Oswald Boelcke, and Max Immelmann; other squadrons were named for such men as Horst Wessel, Hermann Göring, General Walter Wever, and Paul von Hindenburg.[5] While there was certainly no mention in 1961 of honoring Göring or Horst Wessel, Kammhuber apparently believed that the political reputations of Richthofen, Boelcke, and Immelmann were sufficiently neutral to allow a revival. The 51st Reconnaissance Squadron received the name "Immelmann" in honor of the World War I ace; but in this case there was a certain irony, for Hans-Ulrich Rudel had commanded the Dive Bomber Squadron 2 (Immelmann) during the war and was a leading member of its traditions association. Rudel was highly controversial in West Germany. Although he was a man of considerable bravery and enormous skill as a divebomber pilot (among his kills were 519 tanks and a battleship, despite his having been shot down thirty times), he had been unwilling to repudiate National Socialism in the years after 1945 and he was active in the extremist *Sozialistische Reichs Partei* and the later *Deutsche Reichs Partei*.[6]

Rudel's visit of October 1976 took place despite earlier ministerial

[4] Herbert Sewing, "Tradition in den Geschwadern der Luftwaffe: Richthofen, Boelcke, Immelmann," in *Deutscher Soldatenkalender 1962*, ed. Helmut Damerau (München, 1962), pp. 228–30.

[5] Caspar, *Tradition*, p. 278; Oberst E. Tschoeltsch, "Die Tradition in der Luftwaffe," in *Jahrbuch der deutschen Luftwaffe* (Leipzig, 1940), pp. 104–11.

[6] Simon, *Die Integration*, p. 71; Ulrich Mackensen, "Auch der umstrittene Ex-Oberst Rudel wurde eingeladen," *Frankfurter Rundschau*, 23 October 1976.

directives that he not be invited to a Bundeswehr base. Nonetheless, the air force officers at Bremgarten and elsewhere had enlisted the aid of notable parliamentarians, among them CDU members of the defense committee, including Manfred Wörner, himself a reserve officer and pilot. These political figures had apparently convinced the Ministry Parliamentary State Secretary, Hermann Schmidt (SPD), to allow the visit. Schmidt did so with the stipulation that Rudel neither speak nor discredit the air force in any way; he was simply to be one member of the visiting traditions association of the 2nd Dive Bombers. After this news became public, the authority of Defense Minister Georg Leber (Helmut Schmidt's successor in the post) was thrown into doubt; Leber already suffered the reputation among some of his party comrades of being too soft on the generals.[7] Manfred Wörner, on the other hand, later defended Rudel's visit with the observation that "no one can deny that Colonel Rudel was a brave soldier, who fought correctly. . . . Why shouldn't such a man be invited to a harmless, non-political meeting of comrades?" Furthermore, the CDU parliamentarian responded, "military bravery, independent of the personalities involved and their historical context, should have value in and of itself."[8]

The situation became worse, however, when one of the two air force officers responsible for Rudel's visit, Major General Karl-Heinz Franke, commented on the event in an off-the-record discussion with the press. Franke wondered why Rudel should be excluded from an air force traditions celebration, as long as former communists like SPD chairman Herbert Wehner sat in the Bundestag. After all, Franke suggested, Wehner had changed his politics; so had Rudel, who had not made a political statement for over ten years.[9] Asked by a journalist in confidence whether he shared his subordinate's views, Lieutenant General Walter Krupinski, chief of the *Luftflotte*, claimed that he had nothing against Wehner, but that "he was the best example" of the phenomenon of changed political attitudes.

[7] "Eine Generalsaffäre in Bonn: Umstrittene Grenzen der Traditionspflege," *Neue Zürcher Zeitung*, 31 October 1976.
[8] Manfred Wörner, "Vonnöten: etwas mehr Gelassenheit," *Die Zeit*, 12 November 1976, p. 3.
[9] "Eine Generalsaffäre in Bonn: Umstrittene Grenzen der Traditionspflege," *Neue Zürcher Zeitung*, 31 October 1976.

When these observations became public at the end of October, Minister Leber forbade both officers from carrying out their duties and ordered them placed on the retired list.[10] Krupinski responded by making a formal complaint against his being barred from service. State Secretary Schmidt resigned in the wake of the crisis. What had begun as a poorly handled matter of *Traditionspflege* became a crisis of confidence in the civil-military relationship, highlighting the fault-lines within the Social Democratic party.[11]

A week after Leber ordered the two generals retired, federal Chancellor Schmidt commented on the issue of *Traditionspflege* in a television interview.[12] His observations apparently helped to set into motion the revision of the 1965 decree. Responding to the question of whether the Social Democrats should reform the policy of the Bundeswehr toward military tradition, Schmidt recalled that in 1970 he had studied the 1965 document soon after becoming minister of defense. He had found the first sentence, "Tradition is the valid heritage of the past," ambiguous. "What," he asked, "is the valid heritage, and what is the invalid heritage?"[13] The decree, in Schmidt's view, had defined this heritage in an abstract way, which he believed could not succeed. After ten years of experience, a reexamination of the decree was unavoidable. The chancellor suggested that the armed forces should place greater emphasis on its own traditions, developed during the past twenty years.[14] His observations recalled a discussion of 1970, when, as part of his general review of the problems of the Bundeswehr, he suggested to Wagemann that the 1965 decree be withdrawn.[15] The general had warned him against doing so, since such a

---

[10] "Erklärung des Bundesministers der Verteidigung," in *Bundeswehr Aktuell*, 3 November 1976; see the press commentary in Guenther Gillessen, "Lebers Sündenböcke," in *Frankfurter Allgemeine Zeitung*, 3 November 1976, and "Affäre mit alten Kameraden," in *Vorwärts*, 4 November 1976.

[11] See the commentaries in *Sozialdemokratische Sicherheitspolitik* 9 (1976): 1–7; as well as the debate in the Bundestag some weeks later in Deutscher Bundestag, *Stenographische Berichte*, 11. Sitzung, 3 February 1977, pp. 451ff.

[12] ZIF/ZUA, 3.1.2.2., "Deutsches Fernsehen-Bericht aus Bonn-12.11.1976 um 22 Uhr: Bundeskanzler Schmidt zum Traditionsverständnis der Bundeswehr," pp. 14–15.

[13] Ibid., p. 14.

[14] Ibid., pp. 14–15.

[15] For an example of this earlier discussion, see Michael Vollert, "Ist der Traditionserlass noch zeitgemäss?" in *Information für die Truppe* 3 (1971): 372ff.

step would open a "political pandora's box." Schmidt apparently heeded Wagemann's advice—"I kept my fingers off of it"—but the new political situation made a rethinking of the issue necessary. Subsequent events proved Wagemann to have been correct.[16]

The Rudel affair pointed to the mixed fortunes of *Innere Führung* in the mid-1970s and highlighted the continuing threats to its efficacy. The era of open strife associated with the counterreformation gave way in the 1970s to what some observers have called the "technocratic phase" in the development of the Bundeswehr.[17] The growing bureaucratization of military life—a phenomenon by no means unique to the West German military—became a subject of controversy and debate.[18] The cult of high technology and the official enchantment with management techniques loomed ever greater in the armed forces. This trend may have been a greater threat to *Innere Führung* than the counterreformation. Just as the arcane details of nuclear strategy reflect an extraction of war from its political context , the conception of the Bundeswehr as an "organization of technocrats of war"[19] could lead to the idealization of a man like Rudel, whose technical skill in combat could be made to overshadow his obnoxious political goals. The emphasis on technology and bureaucratic perfection in the Bundeswehr of the 1970s seemed to lead some professional soldiers farther away from an understanding of the political and ethical ends of military service.

IN THE WAKE of the Rudel affair, the broader public discussion about military tradition took on a new character, which increasingly disparaged any personal or symbolic connection with the Wehrmacht. This trend against the cold war maintenance of tradition showed itself

[16] Interview with Major General Dr. Eberhard Wagemann, March/April 1984.

[17] Simon, *Die Integration*, pp. 125–36; Peter Balke, "Grenzen von Bürokratie und Technokratie in den Streitkräften," in *De Officio: Zu den ethischen Herausforderungen des Offizierberufs*, ed. Evangelischer Kirchenamt der Bundeswehr (Hannover, 1985), pp. 284–95.

[18] This development in Germany parallels the criticism of American military technocracy that grew steadily in the wake of the Vietnam war and the rise of a self-styled American military reform movement in the late 1970s and early 1980s: see Edward Luttwak, *The Pentagon and the Art of War* (New York, 1985) and Harry Summers, Jr., *On Strategy: A Critical Analysis of the Vietnam War* (New York, 1982).

[19] Simon, *Die Integration*, p. 71.

fully in the ranks of the Social Democrats, who appeared to follow, and indeed, to go well beyond the lead of Helmut Schmidt. In August 1977, the SPD district Mittelrhein in Cologne published ten theses on "Tradition in the Bundeswehr" that can be described as a kind of countertraditions decree.[20] The drafting of the ten theses prompted an exchange among members of the SPD. The authors at first spoke of the Bundeswehr's innovations; it was the first exclusively defensive German military obligated to democracy within the Atlantic alliance. The maintenance of tradition in the Bundeswehr should highlight this mission, as well as the values embodied in the Basic Law and the soldiers law. Values without any relation to a democratic state and its system of beliefs were unworthy of the Bundeswehr. The actions of individuals—an allusion to Rudel—could not be separated from their final purpose. In this sense, there were also no virtues and values unique to soldiers. The Bundeswehr should select persons and symbols principally from its own history. The tradition of the Bundeswehr should begin with the creation of democracy in Germany. As to the veterans and traditions associations, the military should maintain connections only with those groups that had accepted the democratic values of the Federal Republic. Military tradition should aid the integration of the Bundeswehr into society. Here then seemed to be a thoughtful articulation of what Chancellor Schmidt had suggested on television, offered in a nonpolemical style. The chief argument of this side in the debate was the emphasis on the "Bundeswehr's own traditions." The suggestions of the Cologne meeting were taken up by a broader public in the following months. But other participants in the debate were less restrained, and they foreshadowed positions that would soon be taken up by more radical critics of the cold war compromise.

Resurrecting the old agenda of a wing of the SPD from the 1950s, the SPD parliamentarian Karl-Heinz Hansen demanded in October 1977 that the Bundeswehr do away with the oath and ceremonial obligations, as well as abolish the soldier's salute, troop flags, and all military forms—including what was left of old-fashioned drill— which were in opposition to the technical progress of the Bun-

[20] ZIF/ZUA 3.1.2.2., "Thesen zur Tradition in der Bundeswehr," n.d. [ca. August 1977], reprinted as SPD-Bezirk Mittelrhein, "Zehn Thesen zur Traditionspflege," *Sozialdemokratische Sicherheitspolitik* (July/August 1977): 3ff.; "SPD Bezirk erstellt Thesen zur Traditionspflege der Bundeswehr," *Die Welt*, 1 September 1977.

deswehr. Hansen recalled much of Baudissin's proposals of twenty years earlier. So did Bernd Hesslein, a journalist and commentator on military affairs, who revived old criticism of the maintenance of tradition in his work, *The Unconfronted Past of the Bundeswehr*.[21] In particular, Hesslein criticized Leber for having sought a position paper from Baudissin after the Rudel affair broke and then for having ignored Baudissin's work of January 1977.[22] In fact, however, Leber had asked Baudissin's aid for a future commission that would be called to rewrite the decree on tradition.[23] The course of events between 1977 and 1981 had prompted Baudissin's return to the making of policy on *Innere Führung*, after an absence of nearly twenty years. Since his retirement from the Bundeswehr in the late 1960s, Baudissin had become associated with the University of Hamburg, where he had established his reputation as an analyst of peace studies and security affairs.

Baudissin's manuscript of early 1977, which contained ideas roughly comparable to the Mittelrhein theses, was apparently the basis for his later paper "Thoughts on Tradition."[24] In his manuscript, which was also a criticism of the ministerial traditions decree, he wrote that one could offer soldiers neither a "catalogue of virtues,"—a direct reference to the 1965 document—nor a gallery of ancestors. The attempt to award things from the past to the troops was bound to fail. Rather, he suggested that such units as brigades and battalions should conduct research into their own history and find individuals and deeds worthy of emulation. This process would represent an "award of continuity from everyday service into the future."[25]

But not all voices in the SPD had turned against prevailing arrange-

---

[21] Bernd Hesslein, ed., *Die unbewältigte Vergangenheit der Bundeswehr* (Reinbek, 1977).

[22] Peter Henle, "Die Auseinandersetzung über feierliches Gelöbnis, Grossen Zapfenstreich und Tradition in der Bundeswehr," unpublished typescript (Bonn, 1981), p. 50.

[23] Henle, "Tradition," p. 50.

[24] Graf von Baudissin, "Gedanken zur Tradition," 26 July 1978, in the possession of the author, and reprinted in *Sozialdemokratische Sicherheitspolitik* (September 1978): 2ff., and in *Tradition als Last*, ed. Klaus M. Kodalle (Köln, 1981), pp. 189ff.

[25] Graf von Baudissin, "Gedanken zur Tradition," *Sozialdemokratische Sicherheitspolitik* (September 1978): 6. During this writer's time with the Bundeswehr, he found that many units conducted research into their own history. They encountered a shortage or total absence of sources. Unlike the US military with its official history sections at various levels of command, the Bundeswehr's history office (MGFA) does not maintain command historians in peacetime.

ments regarding tradition in the Bundeswehr. A somewhat under-stated defense of the cold war compromise was offered by the leading figure concerned with military affairs in the Bundestag. The parlia-mentary commissioner (*Wehrbeauftragter*) Wilhelm Berkhan (SPD) wrote of military tradition in his 1977 report to parliament.[26] Appar-ently acting on Schmidt's suggestion to reexamine the document of 1965, Berkhan published a discussion of its contents and suggestions for possible changes in his annual commentary on the state of the inner structure. Despite growing criticism, the tradition document still offered soldiers a conception of the values that determined the relationship of the Bundeswehr to tradition. While the overall con-cept and structure of the decree were still acceptable to Berkhan, he suggested that its language and style were out of date. Passages that spoke of a soldier's "discipline of spirit, language and body" no longer appealed to young soldiers. Moreover, the provisions in the decree that dealt with former soldiers of the Wehrmacht and the other armies were distributed at seven different places in the text, adding to the present confusion about veterans.

A defense of the status quo also came from SPD figures in the Min-istry of Defense. The Mittelrhein theses provoked the Parliamentary State Secretary in the Ministry of Defense, Andreas von Bülow, who had replaced Schmidt in December 1976, to make a response in late 1977 and early 1978.[27] Bülow refused to accept the contention that the Bundeswehr should restrict its tradition to its own history. He re-minded his audience that the official birthday of the Bundeswehr, 12 November 1955, recalled the birth of Scharnhorst and was a conscious attempt by the founders to anchor the new military in the spirit of Prussian reform. The age of tradition was unimportant, Bülow sug-

---

[26] BMVg, ed., *Jahresbericht 1977 des Wehrbeauftragten des deutschen Bundestages: mit Bericht und Antrag des Verteidigungsausschusses und Stellungnahme des Bundes-ministeriums der Verteidigung*, in *Schriftenreihe Innere Führung*, no. 9 (Bonn, 1978), pp. 30ff.

[27] ZIF/ZUA, 3.1.2.2., "Rede des Parlamentarischen Staatssekretärs Dr. Andreas von Bülow vor dem SPD Ortsverein Bonn-West am 22. November 1977 zum Thema Bundeswehr und Tradition," reprinted in modified form in *Information für die Truppe* (October 1978): 14ff.; Bülow gained prominence in the mid-1980s with his ideas for a reorganized Bundeswehr with a militia-style force structure and less emphasis on heavy armored maneuver echelons; such a concept was a curious echo of Bonin's ideal of thirty years earlier; see *Protokoll vom Parteitag der SPD in Nürn-berg 25–29. August 1986* (Bonn, 1986), pp. 344ff.

gested, and history knew no zero hours. Rather, tradition required a constant process of reexamination, change, and adjustment.

Another voice against the exclusion of the pre-1945 past was heard in Hamburg in mid-1978. The Armed Forces Chief of Staff, General Harald Wust, addressed the graduates of the Command and Staff Academy on "Tradition in the Bundeswehr."[28] He told the general staff officers that the maintenance of tradition could not be wholly separated from pathos; however, the maintenance of tradition also demanded the use of the intellect. One had to know both history and the political realities of the present. Beyond these useful general observations, the armed forces chief of staff seemed to criticize the advocates of the *bundeswehreigene Tradition*: "it is overlooked that the Federal Republic of Germany has a German and European history that reaches back before 1945, which at the same time forms part of the history of the Bundeswehr."[29] This challenge aside, Wust recognized that the times demanded an ongoing debate about military tradition. The words of Berkhan, Bülow, and Wust notwithstanding, the ministerial leadership now seemed ready to move toward soldierly examples from the post-1945 era.

In 1978, a scandal over the issue of military counterintelligence cost Leber his ministerial portfolio. The intensifying discussion of military tradition, and the trend toward *bundeswehreigene Tradition* may have influenced the choice by the new minister, Hans Apel, in July 1978, to name a barracks in Essen-Kray for former federal President Gustav Heinemann. Citing Theodor Heuss's famous speech of 1959 at the Command and Staff Academy, Apel observed that it was far more difficult to create a tradition than to seek it in an outdated past.[30] Given Heinemann's early and outspoken opposition to rearmament and his reluctant acceptance of the armed forces, the choice of names for the barracks was unconventional. Nevertheless, the naming of the barracks received a generally positive reaction in the press.[31]

---

[28] Harald Wust, "Tradition in der Bundeswehr," *Europäische Wehrkunde* 27, 8 (August 1978): 377–83.

[29] Ibid., p. 377.

[30] Bulletin des Information- und Presseamtes der Bundesregierung, "Gustav Heinemann Kaserne: Ansprache des Bundesministers der Verteidigung," 11 July 1978, pp. 733–34.

[31] "Bundeswehr-Kaserne wird nach Heinemann benannt," *Die Welt*, 7 July 1978, p. 4.

A NEW GENERATION

The trend among SPD critics toward the exclusion of pre-1945 traditions, conventions, and symbols gathered increasing force throughout 1979. During a discussion of security policy at a meeting of SPD leaders in May 1979, several figures in the party, among them Baudissin, appealed to Apel to reform the policy on tradition in the direction of Baudissin's memorandum of 1977–78 with its emphasis on the Bundeswehr's own traditions.[32] These ideas, accompanied apparently with some dissent about Baudissin's involvement, were finally incorporated in an SPD position paper on the Bundeswehr that included statements about *Innere Führung*, tradition, and training in the armed forces.[33] The document followed the same general line of argument as the Mittelrhein theses. The authors argued that since tradition could neither be ordered nor directed, it should not be dealt with in the form of a decree. The integration of the maintenance of military tradition into the democratic order required a constant exchange with the most recent past about the role of the Wehrmacht in National Socialism.[34] This assignment "would remain necessary for the foreseeable future." One had to recall that under National Socialism the "traditions drawn from democratic, liberal, social democratic, and union milieus had been brutally suppressed."[35] Commenting on the purpose of the maintenance of tradition with yet another allusion to Rudel, the Social Democratic authors asserted: "Values without a connection to a democratic state and its system of beliefs are not worthy of tradition. Patterns of behavior, for example, bravery, fulfillment of duty, self-sacrifice and selflessness must be bound to the values of our order of liberty."[36] The Social Democratic critics of existing policy aimed to "integrate the Bundeswehr into society." To do so, however, they sought to prevent a maintenance of tradition that fostered an image of unique soldierly values and elevated the position of the soldier over the state.[37]

Taking up the fight with his fellow Socialists outside of the govern-

[32] Henle, "Tradition," p. 52; Horst Heinemann, "Nach schwerer Geburt ein gesundes Kind: Innere Führung, Tradition, und Ausbildung—was wird aus den wichtigen SPD Forderungen dazu?" in *Vorwärts* 49 (November 1979): 10.
[33] "Positionspapier zu Grundsatzfragen der Bundeswehr," *Sozialdemokratische Sicherheitspolitik* 1/2 (1980): 9–12; Heinemann, "Geburt."
[34] "Positionspapier," p. 10.
[35] Ibid.   [36] Ibid.
[37] Kern et al., "Argumentationsmuster," pp. 22–23.

ment, Hans Apel read a paper at the party congress entitled "Ten Principles on Tradition." Apel's document was supposed to appear in a forthcoming ministerial white paper of 1979.[38] The paper included aspects of Baudissin's work, but it was more circumspect in its approach; most important, it echoed Bülow and Wust in saying that "tradition in the Bundeswehr must not be restricted to the history of the Bundeswehr."[39] There existed "no lack of testimony, attitude, and experience" in the past that were valid for a modern "liberal, republican, and democratic tradition." Nonetheless, the minister concluded his "Ten Principles" by saying that the "Bundeswehr itself must build up and foster its own traditions as well. . . . Tradition is also a matter of patience. It cannot be planned. It has to grow . . . it is not a question that is discussed today and forgotten tomorrow."[40] Apel's further discussion of the decree of 1965 in the white paper of 1979 repeated Berkhan's finding that that document remained the "framework" for tradition in the Bundeswehr. The minister continued with an echo from Wagemann's 1965 explanation of the decree: "It does not lead servicemen by the nose, . . . but leaves room for the men to make their own decisions founded on the Basic Law and the Military Service Act."[41] Referring to the growing calls to suspend the 1965 directive, he offered that "even an amendment to the Directive on Tradition would not ensure that [misunderstandings would be avoided]. Hence we do not anticipate issuing such an amendment." Although there would be no new decree, Apel surely failed to foresee how unwilling many West Germans would be to "forget tradition tomorrow." As the first phase of the new debate about the policy on tradition in the Bundeswehr drew to a close at the end of 1979, critics from the left wing of the SPD were broadly questioning the cold war compromise. They condemned what little continuity existed between the Bundeswehr and the Wehrmacht, and, indeed, between the Bundeswehr and the entire German military past extending back to Frederick the Great. While such critics were often answered by the Socialist party elders serving

[38] *White Paper 1979: The Security of the Federal Republic of Germany and the Development of the Federal Armed Forces*, ed. Federal Minister of Defense (Bonn, 1979), pp. 196ff.; Henle, "Tradition," pp. 67ff.

[39] Minister of Defense, ed., *White Paper 1979*, p. 198.

[40] Ibid., p. 199.   [41] Ibid.

in parliament and the Ministry of Defense, the initiative was swinging toward the opponents of the status quo.

EVENTS in the course of 1980 heralded the opening of the second, more intense phase of debate on military traditions and ceremonies. Developments in the spring and fall of 1980 dramatically changed the character of the government's policy on military tradition. What had previously been a matter for debate in smoke-filled rooms and the pages of newspapers escalated into the object of violent protest in the streets of West German towns. World political tensions added increased passion to the ongoing debate about military tradition. The decision to deploy new intermediate-range nuclear forces in NATO (a move spearheaded by Schmidt to counter the perceived decline of U.S. support of NATO), the Iranian hostage crisis, the Soviet invasion of Afghanistan, political upheavals in Poland, and growing cleavages in Social Democratic policy exacerbated longstanding tensions in the West German civil-military relationship. Was Europe now to lurch back into the cold war after a decade of hard-won advances? Or worse still, would central Europe become the battleground for a Soviet-American limited nuclear war? In the face of these developments, the men who had followed the lead of Kurt Schumacher, Carlo Schmid, and Fritz Erler in military affairs found themselves increasingly isolated and on the defensive. The burden of a coalition government weakening in its resolve and the growing challenge of the antinuclear ecology movement worked against Helmut Schmidt and his cabinet as the 1980s began. The faultlines visible in the intraparty debates about the Bundeswehr and tradition now were thrown into sharp relief as critics focused on the spirit and functions of military pageantry, an aspect of the Bundeswehr that had previously aroused little controversy.[42]

The ceremonial swearing of the oath/solemn obligation and the grand tattoo had been practiced in the Bundeswehr since 1956–57; these customs had taken hold in the German armed forces of the nineteenth century. In the twentieth century, a growing emphasis on military pageantry had filled the swearing of the oath and the grand tat-

[42] The best discussion of the development of symbols and ceremony in the German armed forces is Hans-Peter Stein, *Symbole und Zeremoniell in deutschen Streitkräften vom 18. bis zum 20. Jahrhundert* (Herford/Bonn, 1984).

270

too with ever greater formal and symbolic meaning.[43] After much debate, these customs had been carried over into the Bundeswehr, where they tended to be combined in one event. After 1966, a military regulation spelled out the details of these ceremonies.[44] The swearing of the oath was to take place on the barracks square or at an appropriate place during a field exercise. The regulation stated that chiefs of staff were to restrict the number of such events in public. Swearings of the oath outside of the barracks, according to the regulation, were to strengthen the bond between the local population and the troops. But the regulations often collided with the needs of public relations. In the late 1950s and early 1960s constant local calls for greater military symbolism and pageantry led Bundeswehr units to make more and more public displays. In many cases, the local civilian government insisted that the townspeople wanted to see "their Bundeswehr"; this phenomenon, despite the ideal of an army without pathos, recalled the garrison life of the empire.

But in some German towns, particularly in the north, where the left wing of the SPD was strongest, there was little nostalgia for the brass bands and torchlight processions of the imperial past. The public debate about outdated military traditions of the past that had endured for several months had apparently left a deep impression on numerous local SPD districts. During 1980, public military pageantries led to repeated protests from SPD town organizations as well as from SPD members of local state government.[45] What had begun as an attempt to distance the Bundeswehr from the personalities and symbols of the Wehrmacht now became a general attempt to reform all military symbolism in the Bundeswehr. In particular, people in the local SPD groups objected to the chorale form ("I pray to the power of love") of the grand tattoo as being too resonant of the feudal past. The chorale and the order to "remove cover for prayer" (*Helm ab zum Gebet*) signified the unity of throne and altar, making the grand tattoo a superannuated remnant of a "pre-democratic past," intended for

[43] Ibid., 3:267–73.
[44] Alois Friedel, "Symbole, Feldzeichen, Truppenfahnen," *Truppenpraxis* 5 (1969): 338; BMVg, *Zentrale Dienstvorschrift 10/7, Die Truppenfahnen der Streitkräfte* (Bonn, 1968); BMVg, *Zentrale Dienstvorschrift 10/8, Militärische Formen und Feiern* (Bonn, 1966).
[45] Kern et al., *Argumentationsmuster*, pp. 24–25.

"military freebooters" of the early modern age. Such symbolism was wholly unsuited for "citizens in uniform."[46] The offensive against "pre-democratic symbolism"—a logical outgrowth of the previous debate—became the chief element in the second phase of the public exchanges that began essentially in 1980 and reached a climax in late 1982.

A public swearing of the oath by new soldiers in Bremen in May 1980 was supposed to celebrate the twenty-fifth anniversary of the entry of West Germany into NATO. News of the event triggered a debate in the SPD council in Bremen on tradition and military pageantry. Both the local SPD leaders as well as Bremen's SPD mayor Hans Koschnick took exception to the spirit of the grand tattoo. They argued that the armed forces should find forms and symbols that corresponded to the democratic constitution of the Federal Republic. Opponents of the pageantry decried it as saber rattling during a tense situation in the Middle East and Poland.

The public swearing of the oath that took place on 6 May 1980, with federal President Karl Carstens present, ended in a pitched battle between police and demonstrators at the Weser stadium, a scene that had become all too common in West German life after 1967. The television news program broadcast scenes of riot police protecting soldiers against violent protesters before a backdrop of smoke and wreckage. The political upshot of the conflict in the Weser stadium was mutual recriminations between national and local levels of the SPD as well as widespread allegations that all concerned had betrayed the soldiers.[47] The Ministry of Defense responded to the violence in Bremen by announcing that the public ceremonies for the twenty-fifth anniversary of the Bundeswehr planned for November would be carried out despite protest. The Bundeswehr would undertake a public debate on the military tradition, but the event would be put off until the Spring of 1981. Until the debate was concluded, however, the armed forces would "practice reserve in their public displays of all kinds."[48]

[46] Ibid., p. 25. There is some irony in these assertions, for similar objections were voiced against the grand tattoo of the Wehrmacht by figures in the SA and NSDAP during the Third Reich. See Fritz Wiedemann Papers, Hoover Institution Archives, "Adjutant to the Führer, Correspondence on relations between NSDAP and Wehrmacht, 1934–1938," Boxes 1–3.

[47] Henle, "Tradition," pp. 67ff.

[48] Ibid.

The announcement by the ministry to postpone the official debate failed to prevent others from discussing the problem of tradition. In a July 1980 issue of *Spiegel*, Karl-Heinz Hansen, an SPD member of parliament, forcefully articulated the criticism of the cold war maintenance of military tradition as it had emerged in the second phase of debate.[49] He asserted that the Bundeswehr had generally failed to repudiate the past. The armed forces still engaged in outdated ceremonies with the troop flag, swearings of the oath, and the grand tattoo. Ships, barracks, and air squadrons were named for figures from the empire and the Nazi period who could scarcely be ideals for a republican army. Hansen demanded that these abuses be corrected and that the traditions decree of 1965 be abolished. Voicing the antagonism of the left wing of his party toward existing civil-military relations in West Germany, Hansen further attacked parliament for failing to support Hellmuth Heye in 1964, after Heye (as Hansen would have it) had questioned the Bundeswehr's loyalty to the Bonn democracy. Past ministers of defense had failed by not immediately firing such generals as Grashey and Schnez. He further asserted that the Bonn government had missed the chance to create a revolutionary republican concept of defense, which would have made a connection to the peasants war and the soldier councils. Through half-heartedness, lack of democratic consciousness, and sloth, the government had created a new "unconfronted past." Hansen's article revealed that the regime's critics had now gone well beyond the issue of the symbolic bonds of the Wehrmacht to the Bundeswehr. The opponents were using the maintenance of tradition to call into question nearly all aspects of civil-military relations in the Federal Republic and to question the role of the Social Democrats in the military status quo.

Rising tempers and official anxieties contributed to the violence that surrounded the celebration in Bonn of the twenty-fifth anniversary of the Bundeswehr on 12 November 1980. While Theodor Blank had awarded commissions to the first soldiers of 1955 in the relative obscurity of the garage of the Ermekeil barracks, the Bundeswehr of 1980 was going to hold a public swearing of the oath and grand tattoo on the Muensterplatz in the center of Bonn. For hours before the ceremony, police drawn from all over North Rhine-Westphalia sealed

[49] Karl-Heinz Hansen, "Soldaten und Demokraten," *Spiegel*, 7 July 1980, pp. 38–39.

off the heart of Bonn in the kind of major police action undertaken to protect power plants and airfields against ecological protesters. Over eight thousand police were needed to protect fewer than two hundred soldiers. Despite the best efforts of the police, some three hundred demonstrators managed to slip through the police cordon. The scenes on the television news from the Muensterplatz on the night of 12 November 1980 further undermined the political efficacy of the cold war compromise on the maintenance of tradition. The television cameras recorded an army of green-clad police protecting leading officials of the government and a tiny contingent of gray-uniformed soldiers against a group of shouting demonstrators hurling paint bombs.

The events that took place at Bremen, Bonn, and other major German towns in 1980 suggested that current protests against "pre-democratic" customs in the Bundeswehr differed from the popular debate of the early 1950s, to the extent that they offered more radical groups a cudgel with which to assault the Bonn republic. But the SPD's criticisms also revealed continuities with that earlier debate, and in that they were both desirable and legitimate. Although critics of 1980 often used formulations virtually identical to those used by political figures of the 1950s, the attitude in which certain figures and groups addressed the Bundeswehr bore little resemblance to the bipartisan spirit of twenty-five years before. Rather, in the extreme cases of the protests at Bremen and Bonn, to name just two of several such incidents, specific political groupings capitalized on longstanding anxieties about militarism and an antidemocratic military tradition to assault the West German state and its relationship to the security policy of NATO. That the public symbolism of the Bundeswehr became the object of protest in 1980 is perhaps best explained by the rising tensions between East and West and the faltering struggle of the ruling coalition to respond to this development. Thus, it was not simply the collapse of the cold war consensus about the spirit and symbols of the Bundeswehr that was really at stake when demonstrators hurled rocks at soldiers, but the rejection by a vocal segment of West German society of the most basic tenets of the West German concept of the state and national security—parliamentary democracy integrated into the western alliance.

Minister Apel was caught on the horns of a dilemma, one that increasingly plagued the SPD in the 1980s. On the one hand, he had to pacify a wing of his party increasingly at odds with Helmut Schmidt's policies and eager to practice solidarity with the antinuclear ecological movement. On the other, he had to satisfy the military of which he was peacetime commander-in-chief. This dilemma was a perennial one for German social democracy in relation to military power; in a very real sense, the civil-military problems of the SPD of the early 1980s recalled the war credits vote during the empire and the armored cruiser debate of the Weimar Republic[50]—which had forced earlier generations of German socialists to confront the tension between pacifist internationalism and the desire for power in the state.

THE DRAMATIC escalation in public protests had its effects on policy. As the protests against the intermediate-range missile deployments grew during 1980–81, Apel directed an internal rethinking of existing policy on the maintenance of tradition, in anticipation of the later public seminar.[51] The high point of this process of reflection would come in the seminar on military tradition and security policy to be held in late April at the Ministry of Defense on Bonn's Hardthöhe.[52]

The meeting was preceded by what proved to be a highly controversial article from Manfred Messerschmidt, the chief historian of the

[50] For a discussion of these issues from the mid-1980s, see Harald Mueller and Thomas Risse-Kappen, "Origins of Estrangement: The Peace Movement and the Changed Image of America in Germany," *International Security* 12, 1 (Summer 1987): 52–88; Josef Joffe, "Peace and Populism: Why the European Anti-Nuclear Movement Failed," *International Security* 11, 4 (Spring 1987): 3–40.

[51] For instance, see ZIF/ZUA, 3.1.2.2., "BMVg Fü S I 4 Az 35–08–07 'Traditionspflege in der Bundeswehr: Sofortbericht über die Tagung vom 03.–07.11 1980 in Lohmar,' " 10 November 1980; BMVg Fü S I 4, Az 35–08–07 'Traditionsverständnis, Traditionspflege in den Streitkräften der beiden deutschen Staaten,' " 12 January 1981; "ZInFü/ Ber 3 "Erfahrungsbericht: Impulseminar 'Traditionsverständnis und Traditionspflege in der Bundeswehr,' " 4 March 1981; "Zentrum Innere Führung, 'Positionspapier des ZInFü zu Tradition und Traditionspflege in der Bundeswehr,' " 27 March 1981. The presentations of the Lohmar seminar were published as "Tradition in Bundeswehr und Nationaler Volksarmee," *Sonderheft: Deutsche Studien* (Luneburg, 1981); see in particular, Werner Hahlweg, "Tradition und historisches Bewusstsein," and Günter Kiessling, "Traditionsverständnis und Traditionspflege aus der Sicht eines Truppenführers," pp. 7–16, 53–55.

[52] The transcript is reprinted in *Soldat und Gesellschaft: Die Diskussion des Bundesministers der Verteidigung mit Soldaten und Vertretern gesellschaftlicher Gruppen am 23. und 24. April in Bonn*, in *Schriftenreihe der Bundeszentrale für politische Bildung*, vol. 172 (Bonn, 1981).

Military Historical Research Office in Freiburg (MGFA), in the *Süddeutsche Zeitung*. He succeeded in shifting the debate back to its first considerations with his commentary on the value of the Wehrmacht in the Bundeswehr. His "Not a Valid Heritage" was a critique of the 1965 directive and a synopsis of his earlier research on the inner structure and on political education in the Wehrmacht.[53] Messerschmidt leveled a far more effective attack upon the cold war maintenance of tradition than had any of its previous opponents. He asserted that the key statement in the tradition decree, that the value and achievement of the German soldier rested upon his freedom in obedience, was simply untrue. This ideal had not been the case in relation to the Prussian reforms or afterward. There had never been, in his view, good soldierly traditions of political thought and responsibility in the German armed forces. The abuse of the soldier's virtues in the years 1933–45 posed the greatest problem to the Bundeswehr. Most important, Messerschmidt condemned the Wehrmacht for the role it played in the Nazi state. As the armed protector of the Nazi system, the Wehrmacht had been profoundly anti-Semitic and deeply involved in the slaughter of the Jews. Indeed, next to the SS itself, the military had been the "steel backbone" of Hitler's empire.[54] This article set the tone for the discussion of the historical relationship between the Wehrmacht and Bundeswehr, an important aspect of the seminar on the Hardthöhe held some weeks later.

Apel invited over fifty representatives of nearly all sectors of West German society and politics to the Hardthöhe seminar of 23–24 April 1981. The participants included people from the parties, labor unions, employers associations, youth groups, educational organizations, local government, as well as active duty and retired military men of all ranks.[55] This pluralistic group embraced a wide variety of different opinions on the maintenance of tradition in the Bundeswehr. Nonetheless, the ideas expressed over the course of the two days generally fell into the broad categories of advocates and opponents of the status quo.

The discussion of the first day centered on the growing unwilling-

---

[53] Manfred Messerschmidt, "Kein gültiges Erbe," *Süddeutsche Zeitung*, 21–22 February 1981.
[54] See the insightful discussion of this issue in Buschmann, "Traditionsbruch."
[55] *Soldat und Gesellschaft*, pp. 3–6.

ness of young people to defend the Federal Republic. While many in West German society accepted the Bundeswehr as an institution, a large fraction of the populace could not identify with the mission of the military to deter war in central Europe within the NATO alliance. The present world crisis only exacerbated the increasing tensions between the armed forces and critical members of the younger generation.[56] The general problem of the "will to defense" formed the background to the later discussion of the maintenance of tradition.

Perhaps most important in this exchange was the problem of the Wehrmacht and its relationship to the heritage of the Bundeswehr. The case against the Wehrmacht as a source of tradition was most forcefully articulated by Baudissin, Professor Thomas Ellwein of the University of Konstanz, and Professor Hans-Adolf Jacobsen of the University of Bonn and the speaker of the *Innere Führung* Council.[57] The defenders of select continuities with the Wehrmacht came from among active and retired army officers as well as from the Christian Democratic parties. General a.D. Horst Niemack, representing one of the central veterans organizations, protested against the image of the Wehrmacht offered by Messerschmidt, Ellwein, and Jacobsen. Recalling the issues of the Rudel debate, Niemack asserted that men in war generally cannot choose the political ends they serve. He believed that the military achievements of soldiers must retain "value in themselves," distinct from the political goals of a regime.

Baudissin answered Niemack by commenting on his own experience under National Socialism:

If one wanted to know what went on in the concentration camps in the Third Reich, one could find out. I knew, and pointed it out again and again to my superiors. They answered that it didn't concern us. What's most important for the formation of tradition is Clausewitz's insight that all military deeds and non-deeds have political consequences. Every officer in the Wehrmacht above a certain level was in part responsible for what happened.[58]

[56] Ibid., pp. 13ff.
[57] Ibid., pp. 13ff.; pp. 135ff. Interestingly enough, Baudissin's further comments on the Hardthöhe sought to draw a sharp line between traditions and conventions; this was an echo of his definition offered at Siegburg, Sonthofen, and Koblenz in the years between 1953 and 1956.
[58] Ibid., p. 153.

Jacobsen suggested that the Wehrmacht was more deeply involved in the crimes of the war than many had acknowledged in the past twenty-five years. Among the numerous young opponents of the Wehrmacht were such figure as the head of the Young Socialists (Jusos) Willy Piecyk, the Youth Secretary of the German Labor Union Association, Hans Brauser, and the SPD Deputy Horst Ehmke. They asserted that one could hardly motivate young people to serve the democratic ideals of the Federal Republic by appealing to the memory of such men as Field Marshall Paul von Hindenburg and Admiral Guenther Lütjens.

The problem of the Wehrmacht led Jacobsen and Baudissin to agree that the Bundeswehr should emphasize far more of its "own tradition," but there emerged no clear consensus in the overall group on the details of such a move. Niemack and Ulrich de Maizière responded by recalling that the discontinuity in personnel between the Bundeswehr and Wehrmacht was at best indistinct. Soldiers and officers from the Reichswehr and Wehrmacht had built up the Bundeswehr. De Maizière pointed to the work of the screening boards; their harsh and minute examination of candidates for the senior ranks had been particularly successful.[59] Both Niemack and the Army Chief of Staff Johannes Poeppel reminded the group that in 1955 Blank had chosen Clausewitz, Scharnhorst, and Gneisenau for the heroes of the tradition for the new military. One could not now simply say that there was a new "zero hour" and abandon the Prussian reformers to the pantheon of the East Germans.

The Hardthöhe seminar prompted the various participants to air their views without producing a final consensus—there existed little prospect of finding a common ground between such extremes as the Young Socialists and the Association of Knights Cross Holders. No one side seemed to win over the other.[60] The meeting did, however, herald a shift in policy in favor of the opponents of the cold war maintenance of tradition.[61] The most important outcome of the seminar

[59] Ibid., pp. 174–75.

[60] Ulrich Mackensen, "Auch alte Gegensätze brachen wieder auf: eine schwierige Diskussion auf der Hardthöhe: Bundeswehr und Gesellschaft," *Frankfurter Rundschau*, 27 April 1981 and Karl Feldmeyer, "Halbherzigkeit und Doppelgleisigkeit: Die Bundeswehr porträtrierte die gesellschaftlichen Kräfte," *Frankfurter Allgemeine Zeitung*, 29 April 1981.

[61] *Soldat und Gesellschaft*, pp. 187–92.

was Apel's announcement toward the end of the seminar that the 1965 decree would soon be annulled (*kassiert*), a move against which certain members of the audience voiced immediate protest. The suspension of the decree was but one of several measures that Apel promised in his closing remarks. These steps, intended to improve the public image of the military in the wake of the recent violence, included restrictions on the playing of the grand tattoo at the ceremonial obligation, rethinking the policy on the naming of Bundeswehr barracks, greater emphasis on the military ombudsman (*Vertrauensmann*) in the ranks, as well as steps to make the soldier's everyday service more intellectually and physically challenging. Apel announced that the "understanding of tradition and the maintenance of tradition" needed to be "thought through" again. The results of this ongoing reflection would then be included in the regulations on *Innere Führung* and political education. As soon as this work was concluded, the 1965 decree would be suspended; that document had "deficiencies," especially in its failure to mention that the Bundeswehr "assured peace," the mission at the basis of its soldierly existence and its self-image. While Apel was against any collective damnation of the Wehrmacht, he promised that the armed forces would address and reflect on this phase of German history.

THE CLIMAX of the two-phased reform of the cold war maintenance of tradition came at the end of Helmut Schmidt's tenure in late 1982. The political crisis engendered by the intermediate-range missile deployments and disagreements between the SPD and FDP on social and economic policy was in full fury. The centrifugal forces in Schmidt's party, in the coalition, and within the Atlantic alliance shattered the West German cold war consensus on security and the state that had begun under Schumacher and was codified in the SPD security program of 1960. The results of Apel's initiative appeared on 20 September 1982, on the eve of the break-up of the social-liberal coalition. Apel's "Guidelines for the Understanding of Tradition and the Maintenance of Tradition in the Bundeswehr" was one of his final acts as minister of defense.[62] The new document symbolized the victory of

[62] ZIF/ZUA 3.1.2.2., BMVg Fü S I 3, Az-35–08–07 "Information für Kommandeure Nr. 1/1982 mit Anlage: 'Richtlinien zum Traditionsverständnis und zur Traditionspflege in der Bundeswehr,'" 20 September 1982; "BMVg IP Stab, Material

the critics of the cold war maintenance of tradition over the status quo.

The introduction of the new guidelines at a press conference included comments on the purpose of the new guidelines and a discussion of the deficiencies of the 1965 decree.[63] The authors of the new document, recalling Apel's words of the spring of 1981, had accentuated the "peacekeeping function of the Bundeswehr" as the basis of military tradition; furthermore, they had drawn a sharp distinction between the mission and spirit of the Bundeswehr and that of earlier German armed forces. Finally, the new document sought to describe the issues of tradition and symbolism in terms that would be acceptable to the younger generation.

The 1965 decree, suggested the authors of the press handout, had failed in these three crucial respects. The document prepared under Wagemann, Trettner, and von Hassel suffered from defective historical interpretations. As Messerschmidt had written earlier, the 1965 paper contained errors about the development of German nationalism and the legacy of the Prussian reforms for the "political co-responsibility" of German soldiers. The authors of the earlier work had failed to highlight the "lines of tradition" from the "heritage of liberty and democracy in German history"; from "the tradition worthy of preservation in German military history"; as well as the Bundeswehr's own lines of tradition. Such statements unconsciously recalled the failed effort to choose binding historical examples for the Bundeswehr, especially during the debate of 1961–62 among Meier-Welcker, de Maizière, and Ritter about Franz-Josef Strauss's image of history. But by 1982, that debate was long forgotten.

The new guidelines did indeed differ from the old ones. The overall tone of the guidelines emphasized that soldiers should derive their tradition from democratic examples. Paragraphs one and seven defined tradition as "the passing on of values and norms."[64] No longer

für die Presse: Pressekonferenz am 20. September 1982, 10.30 Uhr zu 'Neue Traditionsrichtlinien der Bundeswehr,' " 20 September 1982; DOKZENT Bw AA 6964, "Pressemeldungen, Kommentare und Stellungnahmen zu den neuen Richtlinien zur Traditionsverständnis und zur Traditionspflege in der Bundeswehr," 1 December 1982.

[63] BMVg, "Material für die Presse: Pressekonferenz am 20. September 1982," pp. 1–2.

[64] BMVg, "Richtlinien," p. 1.

was tradition described as "the handing down of the valid heritage of the past." In the words of the press handout, "tradition is no longer the assumption of things from the past, but requires an exchange with the past that demands intellectual labor."[65] Paragraph two stated that "the measure for the understanding and maintenance of tradition is the Basic Law and the tasks and duties which it assigns to the Bundeswehr. The Basic Law is the answer to German history."[66] This paragraph signified a break with the past, for the authors of the 1965 document had assigned highest priority to the "mission of the Bundeswehr." This new interpretation sought to place due emphasis on the "union of democratic values of liberty between the Federal Republic and its armed forces."[67]

Paragraphs five and six addressed the Third Reich and the continuity and discontinuity of German history; these passages also revealed how effectively the critics of the cold war maintenance of tradition had shaped the new policy. "The history of the German armed forces has developed with deep breaks in its continuity. The armed forces were in part ensnared in guilt in National Socialism and in part they were misused innocently. Such an illegal regime as the Third Reich cannot be the basis of tradition."[68] This was a rather different answer to the issue of the Wehrmacht than had appeared in 1965, after years of debate. Notable for its absence in the new document was any mention of the Twentieth July 1944 attempt on Hitler's life. Paragraph seven offered a reply to the defenders of Rudel: "All military deeds must be oriented to the norms of a state grounded in the law and international law. The duties of the soldier—loyalty, bravery, obedience, comradeship, honesty, confidentiality as well as the care of the exemplary behavior of superiors—achieve their moral standing in our time by being bound to the Basic Law."[69] The eighth paragraph underscored the idea that the Bundeswehr did not seek to glorify war, rather that it "served peace." This mission required that a soldier should be ready to fight in a "state of defense to re-establish peace."

[65] BMVg, "Material für die Presse: Pressekonferenz am 20. September 1982," p. 4.

[66] BMVg, "Richtlinien," p. 1.

[67] BMVg, "Material für die Presse: Pressekonferenz am 20. September 1982," p. 4.

[68] BMVg, "Richtlinien," p. 2.

[69] Ibid.

This "obligation to peace" gave a new "political and ethical dimension to the service of the soldier."[70]

In the remaining paragraphs, the authors drew a sharp distinction between tradition and custom. These lines echoed what Baudissin and his associates had offered at Siegburg and Sonthofen on "tradition and conventions," which more recently had appeared on the Hardthöhe. The authors spoke of recalling the heritage of a "free, republican and democratic Germany" in paragraph sixteen. Worthy of the maintenance of tradition were "soldiers who went beyond proving themselves as military professionals and participated in political revival and who contributed to the rise of an emancipated citizenry."[71] Emphasis on the Bundeswehr's own traditions appeared in paragraph twenty. These traditions included: the "mission to preserve peace"; "the refusal to foster an image of the enemy" in military training and education; "the integration in the Atlantic alliance"; the ideal of the "citizen in uniform"; the "formation of a democracy through the soldier as a citizen"; "readiness to seek contact with civil society," as well as "aid to the civilian population in emergencies and disasters." Yet another break with the cold war maintenance of tradition was to be found in paragraph twenty-two; this passage was also intended to prevent incidents like the one occasioned by the actions of Rudel in 1976. "Meetings for the maintenance of tradition may only take place with persons or associations whose basic attitude accords with the values and aims of our constitutional order. Traditions [lineage and honors] from units of former German armed forces will not be awarded to the Bundeswehr. The flags and standards of earlier German units will neither be trooped nor escorted. Official contacts with the successor organizations of the former Waffen-SS are forbidden."[72] Although the authors of the decree retained the ceremonial swearing-in and the grand tattoo, additional regulations were soon to appear that would restrict these events. The grand tattoo was to be reserved for the retirement ceremonies of high-ranking personalities; it was not to be played together with the ceremonial obligation.

ON THE 20TH OF SEPTEMBER 1982 the new guidelines appeared and the decree of 1965 was thrown out. The critics of the cold war

---

[70] Ibid.   [71] Ibid., p. 3.   [72] Ibid., p. 5.

maintenance of tradition seemed at last to have put their imprint on the spirit and symbols of the Bundeswehr. The ministry had drawn the line between the Wehrmacht and the Bundeswehr afresh; "predemocratic symbols and customs" were now deemphasized. But the impression of having resolved the question was mistaken. Apel's statement about "values and norms" provoked continuing public controversy.[73] The polarization of West German political life assured that the Apel's opponents would quickly take up the fight. Critics of the decree objected strongly to many of the provisions of the new document. They argued that if the 1965 document was filled with archaic language no longer suitable for young soldiers in the 1980s, then the 1982 guidelines contained more than their share of "social scientific jargon" that was little better.

Events now suggested that the advocates of the cold war maintenance of tradition would quickly reestablish themselves. In early October, Helmut Kohl (CDU) became chancellor, naming Manfred Wörner as minister of defense. Wörner, the former CDU defense spokesman and a vehement critic of the policy on tradition articulated under Leber and Apel, announced that he would immediately rescind the Apel guidelines in favor of new ones.[74] Wörner refrained from suspending the new document, however, apparently acting on the advice of one of his senior advisers that a new minister should not immediately overturn the directives of his predecessor. During his first address to the Senior Commanders Conference in October 1982, Wörner commented: "I agree with many points in the directive on tradition issued by my predecessor in office, but I disagree with others. I will have this directive reviewed and in so doing make use of your experience. Until then it will remain in force."[75] Prudence delayed the restoration of the pre-1982 status quo. Certain of the participants, however, worried in private that the issue had become a political foot-

---

[73] DOKZENTBw, "Pressekommentare"; for General Wagemann's answer to the new guidelines, see Dr. Eberhard Wagemann, "Zu den neuen Traditionsrichtlinien der Bundeswehr: Ein Kuckucks-Ei," *Europäische Wehrkunde*, November 1982, pp. 513ff.

[74] "Gelöbnis wieder mit Zapfenstreich," *Frankfurter Rundschau*, 6 October 1982; Adalbert von der Recke, "Last und Chance unserer Geschichte: Gedanken zur Traditionspflege in der Bundeswehr," in *De Officio*, p. 245.

[75] BMVg, *White Paper 1985: The Situation and Development of the Federal Armed Forces* (Bonn, 1985), p. 312.

ball, little more than a contest between competing SPD and CDU/CSU versions of the German military past.

In early December 1983 the armed forces chief of staff set up a working group drawn from members of the three services. The group was to reexamine the Apel guidelines and "take account of the experience of the armed forces" in preparing a "draft summarizing the basic principles and guidelines" on the maintenance of tradition.[76] The members of the group suggested that the results of their work be incorporated in a joint regulation. Among the consultants on this new document were Eberhard Wagemann, whom the correspondent of *Spiegel* tendentiously described as someone embodying the most conservative tendencies in the Bundeswehr; his involvement with the new decree symbolized "the march to the right" of the Bundeswehr, back to a "glorious past."[77] The draft regulation, entitled "Aids for the Maintenance of Tradition," was completed in May 1984 and submitted to the chief of staff.

But well before this draft reached his desk, political developments had diverted Minister Wörner's interest away from the problem of tradition in the Bundeswehr. Publication of the new document was delayed by a scandal that arose in early 1984 about the reputed homosexuality of General Günter Kiessling, the West German deputy supreme allied commander in NATO, whom Wörner suddenly placed on the retired list shortly before he was to have retired from the Bundeswehr.[78] The scandal damaged Wörner's political standing, making him reluctant to confront any renewed political controversy, especially bringing out the tradition regulation when issues of West German security policy and the alliance had become so nationally divisive. Eager to avoid the fate of Blank, Strauss, and Leber, who had to resign from office, Wörner adopted a policy of caution in his leadership of the Bundeswehr. The circle of authors inside and outside the ministry further revised the guidelines, which were still being kept from the public.[79] The problems of historical interpretation and

[76] BMVg, *White Paper 1985*, p. 312; von der Recke, "Last und Chance," pp. 244–45.

[77] "Zurück zur Legende vom besonderen Sterben," *Spiegel*, 10 October 1983, pp. 19–22.

[78] *Zur Sache: Themen Parlamentarischer Beratung*, "Diskussionen und Feststellungen des Deutschen Bundestages in Sachen Kiessling," no. 2, Bonn, 1984.

[79] von der Recke, "Last und Chance," pp. 245–46.

choices of phrasing were no different from those confronted in the protracted drafting of the original decree twenty years earlier.

The document that remained under wraps in the Ministry of Defense was in fact a compromise between the 1965 decree and the 1982 guidelines. This assessment should come as no surprise, for many of the figures who had worked on the 1982 document were involved in writing the new regulation; some had even been involved in writing the original two decades earlier. The new draft signified a restoration in part of the cold war compromise on the maintenance of tradition, overturning the attempts of the period from 1977 to 1982 to maintain chiefly "the Bundeswehr's own traditions." The shape of this restoration was visible in the pages of a 1985 white paper.[80] The section on the maintenance of tradition included these passages, almost certainly drawn from the drafts of the new regulation: "There are many examples of human virtues and military achievement in German history which deserve to be passed on by tradition: the military reforms of the early nineteenth century, the gallantry and sufferings of German soldiers in times of war and captivity, the resistance against the national socialist rule of violence, and the example set by those soldiers of the Bundeswehr who laid down their lives to save those of others."[81] Revising the image of *bundeswehreigene Tradition* in the 1982 guidelines, the authors of the white paper wrote that "the fact that the Bundeswehr came into existence on Scharnhorst's birthday gives evidence of the will of its founders to create a link between the past, present and future. Scharnhorst's postulate that 'all citizens of a state . . . must be its born defenders' and that 'the army and the nation must be linked still more closely together' is just as valid for the Bundeswehr was it was in his day." Thus were the "traditional" Prussian reformers and the Twentieth of July 1944 returned to the pantheon of the Bundeswehr. The authors of the new regulation also sought to draw more subtle distinctions between members of the Wehrmacht who were "ensnared in guilt" and those who had redeemed themselves in the period after the war. The authors of the new regulation—perhaps recalling what Niemack and de Maizière had said on the Hardthöhe—attempted to pay tribute to the generation "that sur-

---

[80] BMVg, *White Paper 1985*, p. 313; also see von der Recke, "Last und Chance," pp. 248–49.
[81] Ibid.

vived the war" and went on to build a democracy in West Germany and to reform the West German military.[82] Nonetheless, the passages that spoke of the "misuse" of the Wehrmacht and its being "ensnared in guilt" provoked intense debate among the drafters, much as this issue had caused for over thirty years.[83] As this internal exchange continued within Bundeswehr staffs, schools, and advisory councils, events on the world scene intervened to place this struggle between the advocates and opponents of the cold war maintenance of tradition in a new light.

WHILE the ministry temporized on the problem of tradition, the German past and the legacy of National Socialism became an issue of international politics during the years 1985–88. Questions about the impact of the Nazi past upon the present, which had long been debated in the Bundeswehr, were caught up in the growing contention between Europe and the United States over the nature of the alliance. The fortieth anniversary of the allied invasion of Normandy in June 1984, the celebration of the fortieth anniversary of the end of World War II in May 1985, the Austrian presidential election campaign of Kurt Waldheim and its aftermath in 1986–88, the trial of the SD chief of Lyon, Klaus Barbie, and the continuing struggle among German historians to interpret the Nazi past all drew the attention of western public opinion to how German-speaking Europe had come to grips with Hitler's legacy. The role of the military in the Third Reich fit easily into this discussion. Despite the passage of time, these issues appeared to be as deeply divisive in the 1980s as they had been in the years immediately after the war. This renewed attention to the legacy

[82] von der Recke, "Last und Chance," pp. 253–54.

[83] "Eine Armee für die Demokratie," *Die Zeit*, 8 November 1985, p. 5. For a discussion of the fate of the guidelines on tradition during 1985–86, see "Bundeswehr: Fettnäpchen aus dem Panzerschrank," *Stern*, 24 October 1985, p. 308; Ulrich Mackensen, "Ein Schritt Zurück," *Frankfurter Rundschau*, 4 November 1985; "Neuer Traditionserlass für die Bundeswehr: 'Schlimmer Rückfall,' " *Die Zeit*, 8 November 1985, p. 13; "Wörner: Neuer Traditionserlass. Es geht auch um die Wehrmacht," *Die Welt*, 12 November 1985, p. 1; "28. Kommandeurtagung der Bundeswehr," *Schriftenreihe Innere Führung*, 1 (Bonn, 1986); Heinz Karst, "Studienzentrum Weikersheim—Geschichte und Tradition in der Bildung der Offiziere der Bundeswehr—Problem Deutsche Wehrmacht," 14 March 1986, consulted by the author; Hans-Wendel von Rabenau, "Tradition und Reform in der Bundeswehr—eine Bestandsaufnahme," *Das Parlament*, 15 March 1986, p. 12.

of Nazism came as the place of the Federal Republic in the European political, strategic, and economic order became increasingly unsettled. The unrest stemmed in part from the progress of events that a few years earlier had overturned the cold war maintenance of tradition in the Bundeswehr.

During the early 1980s, America's increasingly implacable policy toward the Soviet Union and Western European protests against European missile deployments had increased hostility to the NATO alliance on both sides of the Atlantic. This hostility showed the fragility of the cold war consensus that had held the alliance together in its earlier decades. The long-planned celebration of the fortieth anniversary of the allied invasion of Fortress Europe was supposed to take place on 6 June 1984, seven months after NATO had begun the deployment of Pershing II and ground-launched cruise missiles in Western Europe. The anniversary coincided with the election campaign of Ronald Reagan, who decided to visit the ceremonies in France as part of a demonstration of the strength of the alliance. The celebration soon became the object of intense and sophisticated American television coverage.

With the political prestige of the event plainly growing, West German Chancellor Helmut Kohl had allegedly asked to be invited to Normandy as a sign of reconciliation, but the French and the allies refused to do so. After all, many people reasoned, the Germans did not belong at the celebrations, because Nazi Germany had then been the enemy of the Atlantic world and the occupier of France. Because of the domestic political damage that Kohl had sustained from the missile deployments, his absence from the Normandy celebrations further diminished the standing of his government at home. Many West German supporters of the alliance saw the Normandy celebrations as an unwelcome reminder that after forty years, West Germany still occupied the status of an outside nation, one which had the dubious distinction of being the largest nuclear powderkeg in the world.

President François Mitterand sought to lessen the apparent damage to Franco-German relations in the wake of Normandy. He suggested a joint Kohl-Mitterand visit to the battlefield of Verdun in September 1984. Although this French-German commemoration took place without any major incidents, one politically explosive historical celebration seemed to follow another in the mid-1980s. In November

287

1984, Kohl had apparently urged the recently reelected Reagan to emulate Mitterand's gesture of reconciliation on his visit to the economic summit in Bonn in May 1985. The German chancellor suggested a visit to a military cemetery as well as the possibility of a presidential appearance at Dachau. During the winter of 1984–85, the American presidential and the West German chancellery staffs discussed various way to commemorate the anniversary of VE-Day. A visit to the site of a concentration camp was discussed and discarded in favor of a Kohl-Reagan visit to a military cemetery where both American and German war dead were buried together. Since the Americans had moved the remains of their soldiers to cemeteries in France after the war, the staffs dropped this proposal in favor of a visit to the Kolmeshöhe cemetery near Bitburg in the Eifel mountains. The site of a joint U.S.-German garrison, Bitburg was one of many towns in the southwest Federal Republic where Germans and Americans lived side by side in harmony, symbolizing the durability of the alliance. Beginning in the late 1950s, German, French, and American soldiers and airmen from the nearby airbase had regularly honored their war dead in a joint wreath-laying ceremony. Since the 1950s, the care for military cemeteries like the one at Bitburg had come to symbolize an international reconciliation throughout Europe in a way that had never yet excited political controversy. But now the attempt by Kohl and Reagan to honor the war dead turned into political high explosives. The arguments against the commemoration of the memory of the Wehrmacht, which had been offered by the critics of the cold war maintenance of tradition in recent years, were echoed by the opponents of Kohl and Reagan in the United States, who were, of course, unaware of the controversy's long history.

Only the well-known beer from Bitburg (*Bitte ein Bit!*) had caused people outside of the Eifel to mention the town before 1985. But once a growing number of American commentators learned of the planned visit to a cemetery for the "soldiers of Hitler," it provoked considerable outcry in the United States. Long forgotten was Eisenhower's declaration of honor for the German soldier; very few Americans seemed to know or care about how the West German military had struggled with this problem for the past thirty years. The epithet of *Bitburg über alles* signified the perceived indifference of the Reagan government to the Nazi past. When the press learned that the military cemetery at Bitburg contained the remains of Waffen-SS men, particularly from the *Das Reich* division that had laid waste to the French village of Oradour-sur-Glane, the storm of protest in the United States increased still further. During the course of April 1985, the American Congress voted to ask that Reagan abandon the planned visit, which he refused to do.

The Bitburg controversy of 1985 and the outcry in 1986–88 against the concealed Wehrmacht service in the Balkans of Austrian President Kurt Waldheim demonstrated virtually all aspects of the problem of finding a valid military heritage that the Federal Republic had faced since the beginning of rearmament. Bitburg and Waldheim's past prompted contemporaries in the West to reflect on the role of the Wehrmacht in the Third Reich and in the war, as well as on the ethical dimensions of the German soldier's existence. The manner in which these two events quickly became contentious issues of policy suggested why the cold war maintenance of military tradition in the Bundeswehr could not easily reassert itself after 1982. In fact, the difficulties of finding a usable past that had first emerged in the Bundeswehr retained the potential in the 1980s to polarize international political opinion on a large scale. And, in the end, the Bitburg controversy seemed to have been yet another episode in the deterioration of the American-European alliance that at its beginnings had given birth to the West German military. German rearmament within the world context of the cold war had forced the question of military tradition on a people initially unwilling to confront making a choice from the past. Despite the very real success of the Bundeswehr in fashioning a self-image for itself, the events of the 1980s suggest that the problem of carving out a body of usable history from the German past has lost little of its ability to generate violent controversy.

17. Conclusion: A Valid Heritage

THE SUDDEN armament of the Federal Republic in the early
1950s prompted fears that the Germany's new army, drawn from
that of the Third Reich, might endanger the young democracy before
it became firmly established. This anxiety also invested the new soldiers' emblems and customs with exceptional political symbolism—
they became indicators by which to determine whether the spirit of
the old military was reasserting itself. The historical judgment current
in the 1950s blamed the Reichswehr for undermining the first republic
and for paving the way for Hitler. This evaluation of the past made
far-reaching military reforms a political necessity. The reforms known
as *Innere Führung* marked the final triumph of liberal civilian forces
in Germany in their effort to control the army—a struggle that had
begun in the nineteenth century and ended in the 1950s with the creation of the Bundeswehr. But this triumph also raised the dilemma of
finding a valid military heritage. In a bipolar world of nuclear antagonists, a tradition that appealed to the eighteenth and nineteenth centuries, and passed over the Third Reich in silence, seemed bizarre to
many who were critical of the new West German army. As a result,
the government's policy on military tradition compromised between
two extremes: the maintenance of tradition under Seeckt on the one
hand, and the popular revulsion against the military in postwar Germany on the other. The search for a valid tradition occurred within
the confines of these historical memories and anxieties.

THE GERMAN military survived defeat and civil war in 1918 by acting
as the protector of the new regime and as the guarantor of the unity
of the Reich. The spirit and the personalities of the old army survived
and ensured an ambiguous continuity between the forces of the empire and of the republic. After the armed forces were reorganized in
the early 1920s, Hans von Seeckt attempted to preserve what he regarded as the most valuable components of imperial military life and

290

pass them on to the Reichswehr and "a brighter future." His image of the Prussian spirit conceived of the state and the army as two sides of the same entity that must survive the possibly transient republic. Seeckt kept the rank and file out of party politics and formed his soldiers into an elite professional cadre. From the old armies he borrowed conventions and traditions, transforming them into a cult of tradition in the Reichswehr. He sought to create a spirit in the Reichswehr that would become the tradition of a future German army, free of the dictated peace. His policy of *Traditionspflege* was effective, but it nurtured the army as a state within a state, an institution alien to the republic.

Seeckt's concept of military tradition, which served as an ideological bulwark against party politics, later made soldiers susceptible to the appeal of the Nazis, who were clever enough to recognize and use the power of symbols to the fullest. After 1933, maintaining a Prussian and imperial military tradition helped the Nazis to legitimize their rule and to gain the cooperation of military professionals. The victory over France in 1940 could be seen as one of the brightest links in a tradition stretching back for centuries. When the war turned against Germany, military tradition served as an alibi for many officers who either did not recognize or were unwilling to admit their complicity or even guilt. This conflict between conscience and tradition emerged in full force in the failed assassination attempt of the Twentieth of June 1944.

The crimes of the Nazis and the unparalleled defeat broke the hold of German military tradition to a degree that had been unthinkable in 1918. The physical destruction of the German army on the battlefield and its political condemnation in the immediate postwar years at least freed the Federal Republic from this burden. Although humiliated in 1918, the Reich had emerged still fundamentally strong and a great power. In 1945, on the other hand, the state temporarily ceased to exist. Left to its own devices, West Germany would surely not have acquired an army for many years. Instead, the rivalry between the United States and the USSR compelled the young republic, against the will of much of its own population, to establish its own army. It was also the first time that a German democracy had created a conscript army within a multinational alliance. The strategic and operational conditions facing the new West German military constituted a

291

profound discontinuity with its previous armies. The Bundeswehr was organized and equipped solely for a defensive role under international command. Its mission and its role in the state were totally different from that of its predecessors. Could—and should—the past still matter?

FOR POLITICAL and ideological reasons, nonetheless, the prospect of a new army forced West Germany to assess the role of the soldier in the state. The process inevitably constituted a judgment on German history. Much historical writing of the 1950s concentrated on the weaknesses of the Weimar Republic and the role played by soldiers in the rise of Hitler. The German Basic Law and the internal structure of new army were designed with a strong awareness of the failings of the past. The reformed army, as planned and established amid great difficulties in the 1950s and 1960s, reflected a largely honest effort to correct the political failings of the Reichswehr and Wehrmacht. Responsible civilians and soldiers agreed that Seeckt's emphasis on military tradition and the relationship of the Reichswehr to antidemocratic veterans must not be allowed to reappear in the nascent West German democracy, a concern that remained pervasive well into the mid-1960s and was renewed in the late 1970s.

The chief reason for their anxiety lay in the nature of the new army's personnel. Although the era after 1945 revealed many political discontinuities, there were of course important continuities as well. At first, officers and NCOs of Hitler's army and Adenauer's army were one and the same. The officers who began to plan the new West German military at Himmerod in the Fall of 1950 had been senior commanders and general staff officers in the Wehrmacht. Much of what they proposed resembled aspects of the Wehrmacht in detail and recalled some features of the Reichswehr in spirit. But as the army was created, the West German parliament asserted its control over military affairs, and parliamentarians and professional officers learned to collaborate.

The process of building the inner structure of the new army in the 1950s was also without precedent in German history. The group at Himmerod acted in concert with civil servants, legislators, academics, and NATO allies. In so doing, they began to establish a new tradition and defined the image and spirit of the new West German soldier. He was to be a *Staatsbürger in Uniform* who would enjoy the rights he was sworn to defend. Never again could blind obedience to orders become the alibi for crimes. The program of reforms identified with Kielmansegg, Baudissin, and de Maizière contained features that were both old and new. The subordination of the soldier to parliament and the codification of his rights and duties were an innovation; the ideal of a soldier who would follow orders out of conviction and fight with a sense of initiative was not unique to the 1950s. The planners of the new army combined new and old aspects of reform in *Innere Führung* and presented them to the world in a way that raised both high expectations and intense resistance.

From the start, *Innere Führung* had to struggle with the primacy of politics, the need for military efficiency, and the burdens of history. The pace of rearmament combined with the "difficulty of digesting all the new things," as a senior general reflected in 1974, added to the political, strategic and ethical dilemmas of the West German soldier and affected the fortunes of *Innere Führung* in practice. The need to redefine military tradition grew more intense as the reforms were taken from the staff officer's desk to the soldiers' barracks in the midst of the political difficulties of the late 1950s and early 1960s.

The leadership of the new armed forces recognized the danger posed to the nascent army by a revival of Seeckt's *Traditionspflege* early on, but they also feared acting too quickly to regulate tradition. They knew that the reappearance of Prusso-German traditions in field-gray and jack boots would cause anxieties among the allies and the domestic opponents of rearmament, while a total denial of the past would alienate the professional soldiers needed to make the new army combat-ready. By the mid-1950s, the military leadership and their advisers had adopted General Heusinger's motto to let the new German army create its own traditions. Nonetheless, those responsible for the army continued to debate the shape of future policy.

The central dilemma posed by Baudissin's question, "what shall we hand down?" lay in finding an answer that lay between the extremes of Seeckt's concept of military tradition and that of the reeducators. This dilemma was intensified by the fact that, despite the political failings and crimes of the military leadership, the soldiers of the Wehrmacht had fought well against terrible odds. They had mastered their operational craft on the battlefield and in the staff room, and, until the very end, the Wehrmacht retained its cohesion. But excessive

293

pride in these accomplishments, which blinded soldiers to the need for political control over the military, might indeed endanger the new German republic.

Baudissin's academic advisers understood the tension between the need to find a usable past and the politically explosive potential of military tradition in the Federal Republic. As a result, Baudissin chose the Prussian reformers, with whom he felt a spiritual kinship, and the men of the Twentieth of July, who had been comrades to many in the *Amt Blank*. This choice, though appropriate, was not sufficient: it left unanswered questions about the recent past and about the institutional role of the Wehrmacht in National Socialism. Reflecting on his frustrations, Baudissin suggested in 1978 that, once the build-up had begun in the mid-1950s, former professional soldiers had forced the old *Traditionspflege* on the Bundeswehr. The veterans had attempted to salvage their honor in the face of reeducation and the popular backlash against the military. The new officers of the Bundeswehr had faced their former commanders and teachers with mixed feelings, yet still sought contacts between young and old as had been the custom.

Fostered in part by the official policy of "let it grow," a proliferation of traditional forms and practices in the ranks symbolized, in part, the phenomenon of passive resistance to many of the ideas championed by the reformers. Among the innovators, Baudissin was the most prominent and became an object of resentment. The resistance flourished in the difficult first years of the Bundeswehr, in which a wide gap existed between the promises of *Innere Führung* and the realities of everyday life among the troops. In the years since, however, this gap has been closed to a remarkable degree.

Nonetheless, the revival of traditional customs in the ranks of the Bundeswehr seemed to reflect the soldiers' need for symbols and ceremonies. Such a wish does not automatically threaten a democracy, as the military traditions of the United Kingdom, France, and the United States demonstrate. Carlo Schmid recognized in the 1950s that the new soldiers of the Federal Republic had a legitimate right to public displays, a point of view that proved uncongenial to some of his SPD colleagues twenty years later. From the perspective of the present, however, it is clear that the public symbolism of the West German military poses no threat to democracy. The ideal of an "army without pathos" in the hands of some of its more outspoken advocates became an unnecessarily extreme position, especially in the context of an alliance whose other members routinely engage in displays of elaborate pageantry.

THE TENSION between Heusinger's policy of "let the traditions grow" and Baudissin's more abstract idealism finally forced a rethinking of the issue of tradition. The existing confusion and disagreements about symbols, conventions, and traditions compelled the ministry to write the decree that appeared in 1965. It was a document that signified political and human compromises between the extremes of historical memory upon which the Federal Republic and the Bundeswehr had been built. The provisions in the decree included a compromise on the relations of the armed forces with veterans of the old armies that represented a middle path between their complete exclusion, which was impossible, and the restoration of Seeckt's traditions companies, which was unacceptable to West German society. Conscious of the perils inherent in decreeing an official image of history, the authors had obliged the Bundeswehr's officers to judge the past for themselves. To some critics, this seemed to leave unresolved the controversy about the political culpability of the Wehrmacht in National Socialism, a debate that still continues.

The authors of the decree document included many of the founders of the Bundeswehr, as well as a number of academics. There has been remarkable continuity in the circle of men who created the armed forces in the 1950s and who have participated in the traditions debate into the present. For instance, Kielmansegg and Baudissin have now been involved in these undertakings for nearly thirty-five years. The answer they gave to the question of tradition in the 1950s and 1960s was unprecedented in German military history, and further remarkable because no other major social group in West Germany underwent a similar process of historical self-examination. However flawed their reforms may seem to some, in hindsight, they still represented an attempt among professional soldiers to address the past in an intelligent and responsible fashion. Possibly, professional German soldiers have been more thorough in their self-examination than American officers have been in the wake of the Vietnam War.

The change in the political culture of the Federal Republic in the 1960s and 1970s compelled a further reexamination of this heritage, especially in light of the détente between the great powers and the thirteen years in office of the social-liberal coalition. This reevaluation of military tradition condemned the perceived tendency among the founders of the new army to exonerate the Wehrmacht in the process of formulating the traditions policy of the Bundeswehr. This shift in policy, which began to gather force in the wake of the Rudel scandal of 1976, sought to exclude the Wehrmacht from any acceptable tradition. Rather, the West German military was to foster only those traditions formed within the Bundeswehr since the 1950s. Yet more extreme critics on the left advocated the abolition of nearly all military symbols and ceremonies. The climax of this development was Hans Apel's decision to suspend the 1965 decree and to write another, which appeared in late 1982. Ignoring the conditions and choices that had led to the drafting of the 1965 decree, critics of it in the 1970s decried it as hopelessly outdated, forgiving of men like Rudel and a symptom of traditionalism in military leadership. There is some irony in these claims, because the chief author of the decree, Eberhard Wagemann, was the favorite troubleshooter for Helmut Schmidt, the first SPD minister of defense in the Federal Republic. Together with de Maizière, Wagemann confronted perhaps the most serious crisis of spirit of the Bundeswehr, the military counterreformation of the late 1960s and early 1970s, showing himself to be anything but a blinkered traditionalist in his response to Grashey, in his answer to the Schnez study, and in his taking over the 7th Armored Infantry Division at Unna.

Perhaps events in the mid-1980s—President Reagan's visit to Bitburg and Kurt Waldheim's irresponsible election—can place the record of the West German armed forces in a more positive historical light. In contrast to Waldheim's choice not to speak of his past by omitting from his memoirs his service as a Wehrmacht staff officer in the Balkans, the founders and leaders of the West German armed forces have consistently reflected on the both the valid and the invalid aspects of their past. The official publications on tradition, which have been the subject of this study, bear witness to this difficult enterprise. The efforts began in the 1950s within a program intended to integrate the soldier into society, which, as Ulrich de Maizière commented on the thirtieth anniversary of the Bundeswehr in 1985, is no longer a subject of debate. Today's state of affairs reflects the outcome of the struggle between liberal civilian forces and military institutions in German history. But while *Innere Führung* no longer excites controversy as it did in the first years of the Bundeswehr, the discovery of a valid past will remain an issue for each new generation.

Over its thirty-year history—a period of time longer than the existence of the Reichswehr and Wehrmacht combined—the Bundeswehr has laid to rest the widespread anxieties of the 1950s, that once German officers got their crayons and timetables again, they would plan another war. Today, the West German armed forces bear the principal responsibility for the conventional defense of Europe within the Atlantic alliance. The new army has developed principles of leadership and respect for the individual soldier that have now grown into a tradition of modern leadership and command that eludes the armies of the older democracies, especially the United States. These new traditions lie at the center of the valid heritage of the Bundeswehr.

Bibliography

Archival Material

THIS STUDY is based on archival materials in the Bundesarchiv-Militär-archiv, Freiburg; the Bundeswehr-Zwischenarchiv, Freiburg; the Doku-mentationszentrum der Bundeswehr, Bonn; the Zentrales Unterstüt-zungsarchiv, Zentrum Innere Führung, Koblenz; as well as on papers in private hands and on interviews with the participants. Only the most im-portant files consulted by the writer or cited in secondary sources are listed here.

I. Bundesarchiv-Militärarchiv (Bundeswehr-Zwischenarchiv), Freiburg (BA/MA).

Bw 2	982	Bw 9	716
	1267		717
	1302		797
	3949		1248
	3928		1254
	4026		1291
	4238		1324
IV V Min (Bl)			1460
Bw 7	321		2002
Bw 9	221		2527
	482	Bv 3	8119
	505	N	492/11
	714		

II. Dokumentationszentrum der Bundeswehr, Bonn (DOKZENTBW)

AA7123	S2530
F6951	S2786
PA2718	S2791
R5189	S2794
R5452	S3136
R6359	U6671
S2394	U7851
	X2579

III. Zentrales Unterstützung-archiv-Dokumentationsstelle, Zentrum Innere Führung, Ko-blenz (ZIF/ZUA)

0.2.1.	1.2.0.4.
0.2.1.0.	1.2.1.
0.2.1.2.	1.2.1.3.
0.2.1.4.	1.2.1.4.
0.2.2.	1.2.1.5.
0.4.4.4.2.	1.2.1.6.
0.4.4.4.8.	1.2.2.
0.5.	1.2.3.
0.6.	1.2.4.
1.1.	1.2.0.4.
1.1.1.	1.2.4.0.
1.1.3.0.	1.2.4.5.
1.1.4.	2.6.5.4.
1.1.5.	3.1.2.2.
1.1.6.	3.1.2.3.
1.2.	3.1.3.3.
1.2.0.	6.1.
1.2.0.1.	6.2.1.
1.2.0.3.	

Selected Literature

THE LITERATURE on military reform and the maintenance of tradition in the West German armed forces is vast. The annotated bibliography on the subject from 1950 to 1980, *Bibliographie der Inneren Führung*, edited by Streitkräfteamt, Abteilung I (Bonn, 1980), is over six hundred pages in length. The bibliography that follows is selective of the most important recent literature on the subject.

Allemann, Fritz-René. "Die Nemesis der Ohnmacht." *Der Monat* 7, 80 (1955): 99–105.

Bald, Detlef. *Vom Kaiserreich zur Bundeswehr*. Frankfurt a.M., 1981.

———. *Der deutsche Offizier. Sozial- und Bildungsgeschichte des deutschen Offizierkorps im 20. Jahrhundert*. München, 1982.

———. *Generalstabsausbildung in der Demokratie: Die Führungsakademie der Bundeswehr zwischen Traditionalismus und Reform*. Koblenz, 1984.

———, ed. *Militärische Verantwortung für Staat und Gesellschaft: 175 Jahre Generalstabsausbildung in Deutschland*. Koblenz, 1986.

Balke, Peter. *Politische Erziehung in der Bundeswehr: Anmassung oder Chance?* Boppard, 1970.

———. "Tradition als Last? Militär und Gesellschaft in Deutschland." *Aus Politik und Zeitgeschichte* 17 (1981).

———. "Deutsche Geschichte-Konsequenzen für ein zeitgemässes Selbstverständnis des Soldaten." In *Tradition als Last*. Edited by Klaus M. Kodalle. Köln, 1981.

Baring, Arnulf. *Aussenpolitik in Adenauers Kanzlerdemokratie: Westdeutsche Innenpolitik im Zeichen der Europäischen Verteidigungsgemeinschaft*. München, 1971.

Barth, P., et al. *Die Bundeswehr in Staat und Gesellschaft*. München, 1982.

Bastian, H-D. *Bildungsbürger in Uniform: Gedanken zur militärischen Menschenführung und politischen Bildung in den Streitkräften*. München, 1979.

Baudissin, Wolf Graf von. *Soldat für den Frieden: Entwürfe für eine zeitgemässe Bundeswehr*. Edited by Peter von Schubert. München, 1969.

———. *Nie wieder Sieg! Programmatische Schriften 1951–1981*. München, 1982.

Bauer, Karl, ed. *Deutsche Verteidigungspolitik, 1948–1967: Dokumente und Kommentare*. 4th edition. Boppard, 1968.

Becker, Kurt E. *Armee für den Frieden: Aspekte der Bundeswehr, Politisch-militärische Lagebeurteilung*. Hannover, 1980.

Benz, W. *Von der Besatzungsherrschaft zur Bundesrepublik: Stationen einer Staatsgründung 1946–1949.* Frankfurt a.M., 1984.

Berg, H. J. *Der Verteidigungsausschuss des deutschen Bundestages: Kontrollorgan zwischen Macht und Ohnmacht.* München, 1982.

Bericht des Wehrbeauftragten des Deutschen Bundestages. Bonn, 1960ff.

Beste, H. D., ed. *Taschenbuch für Wehrfragen 1977/78.* Vol. 9 of 9 vols. Frankfurt a.M., 1977.

Bethke, Hildburg. *Eid, Gewissen, Treupflicht.* Frankfurt, 1965.

Bieber, Helmut. "Traditionsbewusstsein und Geschichtsbewältigung." In *Jahrbuch der Luftwaffe, 1976–77.* Darmstadt, 1977, pp. 22–24.

Bigler, Rolf. *Der Einsame Soldat.* 3rd edition. Frauenfeld, 1963.

Borgert, H. L., et al. *Dienstgruppen und westdeutscher Verteidigungsbeitrag: Vorüberlegungen zur Bewaffnung der Bundesrepublik Deutschland.* Boppard, 1982.

Borgmeyer, Wolfgang. "Stellung der Bundeswehr zum 20. Juli 1944— Aus Stellungnahmen der Aufbauzeit." *Wehrkunde* 25 (1976): 347–51.

Bracher, Karl Dietrich, et al. *Geschichte der Bundesrepublik Deutschland.* 5 vols. Stuttgart-Wiesbaden, 1981–1986.

Bredow, Wilfried von. *Der Primat militärischen Denkens.* Köln, 1969.

———. *Die unbewältigte Bundeswehr: Zur Prefektionierung eines Anachronismus.* Frankfurt a.M., 1973.

Brill, Heinz. *Bogislaw von Bonin im Spannungsfeld zwischen Wiederbewaffnung—Westintegration—Wiedervereinigung.* Baden-Baden, 1987.

———, ed. *Bogislaw von Bonin: Opposition gegen Adenauers Sicherheitspolitik.* Hamburg, 1976.

Bundesministerium der Verteidigung, ed. *Handbuch Innere Führung: Hilfen zur Klärung der Begriffe.* Bonn, 1957.

———. *Information für die Truppe.* Bonn, 1956ff.

———. *Weisshuch: Zur Sicherheit der Bundesrepublik Deutschland und zur Entwicklung der Bundeswehr.* Bonn, 1969ff.

———. *ZDv/10/1: Hilfen für die Innere Führung.* Bonn, 1972.

———. *ZDv/10/2: Der Vertrauensmann.* Bonn, 1982.

———. *ZDv/10/5: Der Innendienst.* Bonn, 1974.

———. *ZDv/12/1: Politische Bildung in der Bundeswehr.* Bonn, 1973.

———. *ZDv/14/1: Grundgesetz, Soldatengesetz, Wehrbeauftragtergesetz, Vorgesetztenordnung.* Bonn, 1974.

———. *ZDv/14/5: Soldatengesetz, Vertrauensmännerwahlgesetz.* Bonn, 1978.

———. *Schicksalsfragen der Gegenwart: Handbuch politisch-historischer Bildung.* 6 vols. Tübingen, 1957–1961.

Bundeswehr-Demokratie in oliv? Streitkräfte im Wandel. Edited by F. H. Borkenhagen. Berlin, 1986.

Bung, H. *Bildung, Erziehung und Ausbildung in der Bundeswehr.* Regensburg, 1980.

Carsten, Francis L. *Reichswehr und Politik, 1918–1933.* Köln, 1964.

Cioc, Mark. "Pax Atomica: The Nuclear Defense Debate in West Germany during the Adenauer Era," Ph.D. Diss., University of California at Berkeley, 1986.

Craig, Gordon A. *The Politics of the Prussian Army.* New York, 1964.

―――. "NATO and the German Army." In *NATO and American Security.* Edited by William Kaufmann. Princeton, 1956.

Demeter, Karl. *Das Deutsche Offizierkorps in Gesellschaft und Staat, 1650–1945.* 4th edition. Frankfurt, 1965.

Der deutsche Soldat in der Armee von Morgen: Wehrverfassung, Wehrsystem, Inneres Gefüge. München, 1954.

Deutsche Studien, Sonderheft: Tradition in der Bundeswehr und Nationaler Volksarmee. Lüneburg, 1981.

Doepner, Friedrich. *Bundeswehr und Armeereform ein Tabu?* Dorheim, 1969.

―――. "Die 'Innere Führung' im Hunderttausend-Mann-Heer: Die 'Leitgedanken von 1931.'" *Europäische Wehrkunde* 26 (1977): 356–60.

―――. "Über die Traditionspflege in der Bundeswehr." *Europäische Wehrkunde* 27 (1978): 524–26.

Doering-Mantueffel, Anselm. *Katholizismus und Wiederbewaffnung: Die Haltung der deutschen Katholiken gegenüber der Wehrfrage 1948–1955.* Mainz, 1981.

―――. *Die Bundesrepublik Deutschland in der Ära Adenauer.* Darmstadt, 1983.

Dornberg, John. *Schizophrenic Germany.* New York, 1961.

Driftmann, Hans H. *Grundzüge des militärischen Erziehungs- und Bildungswesens in der Zeit 1871–1939.* Regensburg, 1980.

―――, ed. *Allgemeine Führungslehre: Führung in der Bundeswehr Leitfäden für Lehre und Praxis.* Regensburg, 1986.

Eichhorn, Peter. "Tradition in der Bundeswehr." *Deutsche Studien* 5, 20 (1967): 345–60.

Erler, Fritz. "Opposition und Wehrbeitrag." In *Armee gegen den Krieg.* Edited by Wolfram von Raven. Stuttgart, 1966.

―――. "Heer und Staat in der Bundesrepublik." In *Schicksalsfragen der Gegenwart.* Edited by BMVg. 6 vols. Vol. 3, pp. 223–56.

Esser, Martin. *Das Traditionsverständnis des Offizierkorps: eine Empirische Untersuchung zur gesellschaftlichen Integration der Streitkräfte.* Heidelberg/Hamburg, 1982.

Estorff, Eggert von, and Konrad Lehmann. *Dienstunterricht des Offiziers: Anleitung zur Erteilung des Mannschaftsunterrichts in Beispielen*. Berlin, 1913.

Evangelischer Kirchenamt der Bundeswehr, ed. *De Officio: zu den ethischen Herausforderungen des Offizierberufs*. Hannover, 1985.

Fischer, Alexander, ed. *Wiederbewaffnung in Deutschland nach 1945*. Berlin, 1986.

Fischer, Alexander, and Christian Greiner et al., eds. *Entmilitarisierung und Aufrüstung in Mitteleuropa, 1945–1956*. Bonn/Herford, 1983.

Fleckenstein, Bernhard. *Bundeswehr und Industriegesellschaft*. Boppard, 1971.

———. "Das Werden der Bürgerarmee—Die Entwicklung der Bundeswehr von ihren Anfängen bis zur Gegenwart." In *Wie Integriert ist die Bundeswehr?*. Edited by Ralf Zoll. München, 1979.

Fleckenstein, Bernhard, and D. Schoessler. *Bundeswehr und Gesellschaft*. Regensburg, 1986.

Foertsch, Hermann. *Der Offizier der neuen Wehrmacht: Eine Pflichtenlehre*. 2nd edition. Berlin, 1936.

Forster, Thomas. *Die NVA: Kernstück der Landesverteidigung der DDR*. Köln, 1979.

Fröchling, Helmut. "Soldatische Vorbilder—Zum Problem demokratischer Traditionsbildung in der Bundeswehr." *Journal für Geschichte* 2, 3 (1980): 36ff.

Gall, Franz. "Tradition in Uniform." *Feldgrau* 18, 1 (1970): 2–10.

Ganser, Helmut. "Technokraten in Uniform—Zur inneren Krise der Bundeswehr." In *Technokraten in Uniform*. Edited by Helmut Ganser. Reinbek bei Hamburg, 1980.

Geffen, William. "The Role of the Military in West German Defense Policy Making." Ph.D. Diss., University of Denver, 1971.

Genschel, Dietrich. *Wehrreform und Reaktion: die Vorbereitung der Inneren Führung 1951–1956*. Hamburg, 1972.

Giesen, H. *Deutscher Bundeswehr-Verband: Spitzenorganisation der Soldaten*. Wiesbaden, 1984.

Gordon, Harold J. *Die Reichswehr und die Weimarer Republik, 1919–1926*. Frankfurt, 1959.

Grimm, Siegfried. ". . . der Bundesrepublik treu zu Dienen": die geistige Rüstung der Bundeswehr*. Düsseldorf, 1970.

Grosse, Helmut. *Die Bundeswehr in der Gesellschaft der Bundesrepublik Deutschland*. Bonn, 1970.

Haas, Gerhard. "Und nun: der uniformierte Staatsbürger als Soldat." *Truppenpraxis* 6 (1964): 422.

Hamann, Rudolf. *Streit um eine verkannte Reform: Ein Beitrag zur Inneren Führung*. Hamburg, 1970.

———. *Armee in Abseits?* Hamburg, 1972.

Hammerschmidt, Helmut. *Zwanzig Jahre danach. Eine deutsche Bilanz, 1945–1965*. München, 1965.

Harder, H. J., and Norbert Wiggershaus. *Tradition und Reform in den Aufbaujahren der Bundeswehr*. Herford/Bonn, 1985.

Heine, Hans. "Vor dem Abgrund der Geschichte: Bundeswehr ohne Tradition?" *Allgemeines deutsches Sonntagsblatt*, 10 January 1965.

Hesse, Kurt. *Im Banne des Soldatentums*. Frankfurt, 1934.

———. *Die soldatische Tradition*. Frankfurt, 1936.

———. *Der Geist von Potsdam*. Mainz, 1967.

———. "Der alte Soldat und die Bundeswehr: Geschichtsbewusstsein, Traditionspflege und demokratische Mitverantwortung." *Wehrwissenschaftliche Rundschau* 18, 11 (1968): 601–15.

Hessische Stiftung Friedens- und Konfliktforschung, ed. *Unsere Bundeswehr? Zum 25jährigen Bestehen einer umstritten Institution*. Frankfurt a.M., 1981.

Hesslein, Bernd, et al. *Die unbewältigte Vergangenheit der Bundeswehr*. Reinbek bei Hamburg, 1977.

Hessler, Klaus. *Militär-Gehorsam-Meinung: Aktuelle Dokumentation*. Berlin, 1971.

Heusinger, Adolf. *Befehl im Widerstreit. Schicksalsstunden der deutschen Armee 1923–1945*. Tübingen, 1950.

———. *Reden, 1956–1961*. Boppard, 1961.

Heuss, Theodor. *Dank und Bekenntnis: Gedenkrede zum 20. Juli 1944*. Tübingen, 1954.

———. *Soldatentum in unserer Zeit*. Tübingen, 1959.

Heydte, Friedrich August Freiherr von der. "Grundsätze der Menschenführung und Einordnung." In *Der deutsche Soldat in der Armee von Morgen*. München, 1954.

Heye, Hellmuth. "In Sorge um die Bundeswehr." *Quick*, nos. 25–27, June 1964, pp. 14–20, 78–83, 28, 14–20, 66ff., 29, 25–31.

Hillgruber, Andreas. *Deutsche Geschichte, 1945–1982: Die deutsche Frage in der Weltpolitik*. 4th edition. Stuttgart/Berlin, 1983.

Hoffmann, Hanns Hubert, ed. *Das Deutsche Offizierkorps, 1860–1960*. Boppard, 1980.

Höhn, Reinhard. *Verfassungskampf und Heereseid: Der Kampf des Bürgertums um das Heer, 1815–1850*. Leipzig, 1938.

———. *Die Armee als Erziehungsschule der Nation: Das Ende einer Idee*. Bad Harzburg, 1963.

Hornung, Klaus. *Soldat und Staat: Gerechte Massstäbe gegen alte Vorurteile*. Stuttgart, 1956.

———. *Staat und Armee: Studien zur Befehls und Kommandogewalt und zum politisch-militärischen Verhältnis in der Bundesrepublik Deutschland*. Mainz, 1975.

Ilsemann, Carl-Gero von. *Die Bundeswehr in der Demokratie: Zeit der Inneren Führung*. Hamburg, 1971.

———. *Die Innere Führung in den Streitkräften*. Volume 5 in *Die Bundeswehr: eine Gesamtdarstellung*. Edited by Hubert Reinfried und Hubert Walitschek. 14 vols. Regensburg, 1981.

———. *Innere Führung im Meinungsstreit: Beiträge zu ihrer Fortentwicklung in der Bundeswehr*. Grosshesselohe, 1984.

Jacobsen, Hans–Adolf. *1939–1945: Der Zweite Weltkrieg in Chronik und Dokumenten*. Darmstadt, 1961.

———. "Zur Rolle der öffentlichen Meinung bei der Debatte um die Wiederbewaffnung, 1950–1955." In *Aspekte der deutschen Wiederbewaffnung bis 1955*. Edited by the MGFA. Boppard, 1975.

Jacobsen, Hans-Adolf, et al. "Traditionsverständnis und Traditionspflege in der Bundeswehr." *Information für die Truppe* 4 (1981): 1–8.

Jacoby, Hans. *Menschenführung in der Bundeswehr: Ein Beitrag zur Erziehung des jungen Staatsbürgers*. Stuttgart, 1957.

Jaeger, Richard. *Soldat und Bürger—Armee und Staat: Probleme einer demokratischen Wehrverfassung*. 3rd edition. Köln, 1963.

Janssen, Karl-Heinz. "Was ist heute noch soldatische Tradition? Die Bundeswehr zwischen Nostalgie und Geschichtslosigkeit." *Die Zeit*, 22 April 1977.

Karst, Heinz. "Tradition im Atomzeitalter." *Truppenpraxis* 1 (1958): 3–16.

———. *Das Bild des Soldaten*. Boppard, 1964.

Klietmann, Kurt Gerhard. "Überlieferungspflege und Tradition im deutschen Heer." *Feldgrau* 11, 1 (1963): 30ff.

Kirst, Hans Hellmut. *08/15 in der Kaserne*. München, 1954.

Kodalle, Klaus M., et al. *Tradition als Last? Legitimationsprobleme der Bundeswehr*. Köln, 1981.

Kraemmerer, H. J., ed. *Der Reibert. Das Handbuch für den Soldaten*. Ausgabe Heer. Herford, 1982.

Krause, H. Fred. *Das Konzept der Inneren Führung und die Hochschulen der Bundeswehr*. Bochum, 1979.

Krausnick, Helmut, et al. *Die Truppe des Weltanschauungskrieges: Die Einsatzgruppen der Sicherheitspolizei und des SD, 1938–1942*. Stuttgart, 1981.

Lider, Julian. *Problems of Military Policy in the Konrad Adenauer Era, 1949–1956*. Stockholm, 1984.

Lingens, E., and H. Marignoni. *Vorgesetzter und Untergebener.* 2nd edition. Herford, 1984.

Loth, W. *Die Teilung der Welt: Geschichte des kalten Krieges, 1941–1955.* 2nd edition. München, 1982.

Macioszek, Heinz-Georg. "Das Problem der Tradition in der Bundeswehr: Eine empirische Untersuchung unter jungen Offizieren des Heeres." Ph.D. Diss., University of Hamburg, 1969.

Maizière, Ulrich de. *Bekenntnis zum Soldaten.* Hamburg, 1971.

———. *Führen im Frieden: Zwanzig Jahre Dienst für Bundeswehr und Staat.* München, 1974.

Martini, Winfried. *Freiheit auf Abruf.* Köln, 1960.

Meier–Welcker, Hans. *Seeckt.* Frankfurt, 1967.

———. *Soldat und Geschichte.* Freiburg, 1976.

Messerschmidt, Manfred. *Die Wehrmacht im NS Staat: Zeit der Indoktrination.* Hamburg, 1969.

———. "Das Verhältnis von Wehrmacht und NS Staat und die Frage der Traditionsbildung." In *Tradition als Last.* Edited by Klaus M. Kodalle. Köln, 1981.

Meyer, Georg. "Menschenführung im Heer der Bundeswehr, 1955–1969." In *Menschenführung im Heer.* Edited by MGFA. Herford, 1982.

———. "Zur Situation der deutschen militärischen Führungsschicht im Vorfeld des westdeutschen Verteidigungsbeitrages 1945–1950/51." In vol. 1 of *Anfänge westdeutscher Sicherheitspolitik.* Edited by MGFA. München, 1982.

———. "Zu Fragen der personellen Auswahl bei der Vorbereitung eines westdeutschen Verteidigungbeitrages (1950–1956)." In *Das Deutsche Offizierkorps.* Edited by Hanns Hubert Hoffman, pp. 351–56.

———. "Auswirkungen des 20. Juli auf das innere Gefüge der Wehrmacht bis zum Kriegsende und auf das soldatische Selbdstverständnis im Vorfeld des westdeutschen Verteidigungbeitrages bis 1950/1." In *Der militärische Widerstand.* Edited by MGFA. Herford, 1984, pp. 153–86.

Militärgeschichtliches Forschungsamt, ed. *Verteidigung im Bündnis: Planung, Aufbau und Bewährung der Bundeswehr, 1950–72.* München, 1975.

———. *Aspekte der deutschen Wiederbewaffnung bis 1955.* Boppard, 1975.

———. *Handbuch zur deutschen Militärgeschichte, 1648–1939.* 6 vols. München, 1979–1981.

———. *Der Militärische Widerstand gegen Hitler und das NS Regime 1933–1945.* Herford/Bonn, 1984.

———. *Tradition in deutschen Streitkräften bis 1945.* Herford/Bonn, 1986.

———. *Anfänge westdeutscher Sicherheitspolitik 1945–1956: Von der Kapitulation zum Pleven Plan.* München, 1982.

Model, H., and J. Prause. *Generalstab im Wandel: Neue Wege bei der Generalstabsausbildung in der Bundeswehr.* München, 1982.

Morsey, Rudolf. *Die Bundesrepublik Deutschland: Entstehung und Entwicklung bis 1969.* München, 1987.

Mosen, Wido. *Bundeswehr—Elite der Nation?.* Neuwied, 1970.

Müller, Klaus-Jürgen. *Das Heer und Hitler: Armee und nationalsozialistisches Regime 1933–1945.* Stuttgart, 1969.

Müller-Schwefe, Hans-Rudolf. "Tradition im Wandel der Zeiten." *Kampftruppen* 2 (1963): 1–3.

Nobbe, M. *Erziehung und Bildung in der Bundeswehr: Untersuchung über die Schriften zur Bildung in der Truppe und die Konzepte der Inneren Führung.* Köln, 1985.

Obermann, Emil. *Soldaten-Bürger-Militaristen: Militär und Demokratie in Deutschland.* Stuttgart, 1958.

———. *Gesellschaft und Verteidigung: Ein Handbuch.* Stuttgart, 1971.

Park, William. *Defending the West: A History of NATO.* Brighton, 1986.

Paul, Wolfgang. *Das Potsdamer Infanterie Regiment 9, 1918–1945: Preussische Tradition in Krieg und Frieden.* 2 vols. 2nd edition. Osnabrück, 1985.

Picht, Georg, et al. *Studien zur politischen und gesellschaftlichen Situation der Bundeswehr.* 3 vols. Witten, 1965–1966.

Picht, Werner. *Vom Wesen des Krieges und vom Kriegswesen der Deutschen.* Stuttgart, 1952.

———. *Wiederbewaffnung.* Pfullingen, 1954.

Poeggeler, Franz, and Otto Wien, eds. *Soldaten der Demokratie: Die Bundeswehr in Gesellschaft und Staat.* Frankfurt a.M., 1973.

Pohlmann, Hartwig. "Tradition und Bundeswehr—Aus der Sicht eines alten Wehrmachts- und neuen Bundeswehroffiziers." *Alte Kameraden* 9, 10 (1961): 10ff.

Poppitz, Erhard. "Der Antikommunismus in der Traditionspflege der Bundeswehr." Ph.D. Diss., University. of Leipzig, 1967.

Poten, Bernhard. *Geschichte des Militär-Erziehungs und Bildungswesens in den Landen deutscher Zunge.* 4 vols. Reprint. Osnabrück, 1982.

Preuss, Helmut. "Innere Führung—eine zeitgeschichtliche Studie." *Truppenpraxis* 11 (1980).

Rautenberg, Hans-Jürgen. "Planungen zur Offizierausbildung künftiger deutscher Streitkräfte 1950–1954." In *Das deutsche Offizierkorps.* Edited by Hanns Hubert Hoffmann. Boppard, 1980, pp. 367–88.

———. "Aspekte zur Entwicklung der Traditionsfrage in der Bundeswehr." In *Tradition als Last.* Edited by Klaus M. Kodalle. Köln, 1981, pp. 133–51.

———. "Zur Standortbestimmung für künftige deutsche Streitkräfte." In *Anfänge westdeutscher Sicherheitspolitik.* München, 1982.

Rautenberg, Hans-Jürgen, and Norbert Wiggershaus. *"Die Himmeroder Denkshrift" vom Oktober 1950*. Karlsruhe, 1985.

Raven, Wolfram von, ed. *Armee gegen den Krieg: Wert und Wirkung der Bundeswehr*. Stuttgart, 1966.

Rehm, Walter. "Militärtraditionen in der DDR." In *Die DDR und die Tradition*. Edited by Hans Jaschke. Heidelberg, 1981, pp. 163–87.

Richter, M. *Partizipation in der Bundeswehr*. Heidelberg/Hamburg, 1982.

Ritter, F., and H. Ploetz. *Die Bundeswehr: Aufbau, Auftrag, Aufgaben*. Heidelberg, 1986.

Ritter, Gerhard. "Der 20. Juli 1944: Die Wehrmacht und der politische Widerstand gegen Hitler." In vol. 1 of *Schicksalsfragen der Gegenwart*. Edited by BMVg. 6 vols. Tübingen, 1957, pp. 349–81.

Robinson, Hans. "Der Spiegel der Nation—Die Republik und das Traditionsbewusstsein der Bundeswehr." *Vorgänge* 16 (1977): 3–8.

Sadlowski, M., ed. *Handbuch der Bundeswehr und der Verteidigungsindustrie: 1985/86*. Koblenz, 1985.

Scheel, Walter. "Tradition und geschichtliches Denken: Der historische Weg zur Demokratie, Ansprache auf dem deutschen Historikertag, 1976." *Information für die Truppe* 1 (1977): 83–94.

Schenck zu Schweinsberg, Krafft Freiherr von. "Die Soldatenverbände in der Bundesrepublik." In *Studien zur politischen und gesellschaftlichen Situation der Bundeswehr*. Edited by Robert Picht. 3 vols. 1: 96–177.

Scherer, W. *Soldatengesetz und Vorgesetztenverordnung: Kommentar*. München, 1976.

Schlabrendorf, Fabian von. *Offiziere gegen Hitler*. Frankfurt, 1960.

Schlichting, Günter. "Praktische Traditionspflege aus der Sicht eines Marinestützpunktkommandeurs." *Truppenpraxis* 9 (1963): 728ff.

Schmiterlöw, Bertram von. "Gedanken zur Tradition." *Wehrausbildung in Wort und Bild* 7, 5 (1964): 199–202.

Schmückle, Gerd. *Kommiss a.D. Kritische Gänge durch die Kasernen*. Stuttgart, 1972.

———. *Ohne Pauken und Trompeten*. Stuttgart, 1982.

Schramm, Wilhelm Ritter von. "Bundeswehr und Tradition—eine systematische Untersuchung." *Wehrkunde* 8 (1959): 505–13.

Schubert, Klaus von. *Sicherheitspolitik der Bundesrepublik Deutschland: Dokumentation, 1945–1977*. 2 vols. Köln, 1978.

Schulz, Karl-Ernst, et al. *Streitkräfte im gesellschaftlichen Wandel*. Bonn, 1980.

Schumann, Heinz. *Der deutsche Widerstand gegen die NS Diktatur: Seine Darstellung in den Informationsschriften der Bundeswehr zur politischen Bildung*. Unpublished thesis, Führungsakademie, Hamburg, 1978.

Seeckt, Hans. *Die Reichswehr*. Leipzig, 1933.

Simon, Ulrich. *Die Integration der Bundeswehr in die Gesellschaft: Das Ringen um die Innere Führung.* Heidelberg, 1980.

Soell, Harmut. *Fritz Erler: Eine politische Biographie.* 2 vols. Berlin/Bad Godesberg, 1976.

Speier, Hans. *German Rearmament and Atomic War: The Views of the German Military and Political Leaders.* Evanston, 1957.

Sprung, G.M.C. "Gedanken über die militärische Tradition in der heutigen Zeit." *Wehrwissenschaftliche Rundschau* 13, 3 (1963): 121–30.

Stein, H. P. *Symbole und Zeremoniell in deutschen Streitkräften.* 2nd edition. Herford, 1984.

Stuckman, Heinz D. *Es ist so schön, Soldat zu sein oder Staatsbürger in Uniform.* Reinbek bei Hamburg, 1964.

Studnitz, H. G. von. *Rettet die Bundeswehr!* Stuttgart, 1967.

Thayer, Charles W. *The Unquiet Germans.* New York, 1957.

Thielen, Hans-Helmut. *Der Verfall der Inneren Führung: Politische Bewusstseinsbildung in der Bundeswehr.* Hamburg, 1970.

Thomer, E., ed. *Die Bundeswehr heute.* Herford/Bonn, 1985.

Tönnies, Norbert. *Der Weg zu den Waffen: die Geschichte der deutschen Wiederbewaffnung, 1949–1961.* Rastatt, 1961.

Tradition und Reform im militärischen Bildungswesen—von der preussischen Allgemeinen Kriegsschule zur Führungsungsakademie der Bundeswehr: eine Dokumentation. Baden-Baden, 1985.

Vogt, Wolfgang R. *Militär und Demokratie: Funktionen und Konflikte der Institution des Wehrbeauftragten.* Hamburg, 1972.

Volkmann, Hans-Erich, and Walter Schwengler, eds. *Die Europäische Verteidigungsgemeinschaft: Stand und Probleme der Forschung.* Boppard, 1985.

Vollert, Michael, et al. "Ist der Traditionserlass noch zeitgemäss?" *Information für die Truppe* 3 (1971): 372.

Wagemann, Eberhard. "Bundeswehr und Tradition." In *Bundeswehr und Gesellschaft: Ein Wörterbuch.* Edited by Ralf Zoll. Opladen, 1977, pp. 69–73.

Waldman, Eric. *Soldat im Staat: Der Staatsbürger in Uniform, Vorstellung und Wirklichkeit.* Boppard, 1963.

Walitschek, H., and H. Reinfried, eds., *Die Bundeswehr: Eine Gesamtdarstellung.* 14 vols. Regensburg, 1979–1985.

Weinstein, Adelbert. *Armee ohne Pathos: die deutsche Wiederbewaffnung im Urteil ehemaliger Soldaten.* Bonn, 1951.

Weniger, Erich. "Die Gefährdung der Freiheit durch ihre Verteidiger." Vol. 6 of *Schicksalsfragen der Gegenwart.* 6 vols. Tübingen, 1959, pp. 344–381.

Wettig, Gerhard. *Entmilitarisierung und Wiederbewaffnung in Deutschland 1943–1955: Internationale Auseinandersetzungen um die Rolle der Deutschen in Europa.* München, 1967.

Wiggershaus, Norbert. "Überlegungen und Pläne zu einer militärischen Integration Westdeutschlands, 1948–1952." In *Kalter Krieg und Deutsche Frage: Deutschland im Widerstreit der Mächte 1945–1952.* Edited by Josef Foschepoth. Göttingen, 1985, pp. 314–34.

———. "Von Potsdam zum Pleven-Plan. Deutschland in der internationalen Konfrontation 1945–1950." In *Anfänge westdeutscher Sicherheitspolitik.* Edited by MGFA. München, 1982, pp. 325–575.

———. "Zum allierten Pro und Contra eines westdeutschen Militärbeitrages." In *Militärgeschichte. Probleme—Thesen—Wege.* Edited by MGFA. Stuttgart, 1982, pp. 436–51.

———. "Zur Bedeutung und Nachwirkung des militärischen Widerstandes in der Bundesrepublik Deutschland und in der Bundeswehr." In *Aufstand des Gewissens: militärischer Widerstand gegen Hitler und das NS Regime 1933–1945.* Edited by MGFA. Herford, 1984, pp. 501–28.

Zoll, Ralf, et al. *Bundeswehr und Gesellschaft: Ein Wörterbuch.* Opladen, 1977.

Zoll, Ralf, et al. *Wie integriert ist die Bundeswehr? Zum Verhältnis von Militär und Gesellschaft in der Bundesrepublik.* München, 1979.

Zuber, Hubertus. *Innere Führung in Staat, Armee und Gesellschaft.* Regensburg, 1981.

Index